Maid Sama!

Hiro Fujiwara

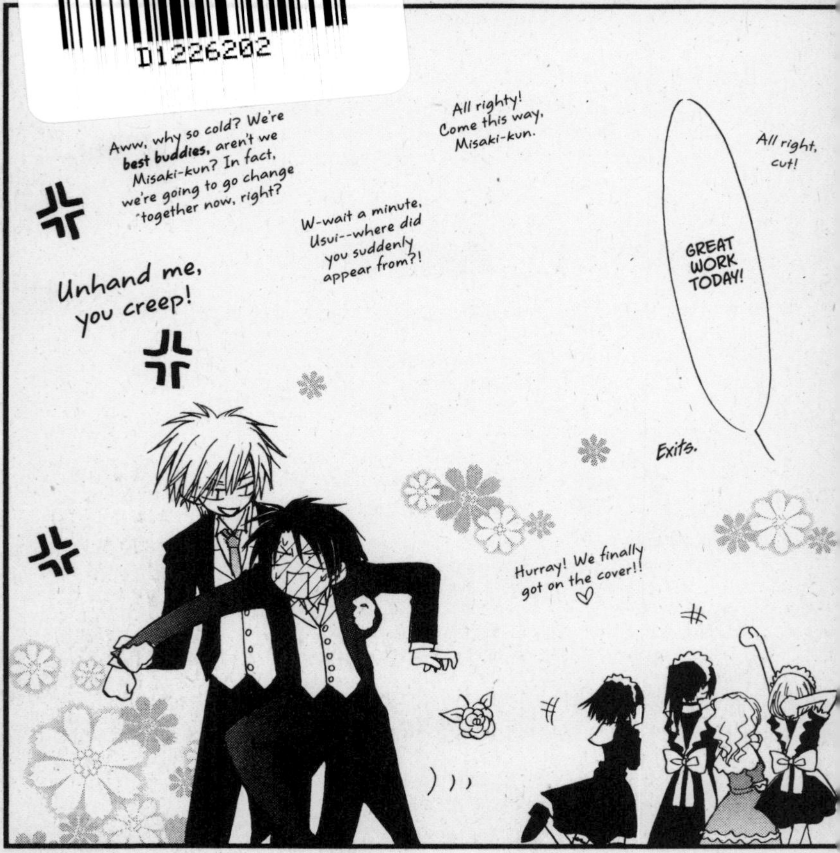
All right, cut!
GREAT WORK TODAY!
Exits.
Hurray! We finally got on the cover!! ♡
All righty! Come this way, Misaki-kun.
W-wait a minute, Usui--where did you suddenly appear from?!
Aww, why so cold? We're **best buddies,** aren't we Misaki-kun? In fact, we're going to go change together now, right?
Unhand me, you creep!

Maid Sama! Volume 3
Created by Hiro Fujiwara

Translation - Su Mon Han
English Adaptation - Karen S. Ahlstrom
Retouch and Lettering - Star Print Brokers
Production Artist - Rui Kyo
Graphic Designer - Louis Csontos

Editor - Lillian Diaz-Przybyl
Print Production Manager - Lucas Rivera
Managing Editor - Vy Nguyen
Senior Designer - Louis Csontos
Art Director - Al-Insan Lashley
Director of Sales and Manufacturing - Allyson De Simone
Associate Publisher - Marco F. Pavia
President and C.O.O. - John Parker
C.E.O. and Chief Creative Officer - Stu Levy

A 🐸 TOKYOPOP® Manga

TOKYOPOP and 🐸 are trademarks or registered trademarks of TOKYOPOP Inc.

TOKYOPOP Inc.
5900 Wilshire Blvd. Suite 2000
Los Angeles, CA 90036

E-mail: info@TOKYOPOP.com
Come visit us online at www.TOKYOPOP.com

ISBN: 978-1-4278-1405-0

First TOKYOPOP printing: January 2010
10 9 8 7 6 5 4 3
Printed in the USA

Maid Sama!™
Hiro Fujiwara

Vol. 3

by
Hiro Fujiwara

TOKYOPOP®

HAMBURG // LONDON // LOS ANGELES // TOKYO

WELCOME HOME, MASTER!

Please allow me to introduce all the ladies and gentlemen who appeared in the previous volume.♥

Maid

President

MISAKI AYUZAWA (HIGH SCHOOL JUNIOR)

AN INDOMITABLE STUDENT COUNCIL PRESIDENT BY DAY, BUT A WAITRESS AT A MAID CAFE BY NIGHT!! BRILLIANT BOTH IN ACADEMICS AND ATHLETICS, HER SPECIALTY IS AIKIDO (ALL ACHIEVED THROUGH MASSIVE HARD WORK AND DEDICATION). AT WORK, THEY CALL HER MISA-CHAN--A SMART, COOL-HEADED MAID!

TAKUMI USUI (HIGH SCHOOL JUNIOR)

THE SCHOOL HEARTTHROB. HE ACCIDENTALLY DISCOVERED MISAKI'S SECRET AND, INTRIGUED, HAS TAKEN TO FOLLOWING HER AROUND. HE'S SUPER SMART, GREAT AT SPORTS, AS GORGEOUS AS THEY COME AND UNBEATABLE IN A FIGHT--THE PERFECT MAN. BUT AS FAR AS MISAKI'S CONCERNED, HE'S ALSO THE DEMON KING OF SEXUAL HARASSMENT. LATELY, HE'S BECOME MAID LATTE'S #1 CUSTOMER.

SEIKA HIGH SCHOOL

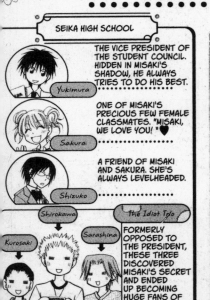

Yukimura

THE VICE PRESIDENT OF THE STUDENT COUNCIL. HIDDEN IN MISAKI'S SHADOW, HE ALWAYS TRIES TO DO HIS BEST.

Sakura

ONE OF MISAKI'S PRECIOUS FEW FEMALE CLASSMATES. "MISAKI, WE LOVE YOU!"♥

Shizuko

A FRIEND OF MISAKI AND SAKURA. SHE'S ALWAYS LEVELHEADED.

The Idiot Trio

Shirokawa

Sarashina

Kurosaki

FORMERLY OPPOSED TO THE PRESIDENT, THESE THREE DISCOVERED MISAKI'S SECRET AND ENDED UP BECOMING HUGE FANS OF MISA-CHAN.

Cafe Maid Latte

MISAKI'S PART-TIME JOB--THE STAFF ALL EAGERLY AWAIT YOUR RETURN, MASTER.♥

Satsuki

THE MANAGER; SATSUKI UNDERSTANDS MISAKI'S SITUATION AND HAS BEEN AS ACCOMMODATING AS POSSIBLE. SHE IS 30 YEARS OLD AND QUITE GIVEN TO FLIGHTS OF FANCY.

Cafe Maid Latte

The Maids

Honoka

Subaru

Erika

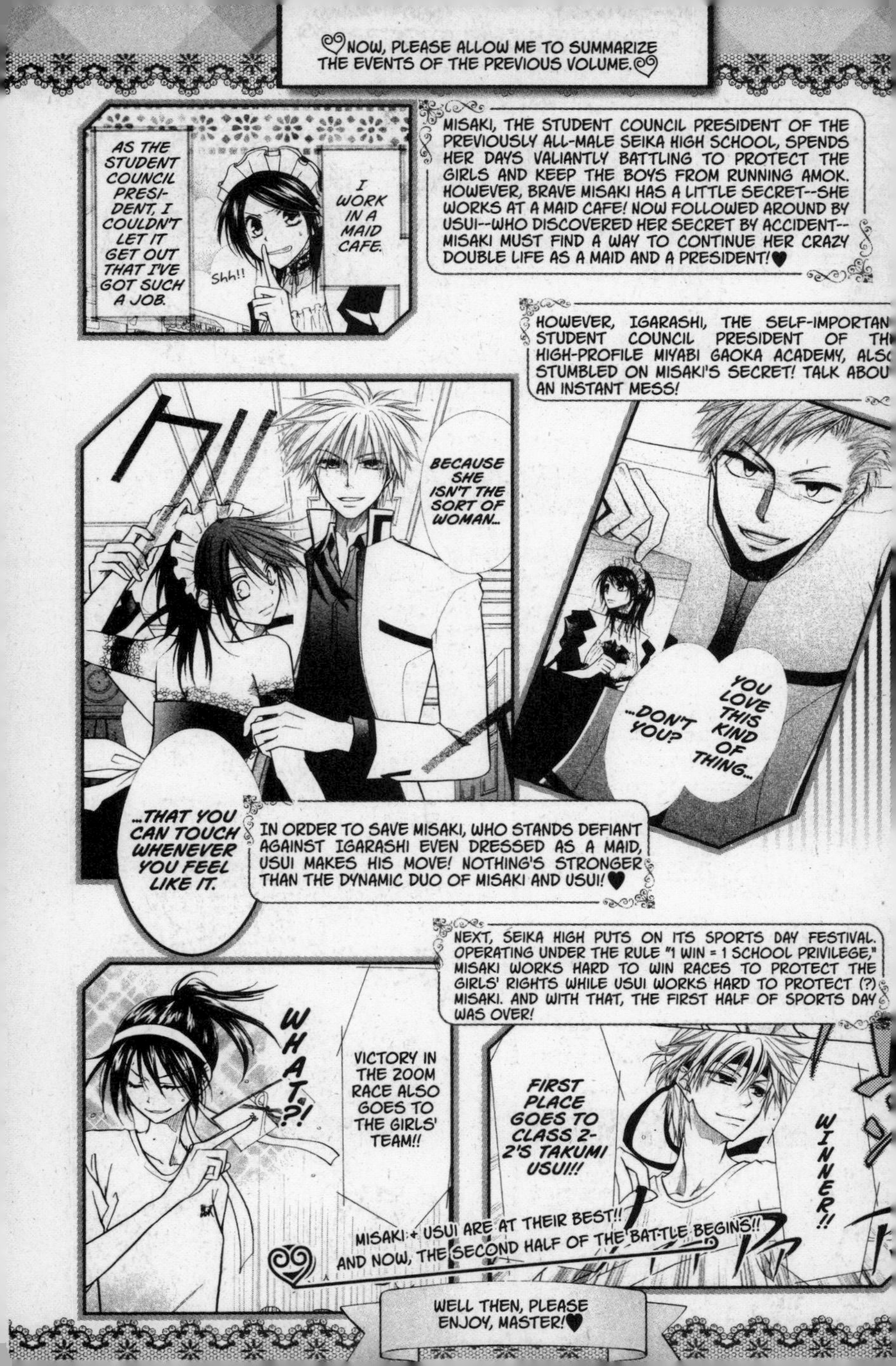
NOW, PLEASE ALLOW ME TO SUMMARIZE THE EVENTS OF THE PREVIOUS VOLUME.
MISAKI, THE STUDENT COUNCIL PRESIDENT OF THE PREVIOUSLY ALL-MALE SEIKA HIGH SCHOOL, SPENDS HER DAYS VALIANTLY BATTLING TO PROTECT THE GIRLS AND KEEP THE BOYS FROM RUNNING AMOK. HOWEVER, BRAVE MISAKI HAS A LITTLE SECRET--SHE WORKS AT A MAID CAFE! NOW FOLLOWED AROUND BY USUI--WHO DISCOVERED HER SECRET BY ACCIDENT--MISAKI MUST FIND A WAY TO CONTINUE HER CRAZY DOUBLE LIFE AS A MAID AND A PRESIDENT!♥
I WORK IN A MAID CAFE.
AS THE STUDENT COUNCIL PRESIDENT, I COULDN'T LET IT GET OUT THAT I'VE GOT SUCH A JOB.
Shh!!
HOWEVER, IGARASHI, THE SELF-IMPORTANT STUDENT COUNCIL PRESIDENT OF THE HIGH-PROFILE MIYABI GAOKA ACADEMY, ALSO STUMBLED ON MISAKI'S SECRET! TALK ABOUT AN INSTANT MESS!
YOU LOVE THIS KIND OF THING...
...DON'T YOU?
BECAUSE SHE ISN'T THE SORT OF WOMAN...
...THAT YOU CAN TOUCH WHENEVER YOU FEEL LIKE IT.
IN ORDER TO SAVE MISAKI, WHO STANDS DEFIANT AGAINST IGARASHI EVEN DRESSED AS A MAID, USUI MAKES HIS MOVE! NOTHING'S STRONGER THAN THE DYNAMIC DUO OF MISAKI AND USUI!♥
NEXT, SEIKA HIGH PUTS ON ITS SPORTS DAY FESTIVAL. OPERATING UNDER THE RULE "1 WIN = 1 SCHOOL PRIVILEGE," MISAKI WORKS HARD TO WIN RACES TO PROTECT THE GIRLS' RIGHTS WHILE USUI WORKS HARD TO PROTECT (?) MISAKI. AND WITH THAT, THE FIRST HALF OF SPORTS DAY WAS OVER!
WINNER!!
FIRST PLACE GOES TO CLASS 2-2'S TAKUMI USUI!!!
VICTORY IN THE 200M RACE ALSO GOES TO THE GIRLS' TEAM!!
WHAT?!
MISAKI + USUI ARE AT THEIR BEST!!
AND NOW, THE SECOND HALF OF THE BATTLE BEGINS!!
WELL THEN, PLEASE ENJOY, MASTER!♥

Cafe Maid Latte

3

CONTENTS

Cafe Maid Latte

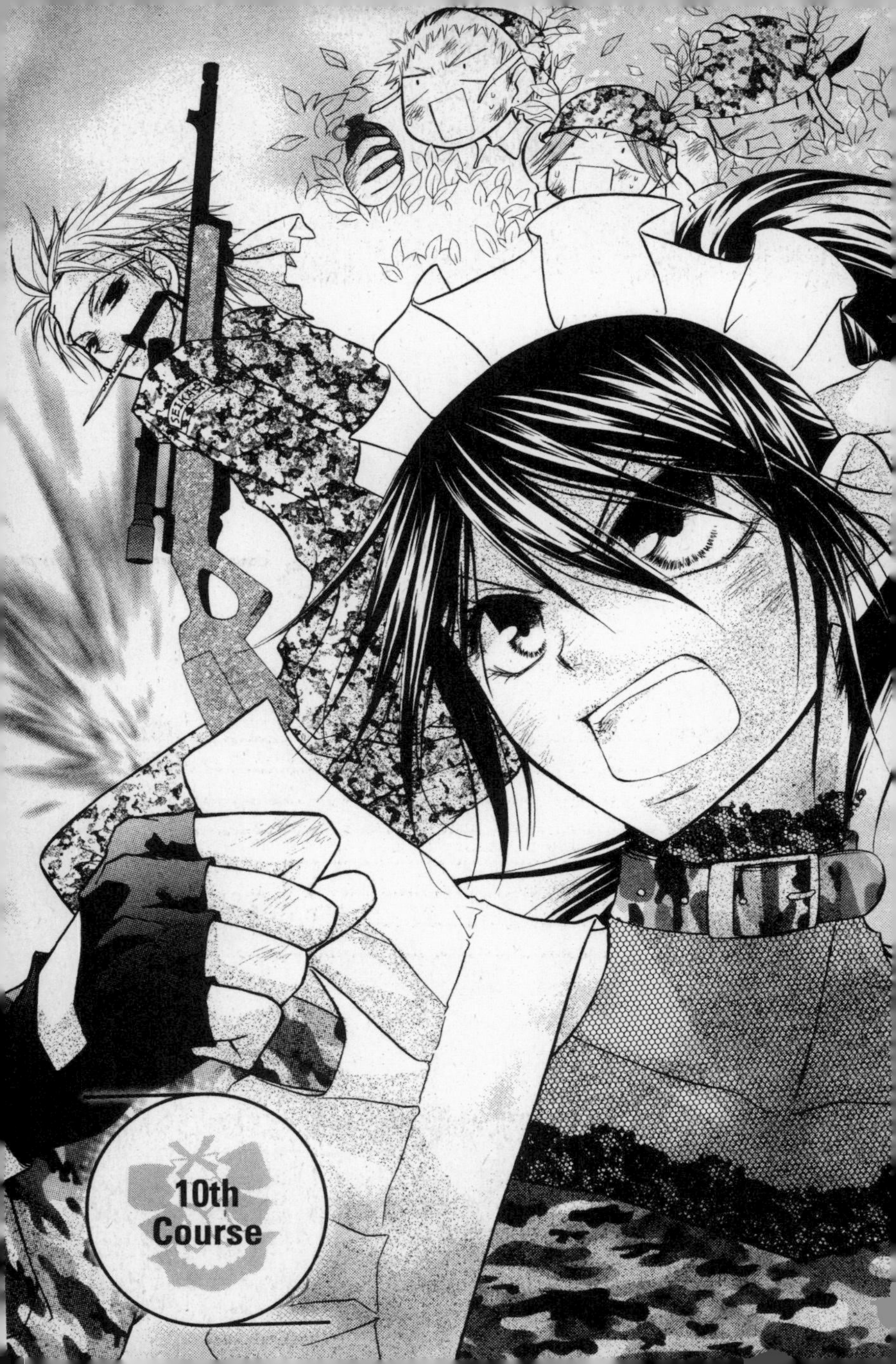
SEIKA
10th Course

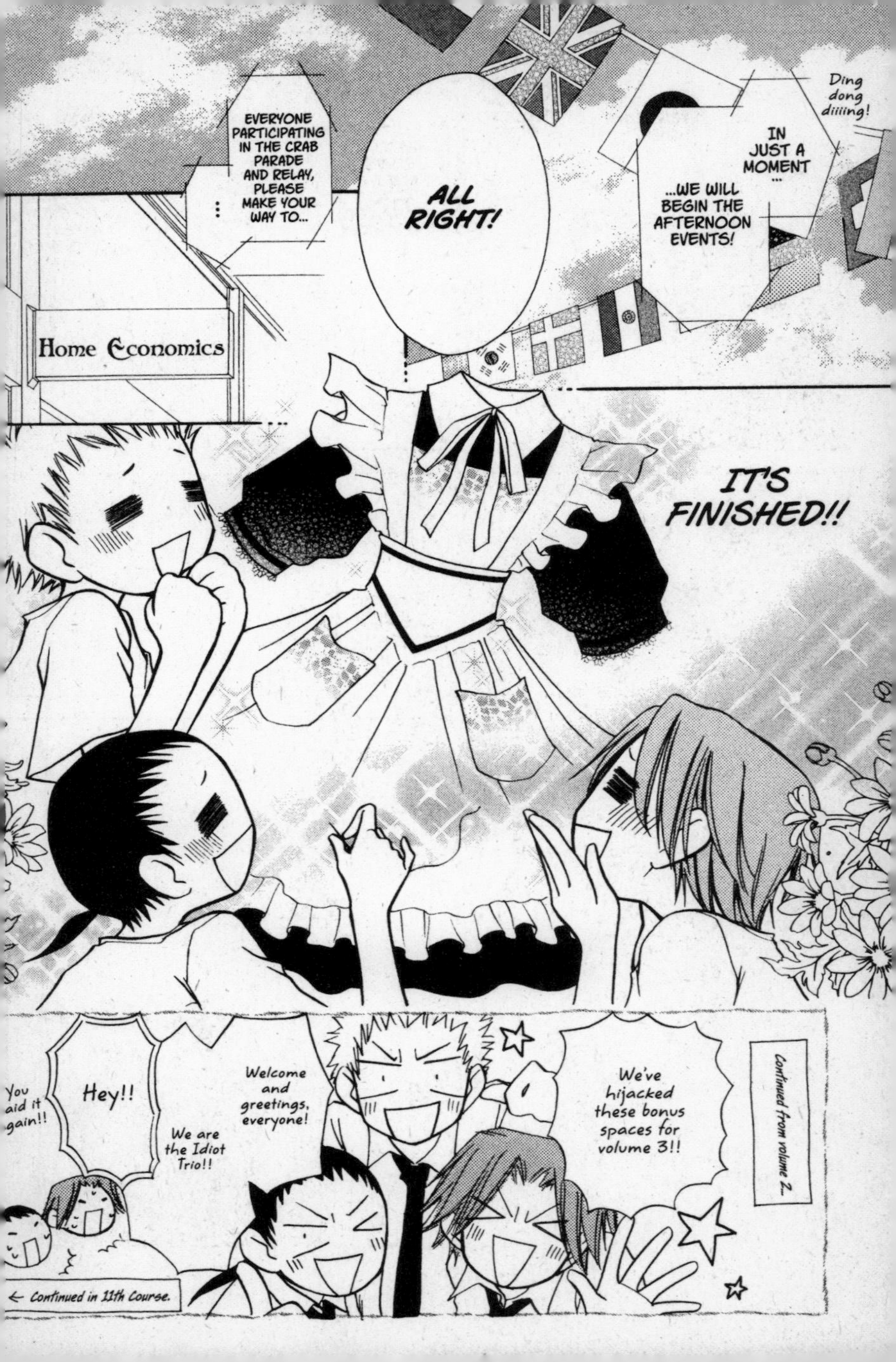

Ding dong diiiing!
IN JUST A MOMENT...
...WE WILL BEGIN THE AFTERNOON EVENTS!
EVERYONE PARTICIPATING IN THE CRAB PARADE AND RELAY, PLEASE MAKE YOUR WAY TO...
Home Economics
ALL RIGHT!
IT'S FINISHED!!
Continued from volume 2.
We've hijacked these bonus spaces for volume 3!!
Welcome and greetings, everyone!
We are the Idiot Trio!!
Hey!!
You aid it gain!!
← Continued in 11th Course.

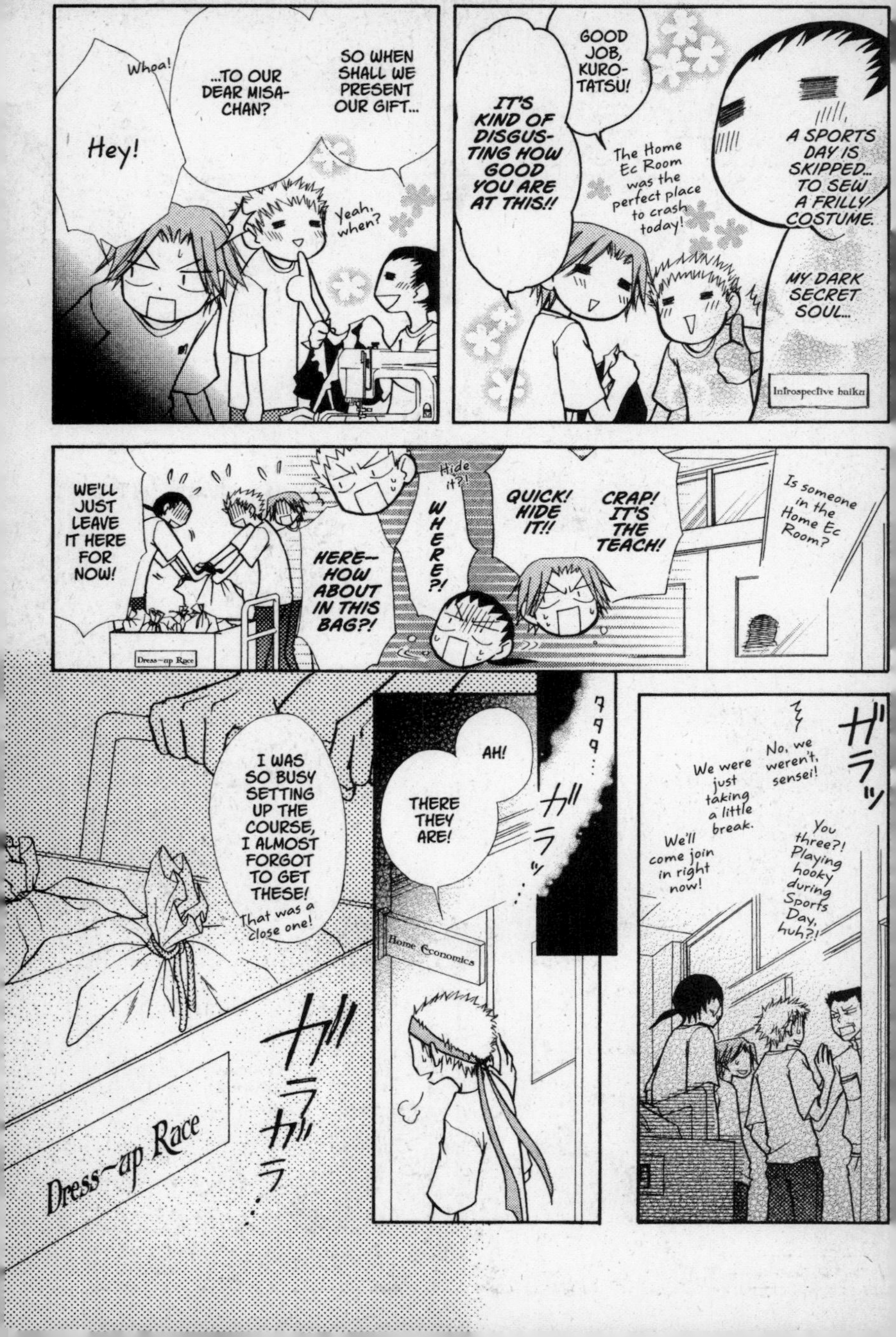
A SPORTS DAY IS SKIPPED... TO SEW A FRILLY COSTUME.
MY DARK SECRET SOUL...
Introspective haiku
GOOD JOB, KURO-TATSU!
The Home Ec Room was the perfect place to crash today!
IT'S KIND OF DISGUSTING HOW GOOD YOU ARE AT THIS!!
SO WHEN SHALL WE PRESENT OUR GIFT...
...TO OUR DEAR MISA-CHAN?
Yeah, when?
Whoa!
Hey!
Is someone in the Home Ec Room?
CRAP! IT'S THE TEACH!
QUICK! HIDE IT!!
Hide it?!
WHERE?!
HERE—HOW ABOUT IN THIS BAG?!
WE'LL JUST LEAVE IT HERE FOR NOW!
Dress-up Race
ガラッ
No, we weren't, sensei!
We were just taking a little break.
You three?! Playing hooky during Sports Day, huh?!
We'll come join in right now!
タタタ...
AH!
THERE THEY ARE!
ガラッ...
Home Economics
I WAS SO BUSY SETTING UP THE COURSE, I ALMOST FORGOT TO GET THESE!
That was a close one!
Dress-up Race
ガラ ガラ...

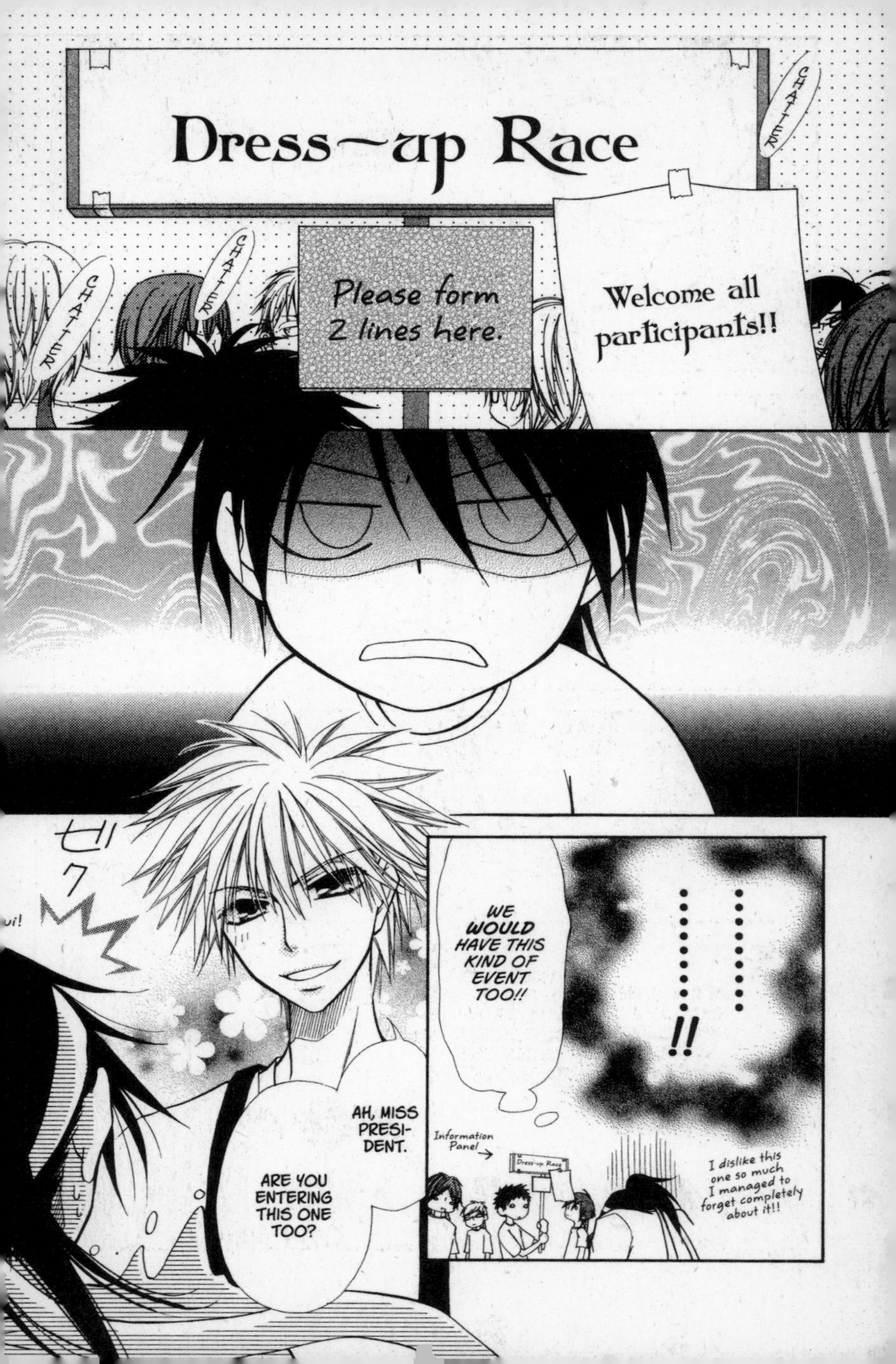
CHATTER
Dress-up Race
Welcome all participants!!
Please form 2 lines here.
CHATTER
CHATTER
......!!
WE WOULD HAVE THIS KIND OF EVENT TOO!!
I dislike this one so much I managed to forget completely about it!!
Information Panel →
Dress-up Race
ギク
AH, MISS PRESIDENT.
ARE YOU ENTERING THIS ONE TOO?

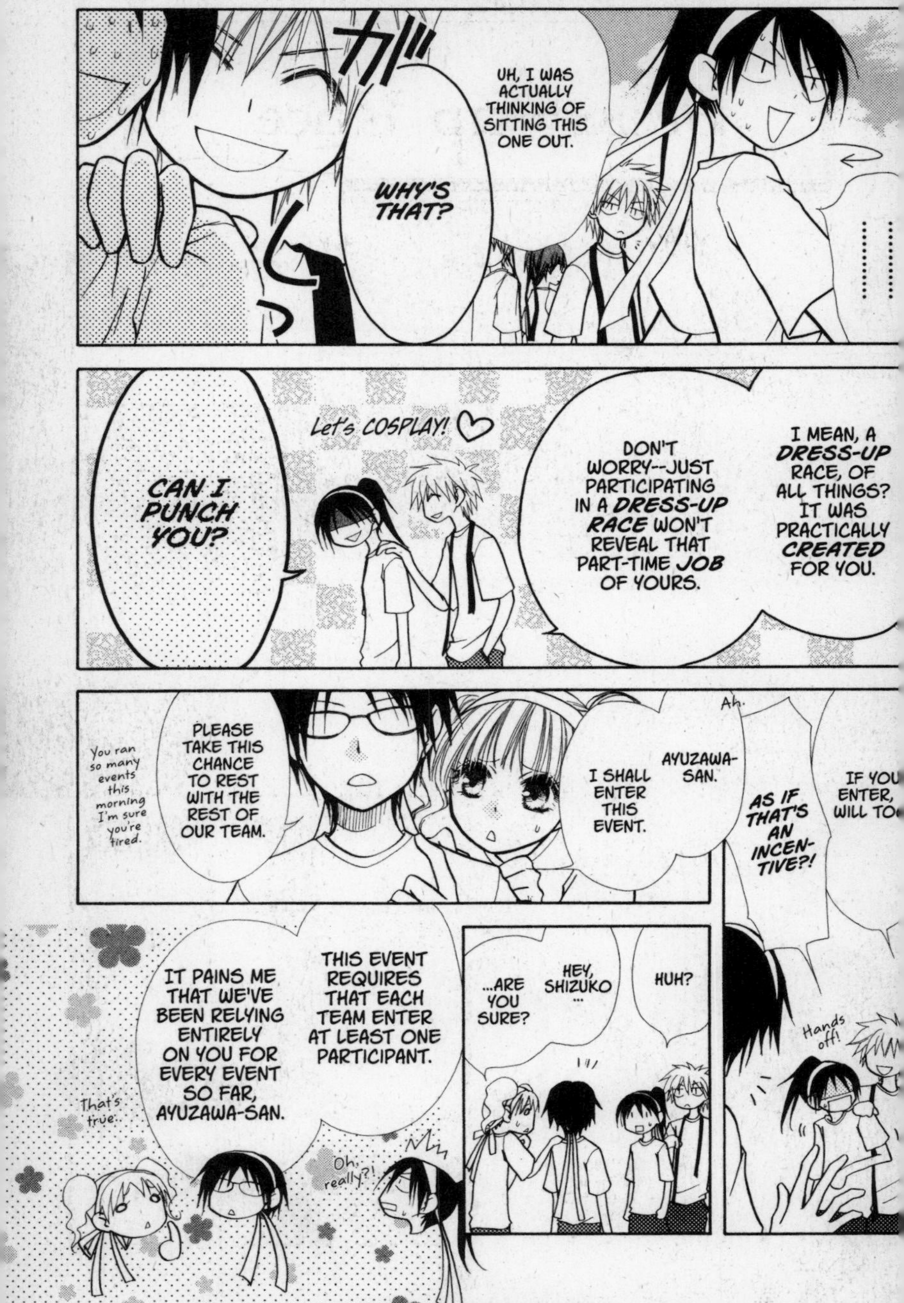
......
UH, I WAS ACTUALLY THINKING OF SITTING THIS ONE OUT.
WHY'S THAT?
I MEAN, A DRESS-UP RACE, OF ALL THINGS? IT WAS PRACTICALLY CREATED FOR YOU.
DON'T WORRY--JUST PARTICIPATING IN A DRESS-UP RACE WON'T REVEAL THAT PART-TIME JOB OF YOURS.
Let's COSPLAY!
CAN I PUNCH YOU?
IF YOU ENTER, WILL TO
AS IF THAT'S AN INCENTIVE?!
Hands off!
Ah.
AYUZAWA-SAN.
I SHALL ENTER THIS EVENT.
PLEASE TAKE THIS CHANCE TO REST WITH THE REST OF OUR TEAM.
You ran so many events this morning I'm sure you're tired.
HUH?
HEY, SHIZUKO...
...ARE YOU SURE?
THIS EVENT REQUIRES THAT EACH TEAM ENTER AT LEAST ONE PARTICIPANT.
IT PAINS ME THAT WE'VE BEEN RELYING ENTIRELY ON YOU FOR EVERY EVENT SO FAR, AYUZAWA-SAN.
That's true.
Oh, really?!

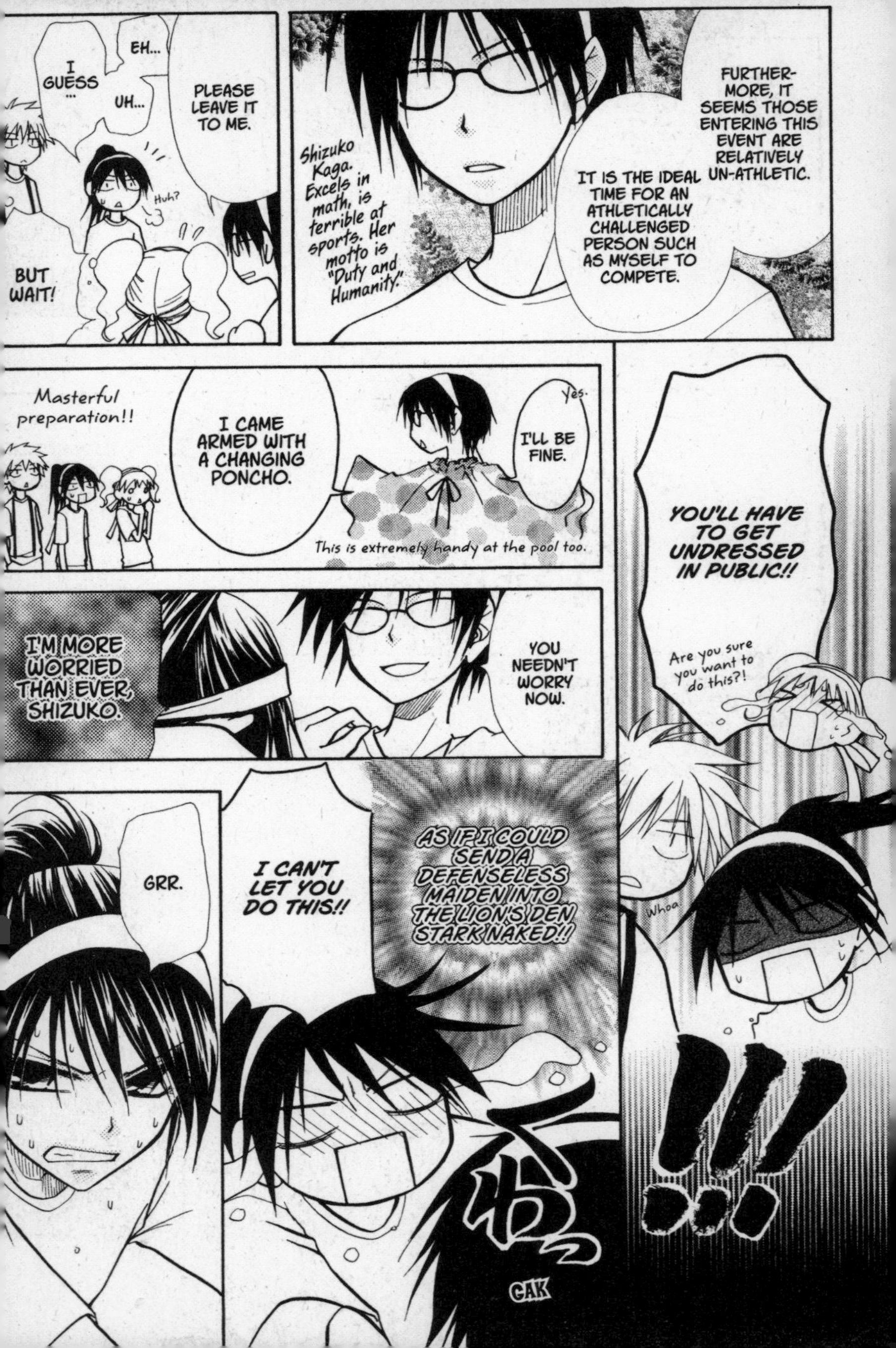
FURTHER-MORE, IT SEEMS THOSE ENTERING THIS EVENT ARE RELATIVELY UN-ATHLETIC.
IT IS THE IDEAL TIME FOR AN ATHLETICALLY CHALLENGED PERSON SUCH AS MYSELF TO COMPETE.
Shizuko Kaga. Excels in math, is terrible at sports. Her motto is "Duty and Humanity."
PLEASE LEAVE IT TO ME.
EH... UH...
I GUESS ...
Huh?
BUT WAIT!
YOU'LL HAVE TO GET UNDRESSED IN PUBLIC!!
Are you sure you want to do this?!
Whoa
!!
Yes.
I'LL BE FINE.
I CAME ARMED WITH A CHANGING PONCHO.
This is extremely handy at the pool too.
Masterful preparation!!
YOU NEEDN'T WORRY NOW.
I'M MORE WORRIED THAN EVER, SHIZUKO.
AS IF I COULD SEND A DEFENSELESS MAIDEN INTO THE LION'S DEN STARK NAKED!!
I CAN'T LET YOU DO THIS!!
GRR.
GAK

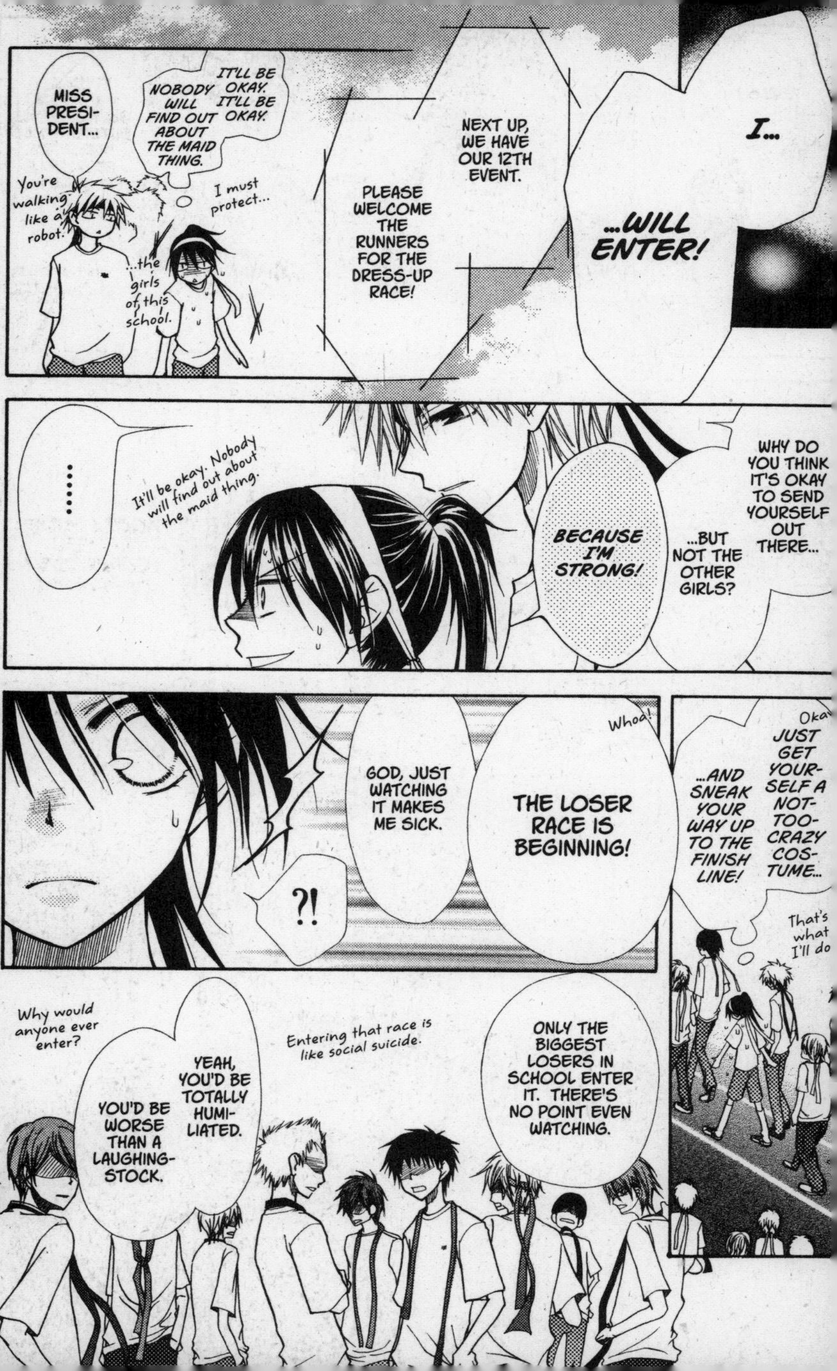
I...
...WILL ENTER!
NEXT UP, WE HAVE OUR 12TH EVENT.
PLEASE WELCOME THE RUNNERS FOR THE DRESS-UP RACE!
IT'LL BE OKAY. IT'LL BE OKAY.
NOBODY WILL FIND OUT ABOUT THE MAID THING.
MISS PRESIDENT...
I must protect...
You're walking like a robot.
...the girls of this school.
WHY DO YOU THINK IT'S OKAY TO SEND YOURSELF OUT THERE...
...BUT NOT THE OTHER GIRLS?
BECAUSE I'M STRONG!
It'll be okay. Nobody will find out about the maid thing.
......
Oka
JUST GET YOURSELF A NOT-TOO-CRAZY COSTUME...
...AND SNEAK YOUR WAY UP TO THE FINISH LINE!
That's what I'll do
Whoa!
THE LOSER RACE IS BEGINNING!
GOD, JUST WATCHING IT MAKES ME SICK.
?!
ONLY THE BIGGEST LOSERS IN SCHOOL ENTER IT. THERE'S NO POINT EVEN WATCHING.
Entering that race is like social suicide.
YEAH, YOU'D BE TOTALLY HUMILIATED.
YOU'D BE WORSE THAN A LAUGHING-STOCK.
Why would anyone ever enter?

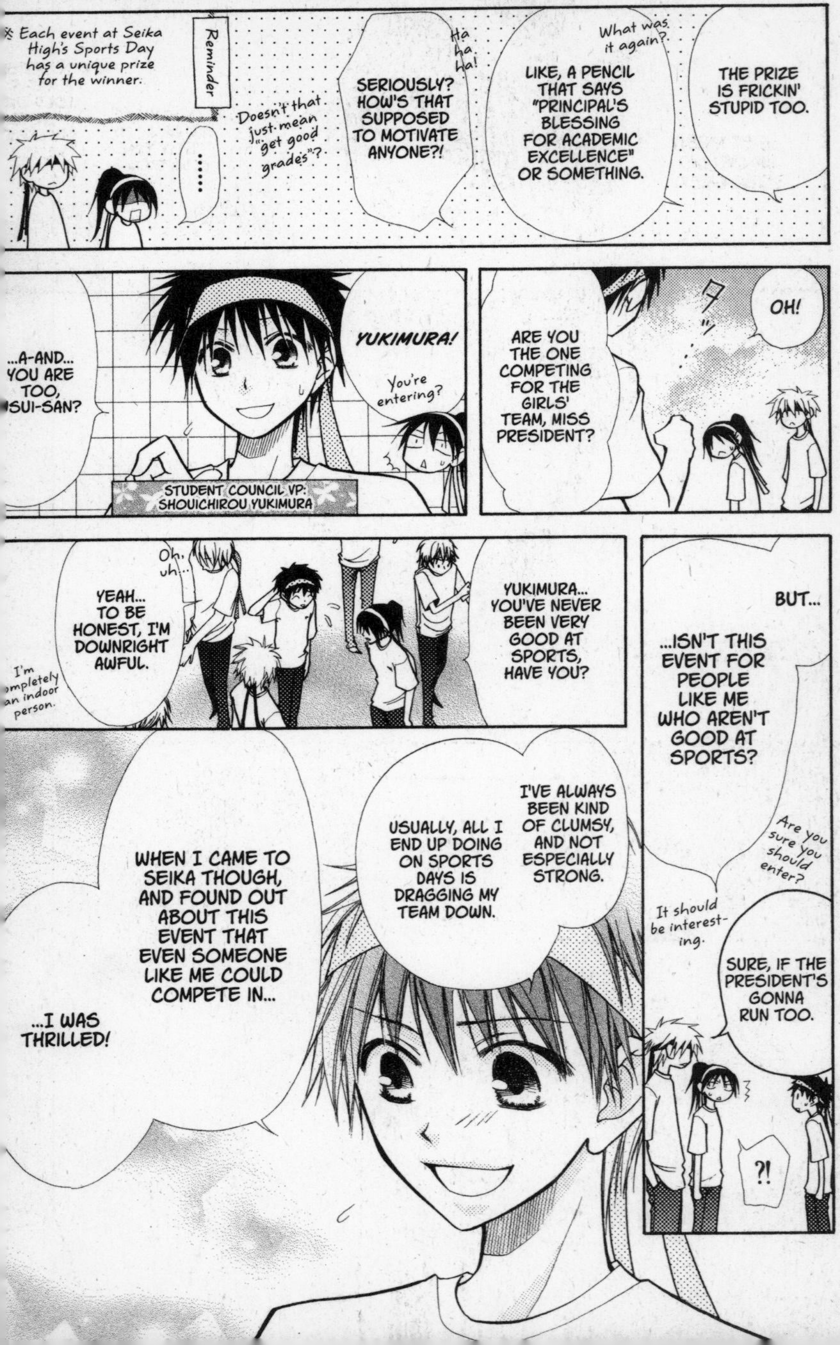
THE PRIZE IS FRICKIN' STUPID TOO.
What was it again?
LIKE, A PENCIL THAT SAYS "PRINCIPAL'S BLESSING FOR ACADEMIC EXCELLENCE" OR SOMETHING.
Ha ha ha!
SERIOUSLY? HOW'S THAT SUPPOSED TO MOTIVATE ANYONE?!
Doesn't that just mean "get good grades"?
......
Reminder
※ Each event at Seika High's Sports Day has a unique prize for the winner.
OH!
ARE YOU THE ONE COMPETING FOR THE GIRLS' TEAM, MISS PRESIDENT?
YUKIMURA!
You're entering?
...A-AND... YOU ARE TOO, SUI-SAN?
STUDENT COUNCIL VP: SHOUICHIROU YUKIMURA
BUT...
...ISN'T THIS EVENT FOR PEOPLE LIKE ME WHO AREN'T GOOD AT SPORTS?
Are you sure you should enter?
It should be interesting.
SURE, IF THE PRESIDENT'S GONNA RUN TOO.
?!
YUKIMURA... YOU'VE NEVER BEEN VERY GOOD AT SPORTS, HAVE YOU?
Oh, uh...
YEAH... TO BE HONEST, I'M DOWNRIGHT AWFUL.
I'm mpletely an indoor person.
I'VE ALWAYS BEEN KIND OF CLUMSY, AND NOT ESPECIALLY STRONG.
USUALLY, ALL I END UP DOING ON SPORTS DAYS IS DRAGGING MY TEAM DOWN.
WHEN I CAME TO SEIKA THOUGH, AND FOUND OUT ABOUT THIS EVENT THAT EVEN SOMEONE LIKE ME COULD COMPETE IN...
...I WAS THRILLED!

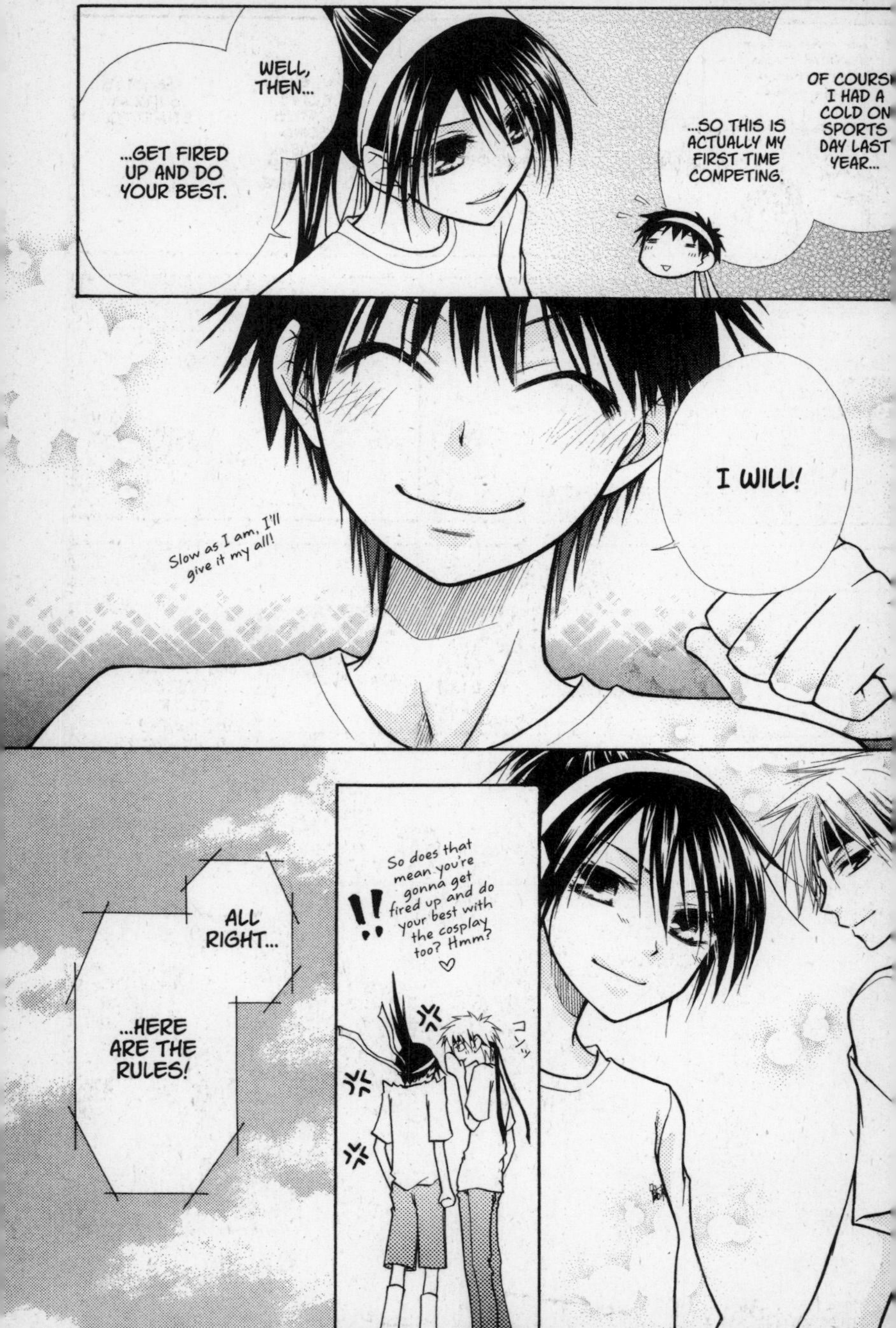
OF COURS I HAD A COLD ON SPORTS DAY LAST YEAR...
...SO THIS IS ACTUALLY MY FIRST TIME COMPETING.
WELL, THEN...
...GET FIRED UP AND DO YOUR BEST.
I WILL!
Slow as I am, I'll give it my all!
So does that mean you're gonna get fired up and do your best with the cosplay too? Hmm? ♡
!!
コンッ
ALL RIGHT...
...HERE ARE THE RULES!

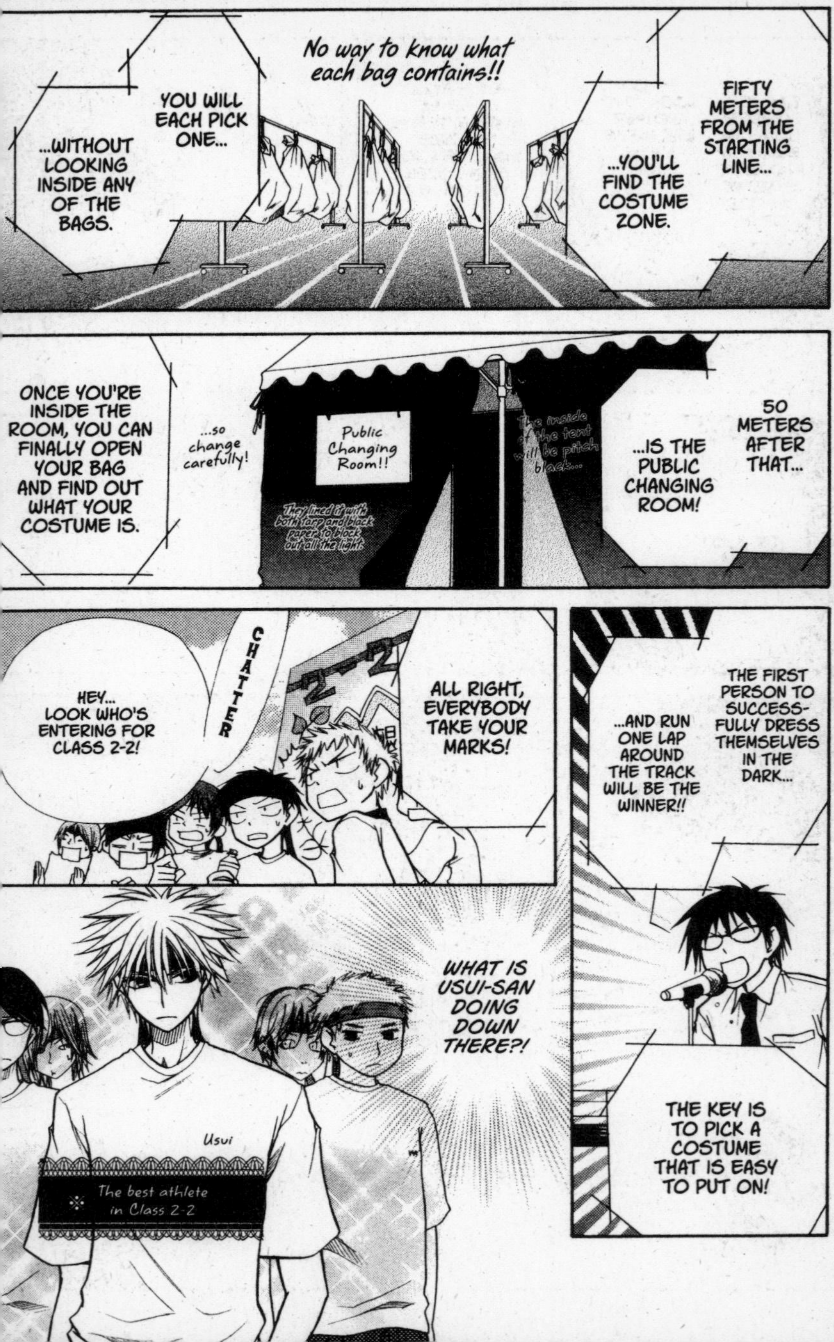
FIFTY METERS FROM THE STARTING LINE...
...YOU'LL FIND THE COSTUME ZONE.
No way to know what each bag contains!!
YOU WILL EACH PICK ONE...
...WITHOUT LOOKING INSIDE ANY OF THE BAGS.
50 METERS AFTER THAT...
...IS THE PUBLIC CHANGING ROOM!
The inside of the tent will be pitch black...
Public Changing Room!!
They lined it with both tarp and black paper to block out all the light.
...so change carefully!
ONCE YOU'RE INSIDE THE ROOM, YOU CAN FINALLY OPEN YOUR BAG AND FIND OUT WHAT YOUR COSTUME IS.
THE FIRST PERSON TO SUCCESSFULLY DRESS THEMSELVES IN THE DARK...
...AND RUN ONE LAP AROUND THE TRACK WILL BE THE WINNER!!
THE KEY IS TO PICK A COSTUME THAT IS EASY TO PUT ON!
ALL RIGHT, EVERYBODY TAKE YOUR MARKS!
CHATTER
HEY... LOOK WHO'S ENTERING FOR CLASS 2-2!
WHAT IS USUI-SAN DOING DOWN THERE?!
Usui
※ The best athlete in Class 2-2

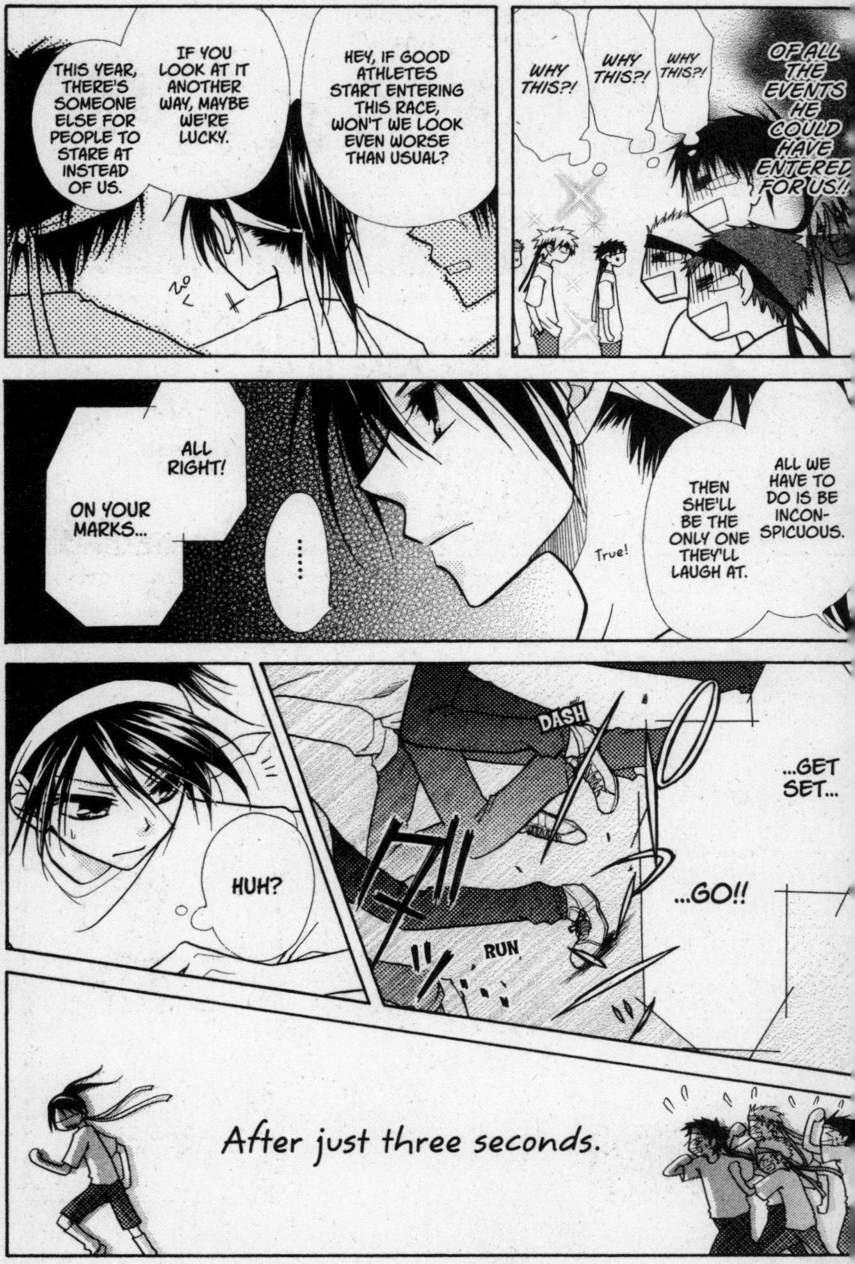
WHY THIS?!
WHY THIS?!
WHY THIS?!
OF ALL THE EVENTS HE COULD HAVE ENTERED FOR US!!
HEY, IF GOOD ATHLETES START ENTERING THIS RACE, WON'T WE LOOK EVEN WORSE THAN USUAL?
IF YOU LOOK AT IT ANOTHER WAY, MAYBE WE'RE LUCKY.
THIS YEAR, THERE'S SOMEONE ELSE FOR PEOPLE TO STARE AT INSTEAD OF US.
ALL WE HAVE TO DO IS BE INCON-SPICUOUS.
THEN SHE'LL BE THE ONLY ONE THEY'LL LAUGH AT.
True!
......
ALL RIGHT!
ON YOUR MARKS...
...GET SET...
DASH
...GO!!
RUN
HUH?
After just three seconds.

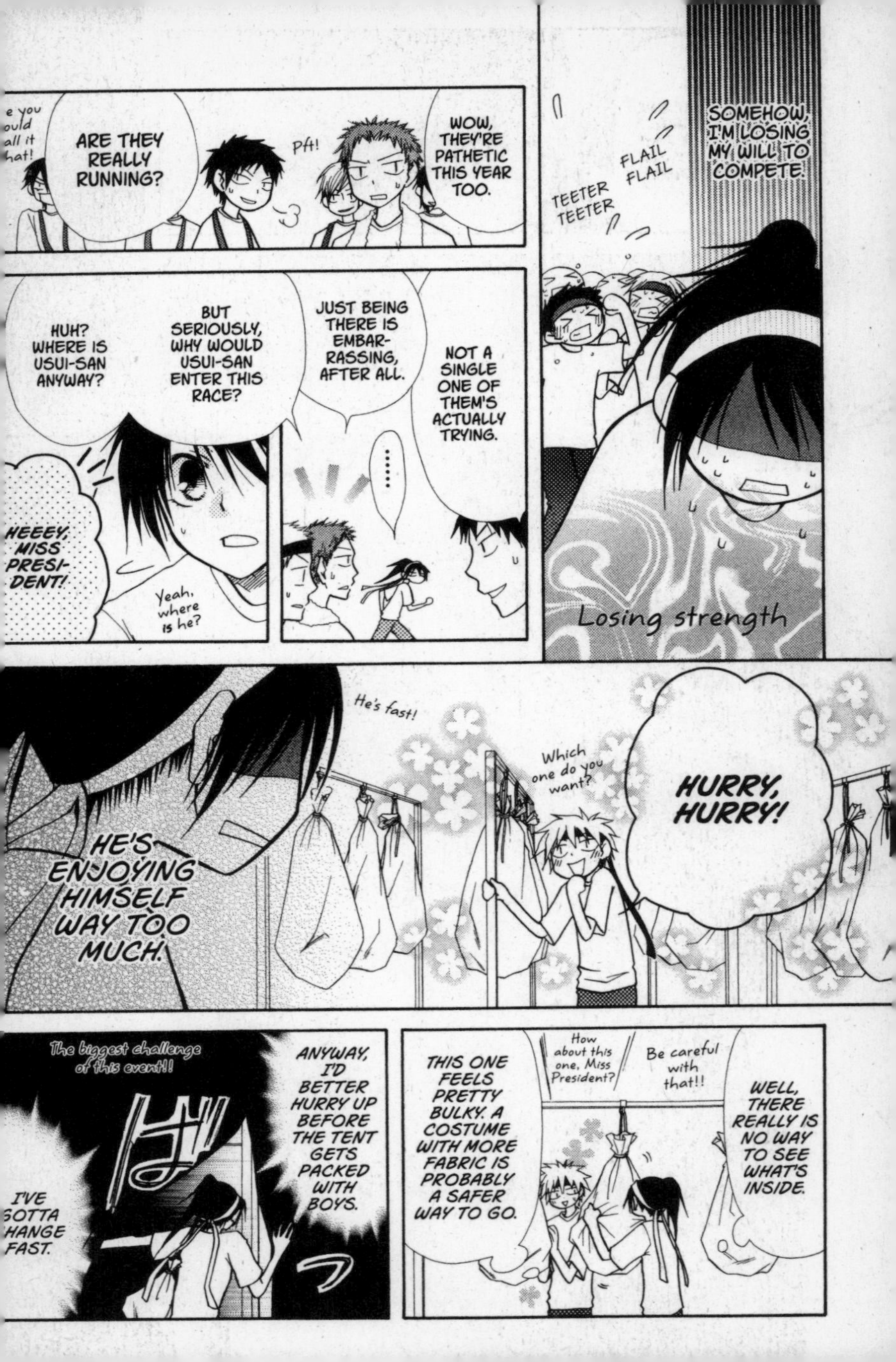
SOMEHOW, I'M LOSING MY WILL TO COMPETE.
FLAIL FLAIL
TEETER TEETER
Losing strength
WOW, THEY'RE PATHETIC THIS YEAR TOO.
Pft!
ARE THEY REALLY RUNNING?
NOT A SINGLE ONE OF THEM'S ACTUALLY TRYING.
JUST BEING THERE IS EMBAR-RASSING, AFTER ALL.
......
BUT SERIOUSLY, WHY WOULD USUI-SAN ENTER THIS RACE?
HUH? WHERE IS USUI-SAN ANYWAY?
HEEEY, MISS PRESI-DENT!
Yeah, where is he?
HURRY, HURRY!
Which one do you want?
He's fast!
HE'S ENJOYING HIMSELF WAY TOO MUCH.
WELL, THERE REALLY IS NO WAY TO SEE WHAT'S INSIDE.
Be careful with that!!
How about this one, Miss President?
THIS ONE FEELS PRETTY BULKY. A COSTUME WITH MORE FABRIC IS PROBABLY A SAFER WAY TO GO.
ANYWAY, I'D BETTER HURRY UP BEFORE THE TENT GETS PACKED WITH BOYS.
The biggest challenge of this event!!
FAST.

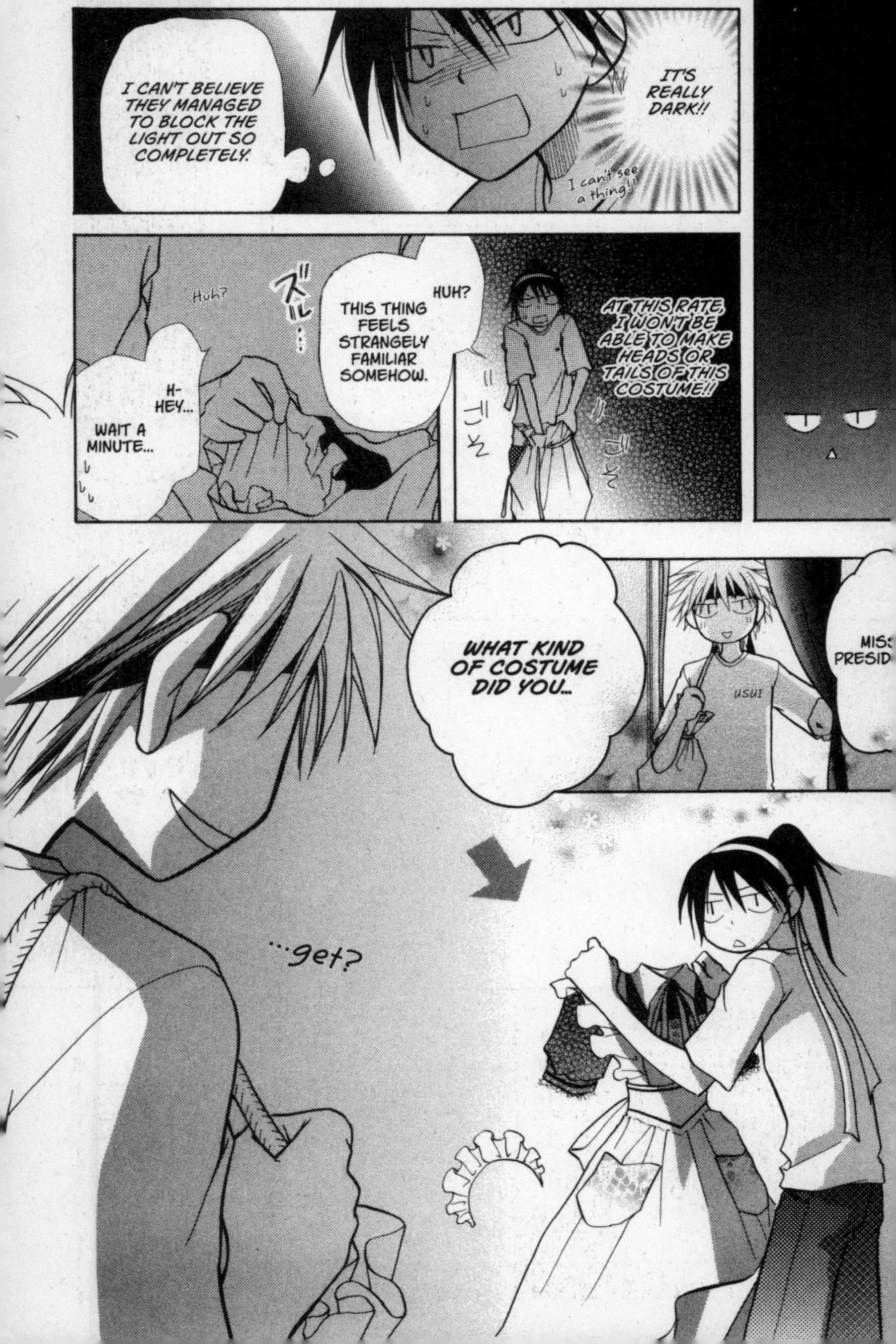
IT'S REALLY DARK!!
I can't see a thing!!
I CAN'T BELIEVE THEY MANAGED TO BLOCK THE LIGHT OUT SO COMPLETELY.
AT THIS RATE, I WON'T BE ABLE TO MAKE HEADS OR TAILS OF THIS COSTUME!!
ゴソ
ゴソ
ズル…
HUH?
THIS THING FEELS STRANGELY FAMILIAR SOMEHOW.
Huh?
H-HEY...
WAIT A MINUTE...
MISS PRESID
WHAT KIND OF COSTUME DID YOU...
...get?

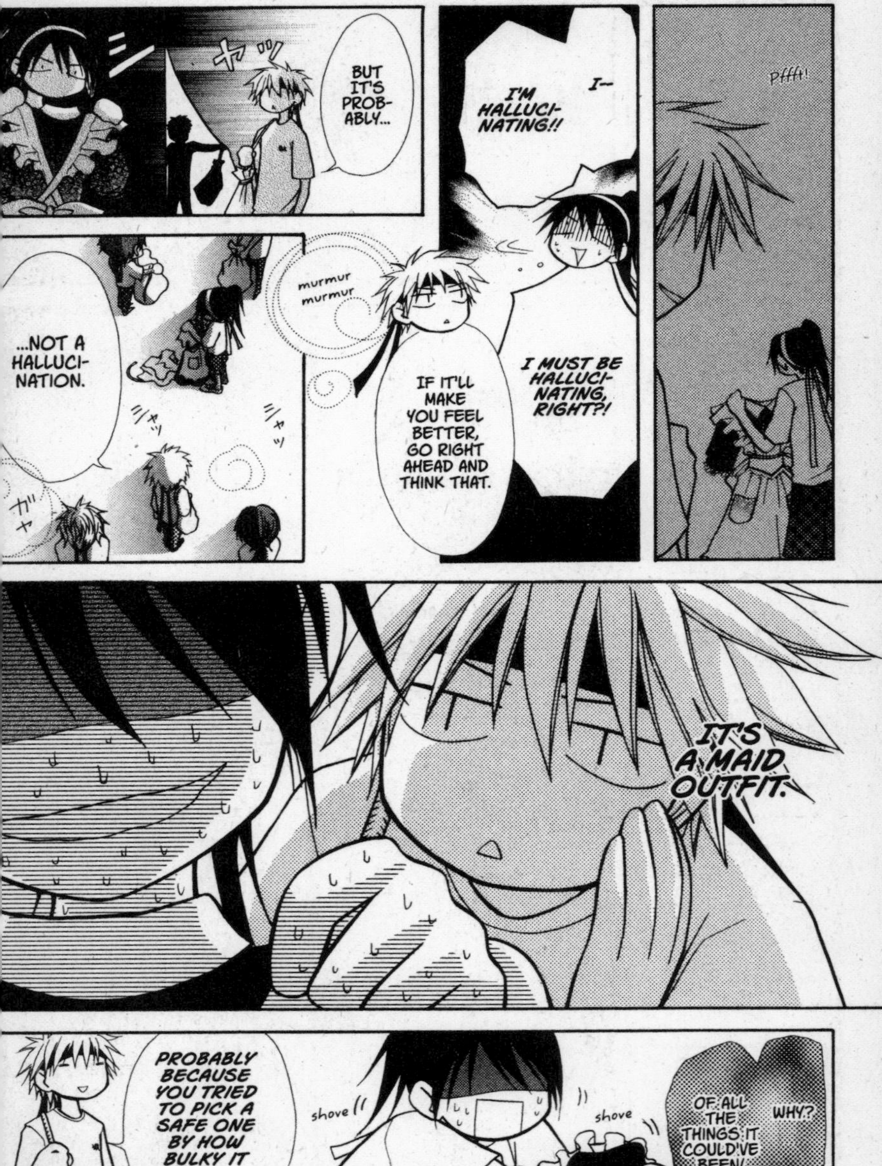
Pffft!
I--
I'M HALLUCINATING!!
I MUST BE HALLUCINATING, RIGHT?!
murmur murmur
IF IT'LL MAKE YOU FEEL BETTER, GO RIGHT AHEAD AND THINK THAT.
ヤッ
BUT IT'S PROBABLY...
...NOT A HALLUCINATION.
シャッ
シャッ
ガヤ
IT'S A MAID OUTFIT.
WHY?!
OF ALL THE THINGS IT COULD'VE BEEN!
shove
shove
Unconsciously stuffing it back in the bag.
PROBABLY BECAUSE YOU TRIED TO PICK A SAFE ONE BY HOW BULKY IT WAS. ☆

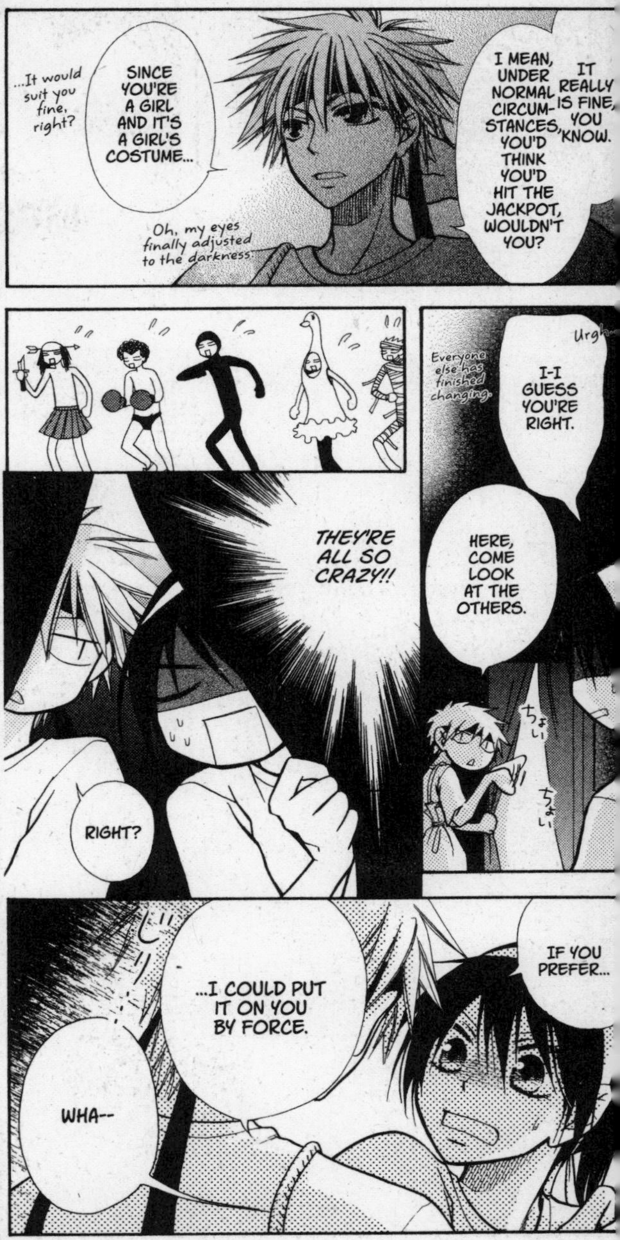
IT REALLY IS FINE, YOU KNOW.
I MEAN, UNDER NORMAL CIRCUM-STANCES, YOU'D THINK YOU'D HIT THE JACKPOT, WOULDN'T YOU?
SINCE YOU'RE A GIRL AND IT'S A GIRL'S COSTUME...
...It would suit you fine, right?
Oh, my eyes finally adjusted to the darkness.
Urgh...
I-I GUESS YOU'RE RIGHT.
Everyone else has finished changing.
HERE, COME LOOK AT THE OTHERS.
ちょい
ちょい
THEY'RE ALL SO CRAZY!!
RIGHT?
IF YOU PREFER...
...I COULD PUT IT ON YOU BY FORCE.
WHA--

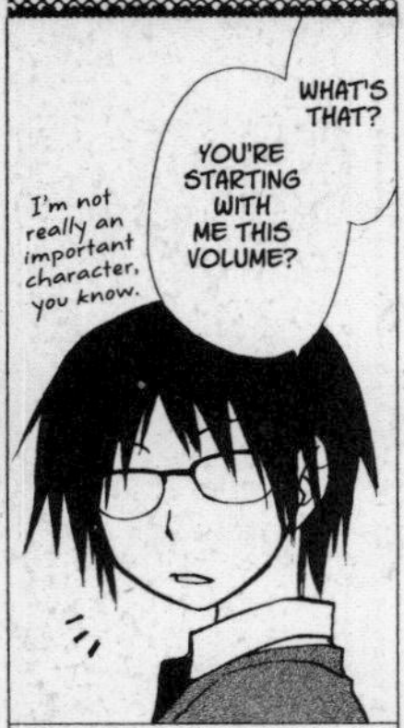
WHAT'S THAT?
YOU'RE STARTING WITH ME THIS VOLUME?
I'm not really an important character, you know.

NAME

Shizuko Kaga

AGE (Class)

16 (Class 2-3)

BLOOD TYPE

A

HEIGHT

158 cm (5ft 2in)

WEIGHT

47 kg (104 lbs)

SPECIAL SKILLS

Flower Arranging

LIKES

Zen Meditation

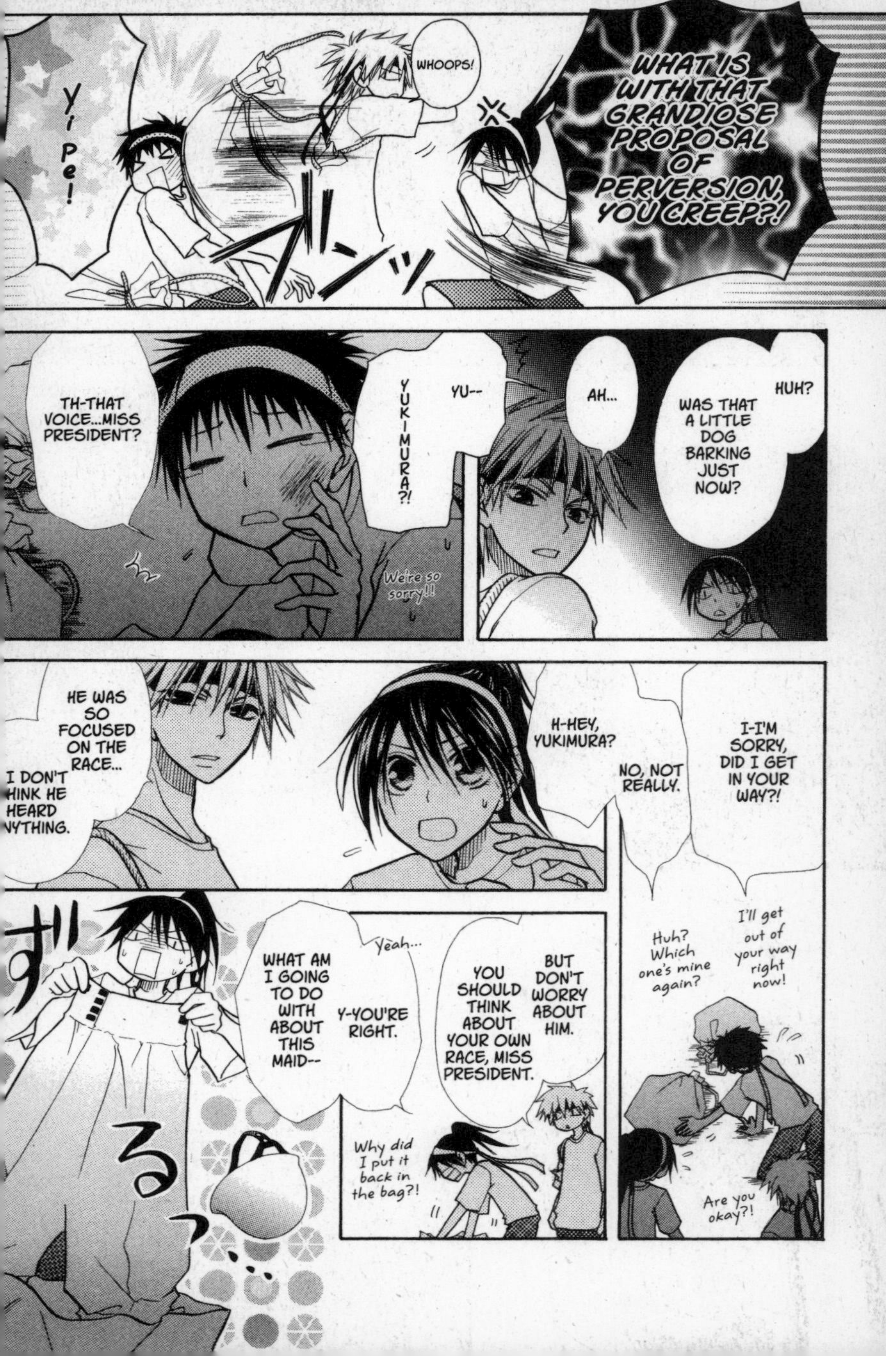
WHAT IS WITH THAT GRANDIOSE PROPOSAL OF PERVERSION, YOU CREEP?!
WHOOPS!
Yipe!
HUH?
WAS THAT A LITTLE DOG BARKING JUST NOW?
AH...
YU--
YUKIMURA?!
TH-THAT VOICE...MISS PRESIDENT?
We're so sorry!!
I-I'M SORRY, DID I GET IN YOUR WAY?!
NO, NOT REALLY.
H-HEY, YUKIMURA?
HE WAS SO FOCUSED ON THE RACE...
I DON'T THINK HE HEARD NYTHING.
I'll get out of your way right now!
Huh? Which one's mine again?
Are you okay?!
BUT DON'T WORRY ABOUT HIM.
YOU SHOULD THINK ABOUT YOUR OWN RACE, MISS PRESIDENT.
Yeah...
Y-YOU'RE RIGHT.
Why did I put it back in the bag?!
WHAT AM I GOING TO DO WITH ABOUT THIS MAID--

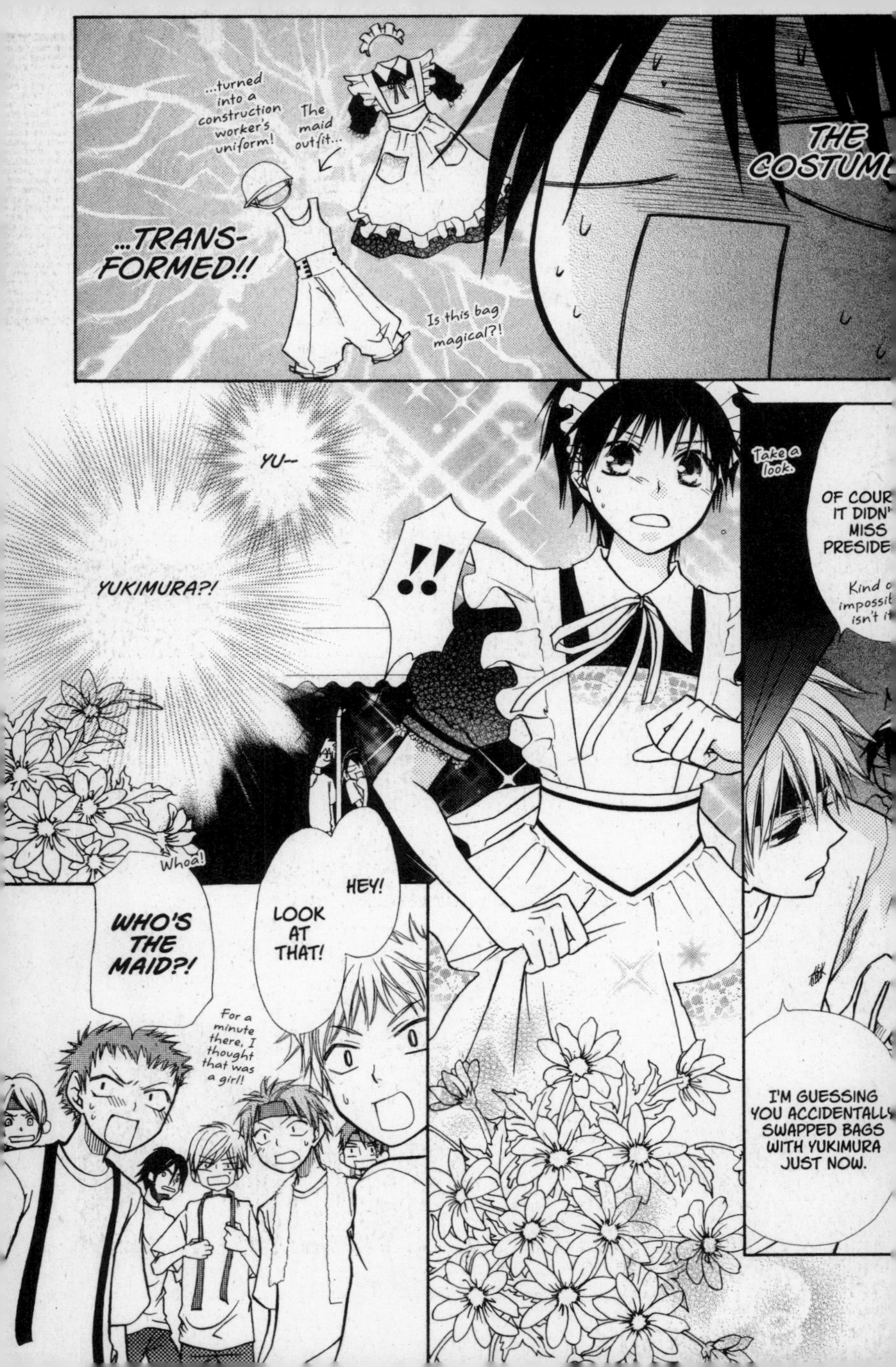
THE COSTUM
The maid outfit...
...turned into a construction worker's uniform!
...TRANS-FORMED!!
Is this bag magical?!
Take a look.
OF COUR IT DIDN' MISS PRESIDE
Kind o impossib isn't i
I'M GUESSING YOU ACCIDENTALLY SWAPPED BAGS WITH YUKIMURA JUST NOW.
!!
YU--
YUKIMURA?!
Whoa!
HEY!
LOOK AT THAT!
WHO'S THE MAID?!
For a minute there, I thought that was a girl!

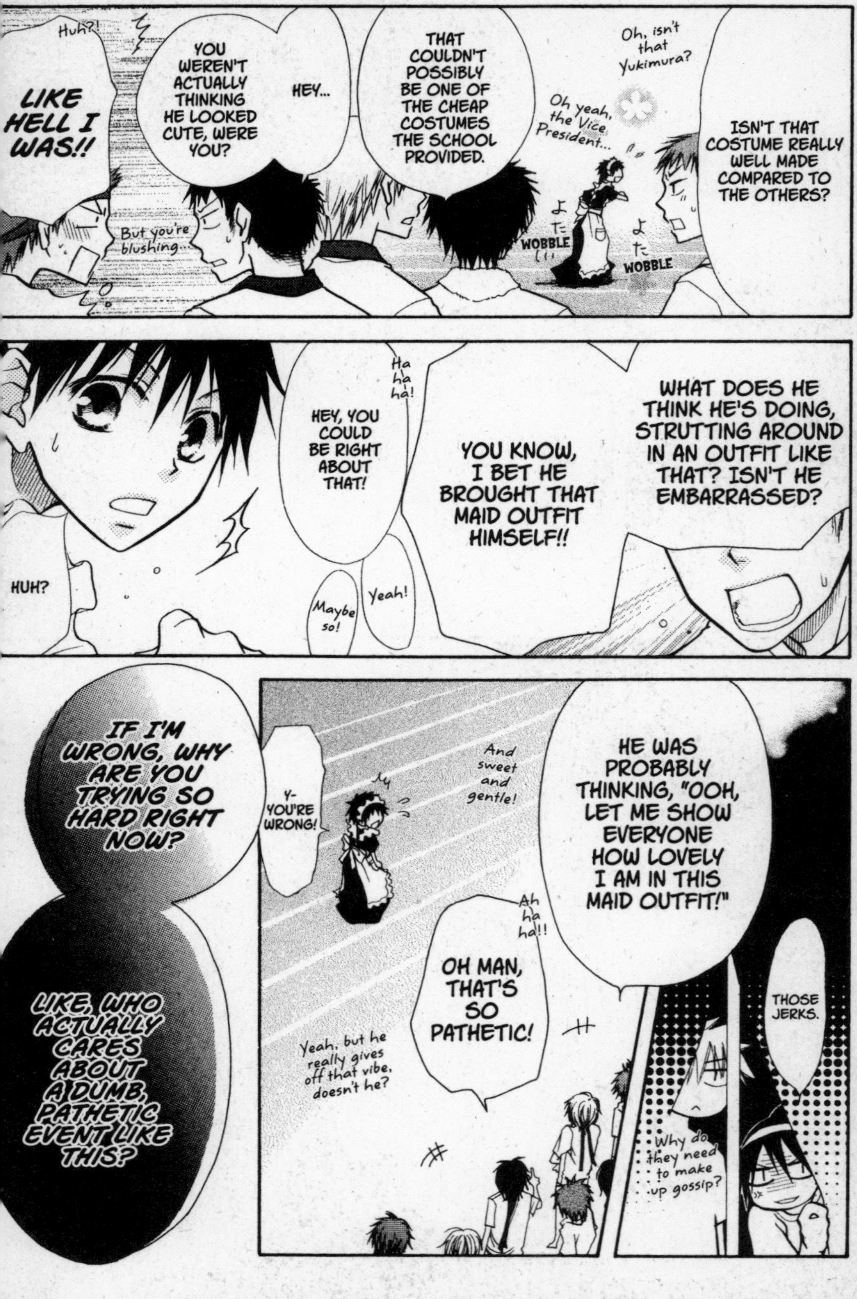
ISN'T THAT COSTUME REALLY WELL MADE COMPARED TO THE OTHERS?
Oh, isn't that Yukimura?
Oh yeah, the Vice President...
よた WOBBLE
よた WOBBLE
THAT COULDN'T POSSIBLY BE ONE OF THE CHEAP COSTUMES THE SCHOOL PROVIDED.
HEY...
YOU WEREN'T ACTUALLY THINKING HE LOOKED CUTE, WERE YOU?
Huh?!
LIKE HELL I WAS!!
But you're blushing...
WHAT DOES HE THINK HE'S DOING, STRUTTING AROUND IN AN OUTFIT LIKE THAT? ISN'T HE EMBARRASSED?
YOU KNOW, I BET HE BROUGHT THAT MAID OUTFIT HIMSELF!!
Ha ha ha!
HEY, YOU COULD BE RIGHT ABOUT THAT!
Yeah!
Maybe so!
HUH?
THOSE JERKS.
Why do they need to make up gossip?
HE WAS PROBABLY THINKING, "OOH, LET ME SHOW EVERYONE HOW LOVELY I AM IN THIS MAID OUTFIT!"
Ah ha ha!!
OH MAN, THAT'S SO PATHETIC!
Yeah, but he really gives off that vibe, doesn't he?
And sweet and gentle!
Y-YOU'RE WRONG!
IF I'M WRONG, WHY ARE YOU TRYING SO HARD RIGHT NOW?
LIKE, WHO ACTUALLY CARES ABOUT A DUMB, PATHETIC EVENT LIKE THIS?

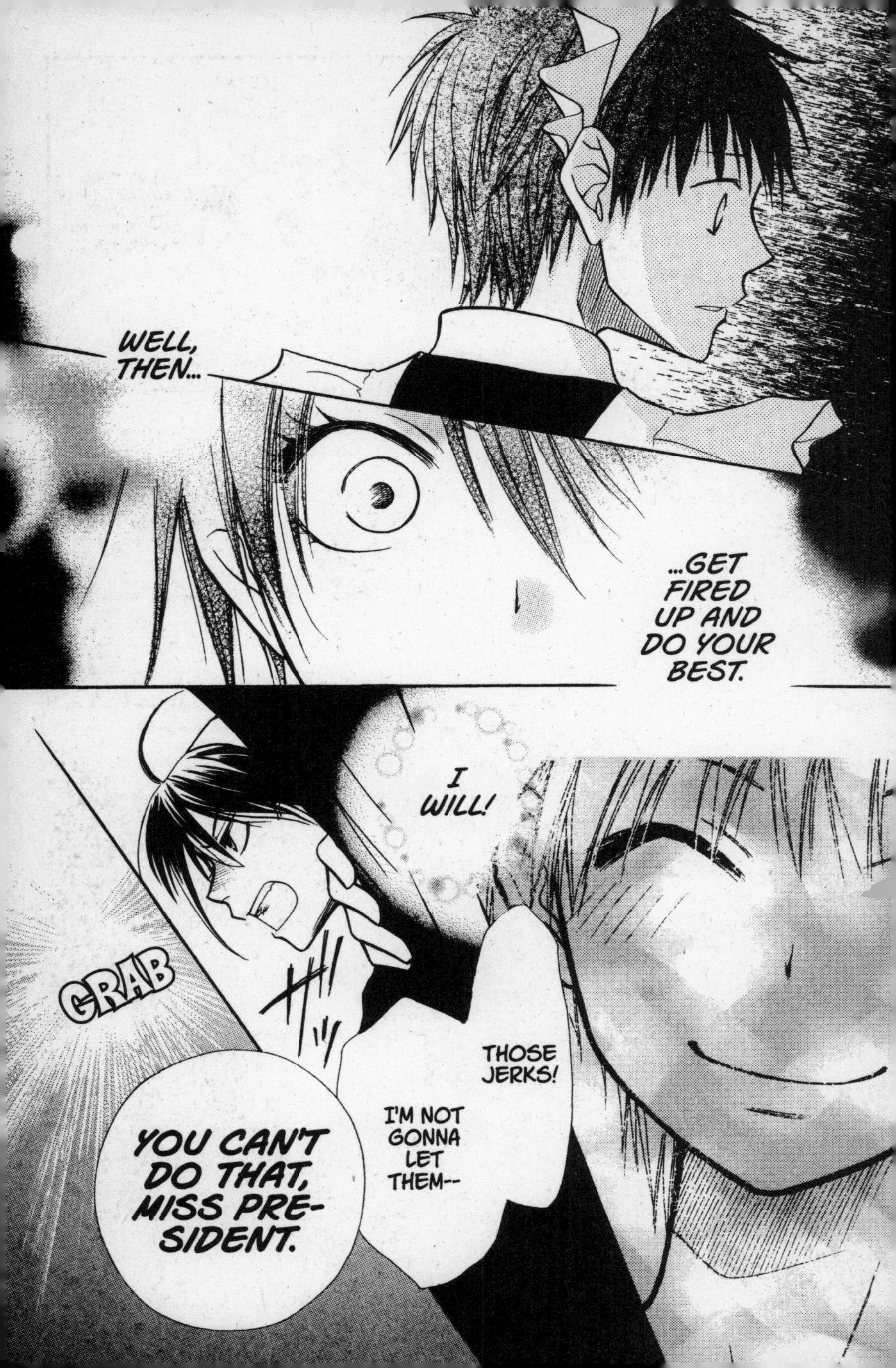
WELL, THEN...
...GET FIRED UP AND DO YOUR BEST.
I WILL!
THOSE JERKS!
I'M NOT GONNA LET THEM--
GRAB
YOU CAN'T DO THAT, MISS PRE-SIDENT.

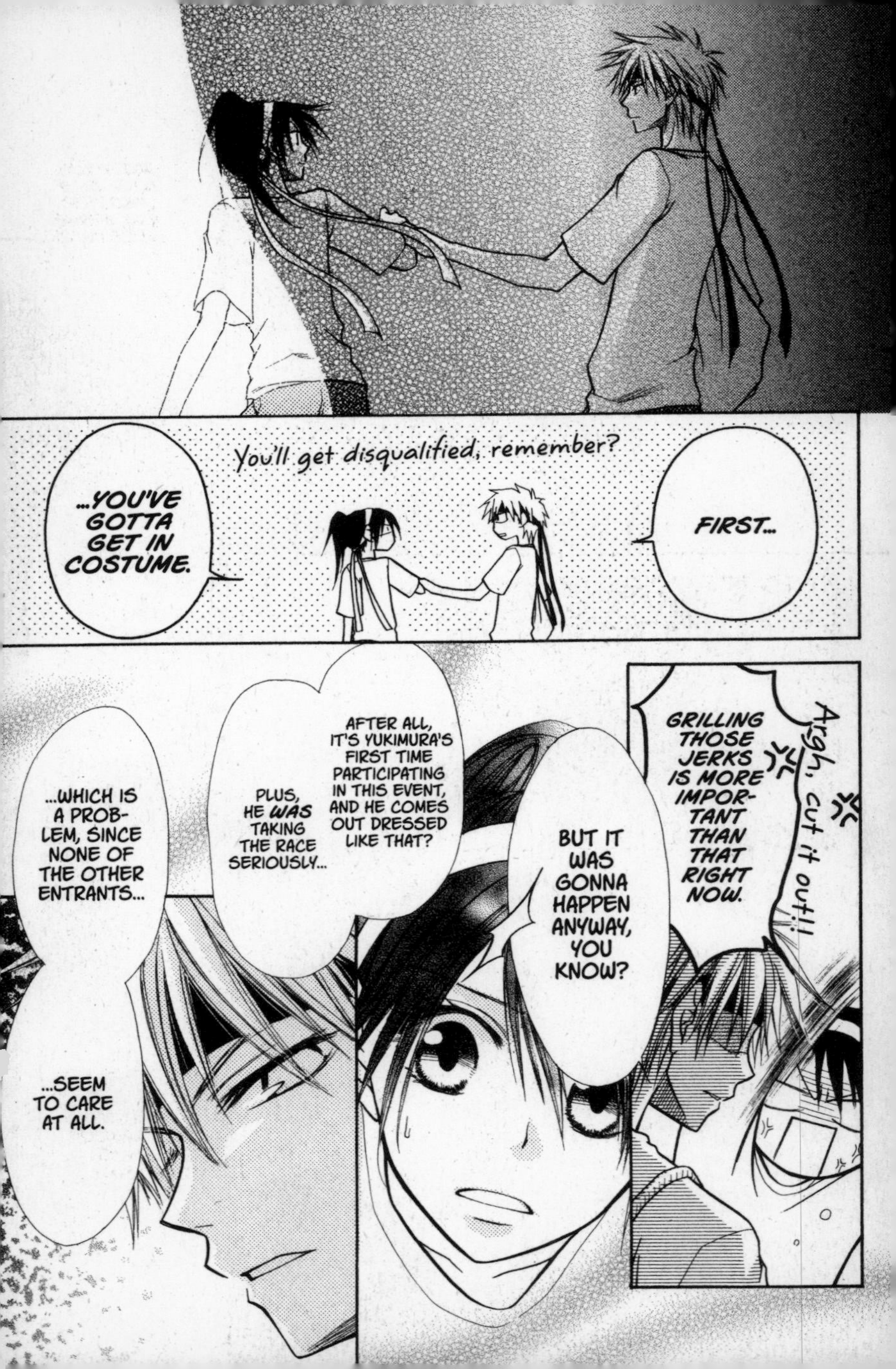
FIRST...
...YOU'VE GOTTA GET IN COSTUME.
You'll get disqualified, remember?
GRILLING THOSE JERKS IS MORE IMPORTANT THAN THAT RIGHT NOW.
Argh, cut it out!!
BUT IT WAS GONNA HAPPEN ANYWAY, YOU KNOW?
AFTER ALL, IT'S YUKIMURA'S FIRST TIME PARTICIPATING IN THIS EVENT, AND HE COMES OUT DRESSED LIKE THAT?
PLUS, HE *WAS* TAKING THE RACE SERIOUSLY...
...WHICH IS A PROBLEM, SINCE NONE OF THE OTHER ENTRANTS...
...SEEM TO CARE AT ALL.

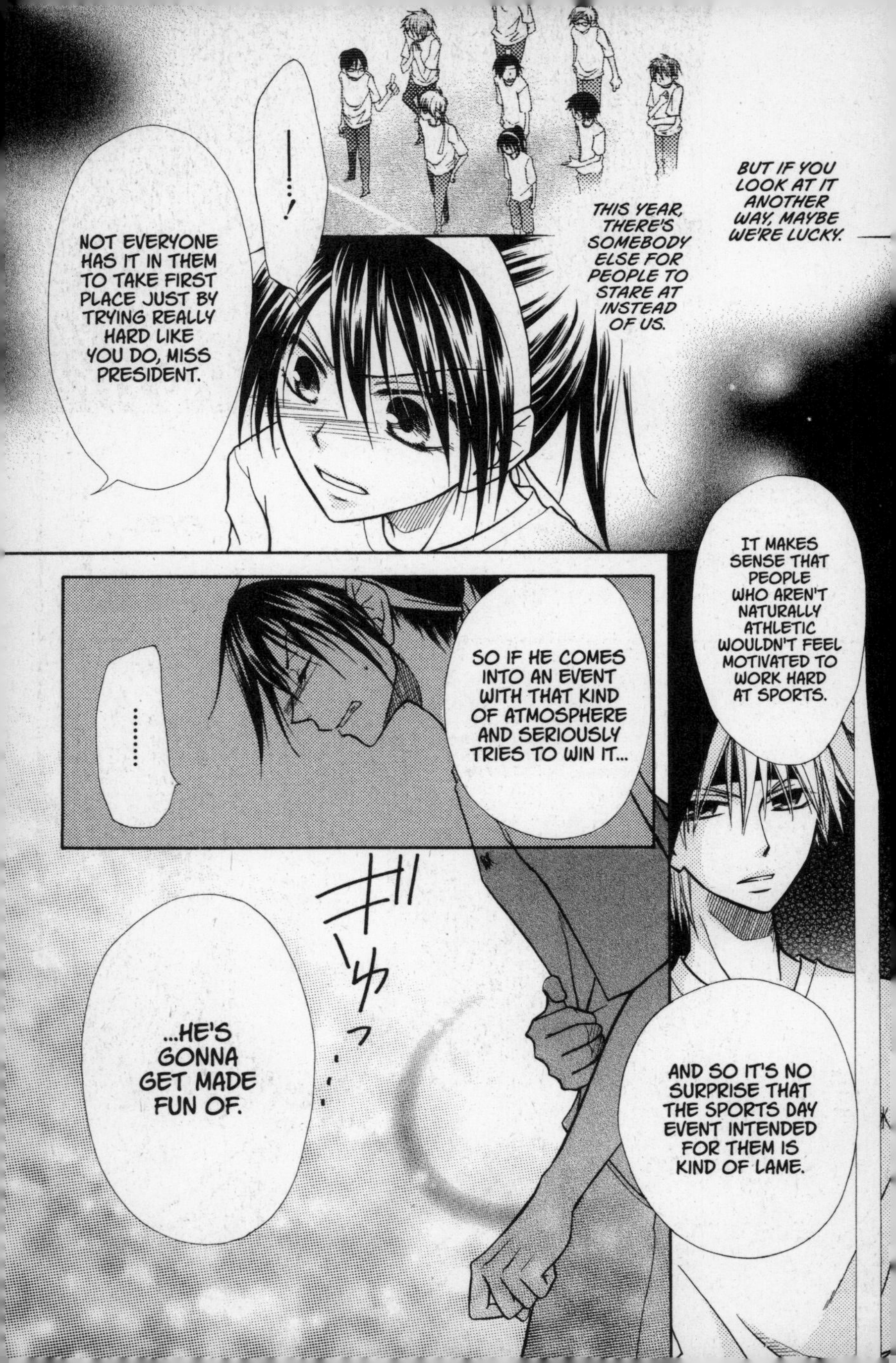
BUT IF YOU LOOK AT IT ANOTHER WAY, MAYBE WE'RE LUCKY.
THIS YEAR, THERE'S SOMEBODY ELSE FOR PEOPLE TO STARE AT INSTEAD OF US.
—!
NOT EVERYONE HAS IT IN THEM TO TAKE FIRST PLACE JUST BY TRYING REALLY HARD LIKE YOU DO, MISS PRESIDENT.
IT MAKES SENSE THAT PEOPLE WHO AREN'T NATURALLY ATHLETIC WOULDN'T FEEL MOTIVATED TO WORK HARD AT SPORTS.
AND SO IT'S NO SURPRISE THAT THE SPORTS DAY EVENT INTENDED FOR THEM IS KIND OF LAME.
SO IF HE COMES INTO AN EVENT WITH THAT KIND OF ATMOSPHERE AND SERIOUSLY TRIES TO WIN IT...
......
...HE'S GONNA GET MADE FUN OF.

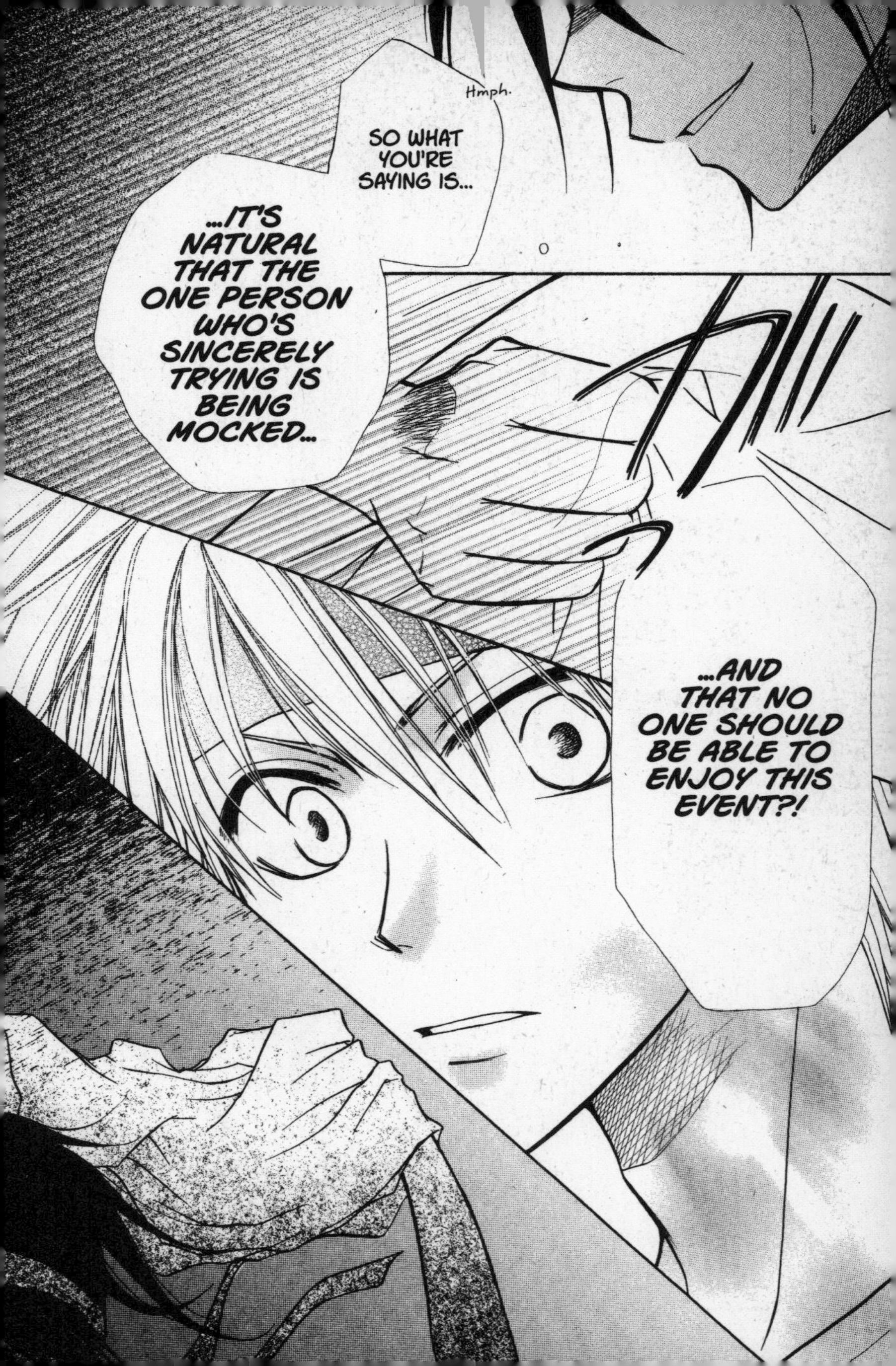
Hmph.
SO WHAT YOU'RE SAYING IS...
...IT'S NATURAL THAT THE ONE PERSON WHO'S SINCERELY TRYING IS BEING MOCKED...
...AND THAT NO ONE SHOULD BE ABLE TO ENJOY THIS EVENT?!

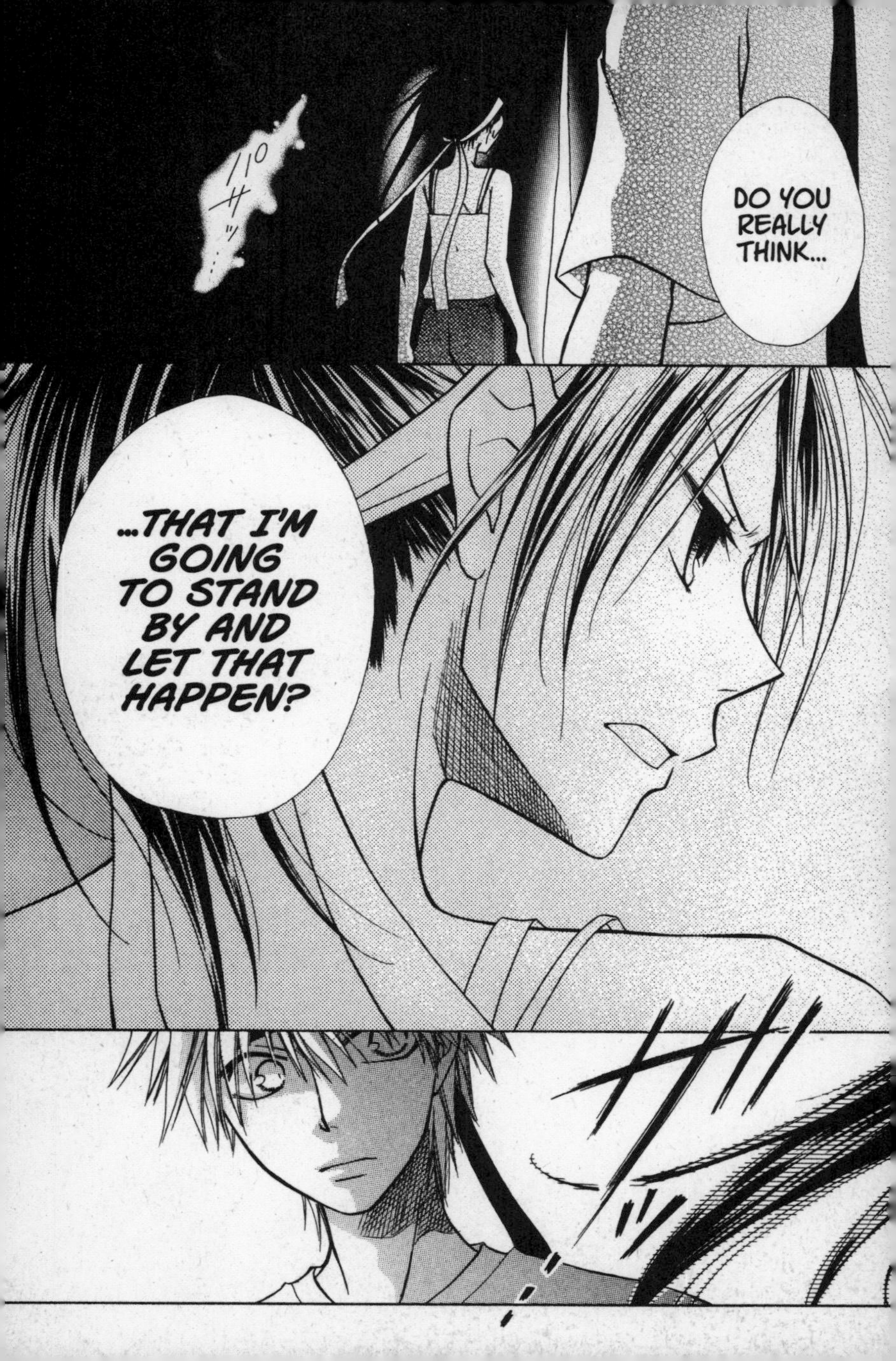
DO YOU REALLY THINK...
パサッ
...THAT I'M GOING TO STAND BY AND LET THAT HAPPEN?

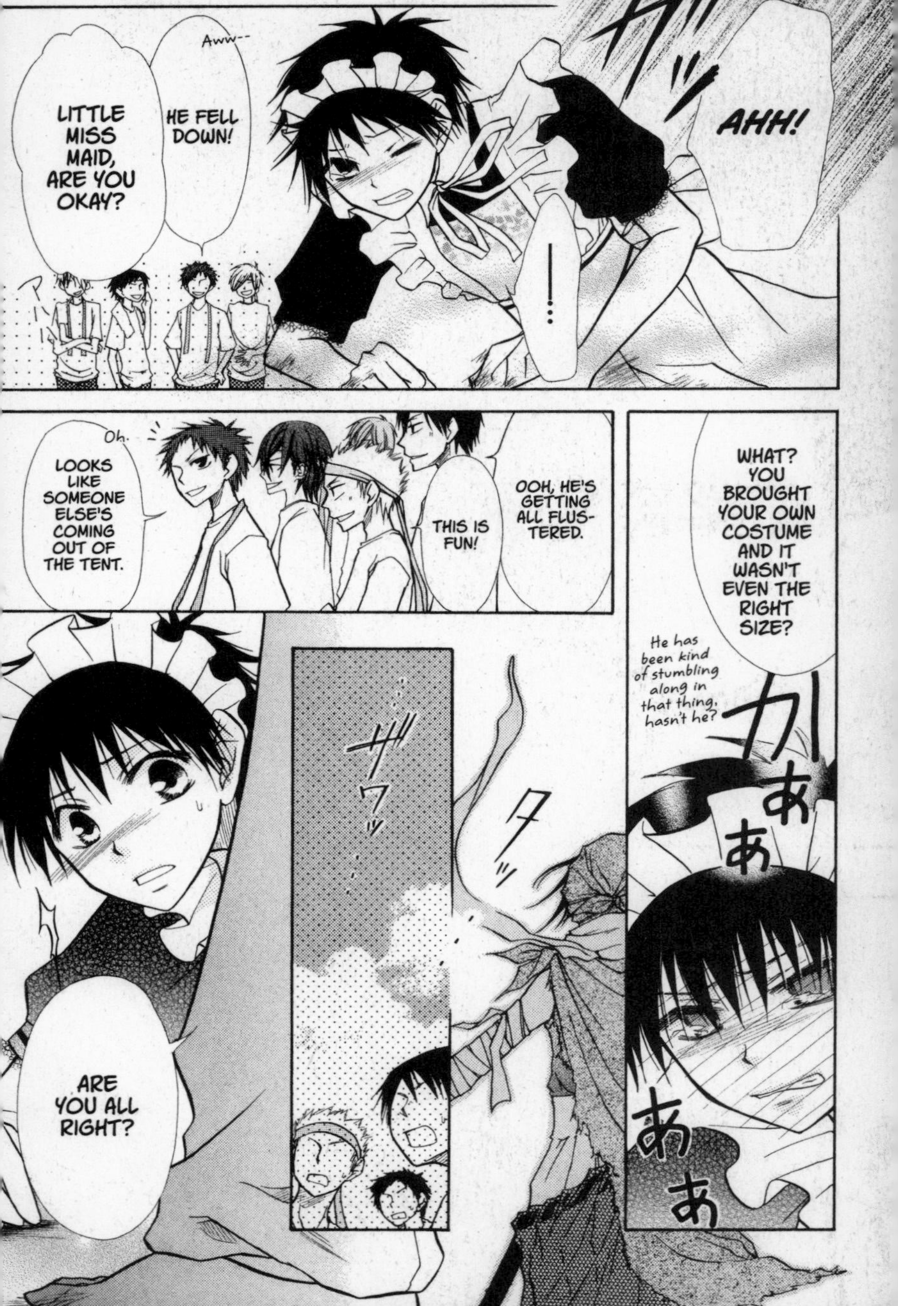
AHH!
!...
Aww--
HE FELL DOWN!
LITTLE MISS MAID, ARE YOU OKAY?
WHAT? YOU BROUGHT YOUR OWN COSTUME AND IT WASN'T EVEN THE RIGHT SIZE?
He has been kind of stumbling along in that thing, hasn't he?
かあああ
OOH, HE'S GETTING ALL FLUS-TERED.
THIS IS FUN!
Oh.
LOOKS LIKE SOMEONE ELSE'S COMING OUT OF THE TENT.
タッ
...ザワッ...
ARE YOU ALL RIGHT?

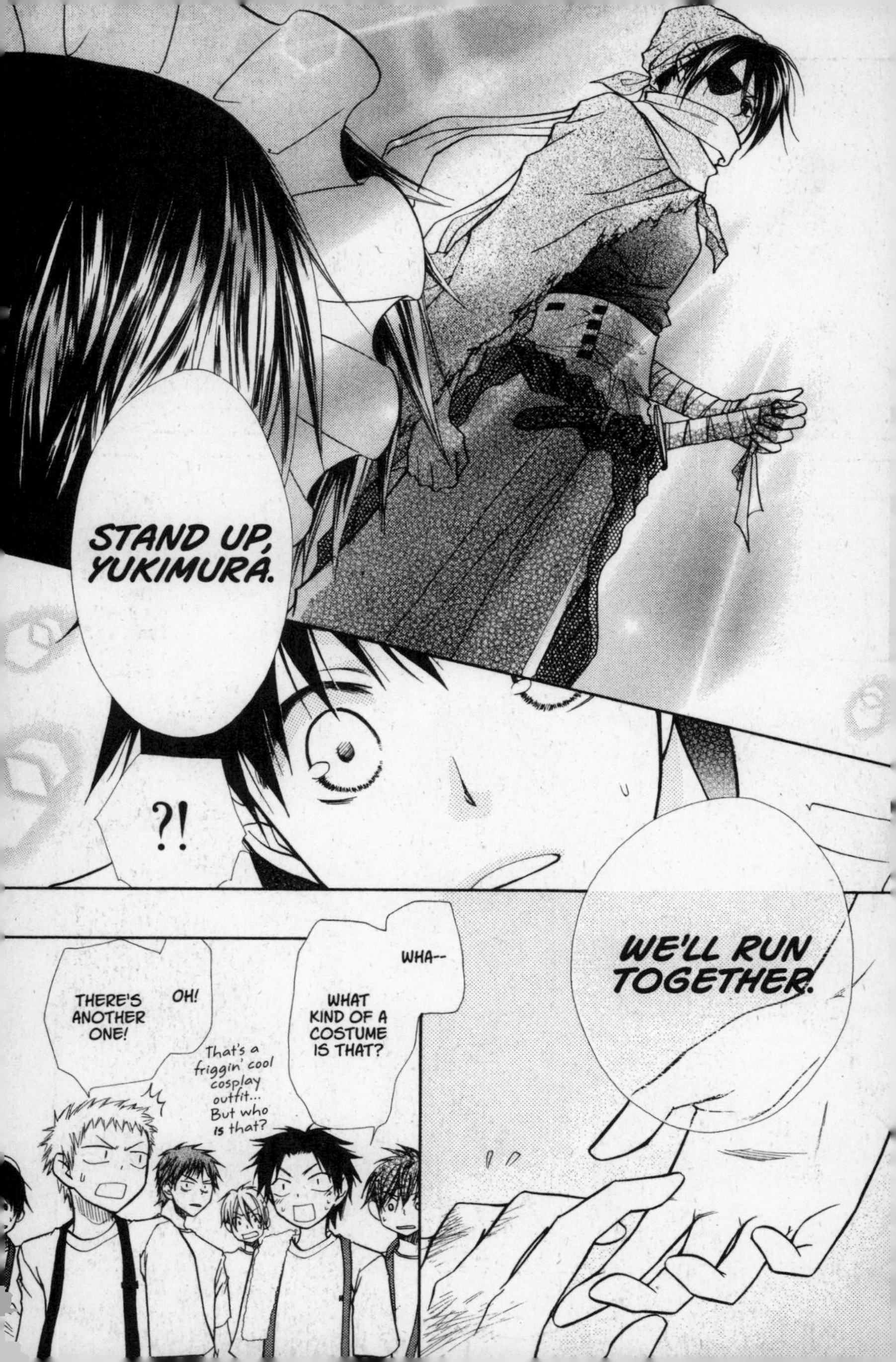
STAND UP, YUKIMURA.
?!
WE'LL RUN TOGETHER.
WHA--
WHAT KIND OF A COSTUME IS THAT?
That's a friggin' cool cosplay outfit... But who is that?
OH!
THERE'S ANOTHER ONE!

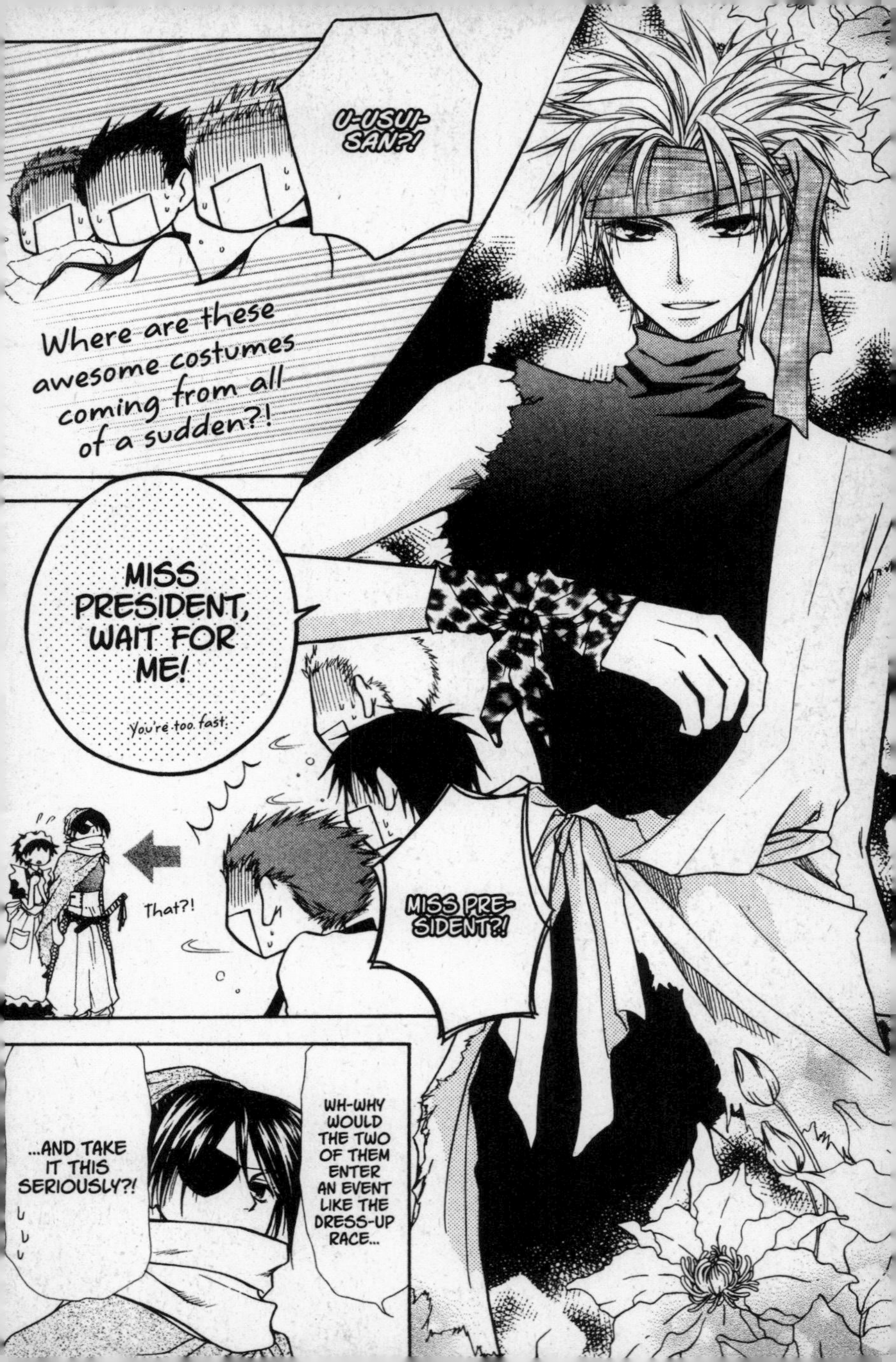
U-USUI-SAN?!
Where are these awesome costumes coming from all of a sudden?!
MISS PRESIDENT, WAIT FOR ME!
You're too fast.
MISS PRESIDENT?!
That?!
WH-WHY WOULD THE TWO OF THEM ENTER AN EVENT LIKE THE DRESS-UP RACE...
...AND TAKE IT THIS SERIOUSLY?!

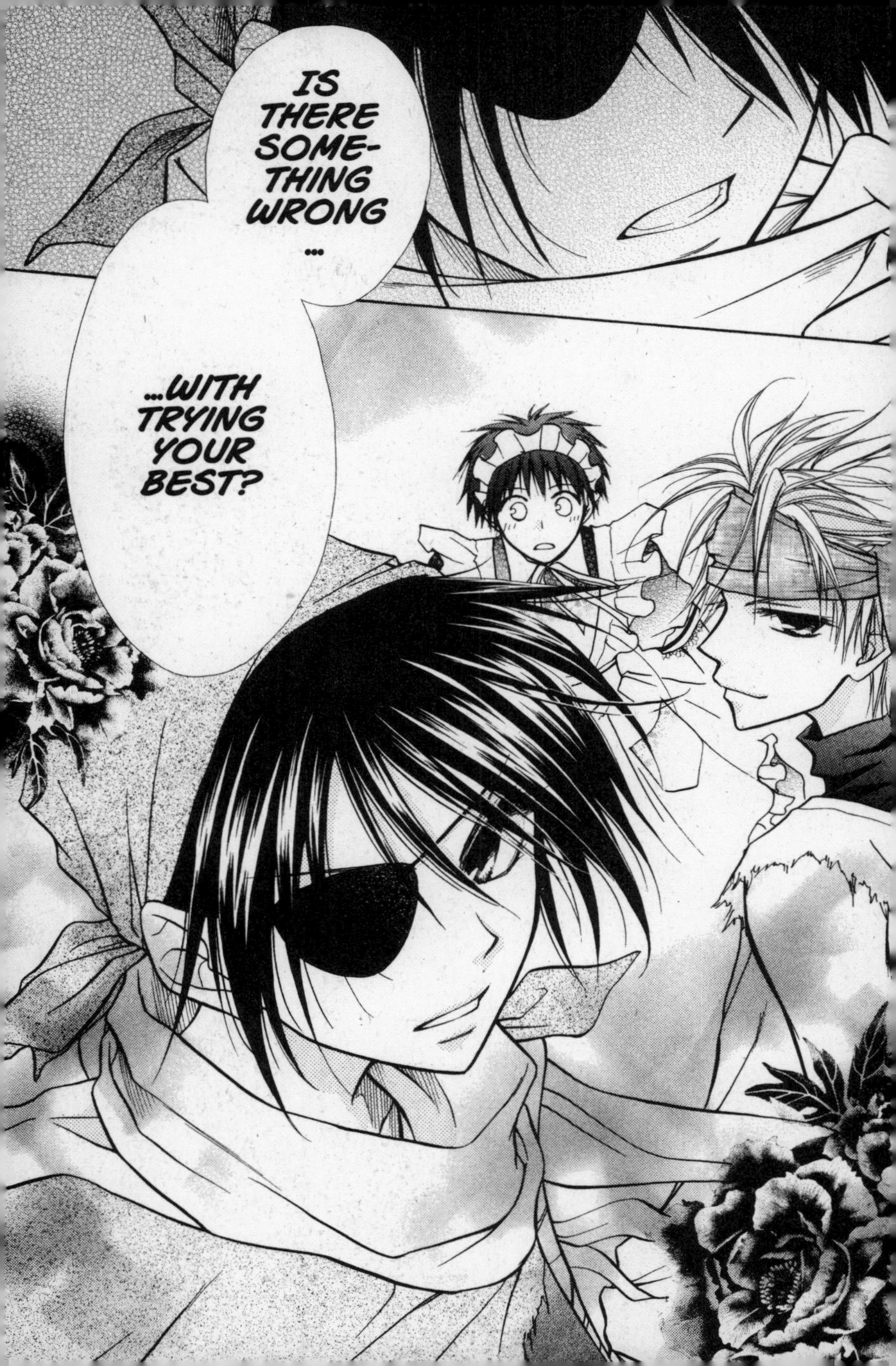
IS THERE SOMETHING WRONG ...
...WITH TRYING YOUR BEST?

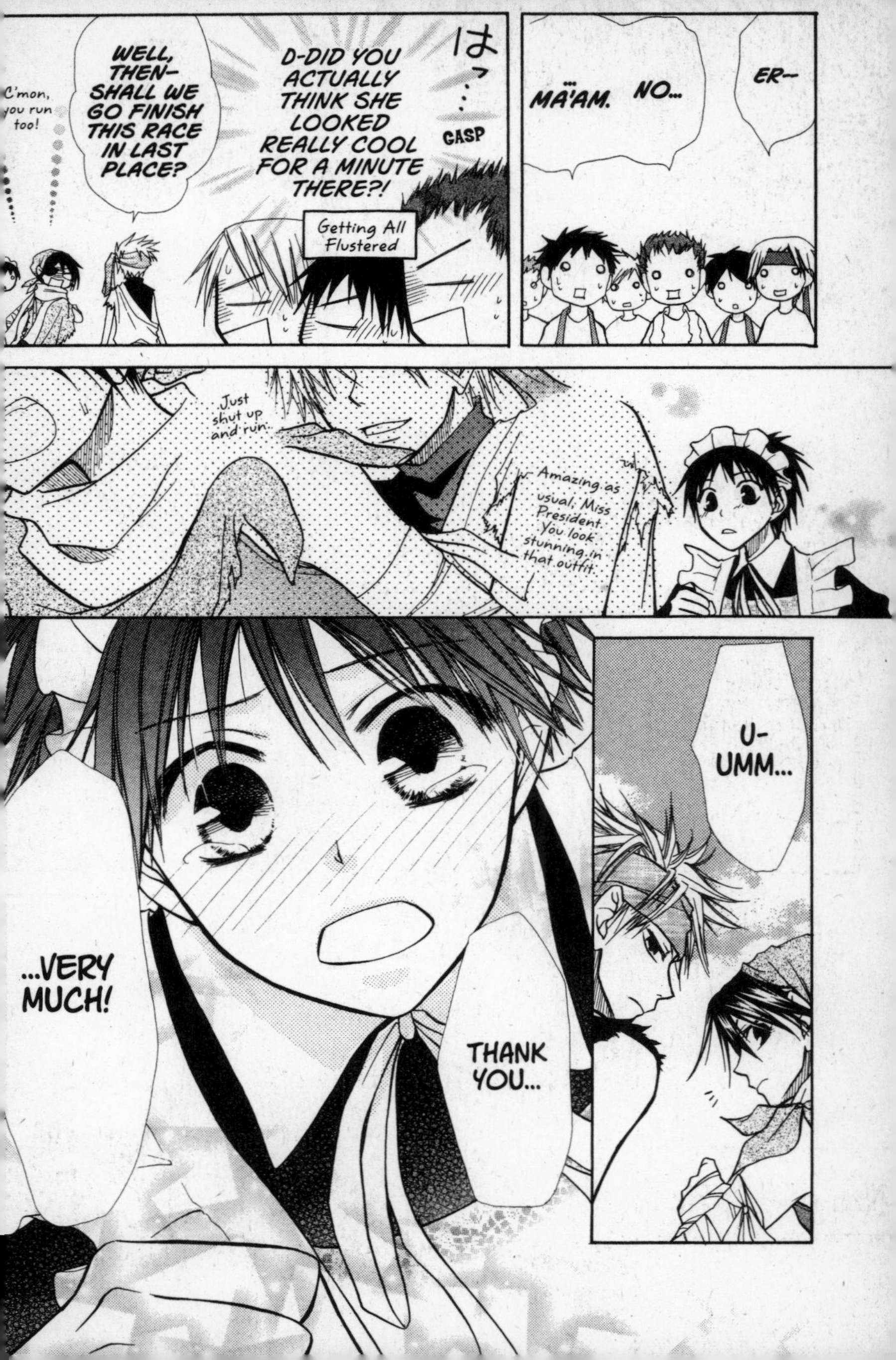
ER–
NO...
...MA'AM.
D-DID YOU ACTUALLY THINK SHE LOOKED REALLY COOL FOR A MINUTE THERE?!
はっ
GASP
Getting All Flustered
WELL, THEN– SHALL WE GO FINISH THIS RACE IN LAST PLACE?
C'mon, you run too!
Amazing as usual, Miss President. You look stunning in that outfit.
Just shut up and run.
U-UMM...
THANK YOU...
...VERY MUCH!

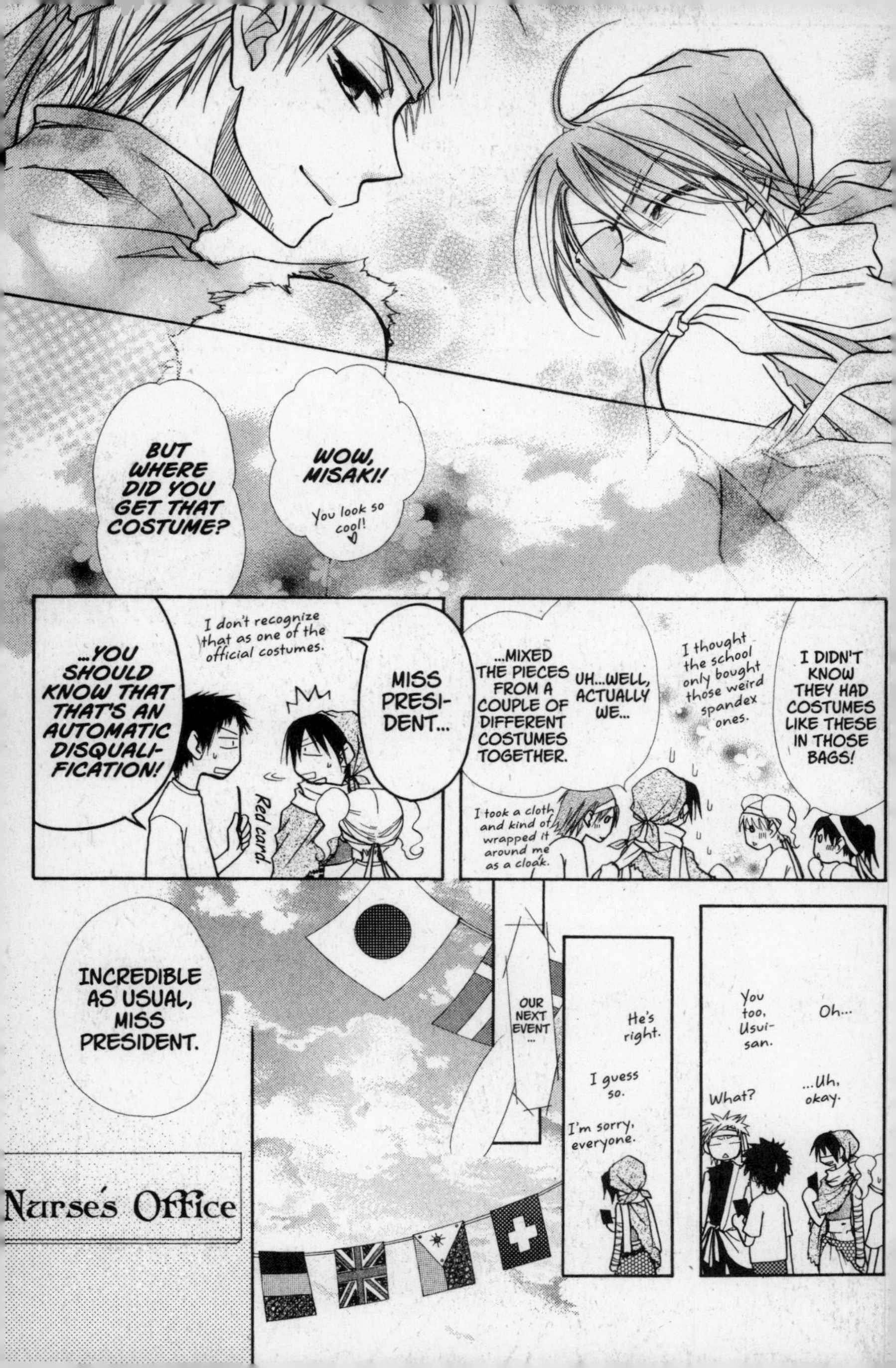
WOW, MISAKI!
You look so cool! ♡
BUT WHERE DID YOU GET THAT COSTUME?
I DIDN'T KNOW THEY HAD COSTUMES LIKE THESE IN THOSE BAGS!
I thought the school only bought those weird spandex ones.
UH...WELL, ACTUALLY WE...
...MIXED THE PIECES FROM A COUPLE OF DIFFERENT COSTUMES TOGETHER.
I took a cloth and kind of wrapped it around me as a cloak.
MISS PRESIDENT...
I don't recognize that as one of the official costumes.
...YOU SHOULD KNOW THAT THAT'S AN AUTOMATIC DISQUALIFICATION!
Red card.
Oh...
You too, Usui-san.
...Uh, okay.
What?
He's right.
I guess so.
I'm sorry, everyone.
OUR NEXT EVENT ...
INCREDIBLE AS USUAL, MISS PRESIDENT.
Nurse's Office

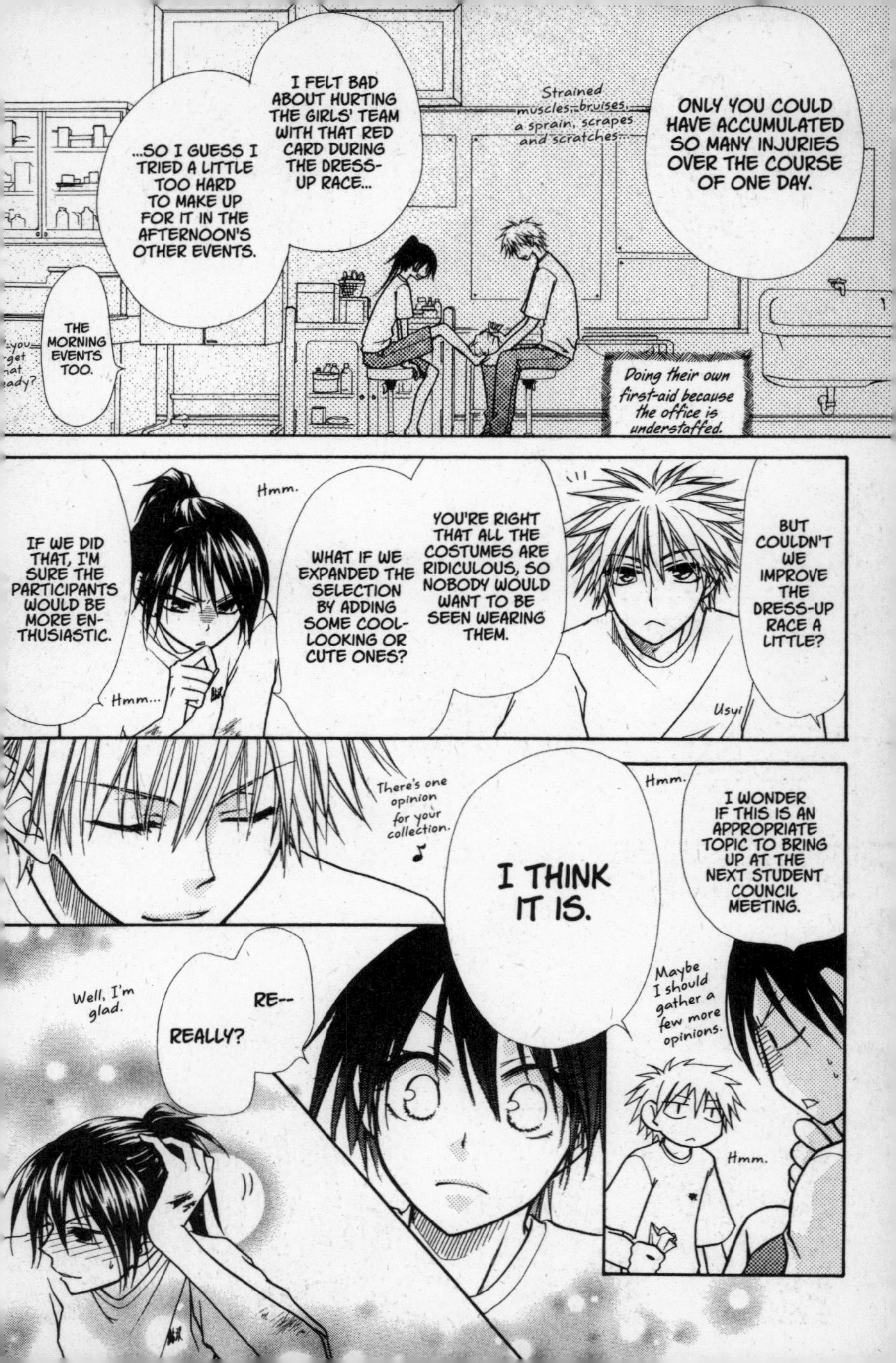
ONLY YOU COULD HAVE ACCUMULATED SO MANY INJURIES OVER THE COURSE OF ONE DAY.
Strained muscles, bruises, a sprain, scrapes and scratches...
I FELT BAD ABOUT HURTING THE GIRLS' TEAM WITH THAT RED CARD DURING THE DRESS-UP RACE...
...SO I GUESS I TRIED A LITTLE TOO HARD TO MAKE UP FOR IT IN THE AFTERNOON'S OTHER EVENTS.
Doing their own first-aid because the office is understaffed.
THE MORNING EVENTS TOO.
BUT COULDN'T WE IMPROVE THE DRESS-UP RACE A LITTLE?
Usui
YOU'RE RIGHT THAT ALL THE COSTUMES ARE RIDICULOUS, SO NOBODY WOULD WANT TO BE SEEN WEARING THEM.
WHAT IF WE EXPANDED THE SELECTION BY ADDING SOME COOL-LOOKING OR CUTE ONES?
Hmm.
IF WE DID THAT, I'M SURE THE PARTICIPANTS WOULD BE MORE EN-THUSIASTIC.
Hmm...
I WONDER IF THIS IS AN APPROPRIATE TOPIC TO BRING UP AT THE NEXT STUDENT COUNCIL MEETING.
Hmm.
I THINK IT IS.
There's one opinion for your collection. ♪
Maybe I should gather a few more opinions.
Hmm.
RE-- REALLY?
Well, I'm glad.

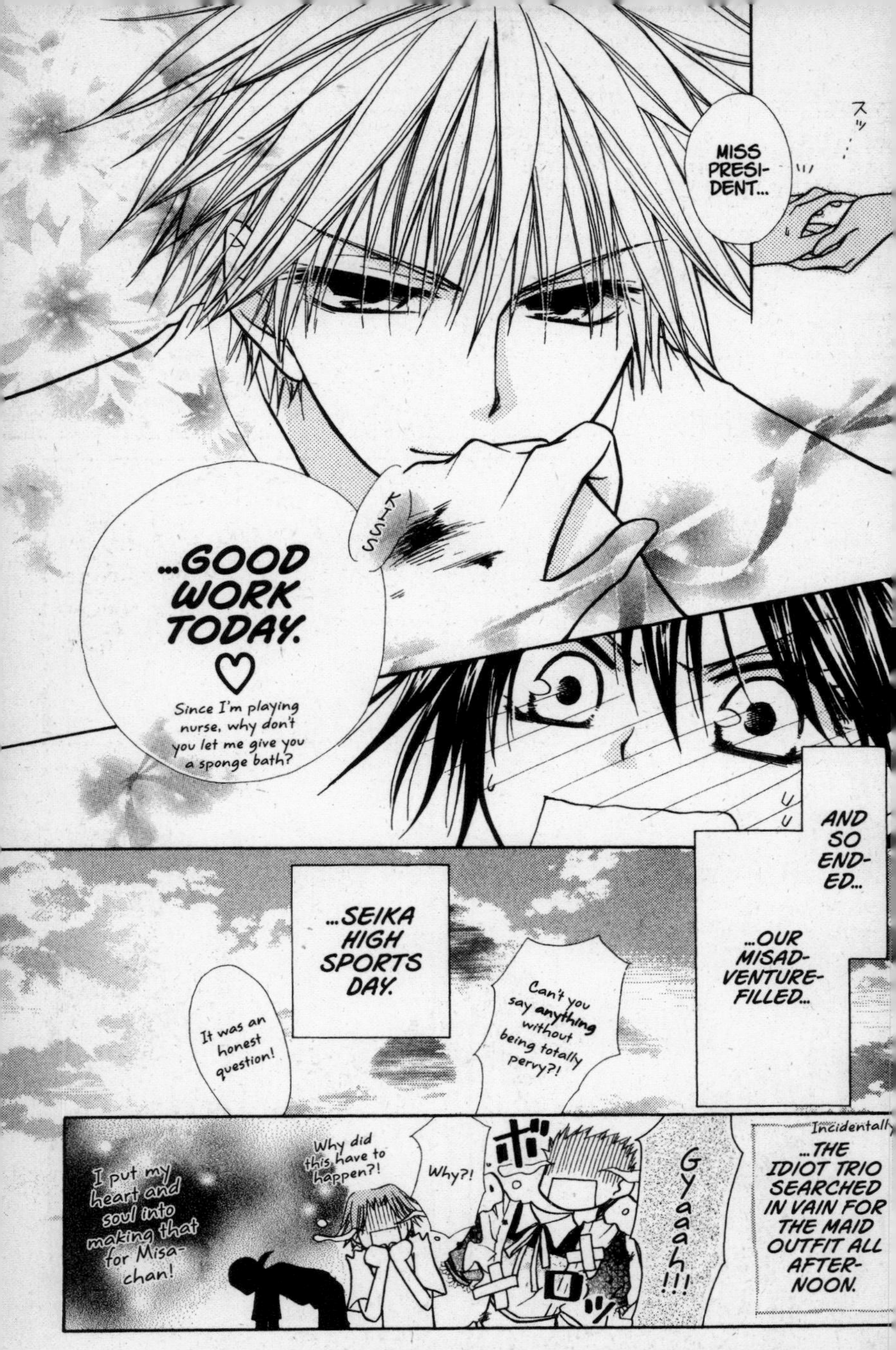
スッ…
MISS PRESIDENT…
KISS
…GOOD WORK TODAY. ♥
Since I'm playing nurse, why don't you let me give you a sponge bath?
AND SO ENDED…
…OUR MISADVENTURE-FILLED…
…SEIKA HIGH SPORTS DAY.
Can't you say anything without being totally pervy?!
It was an honest question!
Incidentally …THE IDIOT TRIO SEARCHED IN VAIN FOR THE MAID OUTFIT ALL AFTERNOON.
Gyaaah!!!
ボ
Why?!
Why did this have to happen?!
I put my heart and soul into making that for Misa-chan!

Where Are They Now?

The Ayuzawa Cram School

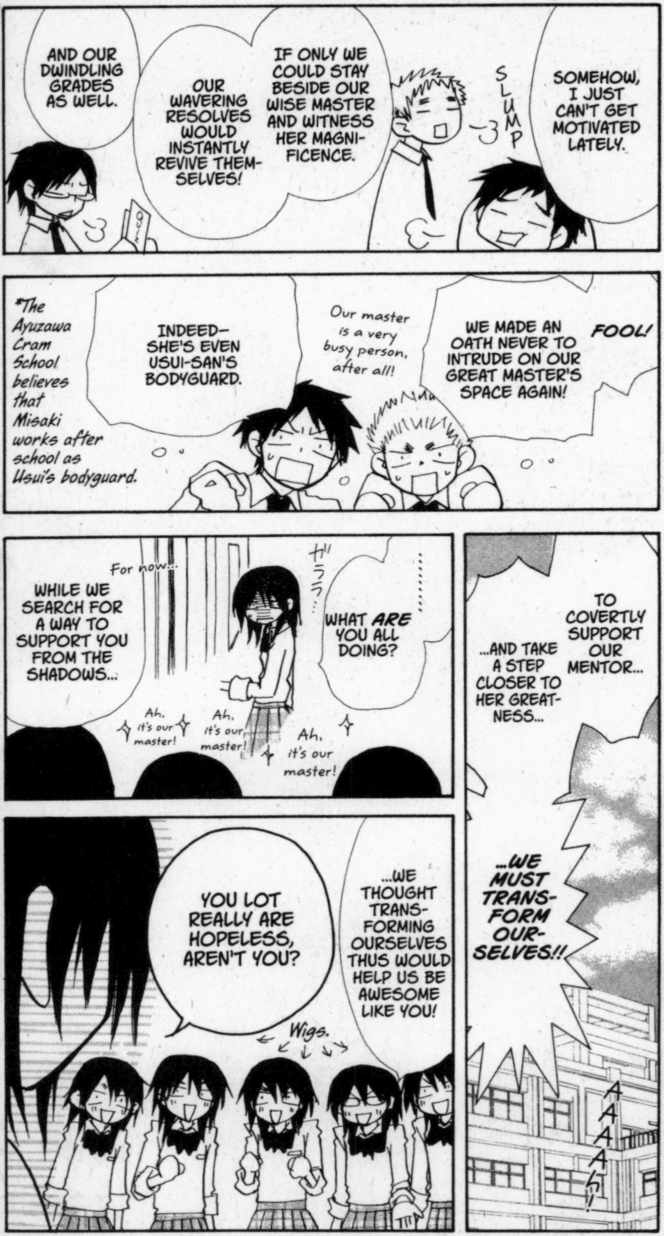
SOMEHOW, I JUST CAN'T GET MOTIVATED LATELY.
SLUMP
IF ONLY WE COULD STAY BESIDE OUR WISE MASTER AND WITNESS HER MAGNIFICENCE.
OUR WAVERING RESOLVES WOULD INSTANTLY REVIVE THEMSELVES!
AND OUR DWINDLING GRADES AS WELL.
QUIZ
FOOL!
WE MADE AN OATH NEVER TO INTRUDE ON OUR GREAT MASTER'S SPACE AGAIN!
Our master is a very busy person, after all!
INDEED—SHE'S EVEN USUI-SAN'S BODYGUARD.
*The Ayuzawa Cram School believes that Misaki works after school as Usui's bodyguard.
TO COVERTLY SUPPORT OUR MENTOR...
...AND TAKE A STEP CLOSER TO HER GREATNESS...
...WE MUST TRANSFORM OURSELVES!!
AAAAAH!
ガラ...
WHAT ARE YOU ALL DOING?
For now...
WHILE WE SEARCH FOR A WAY TO SUPPORT YOU FROM THE SHADOWS...
Ah, it's our master!
Ah, it's our master!
Ah, it's our master!
...WE THOUGHT TRANSFORMING OURSELVES THUS WOULD HELP US BE AWESOME LIKE YOU!
YOU LOT REALLY ARE HOPELESS, AREN'T YOU?
Wigs.

What is the Ayuzawa Cram School?

First appearance: Volume 1, 4th Course. These five boys approached Misaki out of the blue and begged her to make them her disciples. Dubbing her their "mentor," they strove to lead exemplary lives like hers.

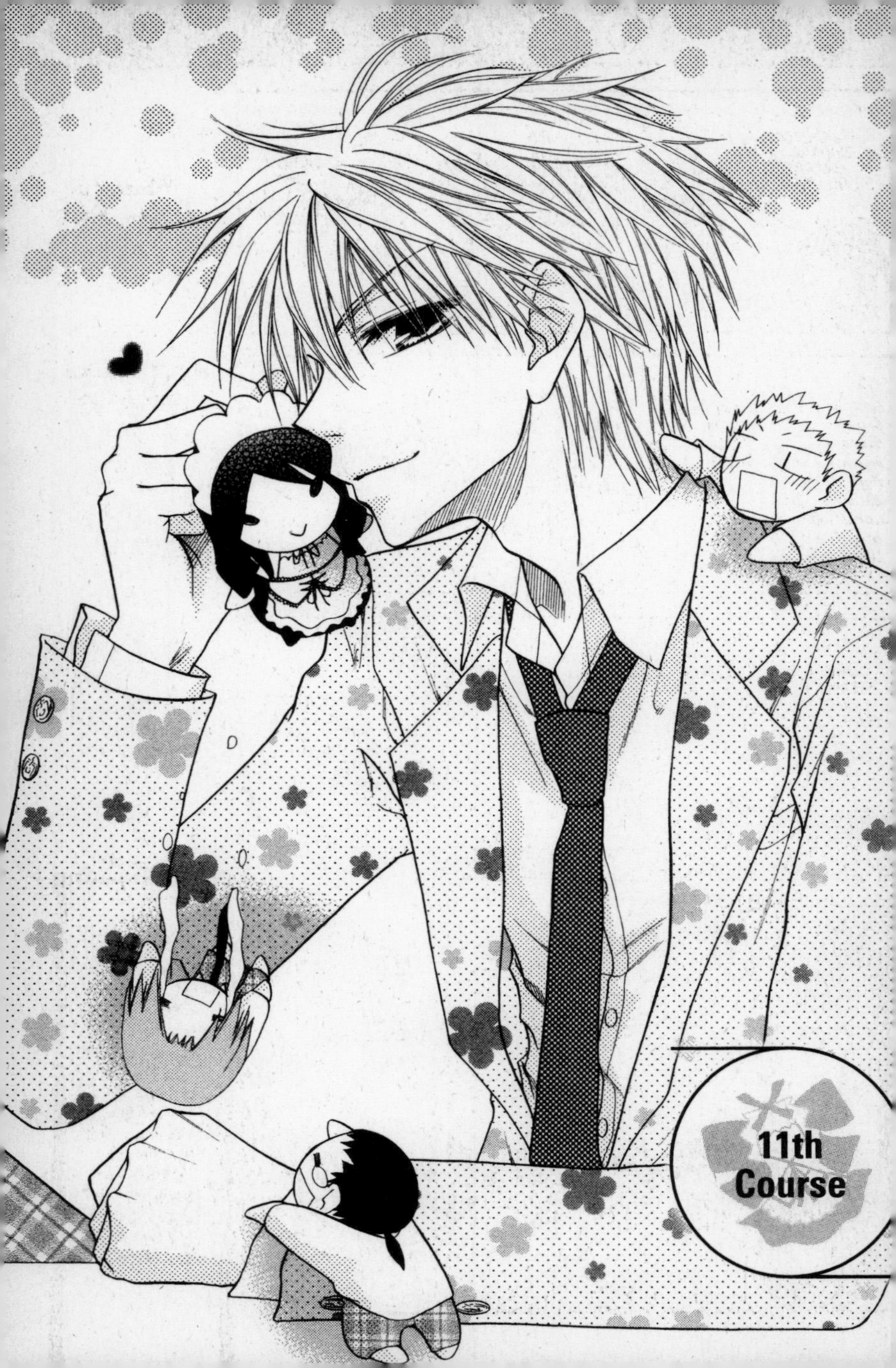
11th
Course

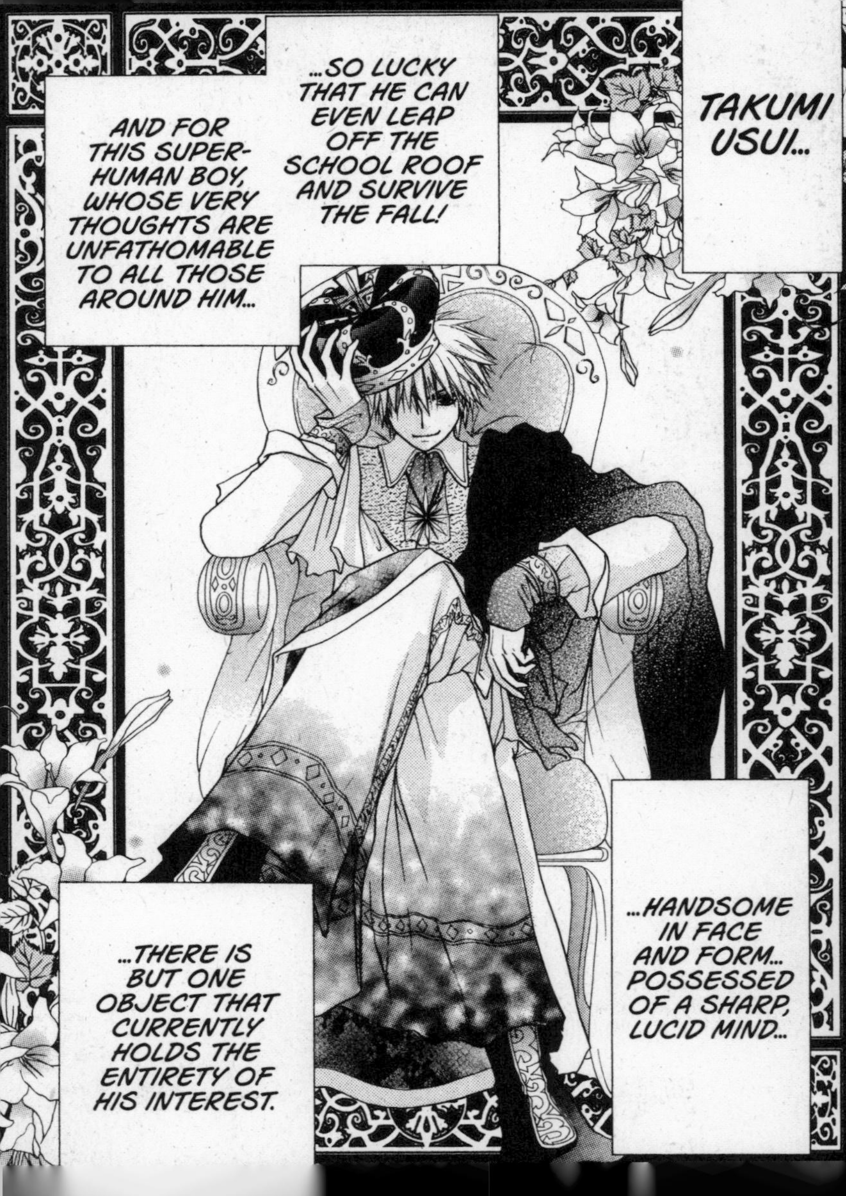
TAKUMI USUI...
...HANDSOME IN FACE AND FORM... POSSESSED OF A SHARP, LUCID MIND...
...SO LUCKY THAT HE CAN EVEN LEAP OFF THE SCHOOL ROOF AND SURVIVE THE FALL!
AND FOR THIS SUPER-HUMAN BOY, WHOSE VERY THOUGHTS ARE UNFATHOMABLE TO ALL THOSE AROUND HIM...
...THERE IS BUT ONE OBJECT THAT CURRENTLY HOLDS THE ENTIRETY OF HIS INTEREST.

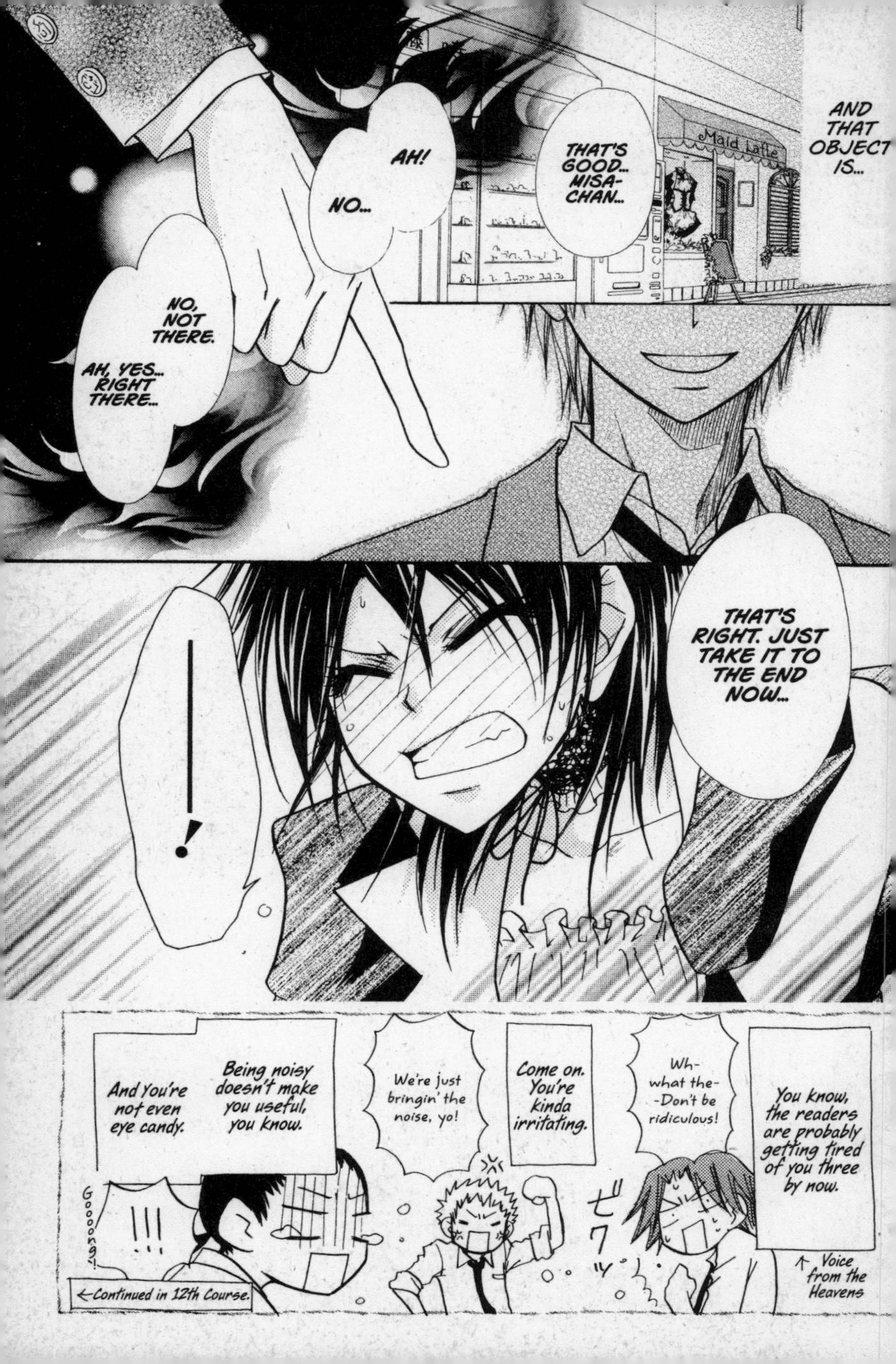
AND THAT OBJECT IS...
THAT'S GOOD... MISA-CHAN...
AH!
NO...
NO, NOT THERE.
AH, YES... RIGHT THERE...
Maid Latte
THAT'S RIGHT. JUST TAKE IT TO THE END NOW...
—!
You know, the readers are probably getting tired of you three by now.
↑ Voice from the Heavens
Wh-what the- -Don't be ridiculous!
ビクッ
Come on. You're kinda irritating.
We're just bringin' the noise, yo!
Being noisy doesn't make you useful, you know.
And you're not even eye candy.
!!!
Gooooong!
←Continued in 12th Course.

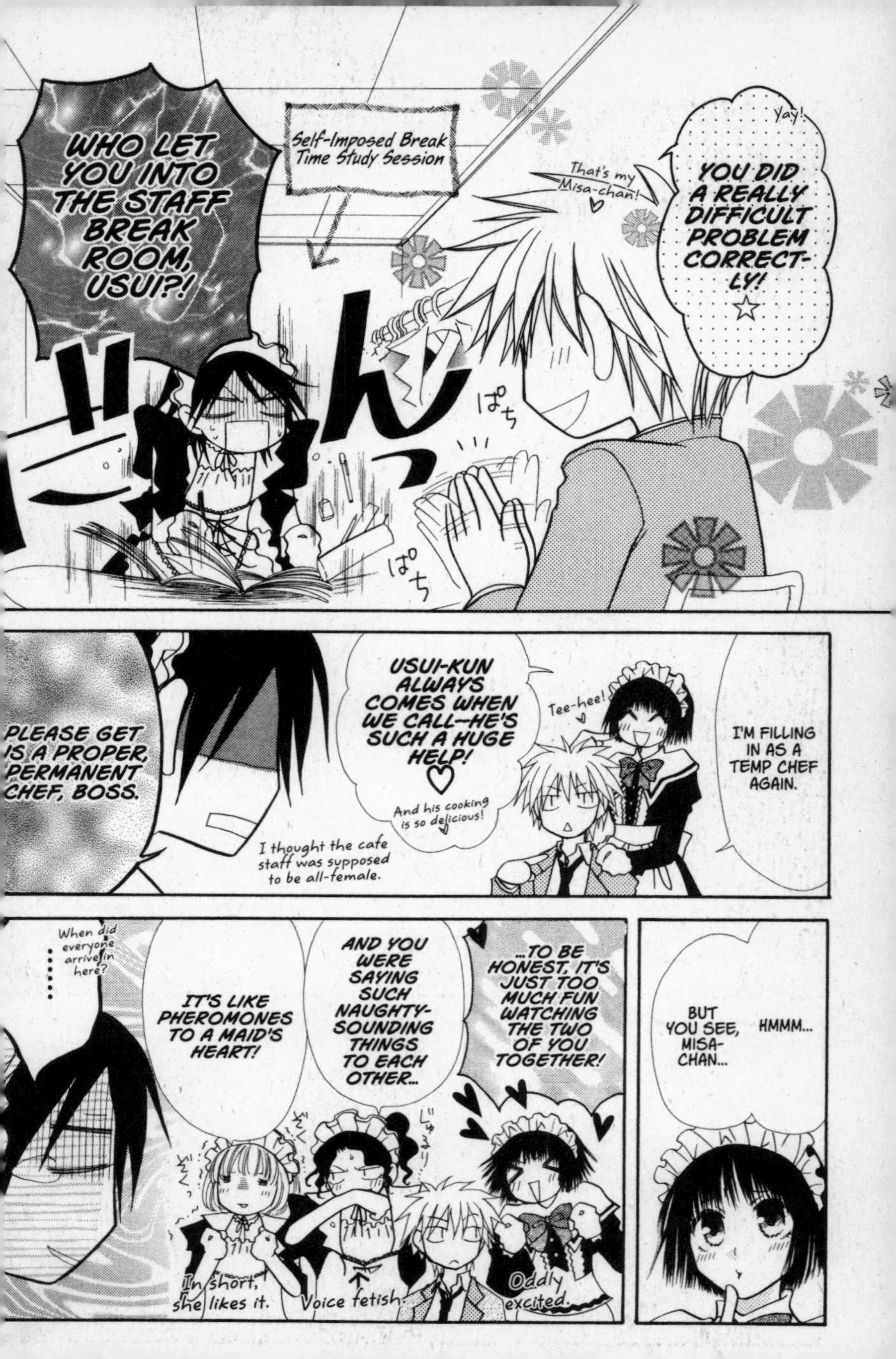
Yay!
YOU DID A REALLY DIFFICULT PROBLEM CORRECT-LY! ☆
That's my Misa-chan! ♡
Self-Imposed Break Time Study Session
ぱち
ぱち
WHO LET YOU INTO THE STAFF BREAK ROOM, USUI?!
I'M FILLING IN AS A TEMP CHEF AGAIN.
Tee-hee! ♡
USUI-KUN ALWAYS COMES WHEN WE CALL--HE'S SUCH A HUGE HELP! ♡
And his cooking is so delicious! ♡
I thought the cafe staff was supposed to be all-female.
PLEASE GET IS A PROPER, PERMANENT CHEF, BOSS.
HMMM...
BUT YOU SEE, MISA-CHAN...
...TO BE HONEST, IT'S JUST TOO MUCH FUN WATCHING THE TWO OF YOU TOGETHER!
じゅるり
AND YOU WERE SAYING SUCH NAUGHTY-SOUNDING THINGS TO EACH OTHER...
ぞくぞく
IT'S LIKE PHEROMONES TO A MAID'S HEART!
When did everyone arrive in here?
Oddly excited.
Voice fetish.
In short, she likes it.

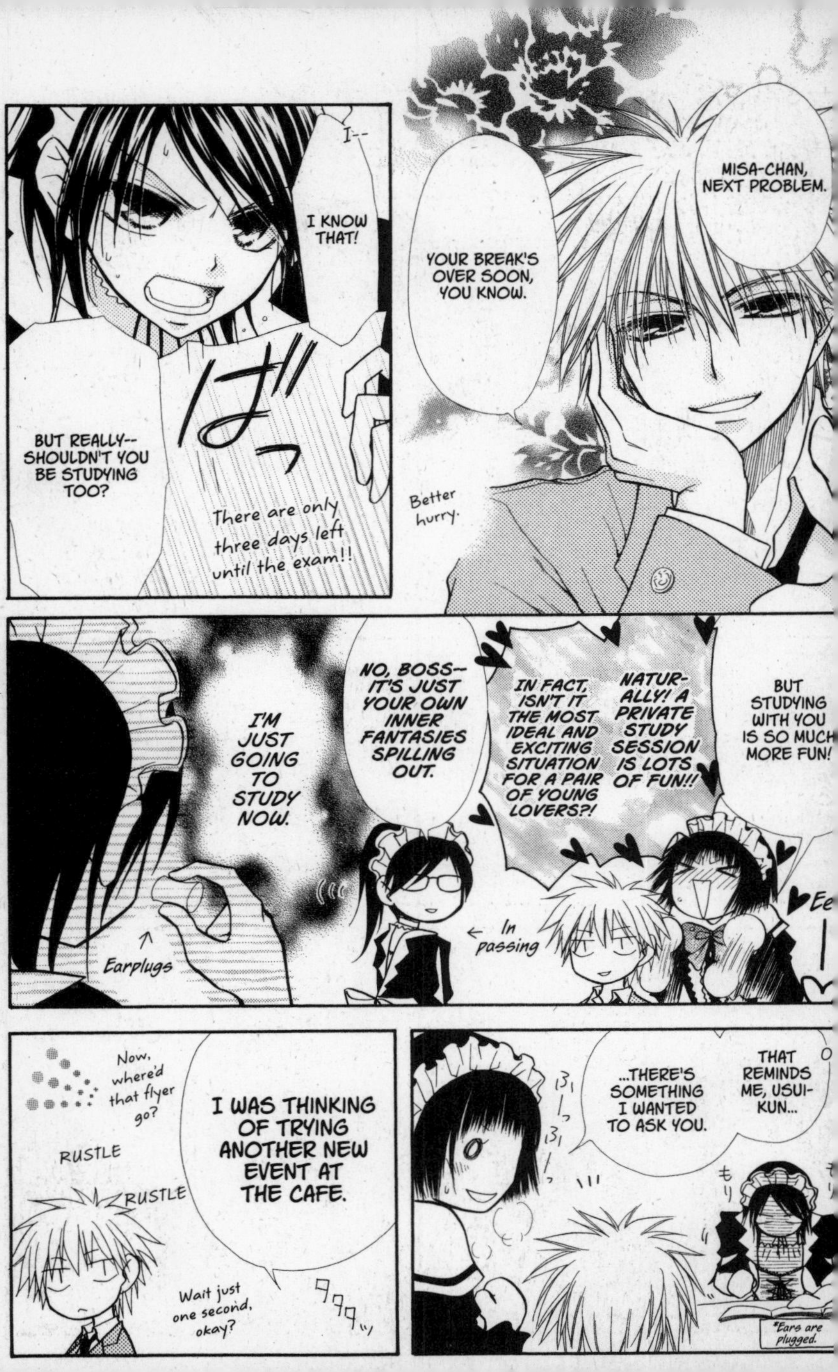
MISA-CHAN, NEXT PROBLEM.
YOUR BREAK'S OVER SOON, YOU KNOW.
Better hurry.
I--
I KNOW THAT!
There are only three days left until the exam!!
BUT REALLY-- SHOULDN'T YOU BE STUDYING TOO?
BUT STUDYING WITH YOU IS SO MUCH MORE FUN!
NATURALLY! A PRIVATE STUDY SESSION IS LOTS OF FUN!!
IN FACT, ISN'T IT THE MOST IDEAL AND EXCITING SITUATION FOR A PAIR OF YOUNG LOVERS?!
NO, BOSS-- IT'S JUST YOUR OWN INNER FANTASIES SPILLING OUT.
In passing
I'M JUST GOING TO STUDY NOW.
Earplugs
THAT REMINDS ME, USUI-KUN...
...THERE'S SOMETHING I WANTED TO ASK YOU.
*Ears are plugged.
I WAS THINKING OF TRYING ANOTHER NEW EVENT AT THE CAFE.
Now, where'd that flyer go?
RUSTLE
RUSTLE
Wait just one second, okay?

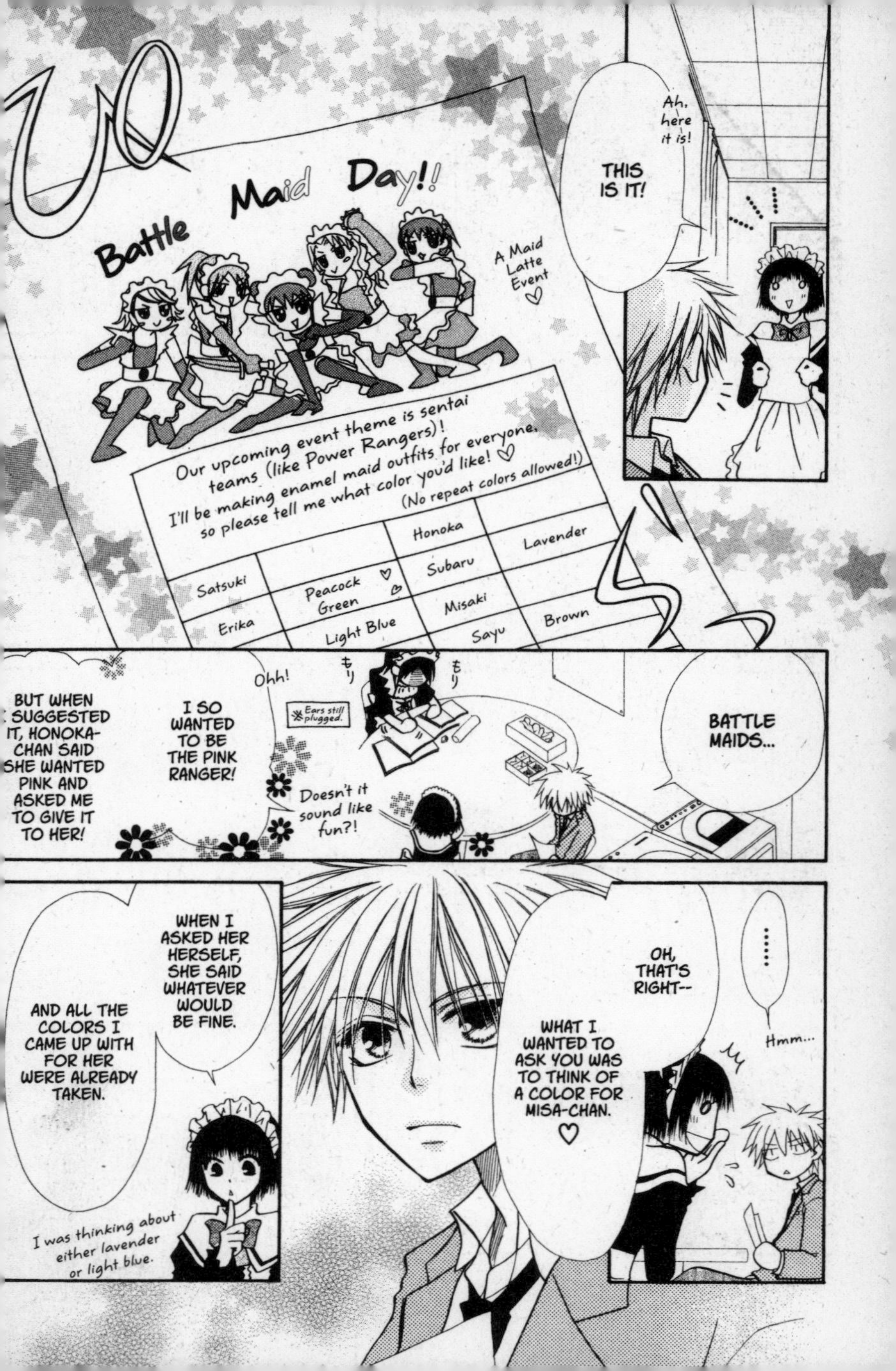
Ah, here it is!
THIS IS IT!
Battle Maid Day!!
A Maid Latte Event
Our upcoming event theme is sentai teams (like Power Rangers)!
I'll be making enamel maid outfits for everyone, so please tell me what color you'd like!
(No repeat colors allowed!)
Honoka
Lavender
Satsuki
Peacock Green
Subaru
Erika
Light Blue
Misaki
Brown
Sayu
BATTLE MAIDS...
Doesn't it sound like fun?!
Ohh!
Ears still plugged.
I SO WANTED TO BE THE PINK RANGER!
BUT WHEN I SUGGESTED IT, HONOKA-CHAN SAID SHE WANTED PINK AND ASKED ME TO GIVE IT TO HER!
......
Hmm...
OH, THAT'S RIGHT--
WHAT I WANTED TO ASK YOU WAS TO THINK OF A COLOR FOR MISA-CHAN.
WHEN I ASKED HER HERSELF, SHE SAID WHATEVER WOULD BE FINE.
AND ALL THE COLORS I CAME UP WITH FOR HER WERE ALREADY TAKEN.
I was thinking about either lavender or light blue.

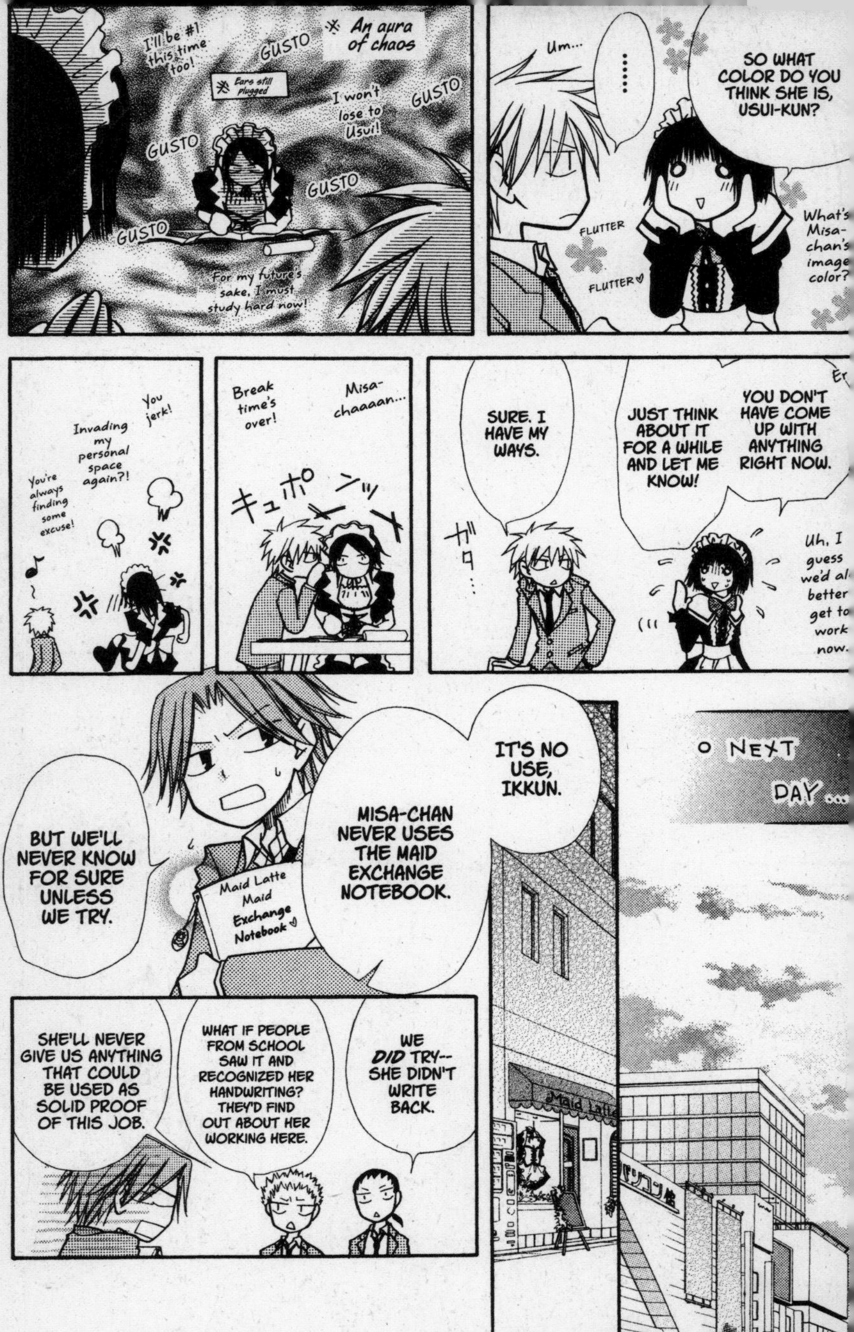
SO WHAT COLOR DO YOU THINK SHE IS, USUI-KUN?
What's Misa-chan's image color?
Um...
......
FLUTTER
FLUTTER♡
※ An aura of chaos
I'll be #1 this time too!
GUSTO
※ Ears still plugged
I won't lose to Usui!
GUSTO
GUSTO
GUSTO
GUSTO
For my future's sake, I must study hard now!
Er
YOU DON'T HAVE COME UP WITH ANYTHING RIGHT NOW.
JUST THINK ABOUT IT FOR A WHILE AND LET ME KNOW!
SURE. I HAVE MY WAYS.
ガタ…
Uh, I guess we'd al better get to work now.
Misa-chaaaan...
Break time's over!
キュポンッ
You jerk!
Invading my personal space again?!
You're always finding some excuse!
○ NEXT DAY ...
Maid Latte
IT'S NO USE, IKKUN.
MISA-CHAN NEVER USES THE MAID EXCHANGE NOTEBOOK.
BUT WE'LL NEVER KNOW FOR SURE UNLESS WE TRY.
Maid Latte Maid Exchange Notebook♡
WE DID TRY-- SHE DIDN'T WRITE BACK.
WHAT IF PEOPLE FROM SCHOOL SAW IT AND RECOGNIZED HER HANDWRITING? THEY'D FIND OUT ABOUT HER WORKING HERE.
SHE'LL NEVER GIVE US ANYTHING THAT COULD BE USED AS SOLID PROOF OF THIS JOB.

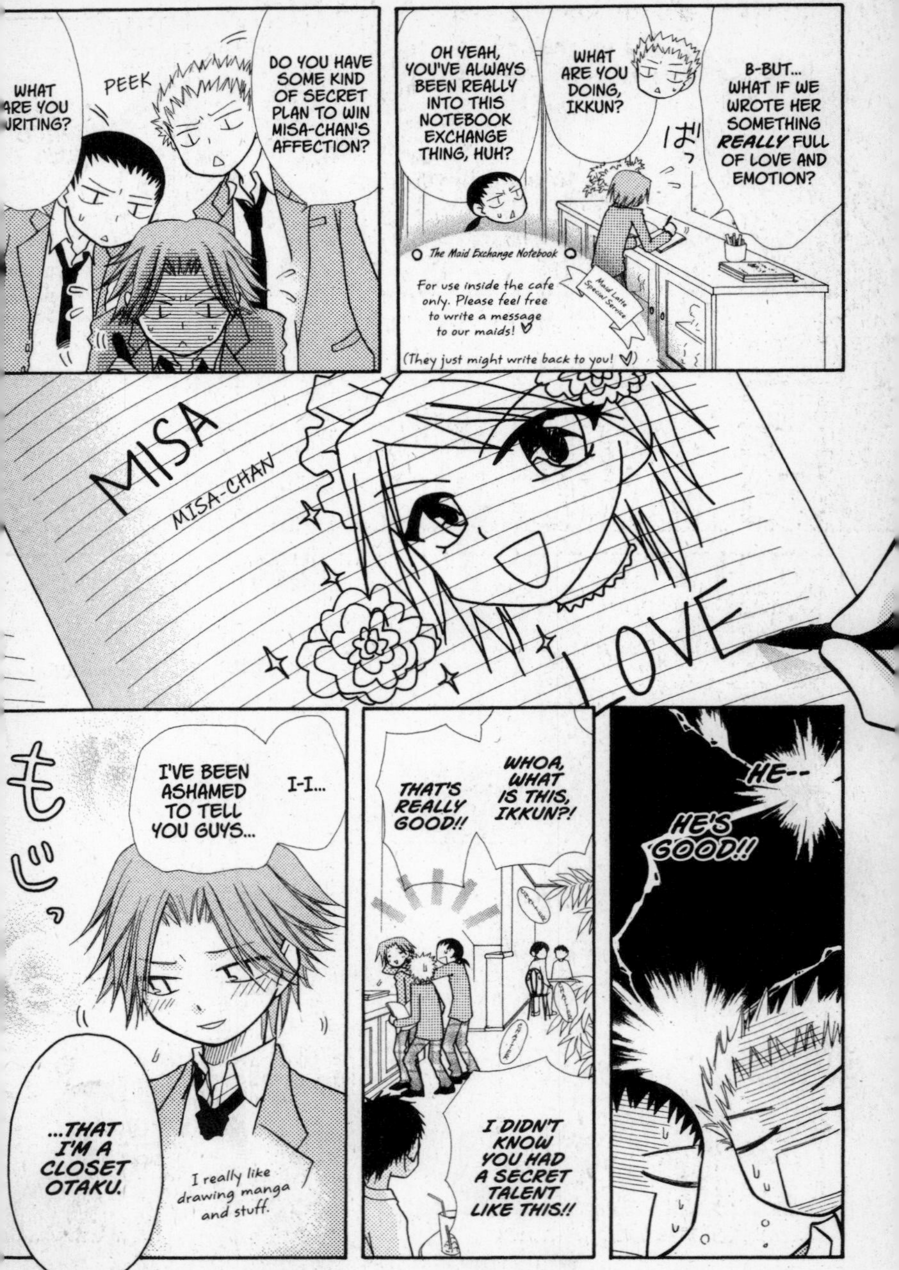
B-BUT... WHAT IF WE WROTE HER SOMETHING *REALLY* FULL OF LOVE AND EMOTION?
ばっ
WHAT ARE YOU DOING, IKKUN?
OH YEAH, YOU'VE ALWAYS BEEN REALLY INTO THIS NOTEBOOK EXCHANGE THING, HUH?
The Maid Exchange Notebook
Maid Latte Special Service
For use inside the cafe only. Please feel free to write a message to our maids! ♡
(They just might write back to you! ♡)
DO YOU HAVE SOME KIND OF SECRET PLAN TO WIN MISA-CHAN'S AFFECTION?
PEEK
WHAT ARE YOU WRITING?
MISA
MISA-CHAN
LOVE
HE--
HE'S GOOD!!
WHOA, WHAT IS THIS, IKKUN?!
THAT'S REALLY GOOD!!
I DIDN'T KNOW YOU HAD A SECRET TALENT LIKE THIS!!
I-I...
I'VE BEEN ASHAMED TO TELL YOU GUYS...
もじっ
...THAT I'M A CLOSET OTAKU.
I really like drawing manga and stuff.

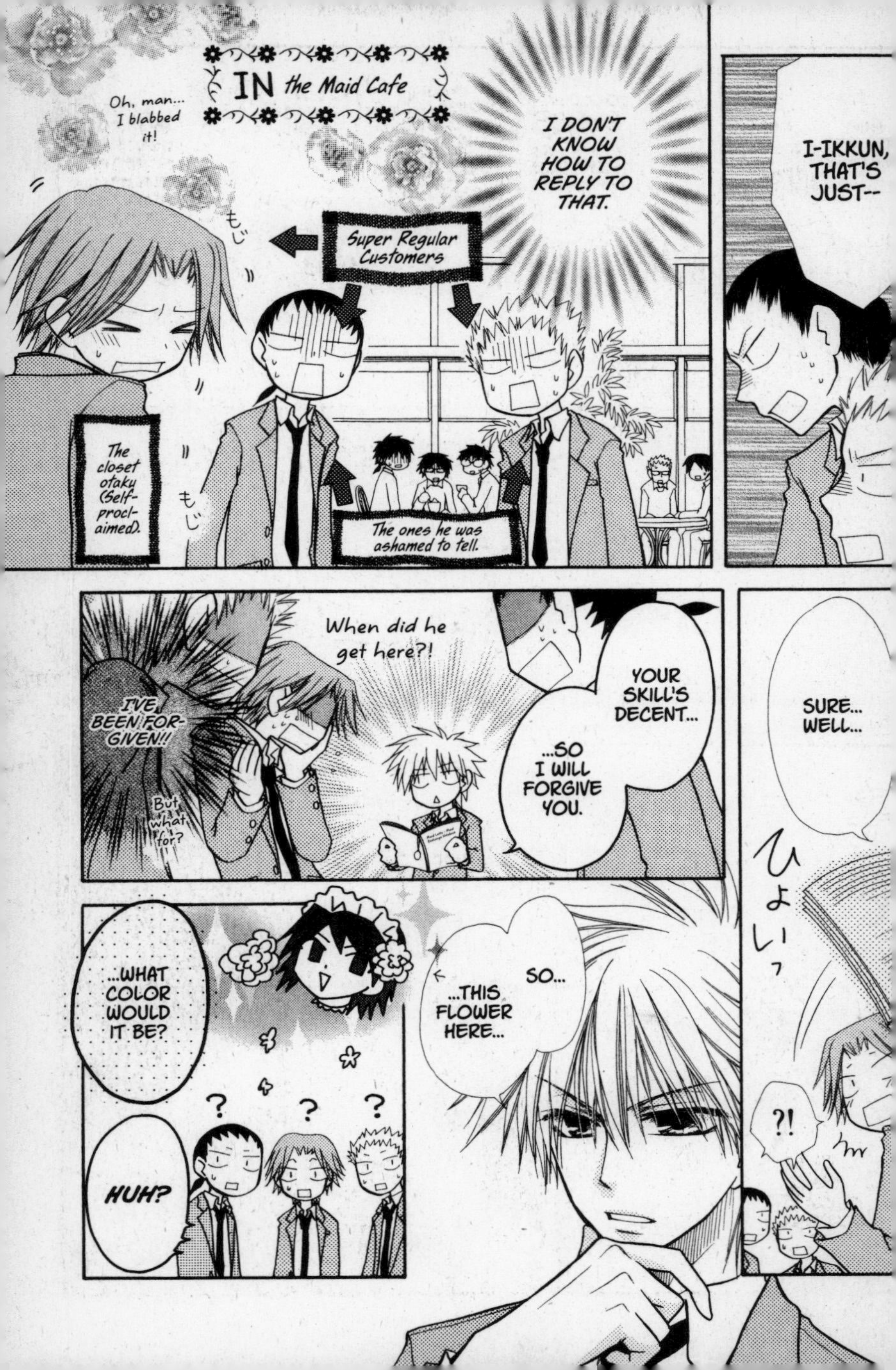
I-IKKUN, THAT'S JUST--
I DON'T KNOW HOW TO REPLY TO THAT.
IN the Maid Cafe
Oh, man... I blabbed it!
もじ
Super Regular Customers
もじ
The closet otaku (Self-proclaimed).
The ones he was ashamed to tell.
SURE... WELL...
ひょいっ
?!
YOUR SKILL'S DECENT...
...SO I WILL FORGIVE YOU.
When did he get here?!
I'VE BEEN FORGIVEN!!
But what for?
SO...
...THIS FLOWER HERE...
...WHAT COLOR WOULD IT BE?
HUH?

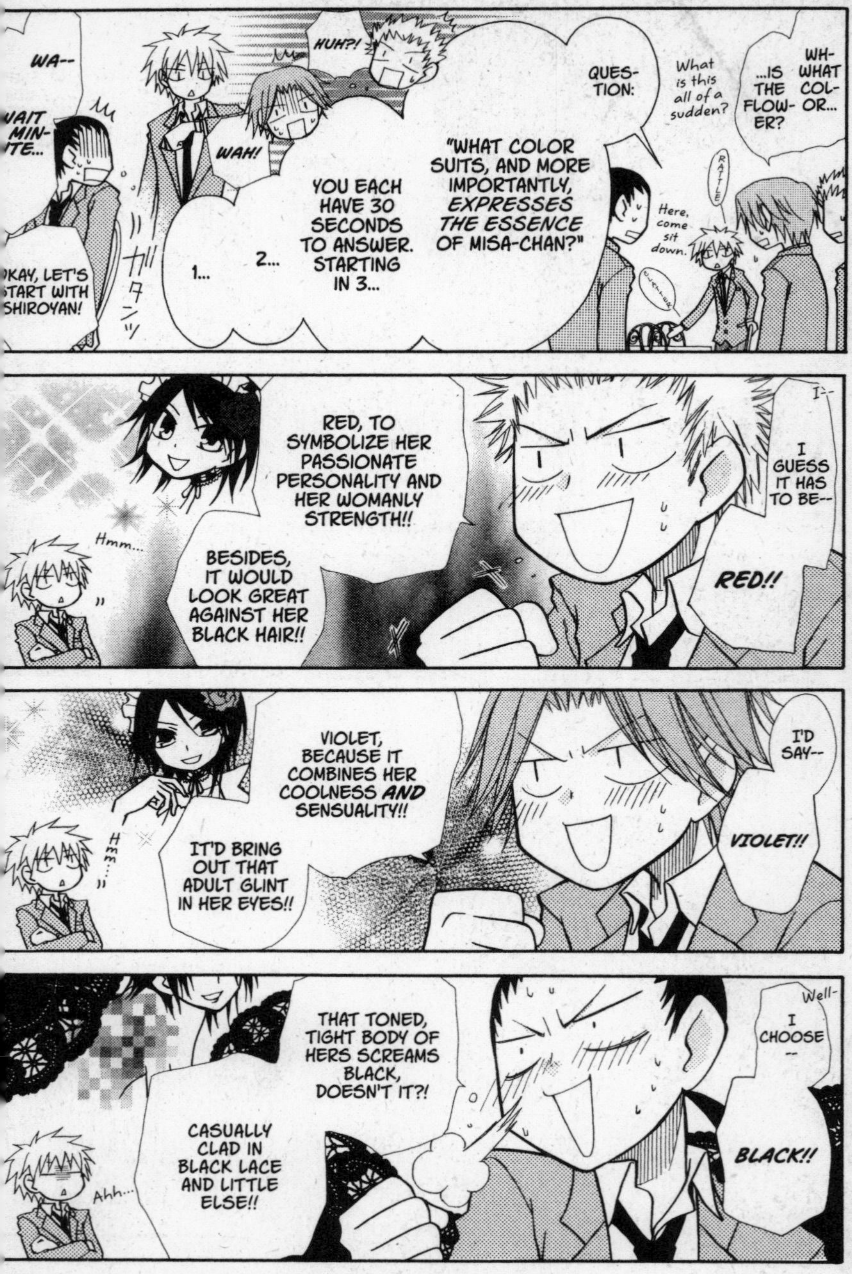
WH-WHAT COL-OR...
...IS THE FLOW-ER?
What is this all of a sudden?
QUES-TION:
"WHAT COLOR SUITS, AND MORE IMPORTANTLY, *EXPRESSES THE ESSENCE* OF MISA-CHAN?"
RATTLE
Here, come sit down.
YOU EACH HAVE 30 SECONDS TO ANSWER. STARTING IN 3...
2...
1...
HUH?!
WAH!
WA--
AIT MIN-ITE...
ガタンッ
OKAY, LET'S START WITH SHIROYAN!
I--
I GUESS IT HAS TO BE--
RED!!
RED, TO SYMBOLIZE HER PASSIONATE PERSONALITY AND HER WOMANLY STRENGTH!!
BESIDES, IT WOULD LOOK GREAT AGAINST HER BLACK HAIR!!
Hmm...
I'D SAY--
VIOLET!!
VIOLET, BECAUSE IT COMBINES HER COOLNESS *AND* SENSUALITY!!
IT'D BRING OUT THAT ADULT GLINT IN HER EYES!!
Hmm...
Well-
I CHOOSE --
BLACK!!
THAT TONED, TIGHT BODY OF HERS SCREAMS BLACK, DOESN'T IT?!
CASUALLY CLAD IN BLACK LACE AND LITTLE ELSE!!
Ahh...

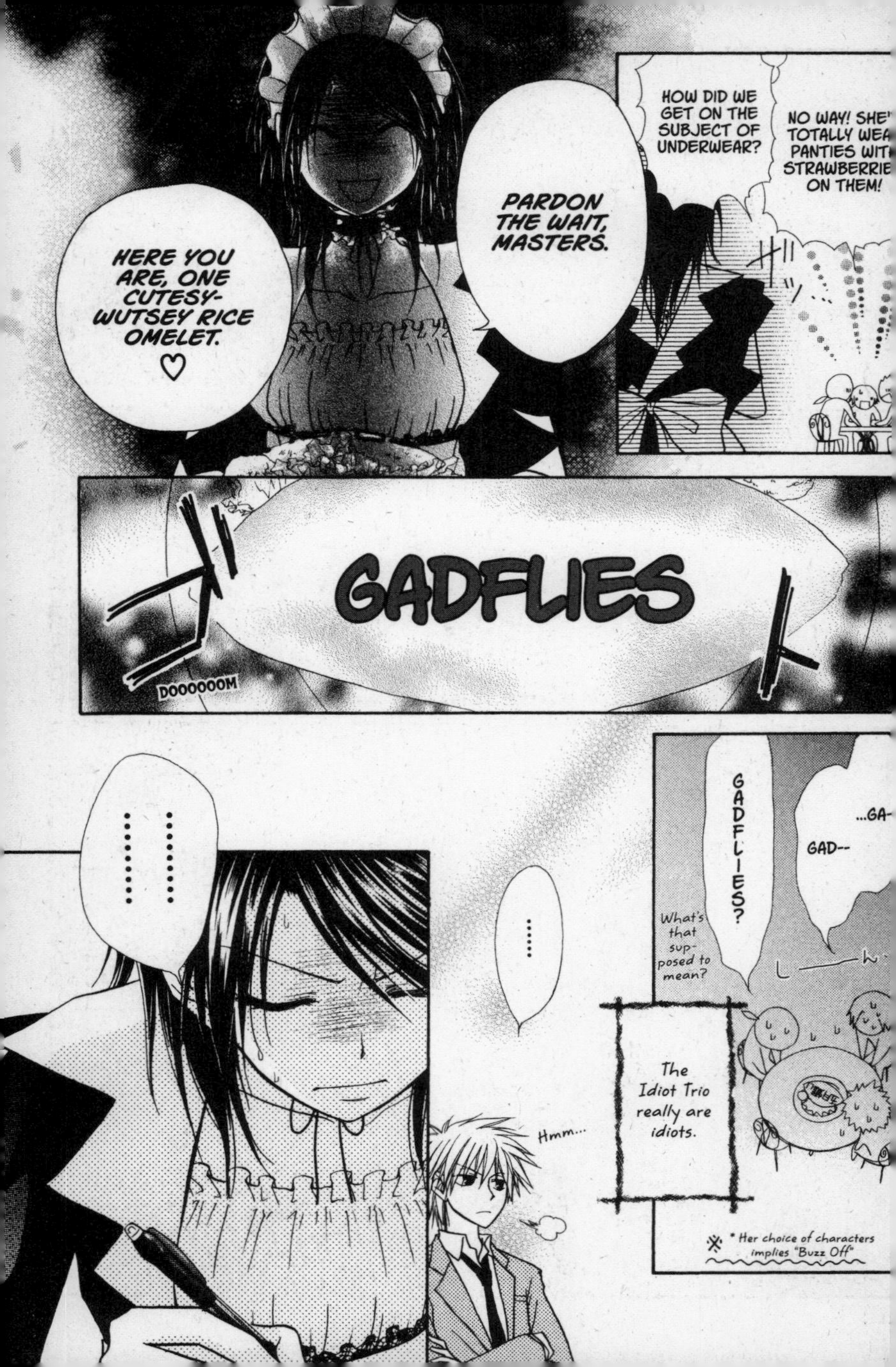
NO WAY! SHE' TOTALLY WEA PANTIES WITH STRAWBERRIE ON THEM!
HOW DID WE GET ON THE SUBJECT OF UNDERWEAR?
PARDON THE WAIT, MASTERS.
HERE YOU ARE, ONE CUTESY-WUTSEY RICE OMELET. ♡
GADFLIES
DOOOOOOM
...GA- GAD--
GADFLIES?
What's that sup-posed to mean?
The Idiot Trio really are idiots.
* Her choice of characters implies "Buzz Off"
......
Hmm...
......

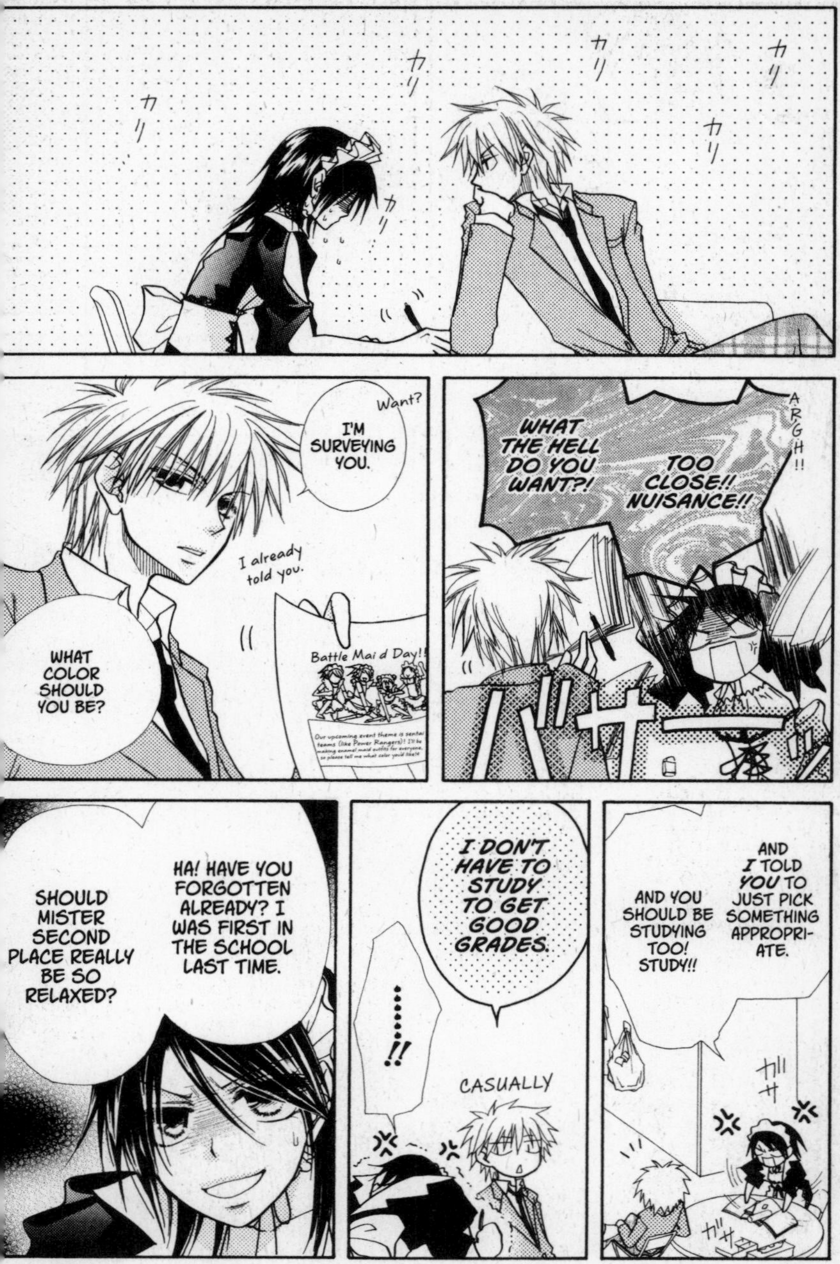
カリ
カリ
カリ
カリ
カリ
カリ
WHAT THE HELL DO YOU WANT?!
TOO CLOSE!! NUISANCE!!
ARGH!!
バサー
Want?
I'M SURVEYING YOU.
I already told you.
Battle Mai d Day!!
Our upcoming event theme is sentai teams (like Power Rangers)! I'll be making enamel maid outfits for everyone, so please tell me what color you'd like!!
WHAT COLOR SHOULD YOU BE?
AND I TOLD YOU TO JUST PICK SOMETHING APPROPRIATE.
AND YOU SHOULD BE STUDYING TOO! STUDY!!
ガサ
ガサ
I DON'T HAVE TO STUDY TO GET GOOD GRADES.
......!!
CASUALLY
HA! HAVE YOU FORGOTTEN ALREADY? I WAS FIRST IN THE SCHOOL LAST TIME.
SHOULD MISTER SECOND PLACE REALLY BE SO RELAXED?

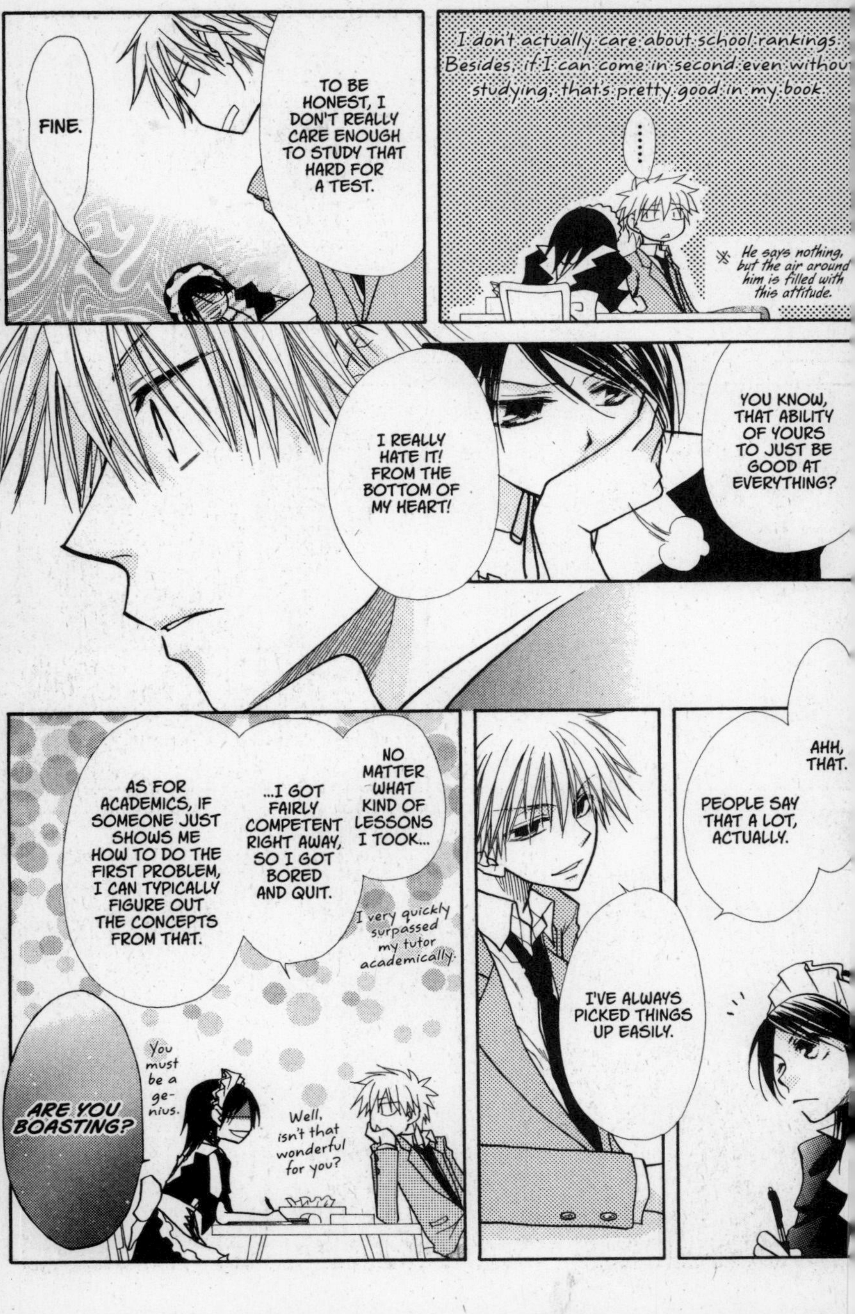
I don't actually care about school rankings. Besides, if I can come in second even withou studying, that's pretty good in my book.
......
※ He says nothing, but the air around him is filled with this attitude.
TO BE HONEST, I DON'T REALLY CARE ENOUGH TO STUDY THAT HARD FOR A TEST.
FINE.
YOU KNOW, THAT ABILITY OF YOURS TO JUST BE GOOD AT EVERYTHING?
I REALLY HATE IT! FROM THE BOTTOM OF MY HEART!
AHH, THAT.
PEOPLE SAY THAT A LOT, ACTUALLY.
I'VE ALWAYS PICKED THINGS UP EASILY.
NO MATTER WHAT KIND OF LESSONS I TOOK...
...I GOT FAIRLY COMPETENT RIGHT AWAY, SO I GOT BORED AND QUIT.
AS FOR ACADEMICS, IF SOMEONE JUST SHOWS ME HOW TO DO THE FIRST PROBLEM, I CAN TYPICALLY FIGURE OUT THE CONCEPTS FROM THAT.
I very quickly surpassed my tutor academically.
You must be a genius.
Well, isn't that wonderful for you?
ARE YOU BOASTING?

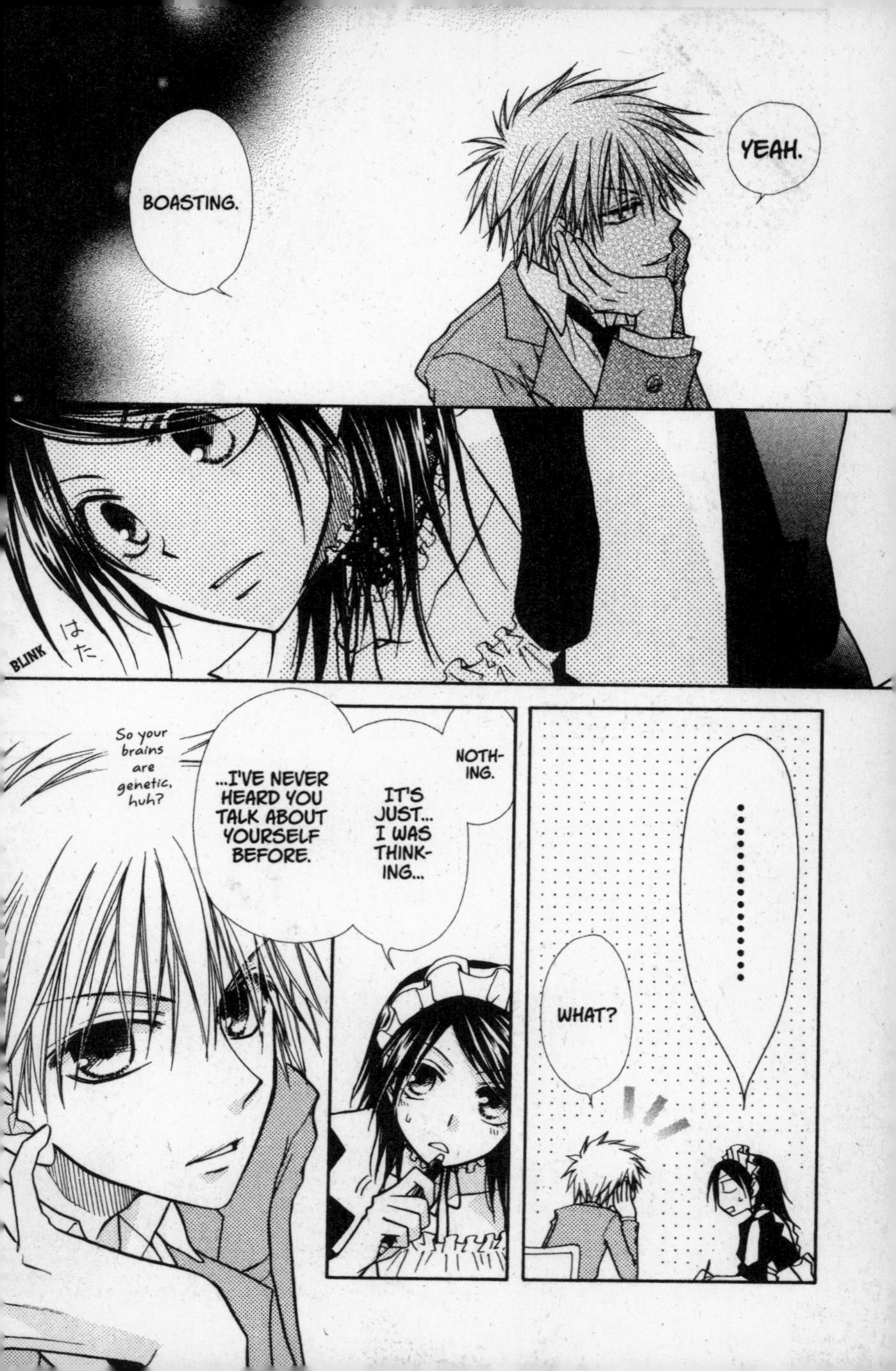
YEAH.
BOASTING.
BLINK
はた
……
WHAT?
NOTHING.
IT'S JUST... I WAS THINKING...
...I'VE NEVER HEARD YOU TALK ABOUT YOURSELF BEFORE.
So your brains are genetic, huh?

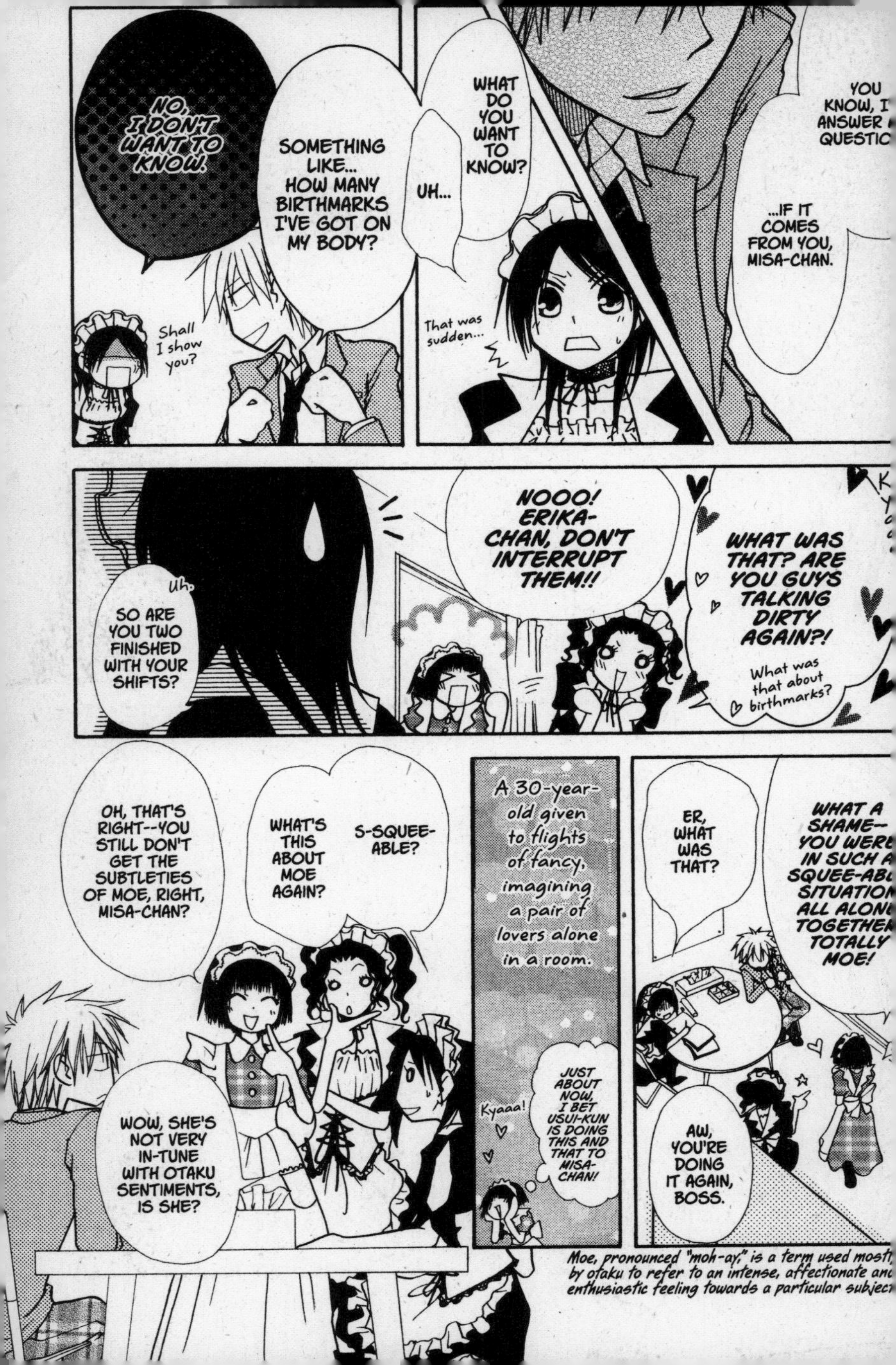
YOU KNOW, I' ANSWER QUESTIC
...IF IT COMES FROM YOU, MISA-CHAN.
WHAT DO YOU WANT TO KNOW?
UH...
That was sudden...
SOMETHING LIKE... HOW MANY BIRTHMARKS I'VE GOT ON MY BODY?
NO, I DON'T WANT TO KNOW.
Shall I show you?
WHAT WAS THAT? ARE YOU GUYS TALKING DIRTY AGAIN?!
What was that about birthmarks?
NOOO! ERIKA-CHAN, DON'T INTERRUPT THEM!!
Uh.
SO ARE YOU TWO FINISHED WITH YOUR SHIFTS?
WHAT A SHAME-- YOU WERE IN SUCH A SQUEE-ABL SITUATION ALL ALONE TOGETHER TOTALLY MOE!
ER, WHAT WAS THAT?
AW, YOU'RE DOING IT AGAIN, BOSS.
A 30-year-old given to flights of fancy, imagining a pair of lovers alone in a room.
JUST ABOUT NOW, I BET USUI-KUN IS DOING THIS AND THAT TO MISA-CHAN!
Kyaaa!
S-SQUEE-ABLE?
WHAT'S THIS ABOUT MOE AGAIN?
OH, THAT'S RIGHT--YOU STILL DON'T GET THE SUBTLETIES OF MOE, RIGHT, MISA-CHAN?
WOW, SHE'S NOT VERY IN-TUNE WITH OTAKU SENTIMENTS, IS SHE?

Moe, pronounced "moh-ay," is a term used mostly by otaku to refer to an intense, affectionate and enthusiastic feeling towards a particular subject.

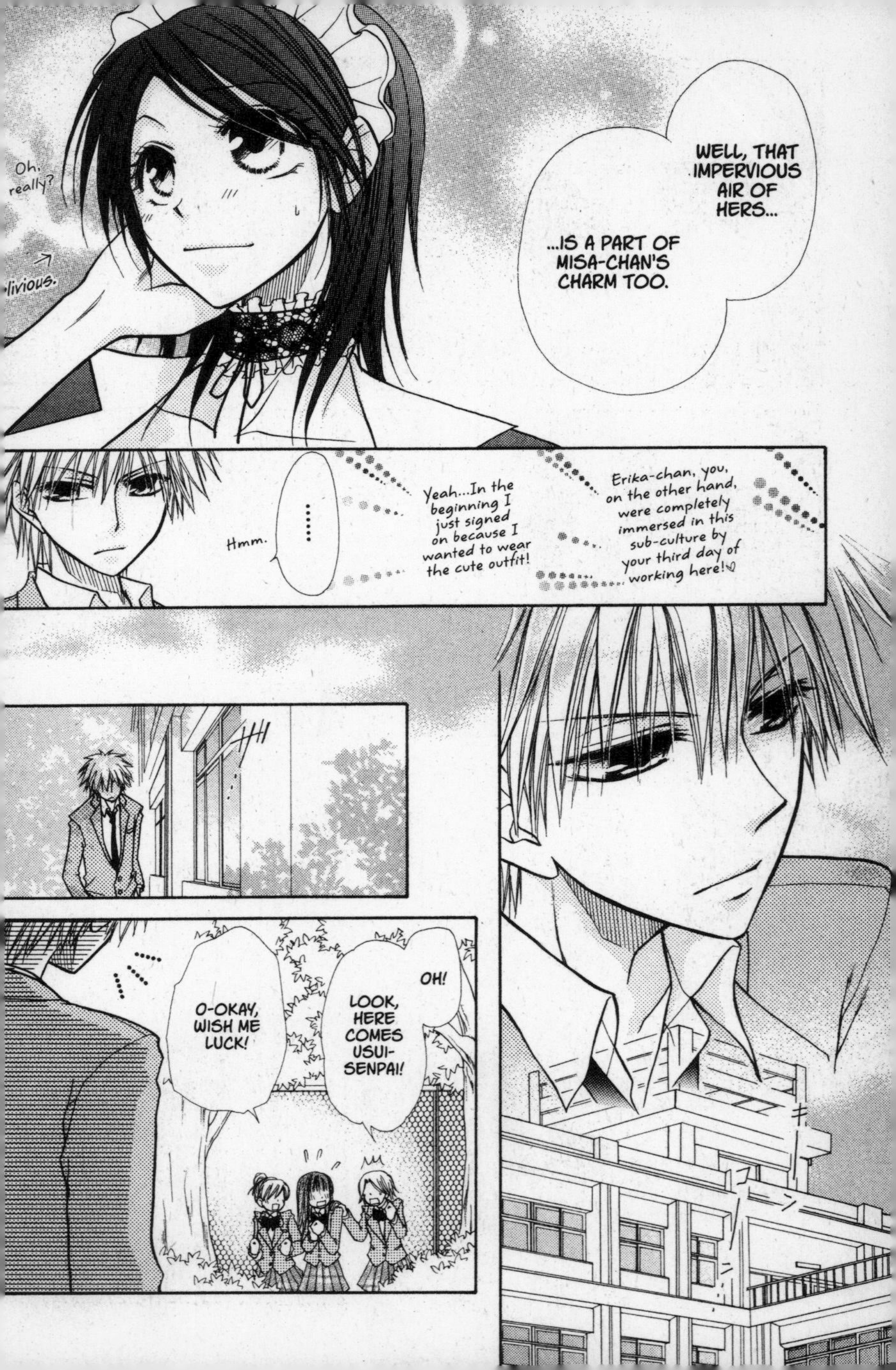

WELL, THAT IMPERVIOUS AIR OF HERS...
...IS A PART OF MISA-CHAN'S CHARM TOO.
Oh, really?
→ livious.
Erika-chan, you, on the other hand, were completely immersed in this sub-culture by your third day of working here!♡
Yeah...In the beginning I just signed on because I wanted to wear the cute outfit!
......
Hmm.
OH!
LOOK, HERE COMES USUI-SENPAI!
O-OKAY, WISH ME LUCK!
.....

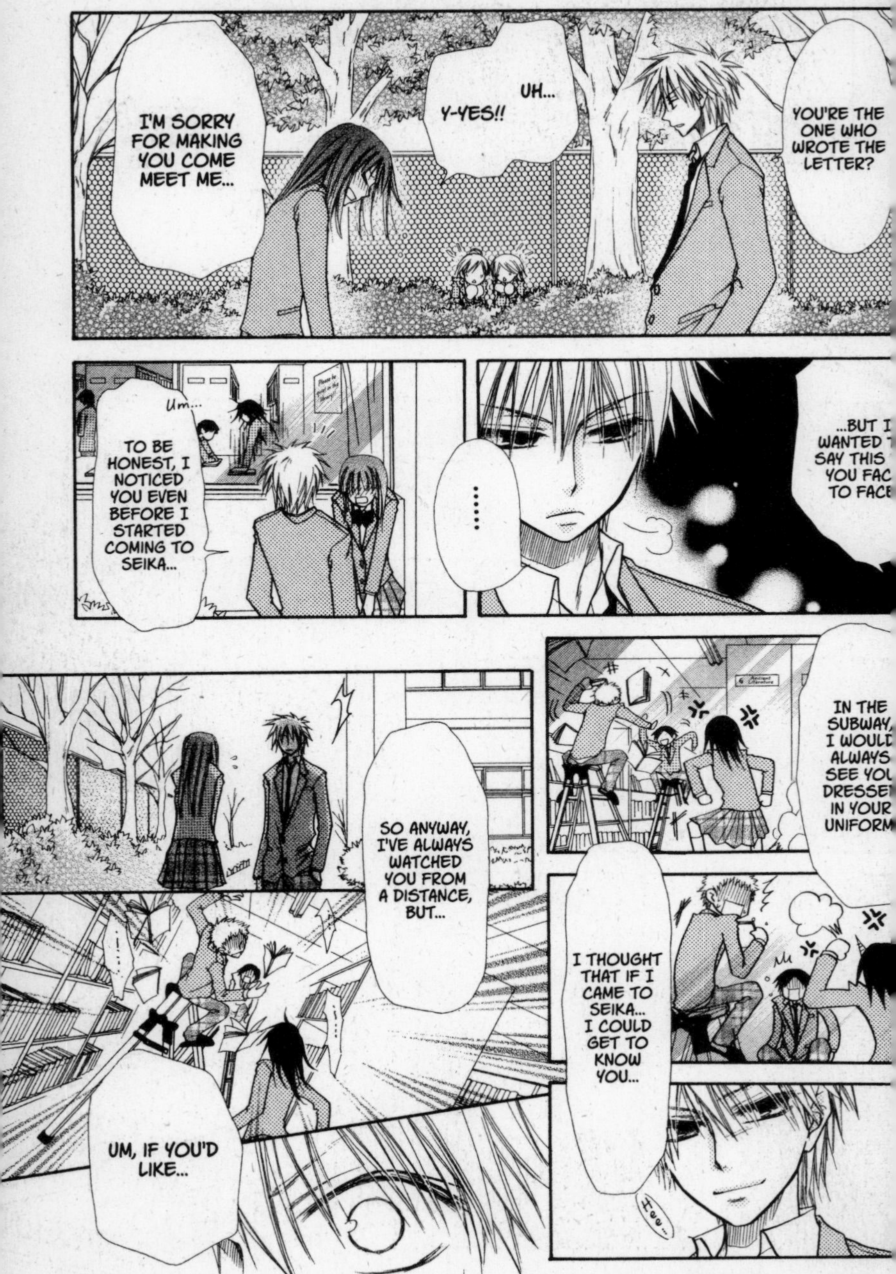
YOU'RE THE ONE WHO WROTE THE LETTER?
UH... Y-YES!!
I'M SORRY FOR MAKING YOU COME MEET ME...
...BUT I WANTED T SAY THIS YOU FAC TO FACE
......
Um...
TO BE HONEST, I NOTICED YOU EVEN BEFORE I STARTED COMING TO SEIKA...
IN THE SUBWAY, I WOULD ALWAYS SEE YOU DRESSE IN YOUR UNIFORM
Ancient Literature
SO ANYWAY, I'VE ALWAYS WATCHED YOU FROM A DISTANCE, BUT...
I THOUGHT THAT IF I CAME TO SEIKA... I COULD GET TO KNOW YOU...
Hee...
UM, IF YOU'D LIKE...

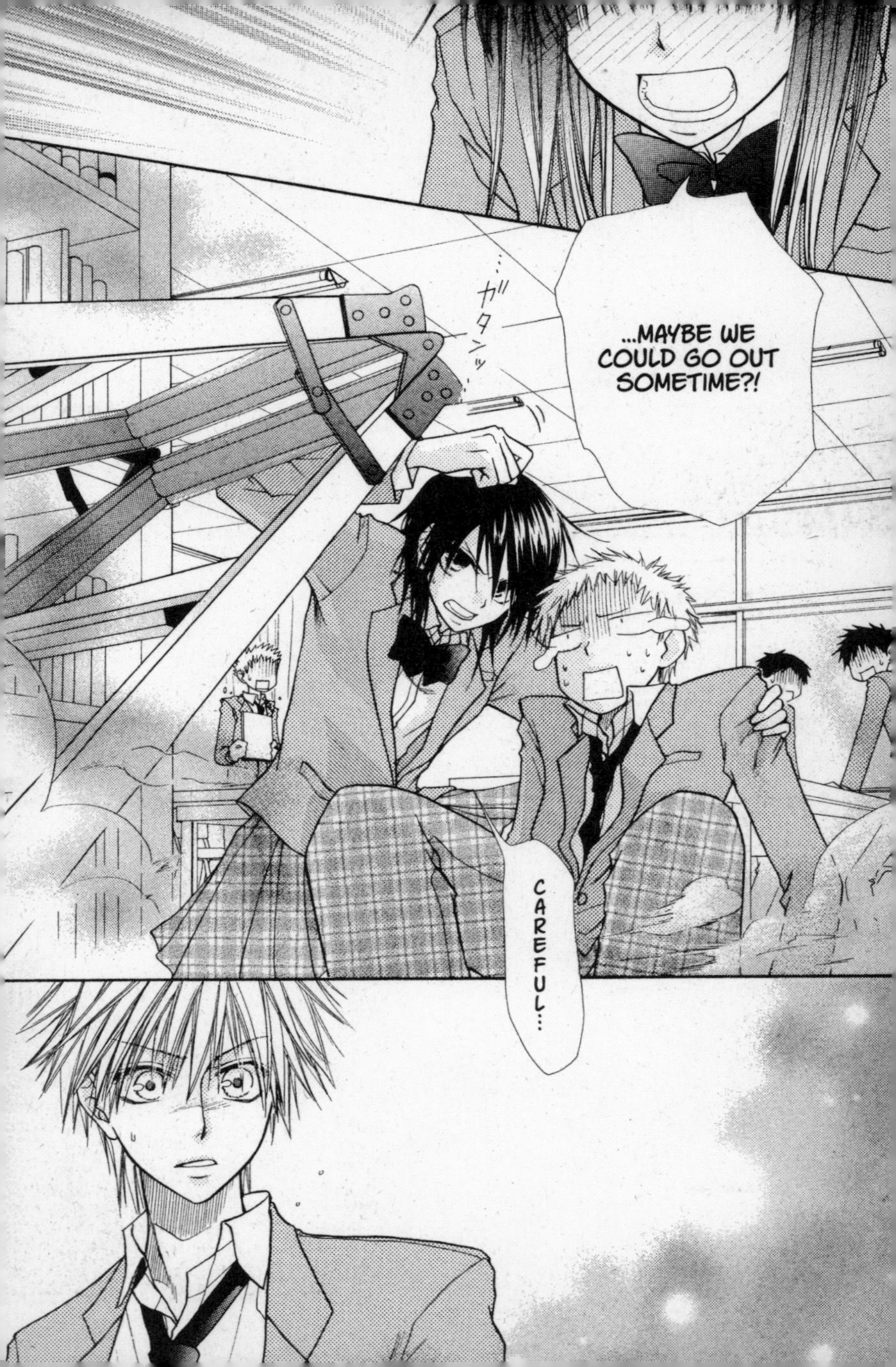
...MAYBE WE COULD GO OUT SOMETIME?!
…ガタンッ…
CAREFUL...

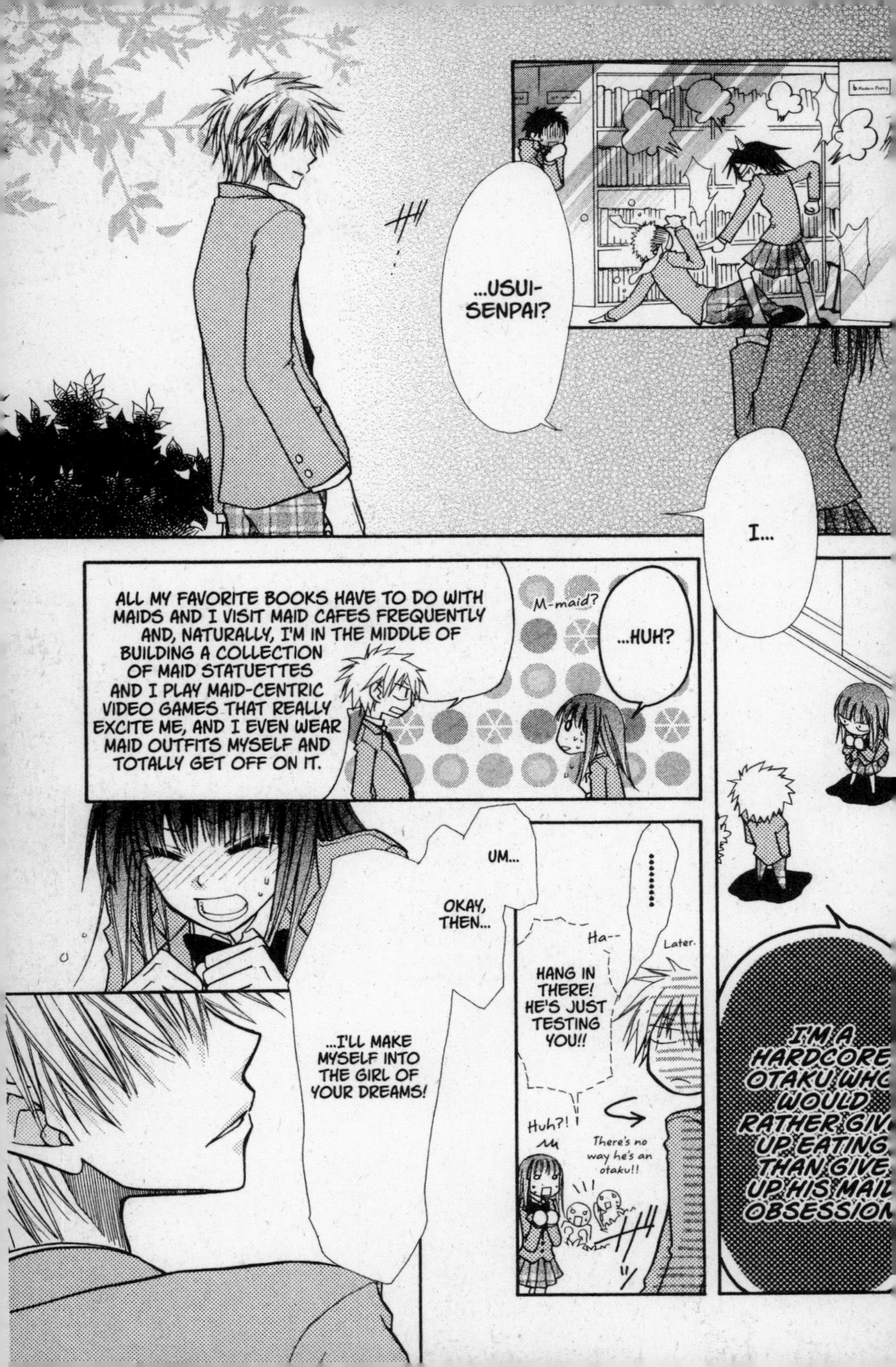

...USUI-SENPAI?
I...
I'M A HARDCORE OTAKU WHO WOULD RATHER GIVE UP EATING THAN GIVE UP HIS MAID OBSESSION
...HUH?
M-maid?
ALL MY FAVORITE BOOKS HAVE TO DO WITH MAIDS AND I VISIT MAID CAFES FREQUENTLY AND, NATURALLY, I'M IN THE MIDDLE OF BUILDING A COLLECTION OF MAID STATUETTES AND I PLAY MAID-CENTRIC VIDEO GAMES THAT REALLY EXCITE ME, AND I EVEN WEAR MAID OUTFITS MYSELF AND TOTALLY GET OFF ON IT.
....
Later.
Ha--
HANG IN THERE! HE'S JUST TESTING YOU!!
Huh?!
There's no way he's an otaku!!
UM...
OKAY, THEN...
...I'LL MAKE MYSELF INTO THE GIRL OF YOUR DREAMS!

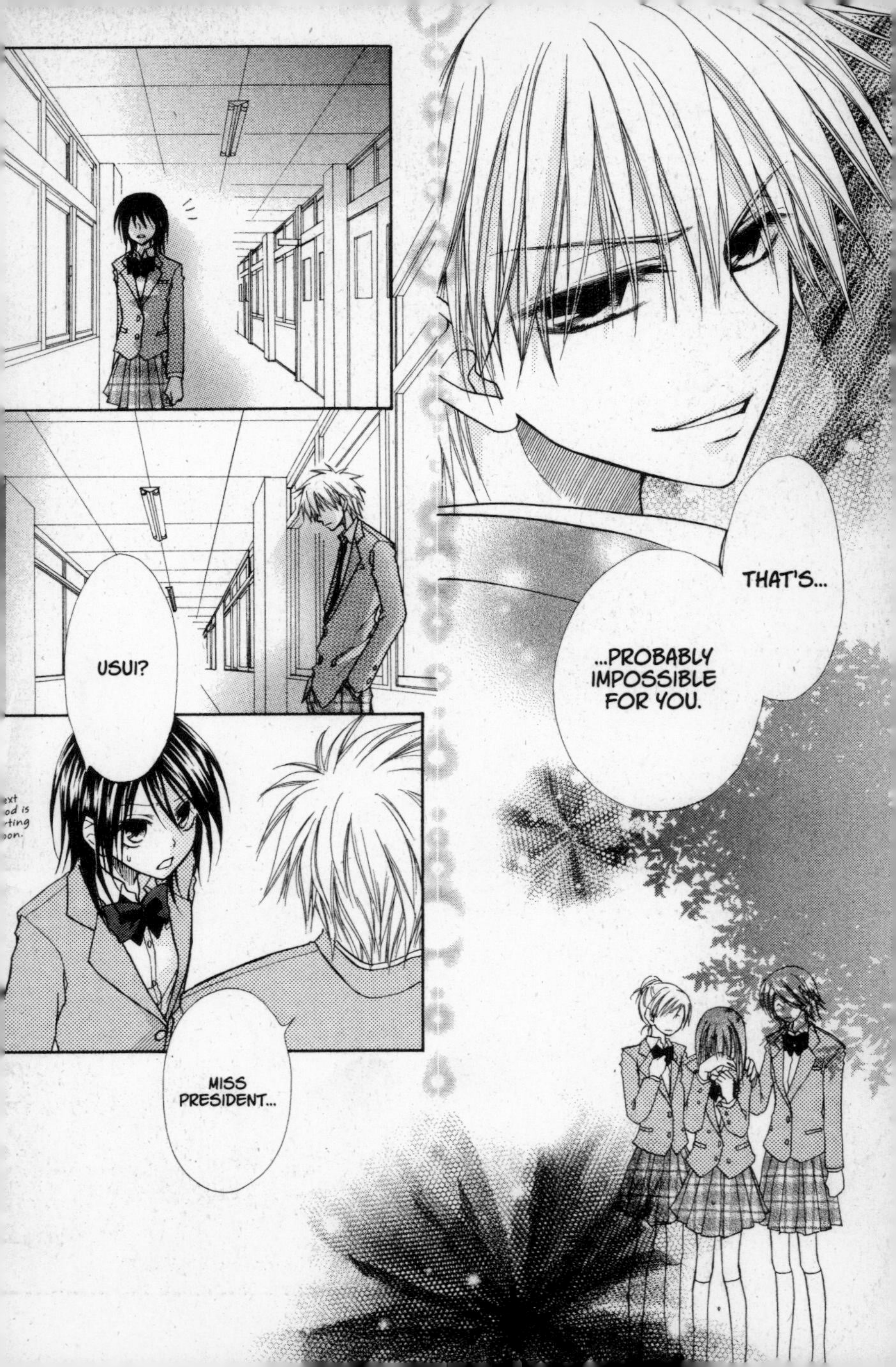
THAT'S...
...PROBABLY IMPOSSIBLE FOR YOU.
USUI?
MISS PRESIDENT...

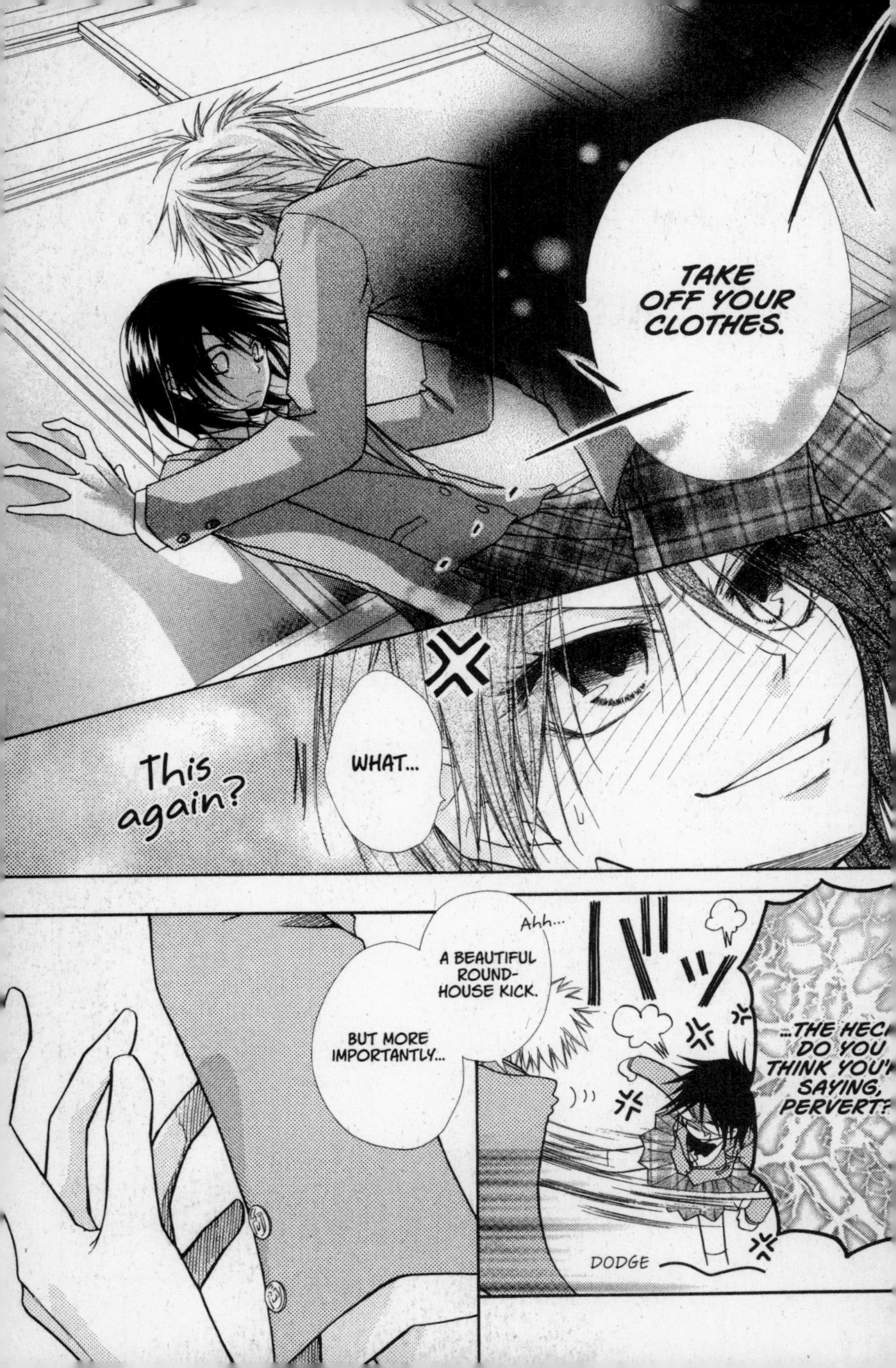

TAKE OFF YOUR CLOTHES.
WHAT...
This again?
...THE HEC DO YOU THINK YOU' SAYING, PERVERT?!
DODGE
Ahh...
A BEAUTIFUL ROUND-HOUSE KICK.
BUT MORE IMPORTANTLY...

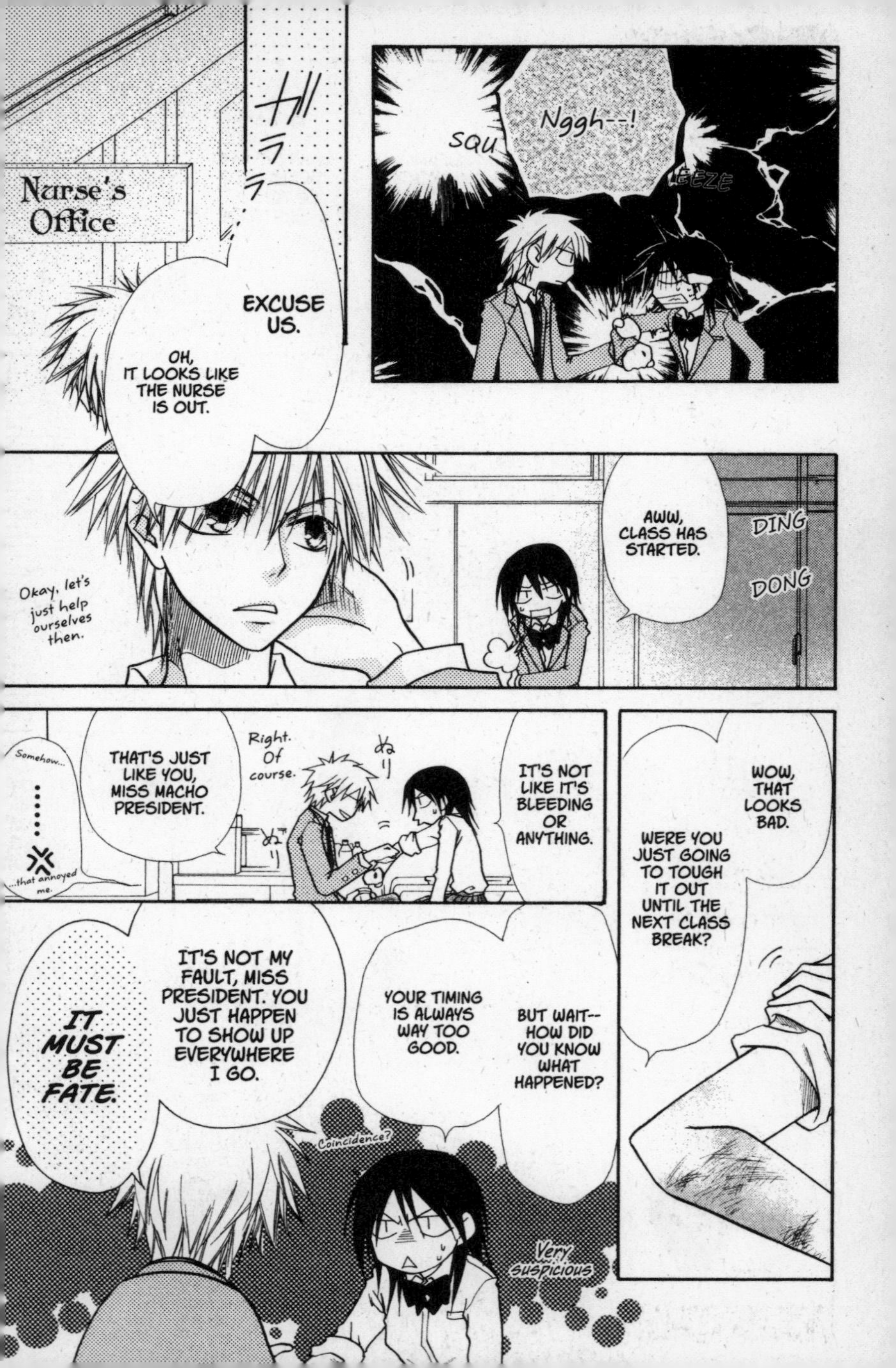
Nggh--!
SQU
EEZE
Nurse's Office
ガララ…
EXCUSE US.
OH, IT LOOKS LIKE THE NURSE IS OUT.
DING
DONG
AWW, CLASS HAS STARTED.
Okay, let's just help ourselves then.
WOW, THAT LOOKS BAD.
WERE YOU JUST GOING TO TOUGH IT OUT UNTIL THE NEXT CLASS BREAK?
IT'S NOT LIKE IT'S BLEEDING OR ANYTHING.
Right. Of course.
ぬり
ぬり
THAT'S JUST LIKE YOU, MISS MACHO PRESIDENT.
Somehow...
......
...that annoyed me.
BUT WAIT-- HOW DID YOU KNOW WHAT HAPPENED?
YOUR TIMING IS ALWAYS WAY TOO GOOD.
IT'S NOT MY FAULT, MISS PRESIDENT. YOU JUST HAPPEN TO SHOW UP EVERYWHERE I GO.
IT MUST BE FATE.
Coincidence?
Very suspicious

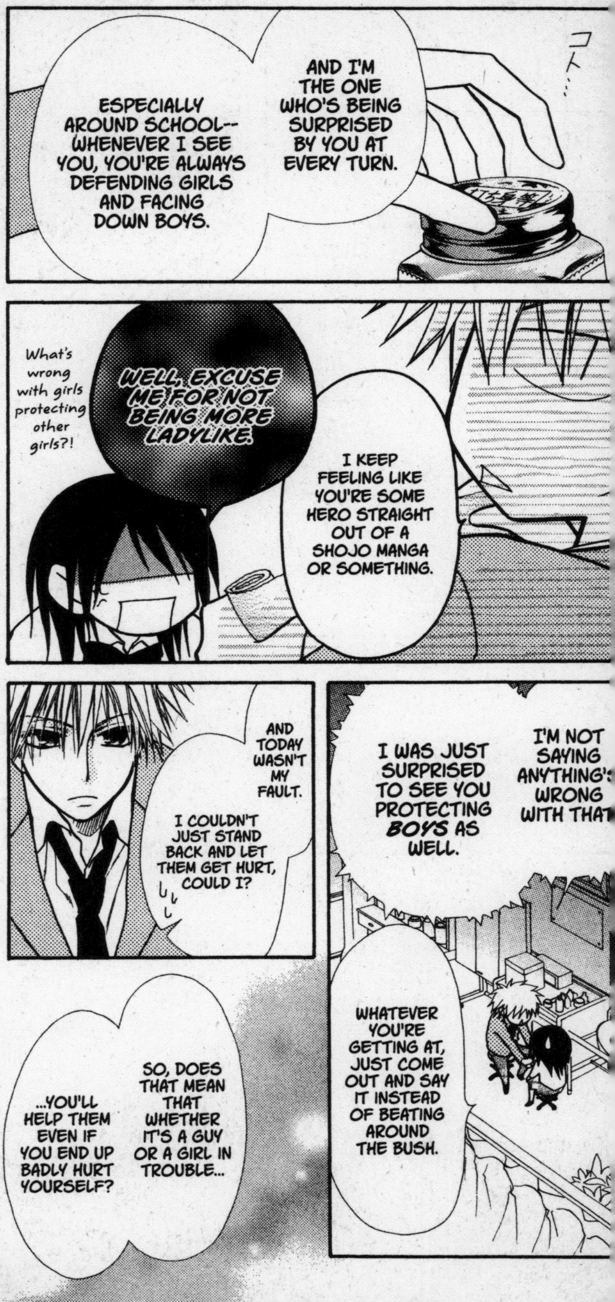
コト…
AND I'M THE ONE WHO'S BEING SURPRISED BY YOU AT EVERY TURN.
ESPECIALLY AROUND SCHOOL-- WHENEVER I SEE YOU, YOU'RE ALWAYS DEFENDING GIRLS AND FACING DOWN BOYS.
I KEEP FEELING LIKE YOU'RE SOME HERO STRAIGHT OUT OF A SHOJO MANGA OR SOMETHING.
WELL, EXCUSE ME FOR NOT BEING MORE LADYLIKE.
What's wrong with girls protecting other girls?!
I'M NOT SAYING ANYTHING'S WRONG WITH THAT
I WAS JUST SURPRISED TO SEE YOU PROTECTING BOYS AS WELL.
WHATEVER YOU'RE GETTING AT, JUST COME OUT AND SAY IT INSTEAD OF BEATING AROUND THE BUSH.
AND TODAY WASN'T MY FAULT.
I COULDN'T JUST STAND BACK AND LET THEM GET HURT, COULD I?
SO, DOES THAT MEAN THAT WHETHER IT'S A GUY OR A GIRL IN TROUBLE...
...YOU'LL HELP THEM EVEN IF YOU END UP BADLY HURT YOURSELF?

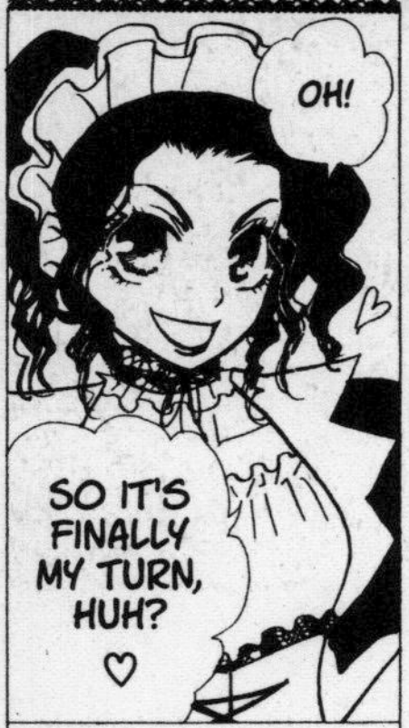
OH!
SO IT'S FINALLY MY TURN, HUH? ♡

NAME

Erika

AGE (CLASS)

19

BLOOD TYPE

O

HEIGHT

162 cm (5 ft 4 in)

WEIGHT

50 kg (110 lbs)

SPECIAL SKILLS

Seduction ♡

LIKES

I like anything as long as it's fun!

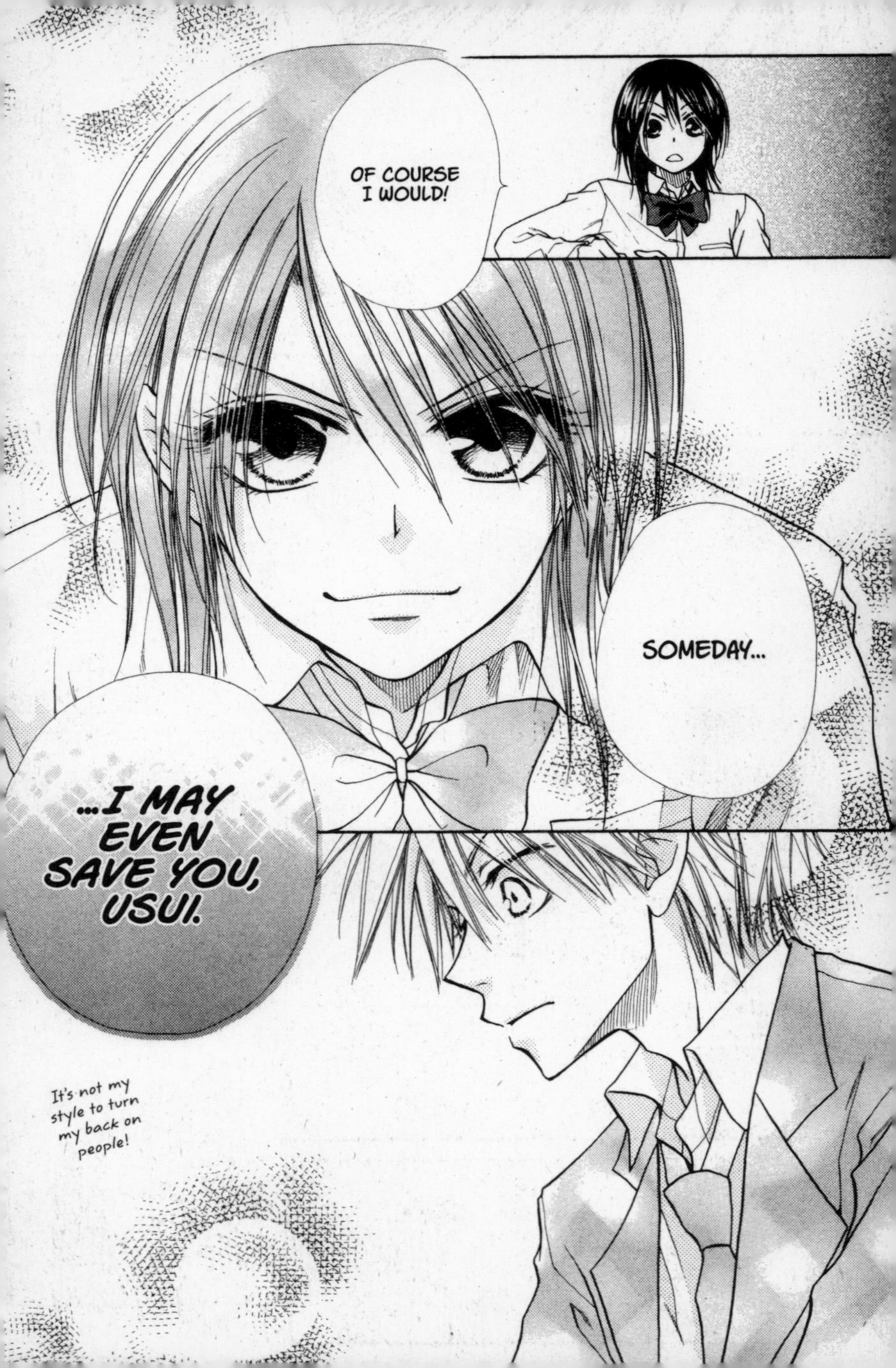
OF COURSE I WOULD!
SOMEDAY...
...I MAY EVEN SAVE YOU, USUI.
It's not my style to turn my back on people!

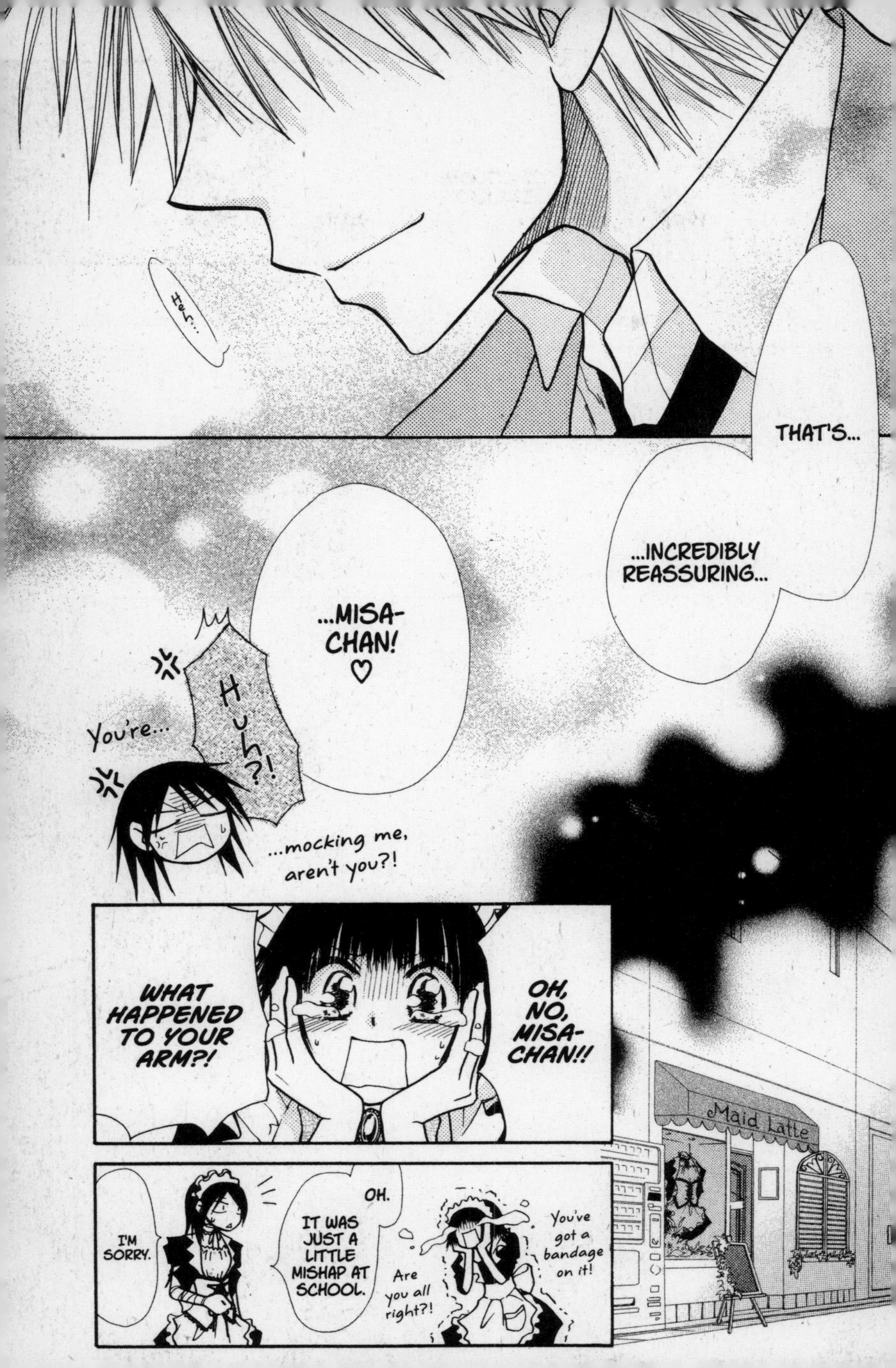
Heh...
THAT'S...
...INCREDIBLY REASSURING...
...MISA-CHAN! ♡
Huh?!
You're...
...mocking me, aren't you?!
OH, NO, MISA-CHAN!!
WHAT HAPPENED TO YOUR ARM?!
Maid Latte
You've got a bandage on it!
Are you all right?!
OH.
IT WAS JUST A LITTLE MISHAP AT SCHOOL.
I'M SORRY.

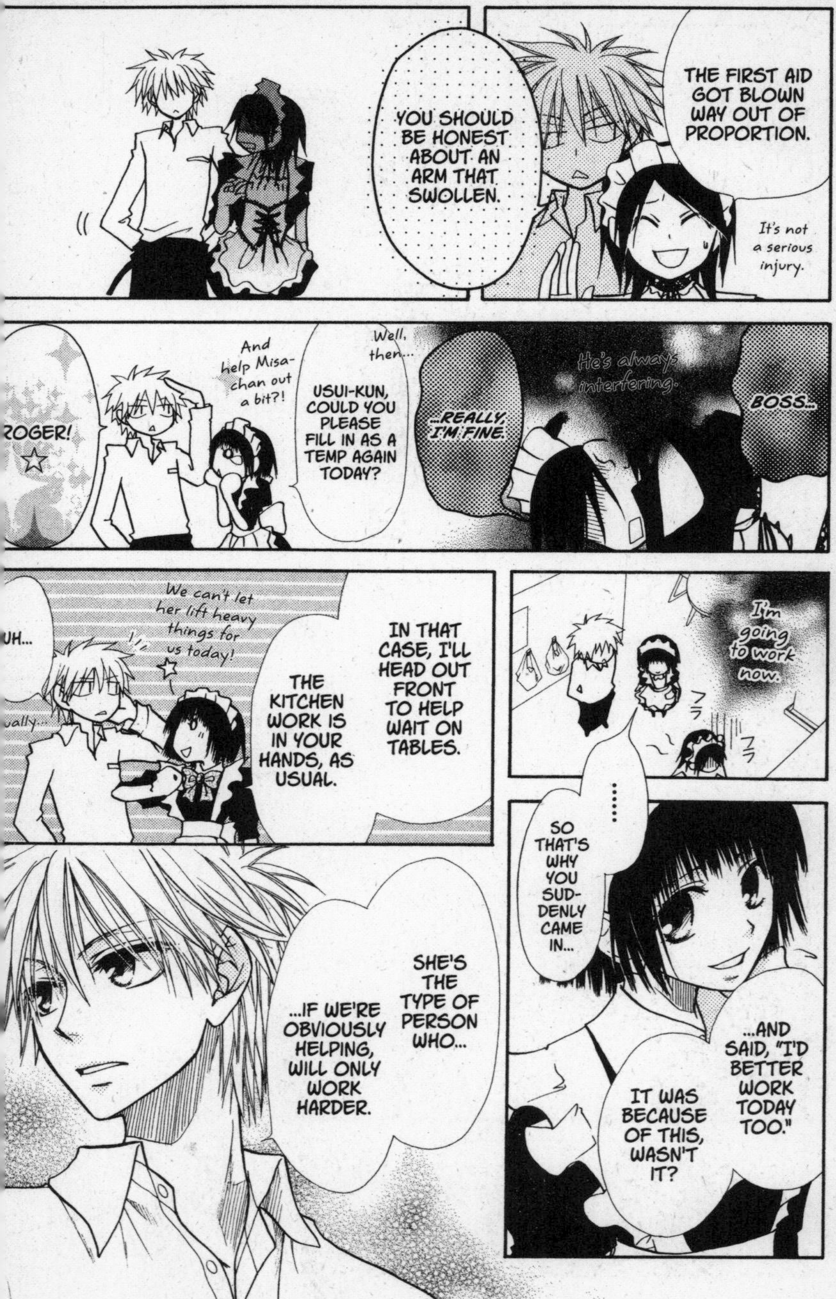
THE FIRST AID GOT BLOWN WAY OUT OF PROPORTION.
It's not a serious injury.
YOU SHOULD BE HONEST ABOUT AN ARM THAT SWOLLEN.
BOSS...
He's always interfering.
...REALLY, I'M FINE.
Well, then...
USUI-KUN, COULD YOU PLEASE FILL IN AS A TEMP AGAIN TODAY?
And help Misa-chan out a bit?!
ROGER!
I'm going to work now.
IN THAT CASE, I'LL HEAD OUT FRONT TO HELP WAIT ON TABLES.
THE KITCHEN WORK IS IN YOUR HANDS, AS USUAL.
We can't let her lift heavy things for us today!
......
SO THAT'S WHY YOU SUDDENLY CAME IN...
...AND SAID, "I'D BETTER WORK TODAY TOO."
IT WAS BECAUSE OF THIS, WASN'T IT?
SHE'S THE TYPE OF PERSON WHO...
...IF WE'RE OBVIOUSLY HELPING, WILL ONLY WORK HARDER.

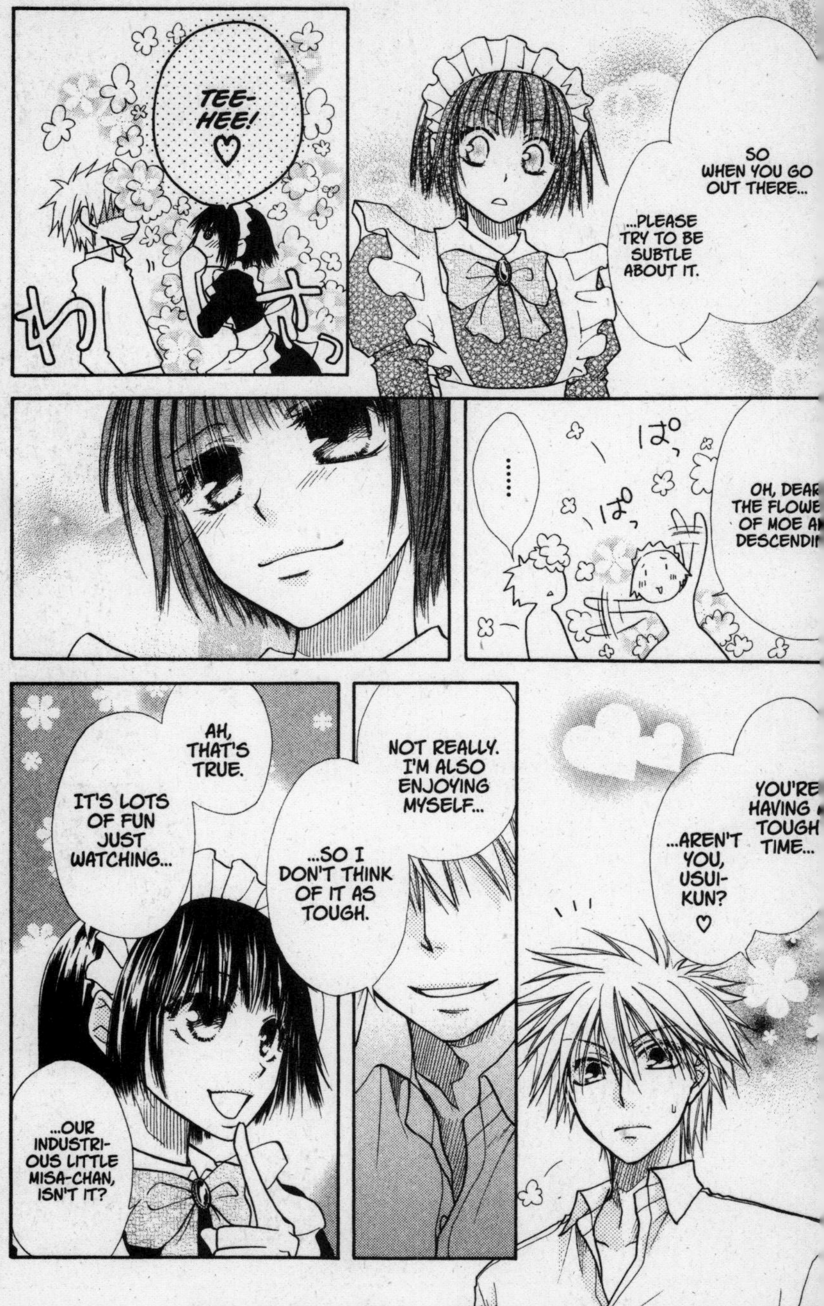
SO WHEN YOU GO OUT THERE...
...PLEASE TRY TO BE SUBTLE ABOUT IT.
TEE-HEE! ♡
OH, DEAR THE FLOWE OF MOE A DESCENDI
ぱっ
ぱっ
......
YOU'RE HAVING TOUGH TIME...
...AREN'T YOU, USUI-KUN? ♡
NOT REALLY. I'M ALSO ENJOYING MYSELF...
...SO I DON'T THINK OF IT AS TOUGH.
AH, THAT'S TRUE.
IT'S LOTS OF FUN JUST WATCHING...
...OUR INDUSTRIOUS LITTLE MISA-CHAN, ISN'T IT?

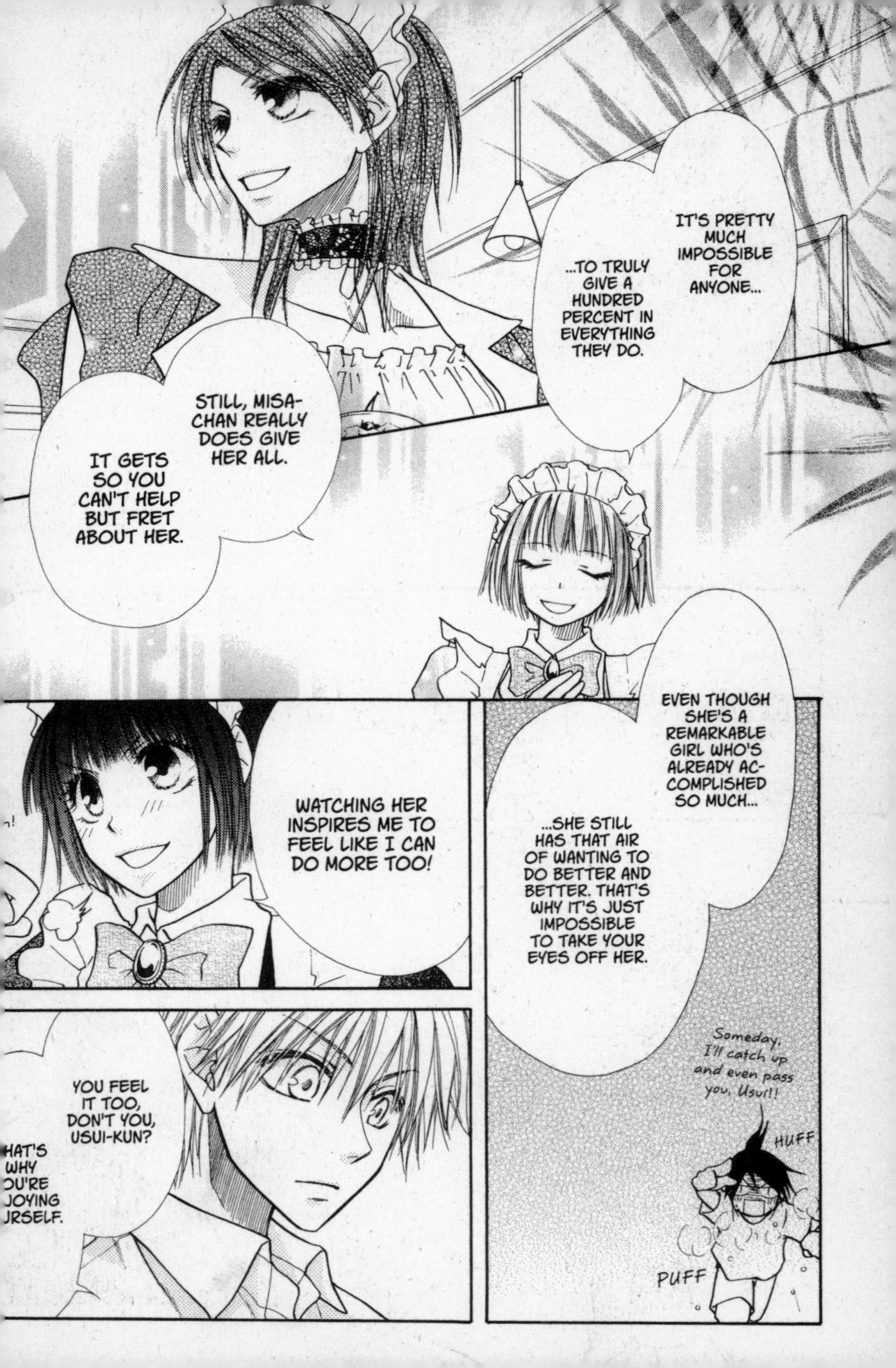

IT'S PRETTY MUCH IMPOSSIBLE FOR ANYONE...
...TO TRULY GIVE A HUNDRED PERCENT IN EVERYTHING THEY DO.
STILL, MISA-CHAN REALLY DOES GIVE HER ALL.
IT GETS SO YOU CAN'T HELP BUT FRET ABOUT HER.
EVEN THOUGH SHE'S A REMARKABLE GIRL WHO'S ALREADY AC-COMPLISHED SO MUCH...
...SHE STILL HAS THAT AIR OF WANTING TO DO BETTER AND BETTER. THAT'S WHY IT'S JUST IMPOSSIBLE TO TAKE YOUR EYES OFF HER.
Someday, I'll catch up and even pass you, Usui!!
HUFF
PUFF
WATCHING HER INSPIRES ME TO FEEL LIKE I CAN DO MORE TOO!
YOU FEEL IT TOO, DON'T YOU, USUI-KUN?
HAT'S WHY OU'RE JOYING URSELF.

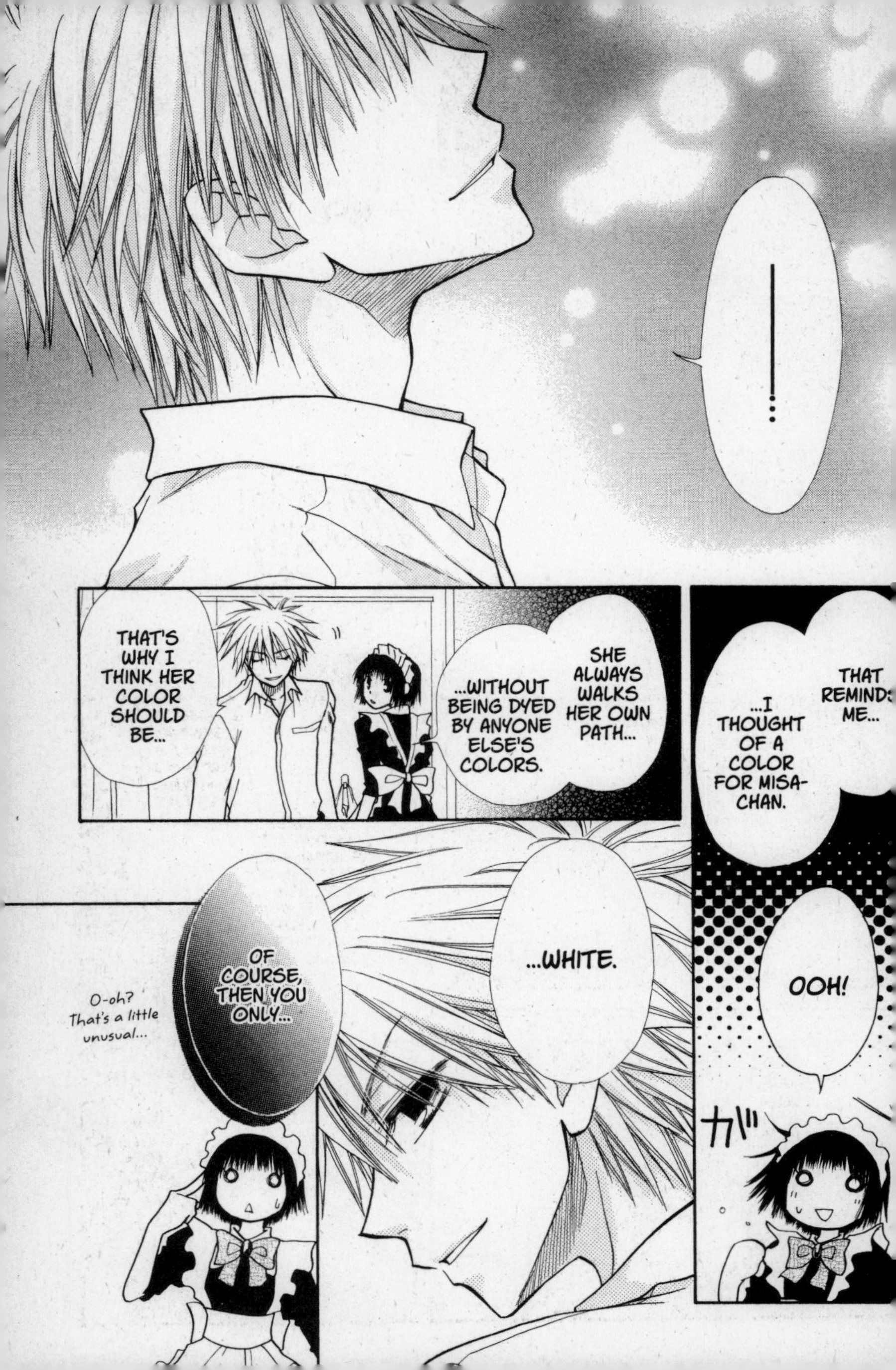
......
THAT REMINDS ME...
...I THOUGHT OF A COLOR FOR MISA-CHAN.
SHE ALWAYS WALKS HER OWN PATH...
...WITHOUT BEING DYED BY ANYONE ELSE'S COLORS.
THAT'S WHY I THINK HER COLOR SHOULD BE...
ガ
OOH!
...WHITE.
OF COURSE, THEN YOU ONLY...
O-oh? That's a little unusual...

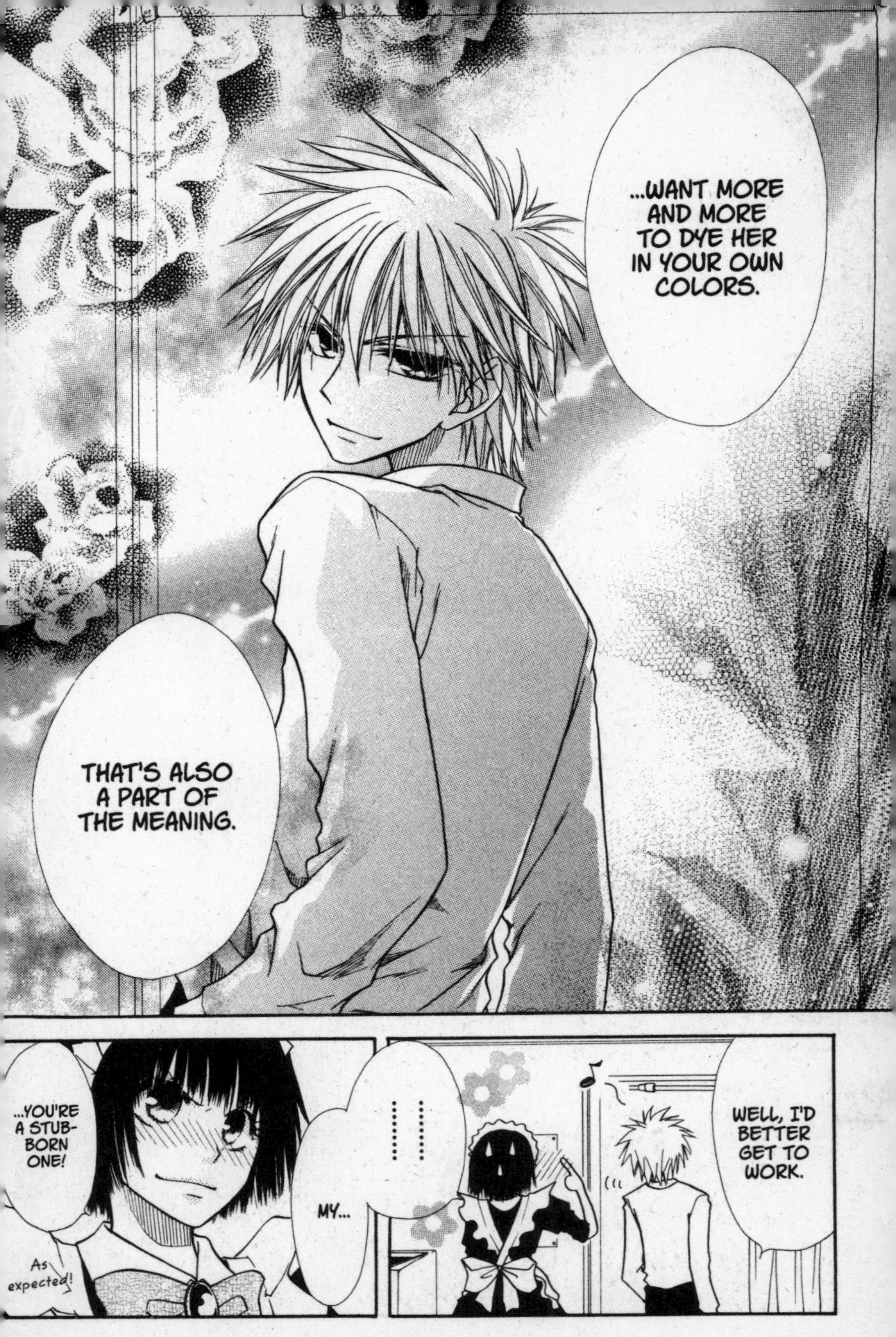
...WANT MORE AND MORE TO DYE HER IN YOUR OWN COLORS.
THAT'S ALSO A PART OF THE MEANING.
WELL, I'D BETTER GET TO WORK.
......
MY...
...YOU'RE A STUB-BORN ONE!
As expected!

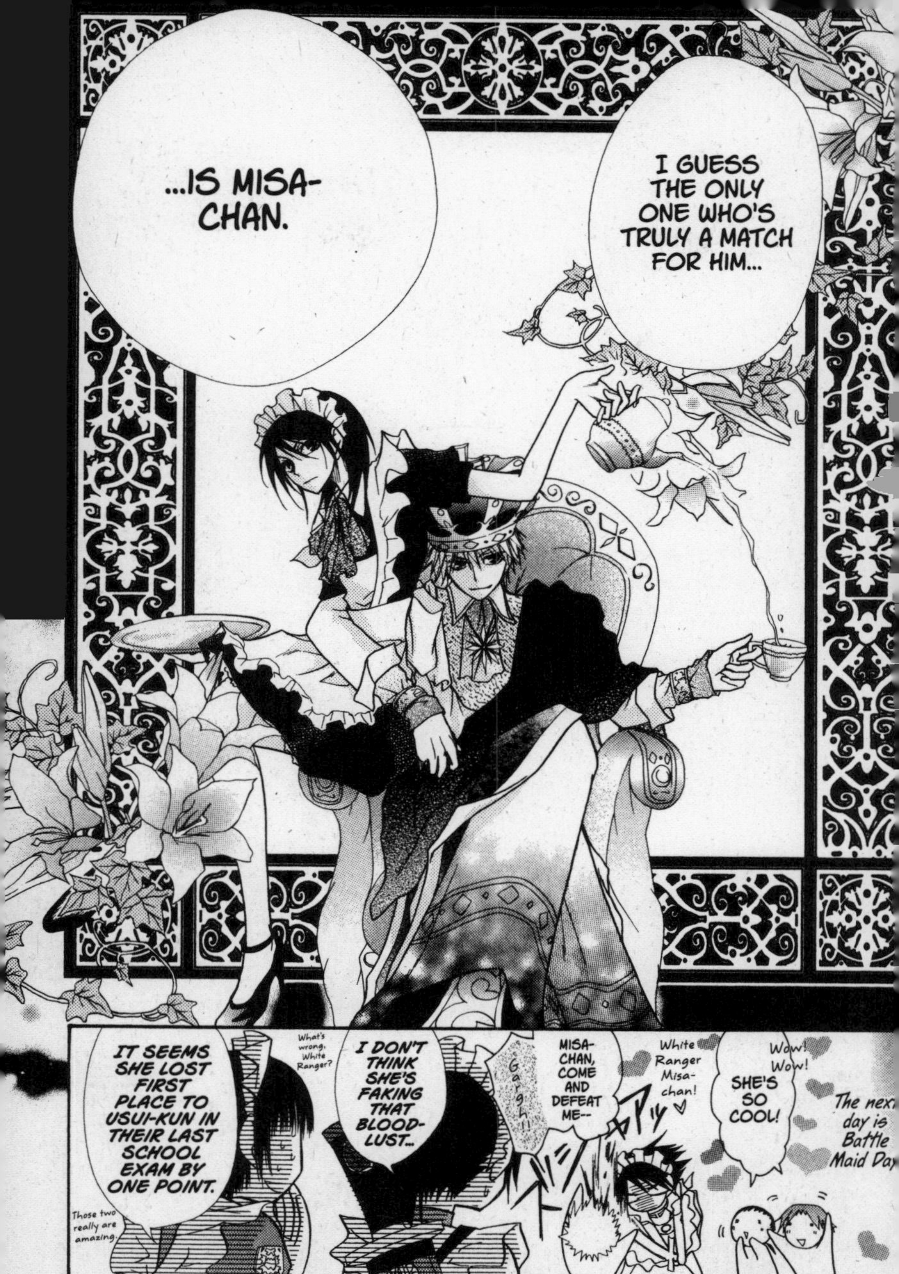
I GUESS THE ONLY ONE WHO'S TRULY A MATCH FOR HIM...
...IS MISA-CHAN.
The nex day is Battle Maid Day
Wow! Wow!
SHE'S SO COOL!
White Ranger Misa-chan! ♥
MISA-CHAN, COME AND DEFEAT ME--
Gargh!!
I DON'T THINK SHE'S FAKING THAT BLOODLUST...
What's wrong, White Ranger?
IT SEEMS SHE LOST FIRST PLACE TO USUI-KUN IN THEIR LAST SCHOOL EXAM BY ONE POINT.
Those two really are amazing.

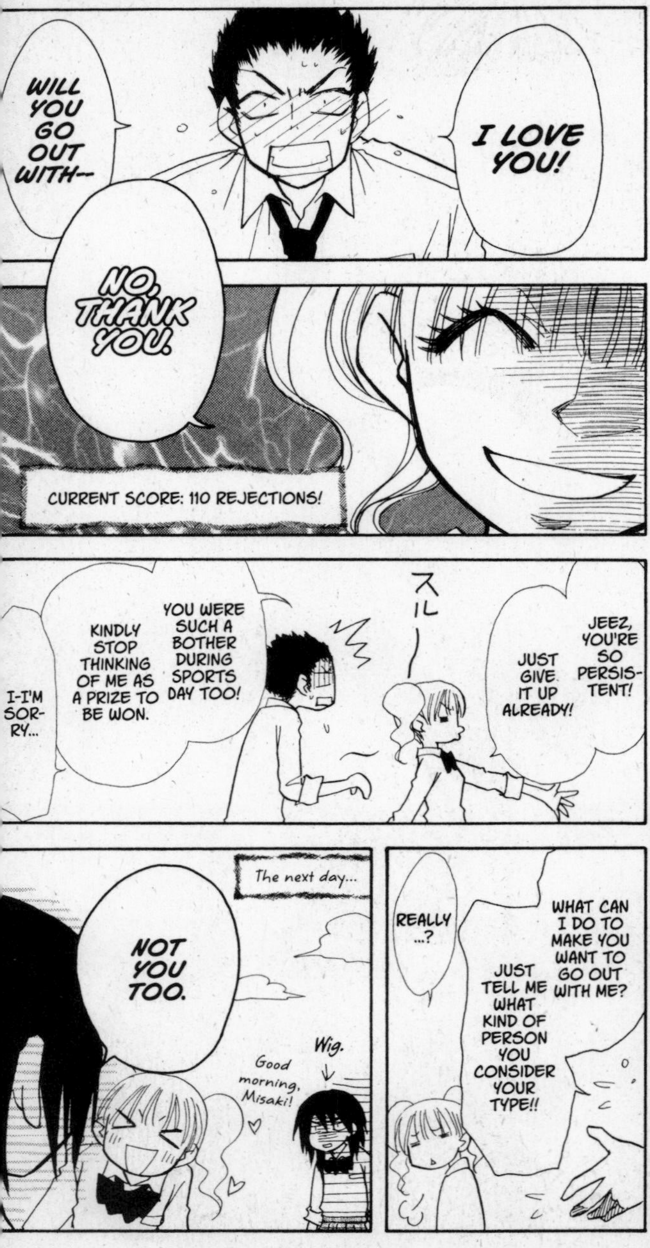
I LOVE YOU!
WILL YOU GO OUT WITH--
NO, THANK YOU.
CURRENT SCORE: 110 REJECTIONS!
JEEZ, YOU'RE SO PERSISTENT!
JUST GIVE IT UP ALREADY!
スルー
YOU WERE SUCH A BOTHER DURING SPORTS DAY TOO!
KINDLY STOP THINKING OF ME AS A PRIZE TO BE WON.
I-I'M SORRY...
WHAT CAN I DO TO MAKE YOU WANT TO GO OUT WITH ME?
JUST TELL ME WHAT KIND OF PERSON YOU CONSIDER YOUR TYPE!!
REALLY...?
The next day...
NOT YOU TOO.
Wig.
Good morning, Misaki!

Where Are They Now?

The Earnest Kouda-senpai

Who is Kouda?

First appearance: Volume 2, 9th Course. Kouda-senpai is passionately in love with Sakura Hanazono. He still won't give up on her even after she's rejected him a hundred times. He was formerly captain of the rugby team.

12th Course

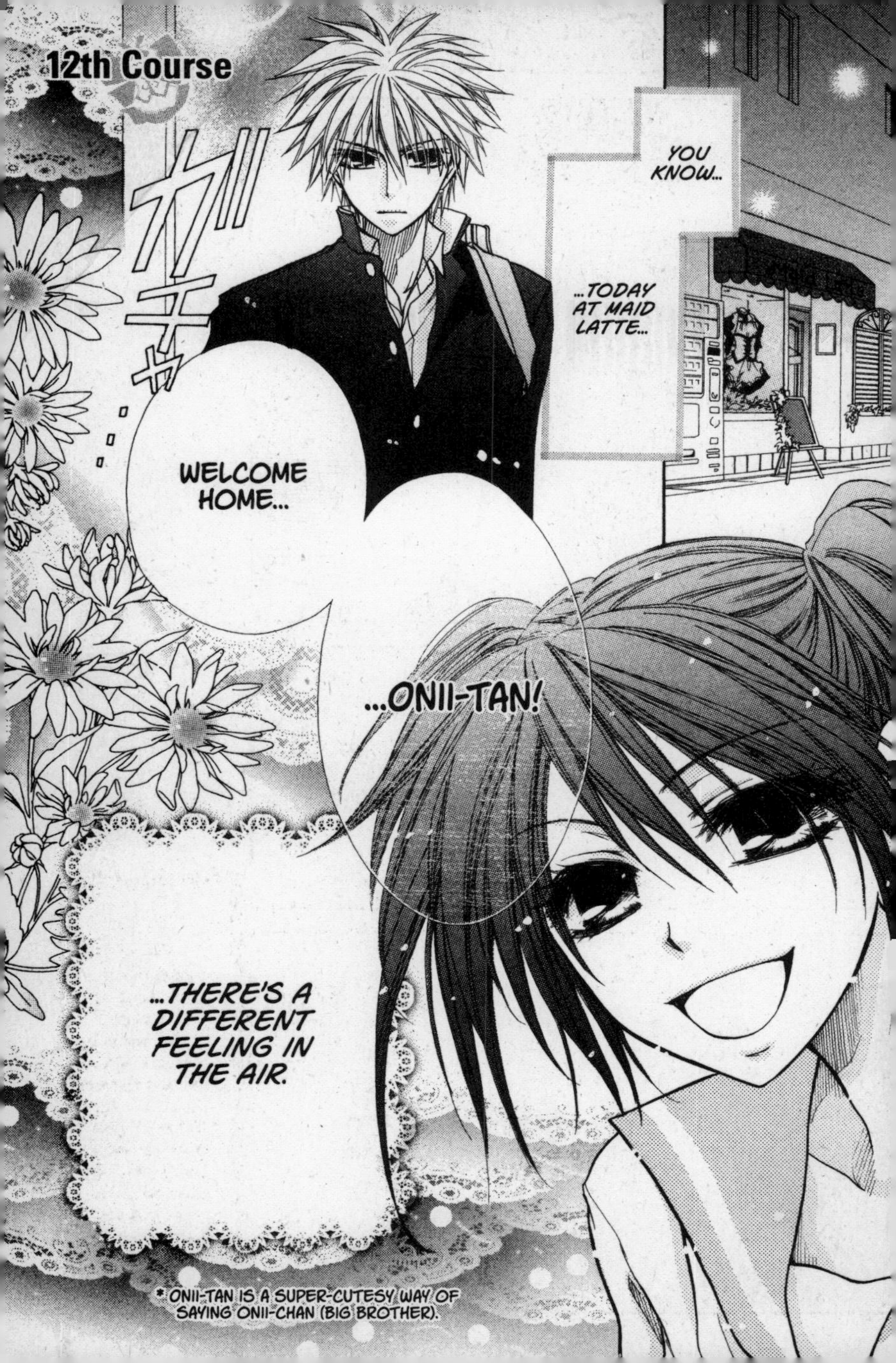
YOU KNOW...
...TODAY AT MAID LATTE...
ガチャ
WELCOME HOME...
...ONII-TAN!
...THERE'S A DIFFERENT FEELING IN THE AIR.

* ONII-TAN IS A SUPER-CUTESY WAY OF SAYING ONII-CHAN (BIG BROTHER).

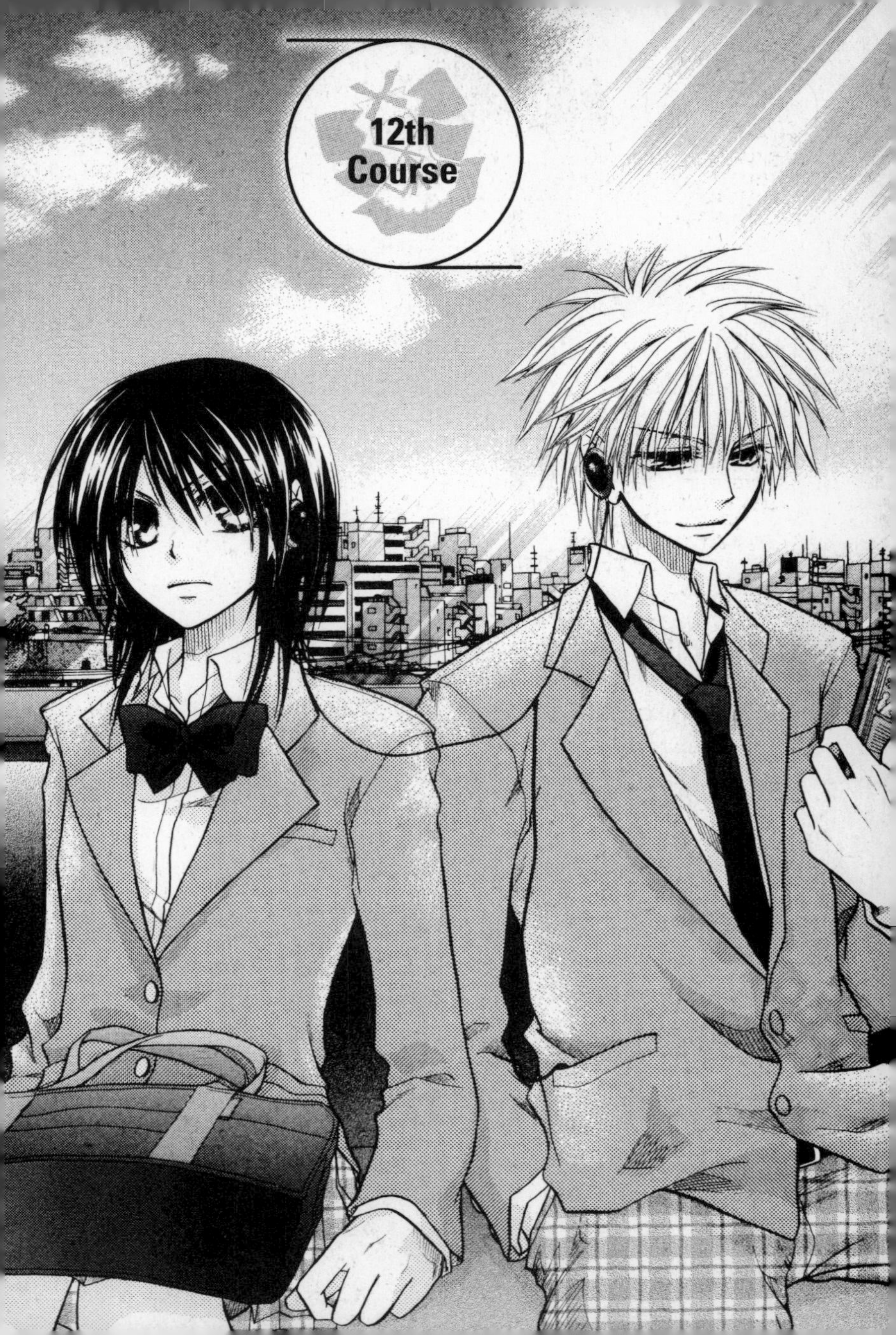
12th
Course

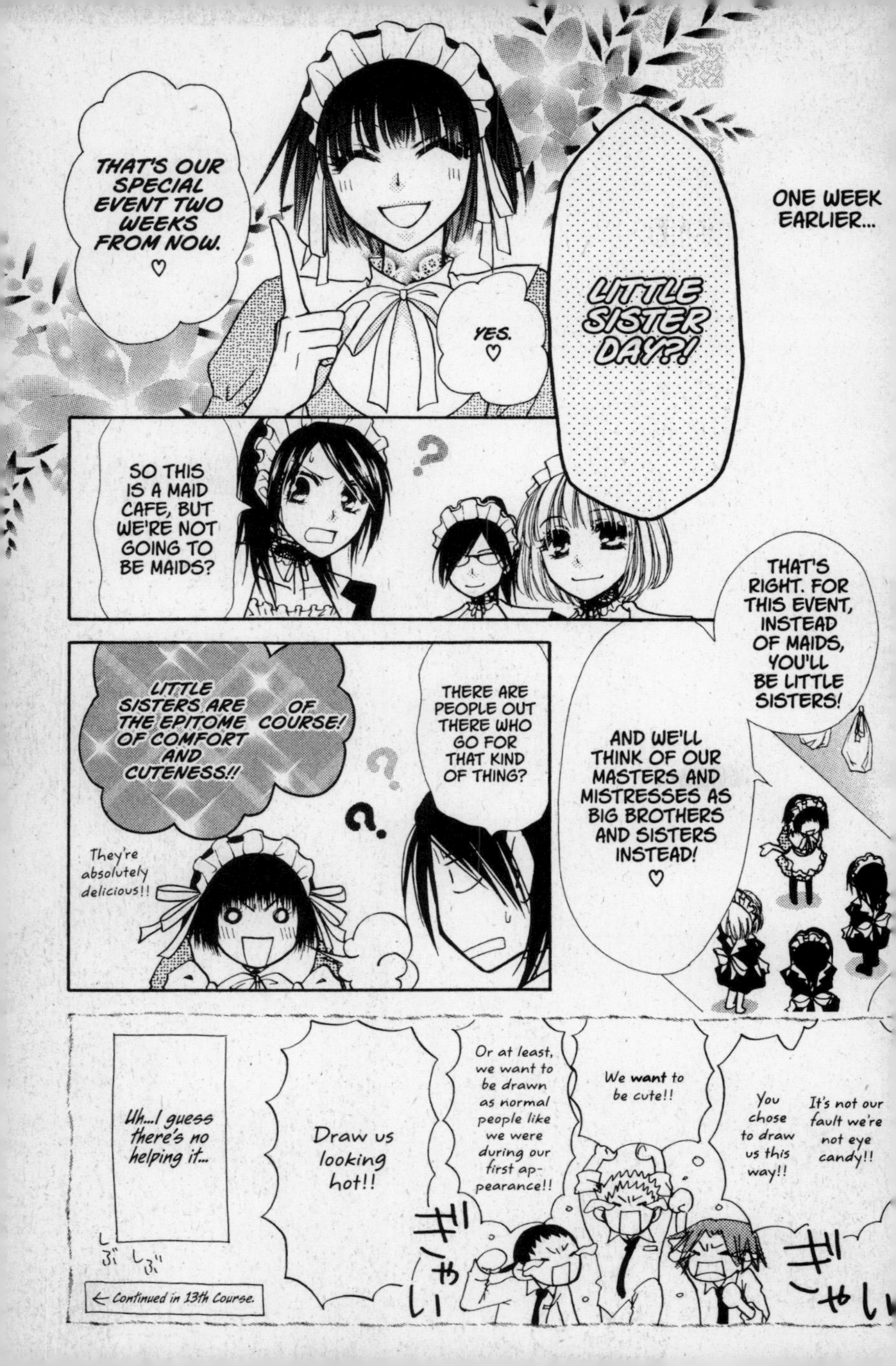
ONE WEEK EARLIER...
LITTLE SISTER DAY?!
YES. ♡
THAT'S OUR SPECIAL EVENT TWO WEEKS FROM NOW. ♡
SO THIS IS A MAID CAFE, BUT WE'RE NOT GOING TO BE MAIDS?
THAT'S RIGHT. FOR THIS EVENT, INSTEAD OF MAIDS, YOU'LL BE LITTLE SISTERS!
AND WE'LL THINK OF OUR MASTERS AND MISTRESSES AS BIG BROTHERS AND SISTERS INSTEAD! ♡
THERE ARE PEOPLE OUT THERE WHO GO FOR THAT KIND OF THING?
OF COURSE!
LITTLE SISTERS ARE THE EPITOME OF COMFORT AND CUTENESS!!
They're absolutely delicious!!
It's not our fault we're not eye candy!!
You chose to draw us this way!!
ぎゃい
We want to be cute!!
Or at least, we want to be drawn as normal people like we were during our first appearance!!
ぎゃい
Draw us looking hot!!
Uh...I guess there's no helping it...
しぶしぶ

← Continued in 13th Course.

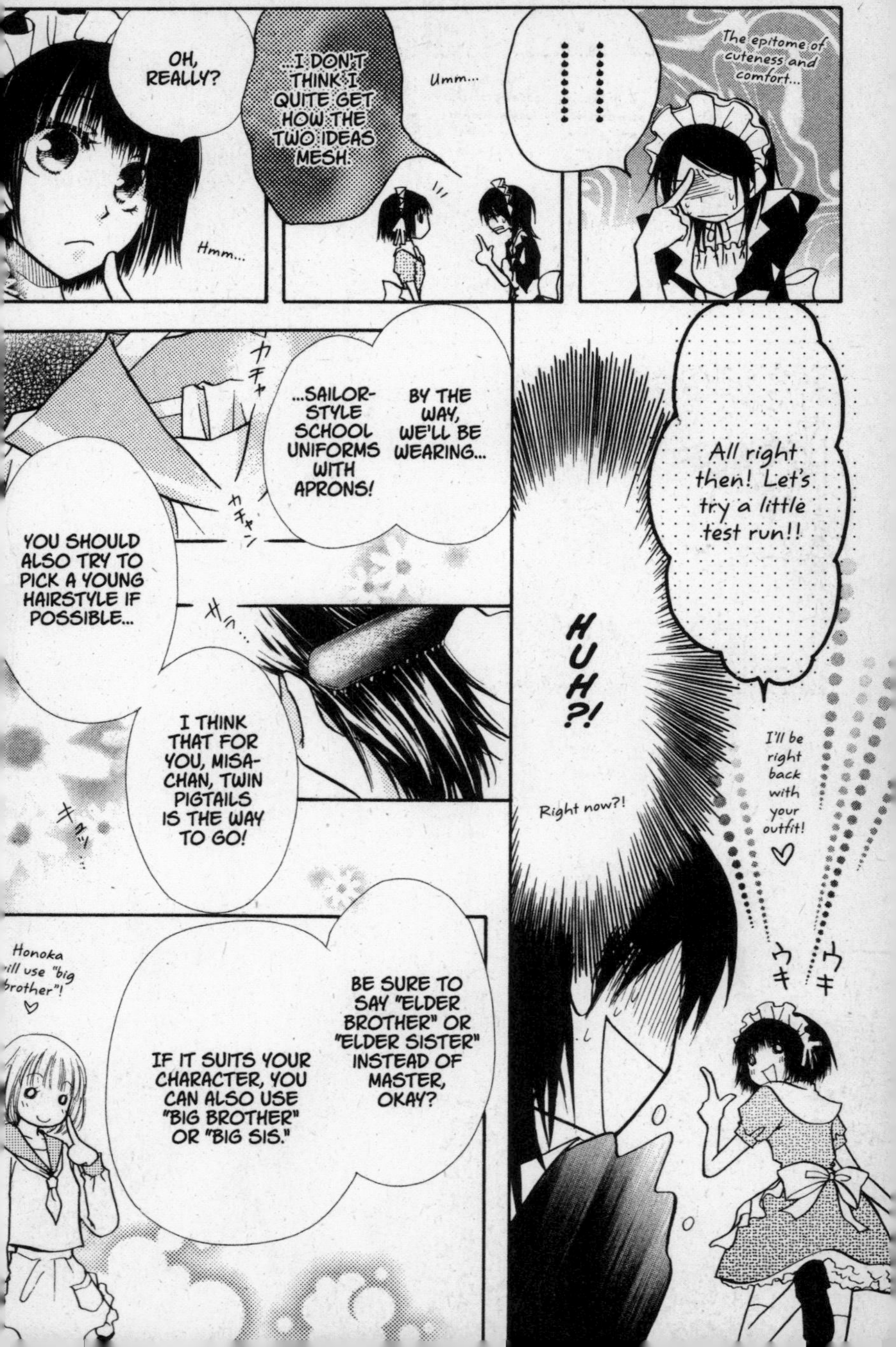
The epitome of cuteness and comfort...
!!
Umm...
...I DON'T THINK I QUITE GET HOW THE TWO IDEAS MESH.
OH, REALLY?
Hmm...
All right then! Let's try a little test run!!
HUH?!
Right now?!
I'll be right back with your outfit! ♡
ウキウキ
カチャ
BY THE WAY, WE'LL BE WEARING...
...SAILOR-STYLE SCHOOL UNIFORMS WITH APRONS!
カチャン
YOU SHOULD ALSO TRY TO PICK A YOUNG HAIRSTYLE IF POSSIBLE...
I THINK THAT FOR YOU, MISA-CHAN, TWIN PIGTAILS IS THE WAY TO GO!
キュッ
BE SURE TO SAY "ELDER BROTHER" OR "ELDER SISTER" INSTEAD OF MASTER, OKAY?
IF IT SUITS YOUR CHARACTER, YOU CAN ALSO USE "BIG BROTHER" OR "BIG SIS."
Honoka ill use "big brother"! ♡

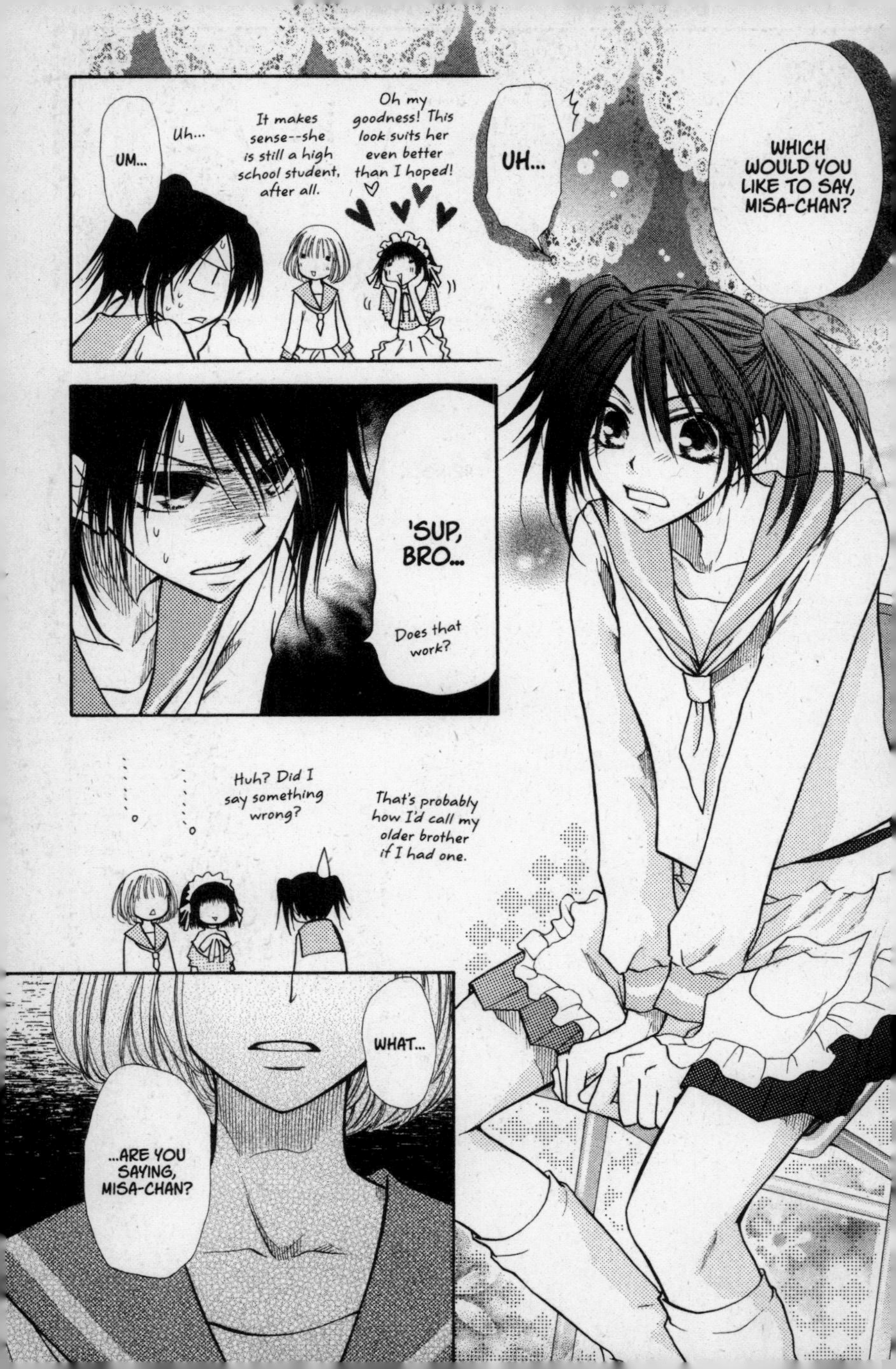
WHICH WOULD YOU LIKE TO SAY, MISA-CHAN?
UH...
Oh my goodness! This look suits her even better than I hoped!
It makes sense--she is still a high school student, after all.
Uh...
UM...
'SUP, BRO...
Does that work?
That's probably how I'd call my older brother if I had one.
Huh? Did I say something wrong?
WHAT...
...ARE YOU SAYING, MISA-CHAN?

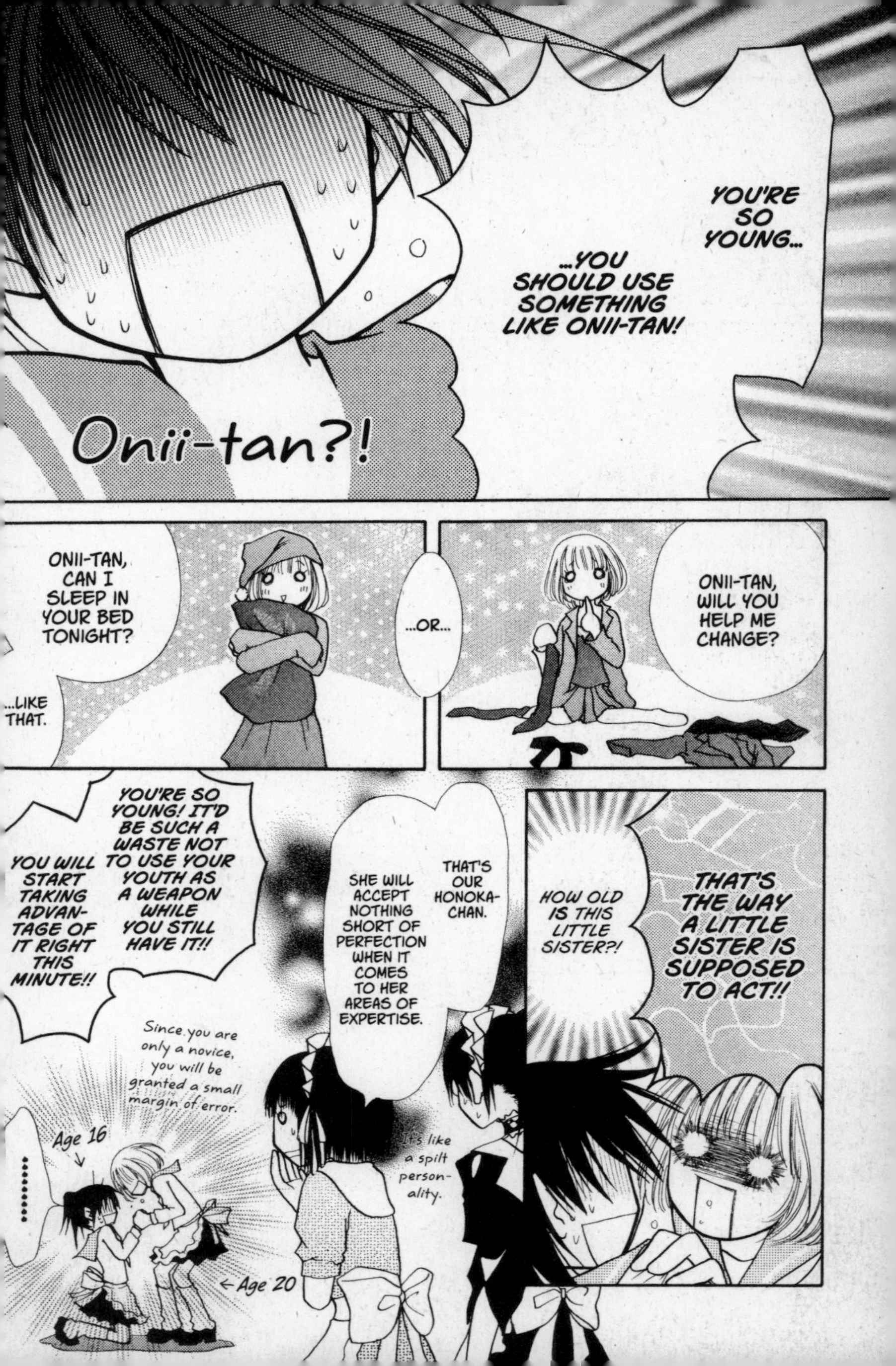
YOU'RE SO YOUNG...
...YOU SHOULD USE SOMETHING LIKE ONII-TAN!
Onii-tan?!
ONII-TAN, WILL YOU HELP ME CHANGE?
...OR...
ONII-TAN, CAN I SLEEP IN YOUR BED TONIGHT?
...LIKE THAT.
THAT'S THE WAY A LITTLE SISTER IS SUPPOSED TO ACT!!
HOW OLD IS THIS LITTLE SISTER?!
THAT'S OUR HONOKA-CHAN.
SHE WILL ACCEPT NOTHING SHORT OF PERFECTION WHEN IT COMES TO HER AREAS OF EXPERTISE.
It's like a spilt personality.
YOU'RE SO YOUNG! IT'D BE SUCH A WASTE NOT TO USE YOUR YOUTH AS A WEAPON WHILE YOU STILL HAVE IT!!
YOU WILL START TAKING ADVANTAGE OF IT RIGHT THIS MINUTE!!
Since you are only a novice, you will be granted a small margin of error.
Age 16
....
← Age 20

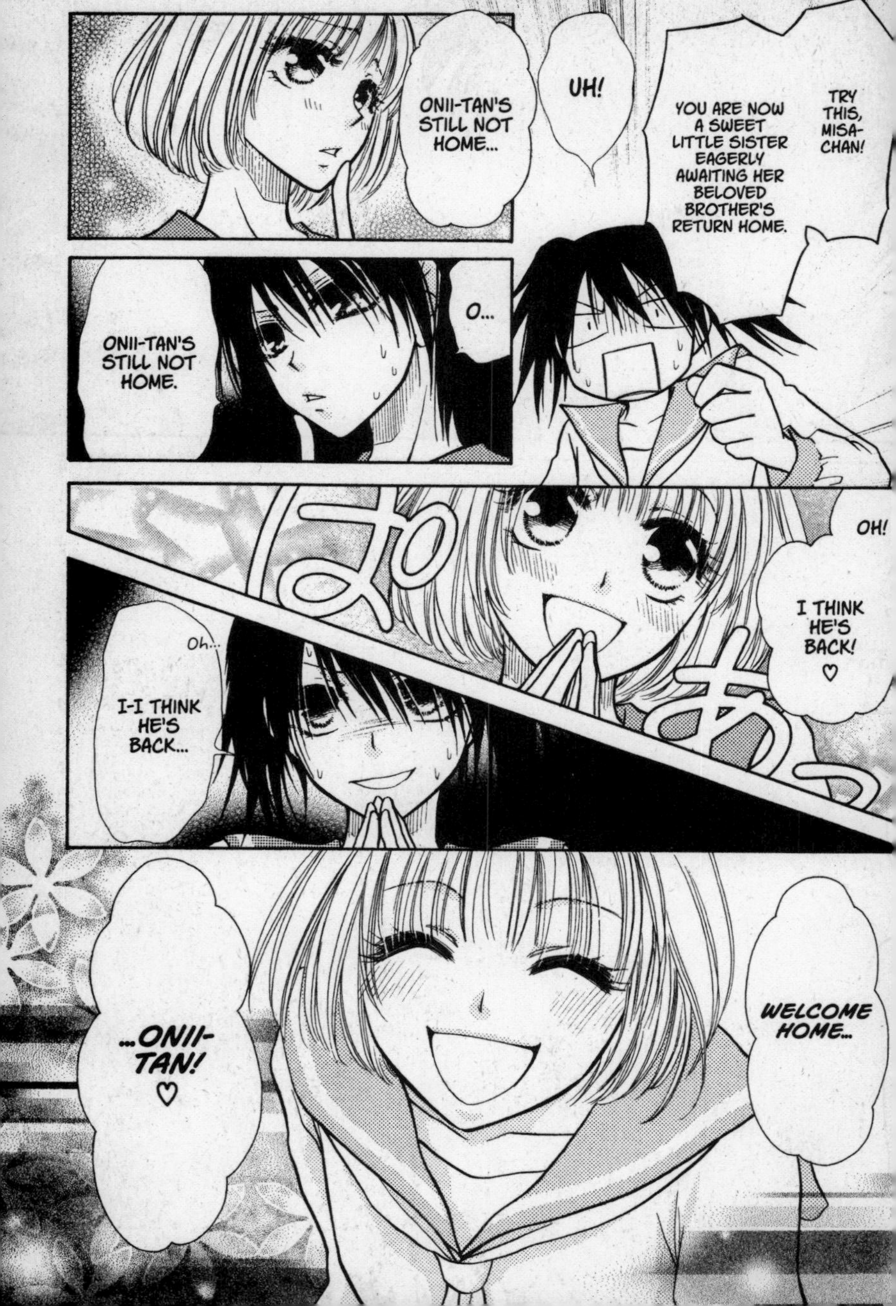
TRY THIS, MISA-CHAN!
YOU ARE NOW A SWEET LITTLE SISTER EAGERLY AWAITING HER BELOVED BROTHER'S RETURN HOME.
UH!
ONII-TAN'S STILL NOT HOME...
O...
ONII-TAN'S STILL NOT HOME.
OH!
I THINK HE'S BACK! ♡
Oh...
I-I THINK HE'S BACK...
WELCOME HOME...
...ONII-TAN! ♡

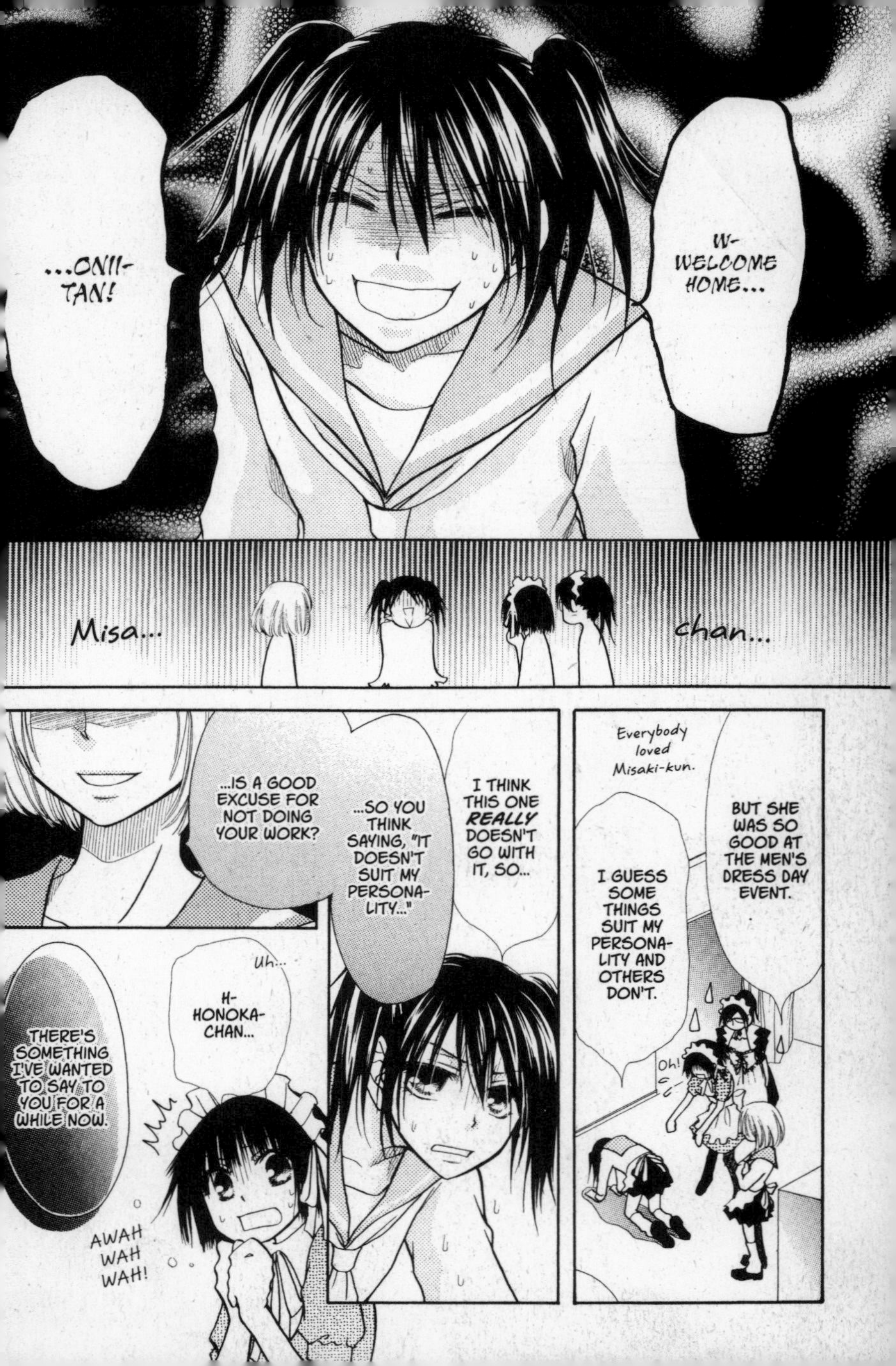
W-WELCOME HOME...
...ONII-TAN!
Misa...
chan...
Everybody loved Misaki-kun.
BUT SHE WAS SO GOOD AT THE MEN'S DRESS DAY EVENT.
I GUESS SOME THINGS SUIT MY PERSONALITY AND OTHERS DON'T.
Oh!
I THINK THIS ONE REALLY DOESN'T GO WITH IT, SO...
...SO YOU THINK SAYING, "IT DOESN'T SUIT MY PERSONALITY..."
...IS A GOOD EXCUSE FOR NOT DOING YOUR WORK?
Uh...
H-HONOKA-CHAN...
THERE'S SOMETHING I'VE WANTED TO SAY TO YOU FOR A WHILE NOW.
AWAH WAH WAH!

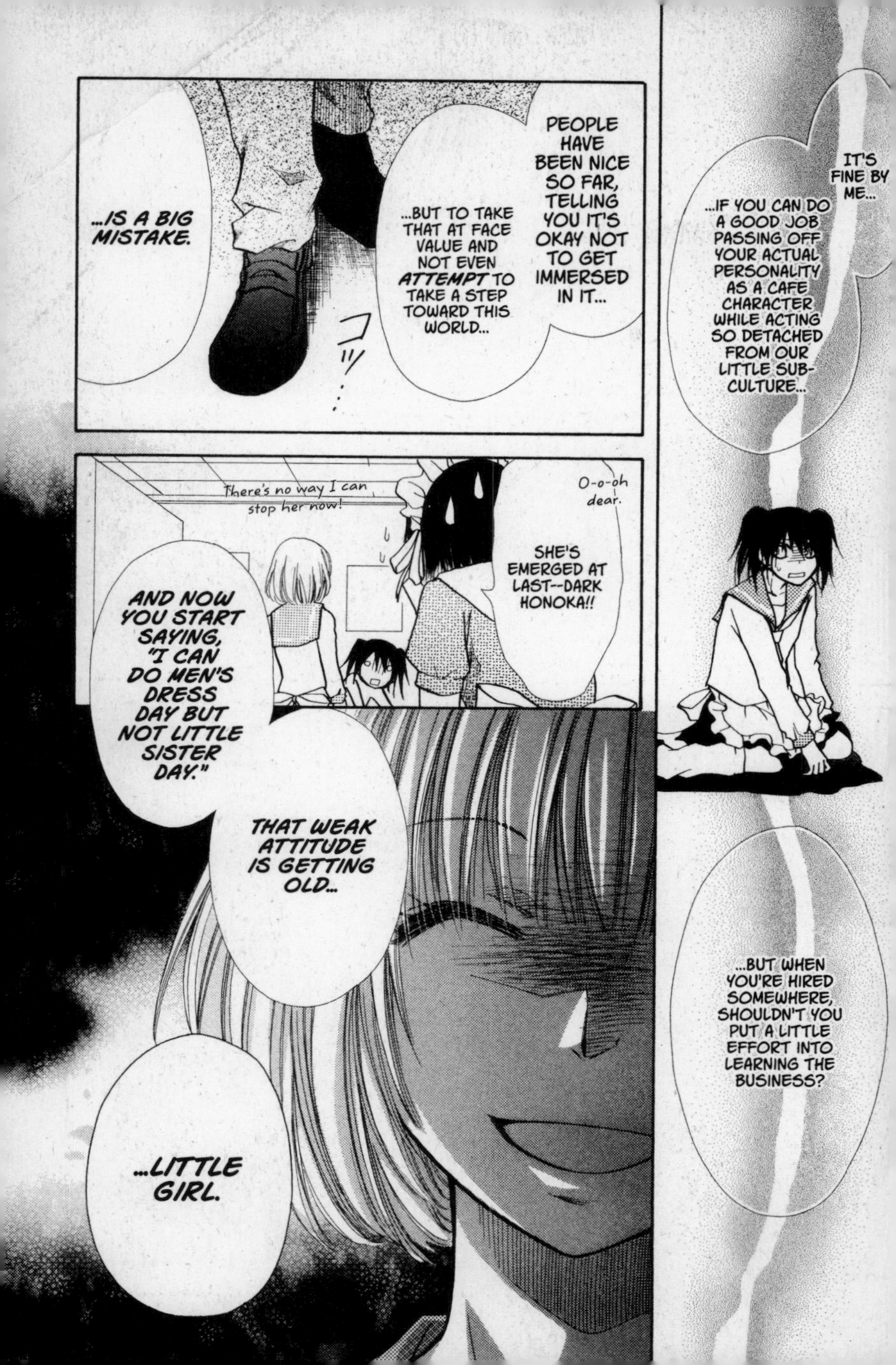
IT'S FINE BY ME...
...IF YOU CAN DO A GOOD JOB PASSING OFF YOUR ACTUAL PERSONALITY AS A CAFE CHARACTER WHILE ACTING SO DETACHED FROM OUR LITTLE SUB-CULTURE...
...BUT WHEN YOU'RE HIRED SOMEWHERE, SHOULDN'T YOU PUT A LITTLE EFFORT INTO LEARNING THE BUSINESS?
PEOPLE HAVE BEEN NICE SO FAR, TELLING YOU IT'S OKAY NOT TO GET IMMERSED IN IT...
...BUT TO TAKE THAT AT FACE VALUE AND NOT EVEN *ATTEMPT* TO TAKE A STEP TOWARD THIS WORLD...
コツ...
...IS A BIG MISTAKE.
O-o-oh dear.
SHE'S EMERGED AT LAST--DARK HONOKA!!
There's no way I can stop her now!
AND NOW YOU START SAYING, "I CAN DO MEN'S DRESS DAY BUT NOT LITTLE SISTER DAY."
THAT WEAK ATTITUDE IS GETTING OLD...
...LITTLE GIRL.

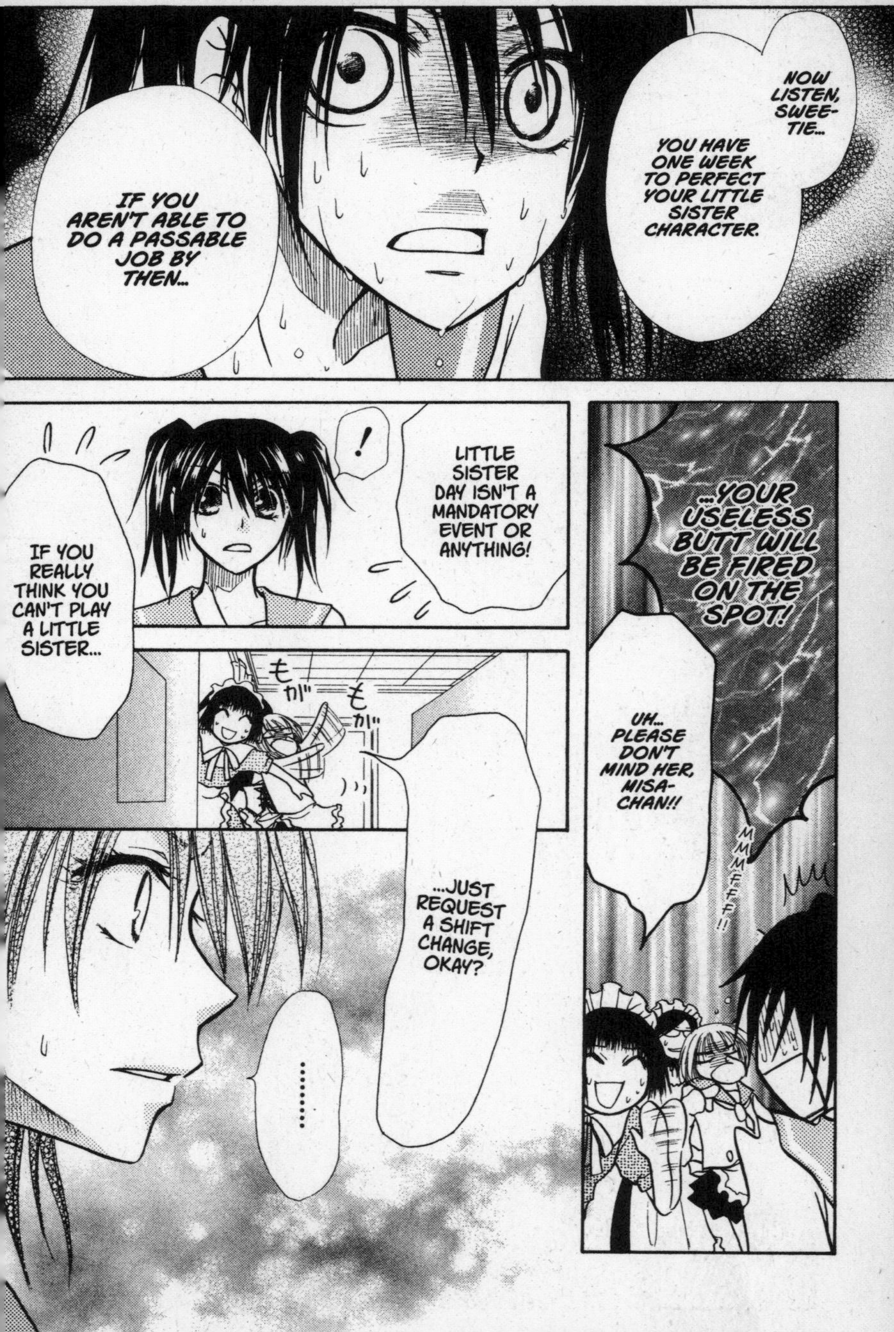
NOW LISTEN, SWEETIE...
YOU HAVE ONE WEEK TO PERFECT YOUR LITTLE SISTER CHARACTER.
IF YOU AREN'T ABLE TO DO A PASSABLE JOB BY THEN...
...YOUR USELESS BUTT WILL BE FIRED ON THE SPOT!
UH... PLEASE DON'T MIND HER, MISA-CHAN!!
MMMFFF!!
!
LITTLE SISTER DAY ISN'T A MANDATORY EVENT OR ANYTHING!
IF YOU REALLY THINK YOU CAN'T PLAY A LITTLE SISTER...
もが
もが
...JUST REQUEST A SHIFT CHANGE, OKAY?
......

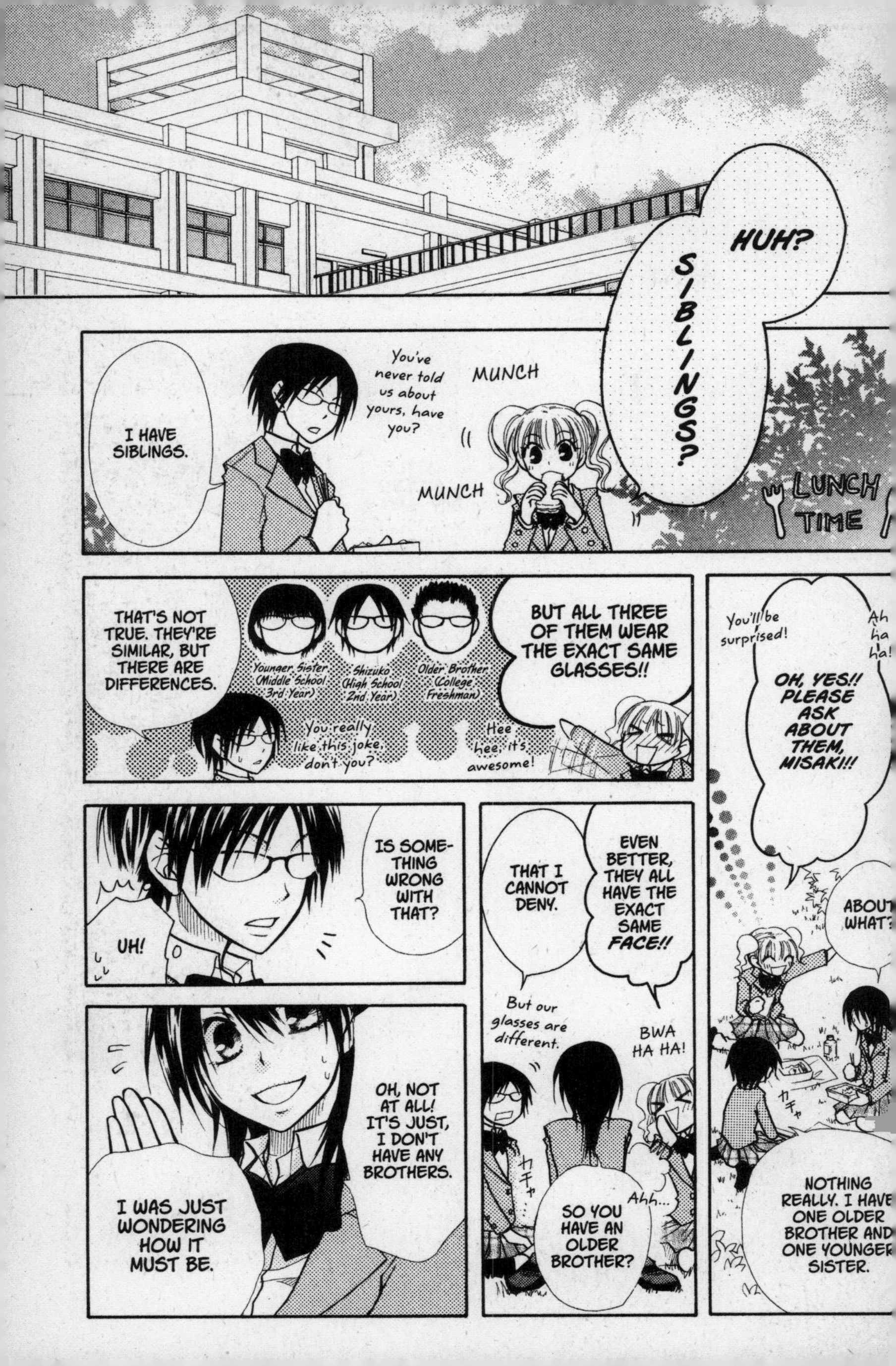
HUH?
SIBLINGS?
LUNCH TIME
MUNCH
MUNCH
You've never told us about yours, have you?
I HAVE SIBLINGS.
You'll be surprised!
Ah ha ha!
OH, YES!! PLEASE ASK ABOUT THEM, MISAKI!!
ABOUT WHAT?
カチャ
NOTHING REALLY. I HAVE ONE OLDER BROTHER AND ONE YOUNGER SISTER.
BUT ALL THREE OF THEM WEAR THE EXACT SAME GLASSES!!
Hee hee, it's awesome!
Older Brother (College Freshman)
Shizuko (High School 2nd Year)
Younger Sister (Middle School 3rd Year)
You really like this joke, don't you?
THAT'S NOT TRUE. THEY'RE SIMILAR, BUT THERE ARE DIFFERENCES.
EVEN BETTER, THEY ALL HAVE THE EXACT SAME FACE!!
THAT I CANNOT DENY.
BWA HA HA!
But our glasses are different.
カチャ
Ahh...
SO YOU HAVE AN OLDER BROTHER?
IS SOME-THING WRONG WITH THAT?
UH!
OH, NOT AT ALL! IT'S JUST, I DON'T HAVE ANY BROTHERS.
I WAS JUST WONDERING HOW IT MUST BE.

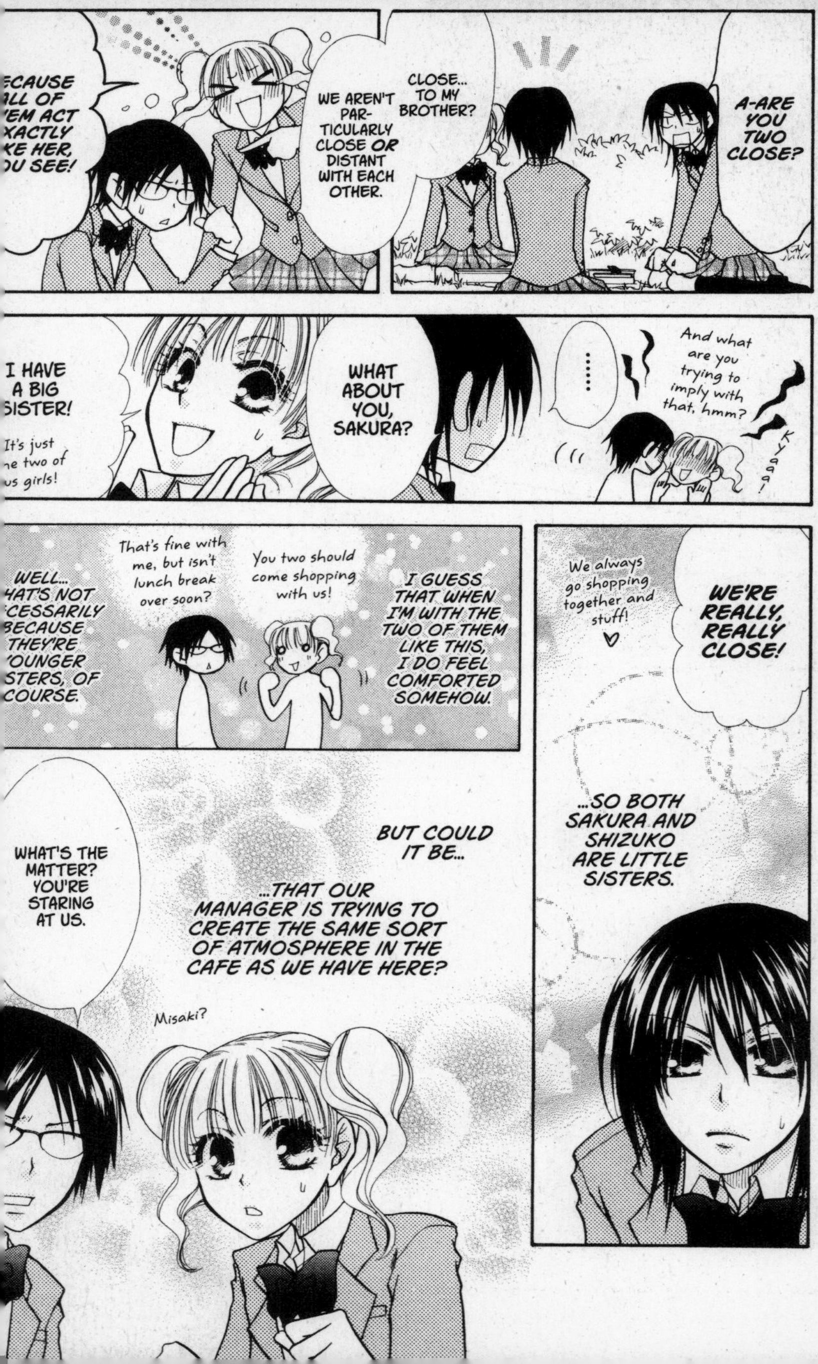
A-ARE YOU TWO CLOSE?
CLOSE... TO MY BROTHER?
WE AREN'T PARTICULARLY CLOSE OR DISTANT WITH EACH OTHER.
ECAUSE ALL OF EM ACT XACTLY KE HER, OU SEE!
And what are you trying to imply with that, hmm?
......
Kyaaa!
WHAT ABOUT YOU, SAKURA?
I HAVE A BIG SISTER!
It's just ne two of us girls!
WE'RE REALLY, REALLY CLOSE!
We always go shopping together and stuff!
...SO BOTH SAKURA AND SHIZUKO ARE LITTLE SISTERS.
I GUESS THAT WHEN I'M WITH THE TWO OF THEM LIKE THIS, I DO FEEL COMFORTED SOMEHOW.
You two should come shopping with us!
That's fine with me, but isn't lunch break over soon?
WELL... HAT'S NOT ECESSARILY BECAUSE THEY'RE OUNGER STERS, OF COURSE.
BUT COULD IT BE...
...THAT OUR MANAGER IS TRYING TO CREATE THE SAME SORT OF ATMOSPHERE IN THE CAFE AS WE HAVE HERE?
Misaki?
WHAT'S THE MATTER? YOU'RE STARING AT US.

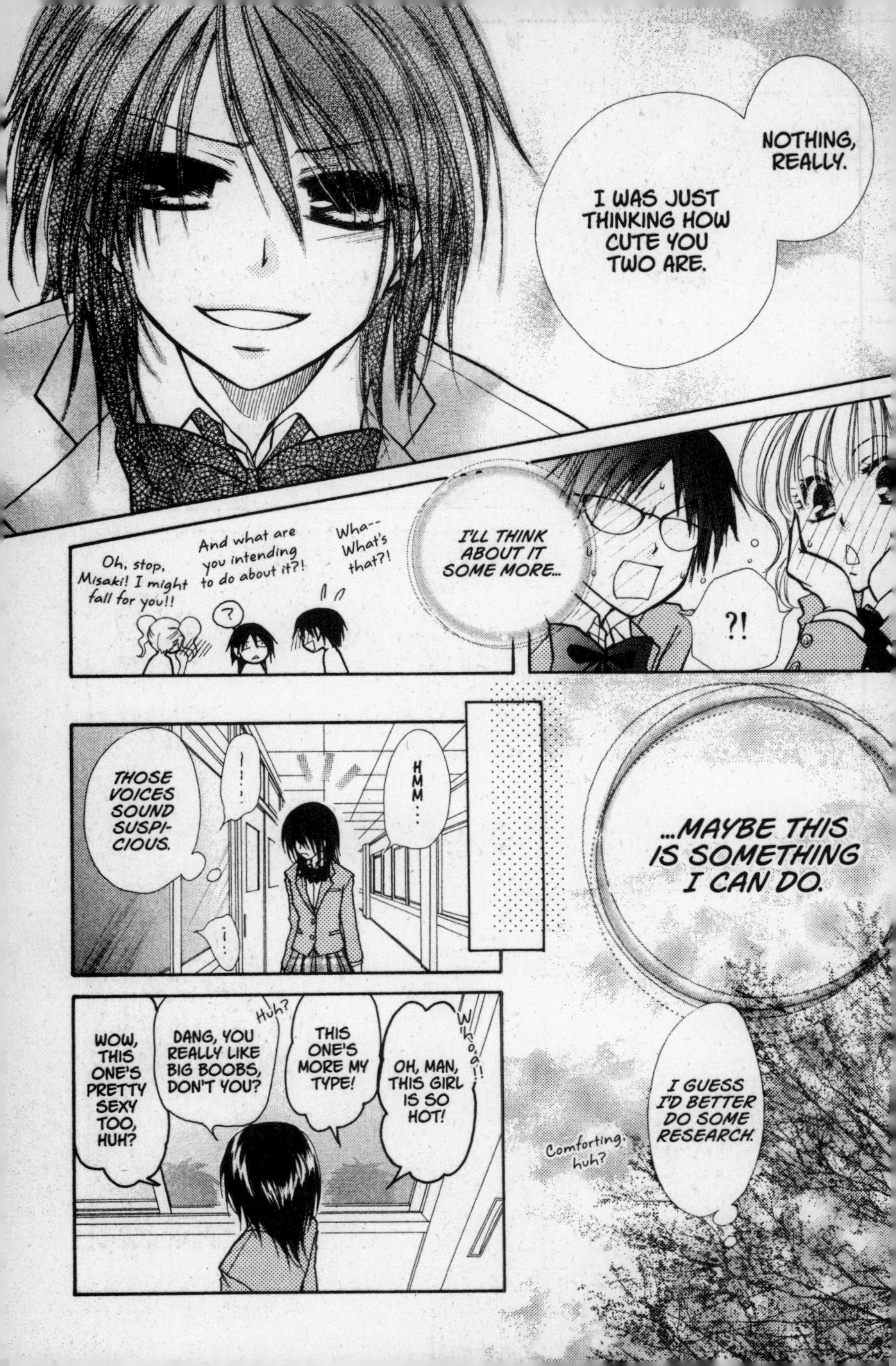
NOTHING, REALLY.
I WAS JUST THINKING HOW CUTE YOU TWO ARE.
I'LL THINK ABOUT IT SOME MORE...
?!
Wha-- What's that?!
And what are you intending to do about it?!
Oh, stop, Misaki! I might fall for you!!
?
...MAYBE THIS IS SOMETHING I CAN DO.
I GUESS I'D BETTER DO SOME RESEARCH.
Comforting, huh?
HMM...
THOSE VOICES SOUND SUSPICIOUS.
Whoa!!
OH, MAN, THIS GIRL IS SO HOT!
THIS ONE'S MORE MY TYPE!
Huh?
DANG, YOU REALLY LIKE BIG BOOBS, DON'T YOU?
WOW, THIS ONE'S PRETTY SEXY TOO, HUH?

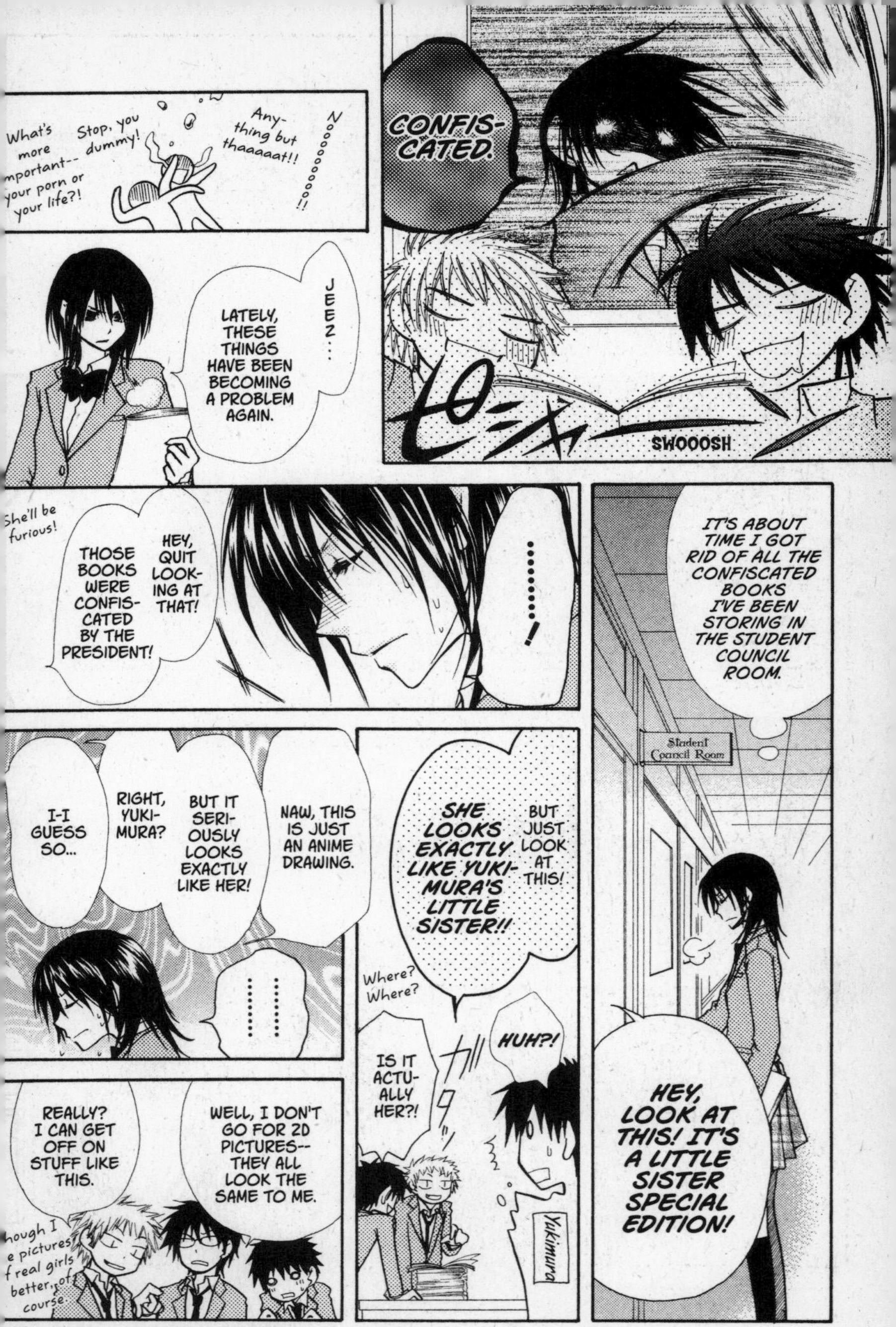
CONFIS-CATED.
SWOOOSH
Noooooooooo!!
Any-thing but thaaaaat!!
Stop, you dummy!
What's more mportant-- your porn or your life?!
JEEZ...
LATELY, THESE THINGS HAVE BEEN BECOMING A PROBLEM AGAIN.
IT'S ABOUT TIME I GOT RID OF ALL THE CONFISCATED BOOKS I'VE BEEN STORING IN THE STUDENT COUNCIL ROOM.
Student Council Room
HEY, LOOK AT THIS! IT'S A LITTLE SISTER SPECIAL EDITION!
.........!
HEY, QUIT LOOKING AT THAT!
THOSE BOOKS WERE CONFISCATED BY THE PRESIDENT!
She'll be furious!
BUT JUST LOOK AT THIS!
SHE LOOKS EXACTLY LIKE YUKIMURA'S LITTLE SISTER!!
Where? Where?
HUH?!
IS IT ACTUALLY HER?!
Yukimura
NAW, THIS IS JUST AN ANIME DRAWING.
BUT IT SERIOUSLY LOOKS EXACTLY LIKE HER!
RIGHT, YUKIMURA?
I-I GUESS SO...
....
WELL, I DON'T GO FOR 2D PICTURES-- THEY ALL LOOK THE SAME TO ME.
REALLY? I CAN GET OFF ON STUFF LIKE THIS.
hough I e pictures f real girls better, of course.

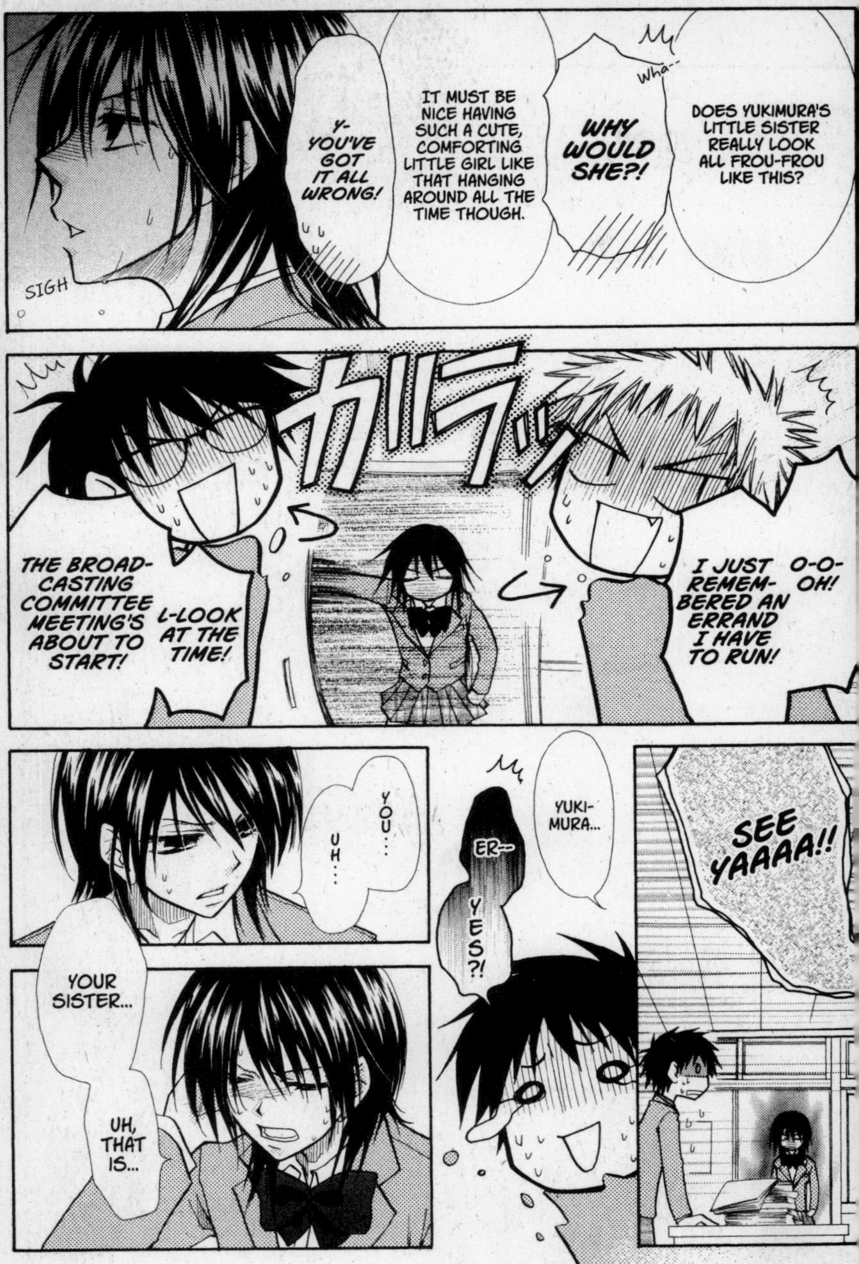
DOES YUKIMURA'S LITTLE SISTER REALLY LOOK ALL FROU-FROU LIKE THIS?
Wha--
WHY WOULD SHE?!
IT MUST BE NICE HAVING SUCH A CUTE, COMFORTING LITTLE GIRL LIKE THAT HANGING AROUND ALL THE TIME THOUGH.
Y-YOU'VE GOT IT ALL WRONG!
SIGH
ガラッ
O-O-OH!
I JUST REMEMBERED AN ERRAND I HAVE TO RUN!
L-LOOK AT THE TIME!
THE BROADCASTING COMMITTEE MEETING'S ABOUT TO START!
SEE YAAAA!!
YUKIMURA...
ER-- YES?!
YOU... UH...
YOUR SISTER...
UH, THAT IS...

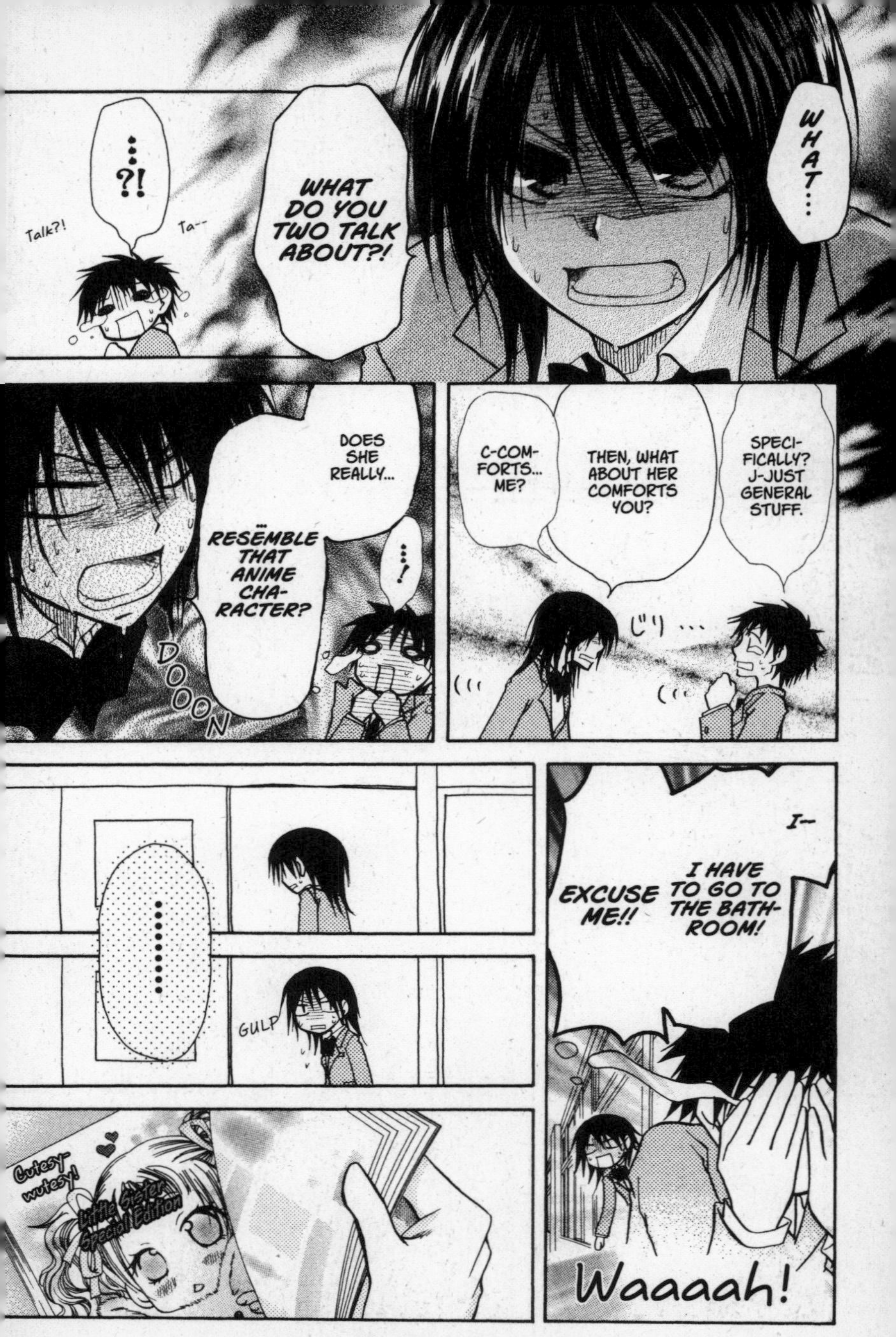
WHAT...
WHAT DO YOU TWO TALK ABOUT?!
Ta--
...?!
Talk?!
SPECIFICALLY? J-JUST GENERAL STUFF.
THEN, WHAT ABOUT HER COMFORTS YOU?
C-COMFORTS... ME?
じり...
DOES SHE REALLY...
...!
...RESEMBLE THAT ANIME CHARACTER?
DOOOON
I--
I HAVE TO GO TO THE BATHROOM!
EXCUSE ME!!
Waaaah!
....
GULP
Cutesy-wutesy!
Little Sister Special Edition

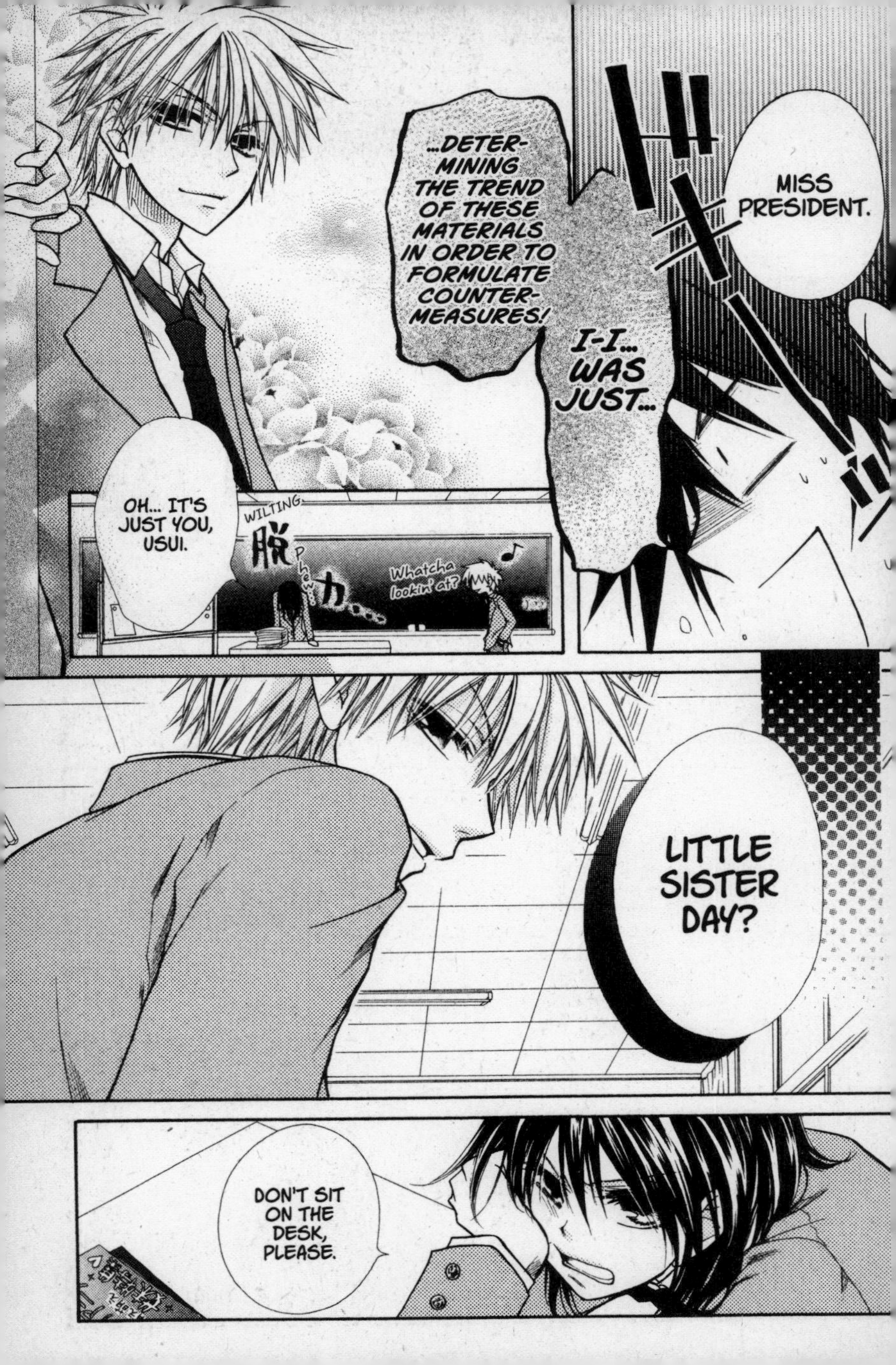
MISS PRESIDENT.
I-I... WAS JUST...
...DETER-MINING THE TREND OF THESE MATERIALS IN ORDER TO FORMULATE COUNTER-MEASURES!
OH... IT'S JUST YOU, USUI.
WILTING
Phew...
Whatcha lookin' at?
LITTLE SISTER DAY?
DON'T SIT ON THE DESK, PLEASE.

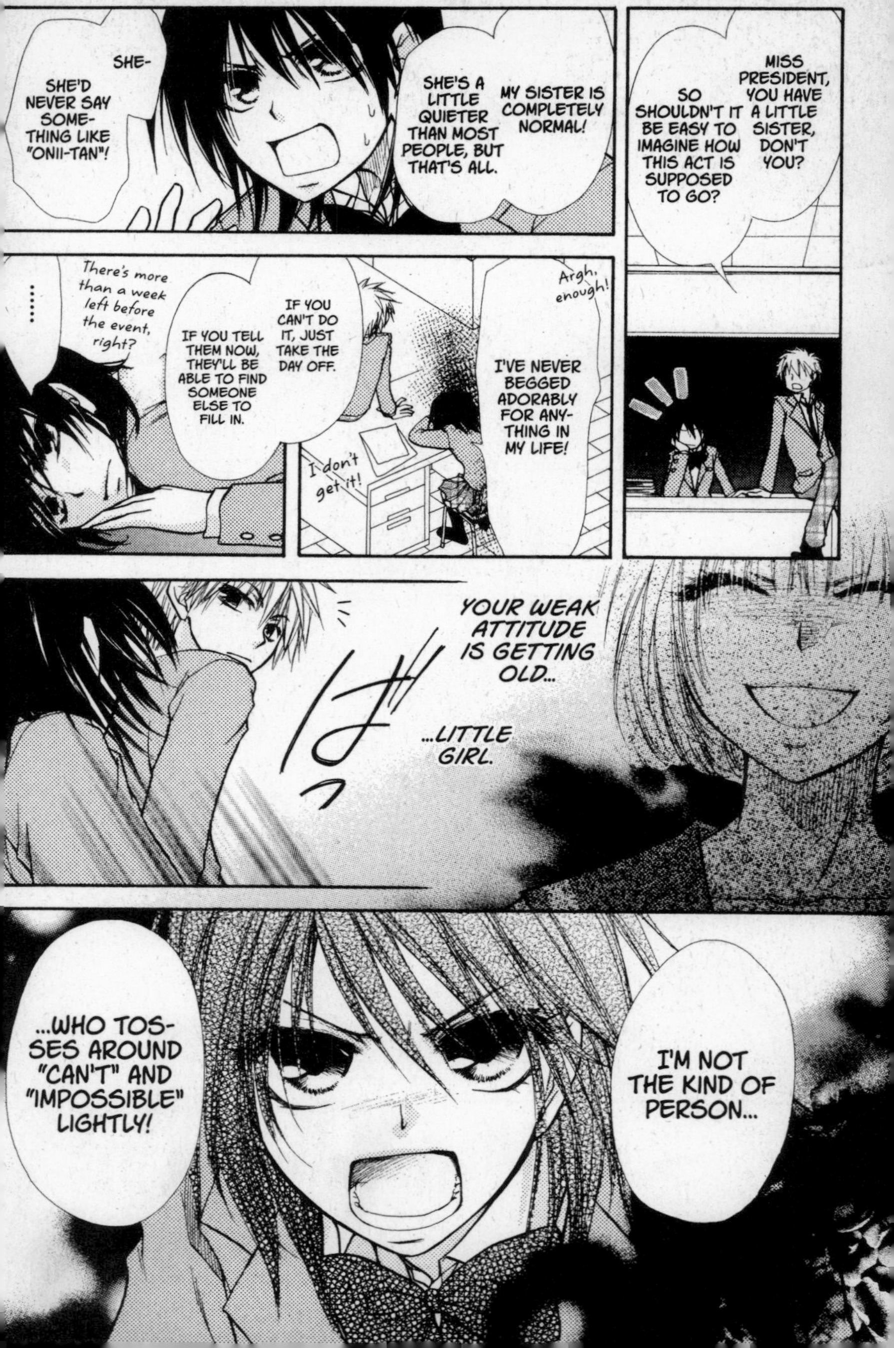
MISS PRESIDENT, YOU HAVE A LITTLE SISTER, DON'T YOU?
SO SHOULDN'T IT BE EASY TO IMAGINE HOW THIS ACT IS SUPPOSED TO GO?
MY SISTER IS COMPLETELY NORMAL!
SHE'S A LITTLE QUIETER THAN MOST PEOPLE, BUT THAT'S ALL.
SHE-
SHE'D NEVER SAY SOMETHING LIKE "ONII-TAN"!
Argh, enough!
I'VE NEVER BEGGED ADORABLY FOR ANYTHING IN MY LIFE!
I don't get it!
IF YOU CAN'T DO IT, JUST TAKE THE DAY OFF.
IF YOU TELL THEM NOW, THEY'LL BE ABLE TO FIND SOMEONE ELSE TO FILL IN.
There's more than a week left before the event, right?
......
YOUR WEAK ATTITUDE IS GETTING OLD...
...LITTLE GIRL.
I'M NOT THE KIND OF PERSON...
...WHO TOSSES AROUND "CAN'T" AND "IMPOSSIBLE" LIGHTLY!

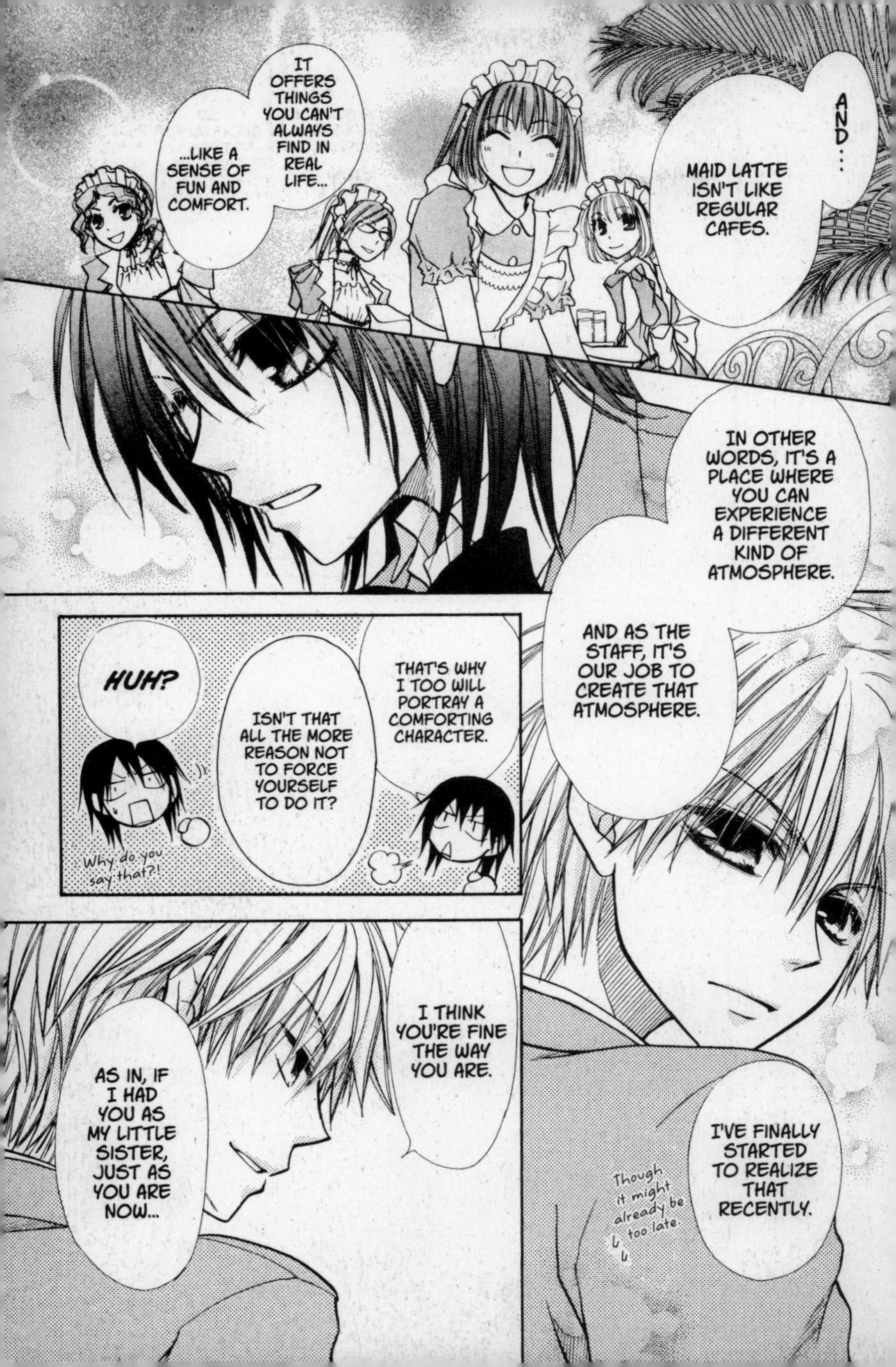
AND...
MAID LATTE ISN'T LIKE REGULAR CAFES.
IT OFFERS THINGS YOU CAN'T ALWAYS FIND IN REAL LIFE...
...LIKE A SENSE OF FUN AND COMFORT.
IN OTHER WORDS, IT'S A PLACE WHERE YOU CAN EXPERIENCE A DIFFERENT KIND OF ATMOSPHERE.
AND AS THE STAFF, IT'S OUR JOB TO CREATE THAT ATMOSPHERE.
I'VE FINALLY STARTED TO REALIZE THAT RECENTLY.
Though it might already be too late.
THAT'S WHY I TOO WILL PORTRAY A COMFORTING CHARACTER.
ISN'T THAT ALL THE MORE REASON NOT TO FORCE YOURSELF TO DO IT?
HUH?
Why do you say that?!
I THINK YOU'RE FINE THE WAY YOU ARE.
AS IN, IF I HAD YOU AS MY LITTLE SISTER, JUST AS YOU ARE NOW...

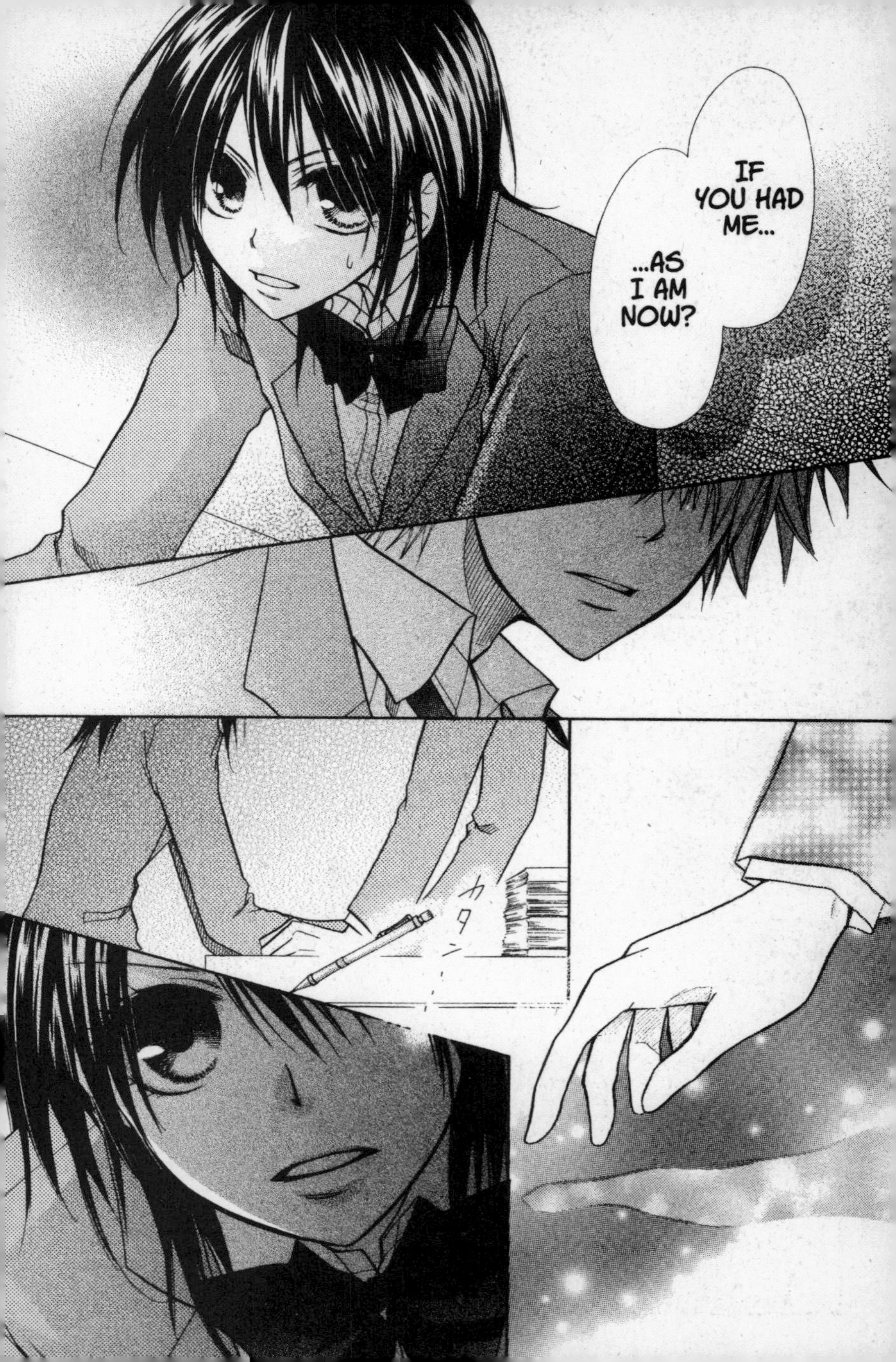
IF YOU HAD ME...
...AS I AM NOW?
カタン

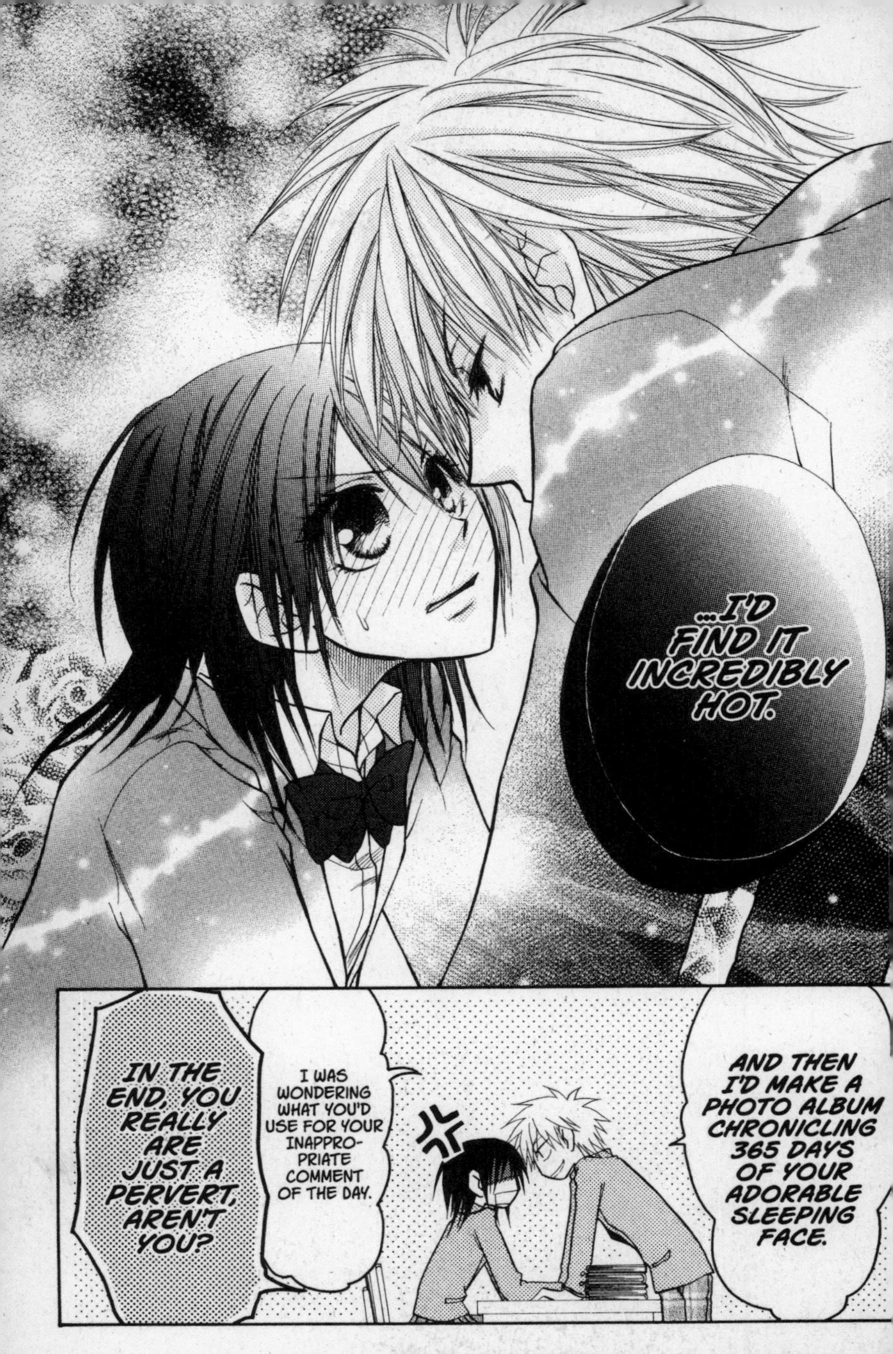
...I'D FIND IT INCREDIBLY HOT.
AND THEN I'D MAKE A PHOTO ALBUM CHRONICLING 365 DAYS OF YOUR ADORABLE SLEEPING FACE.
I WAS WONDERING WHAT YOU'D USE FOR YOUR INAPPRO-PRIATE COMMENT OF THE DAY.
IN THE END, YOU REALLY ARE JUST A PERVERT, AREN'T YOU?

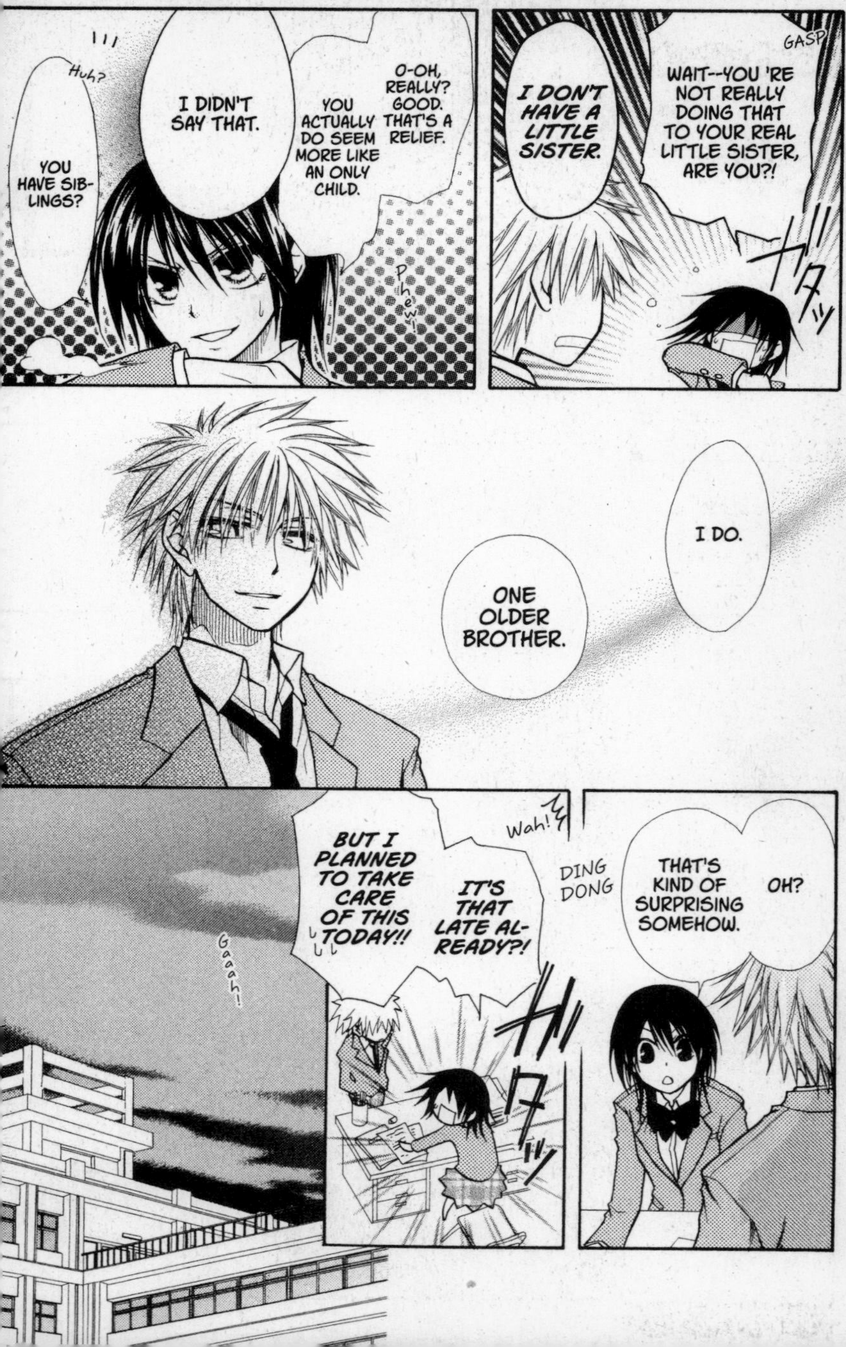
GASP
WAIT--YOU 'RE NOT REALLY DOING THAT TO YOUR REAL LITTLE SISTER, ARE YOU?!
I DON'T HAVE A LITTLE SISTER.
O-OH, REALLY? GOOD. THAT'S A RELIEF.
YOU ACTUALLY DO SEEM MORE LIKE AN ONLY CHILD.
Phew!
I DIDN'T SAY THAT.
Huh?
YOU HAVE SIB-LINGS?
I DO.
ONE OLDER BROTHER.
OH?
THAT'S KIND OF SURPRISING SOMEHOW.
DING DONG
Wah!
IT'S THAT LATE AL-READY?!
BUT I PLANNED TO TAKE CARE OF THIS TODAY!!
Gaaah!

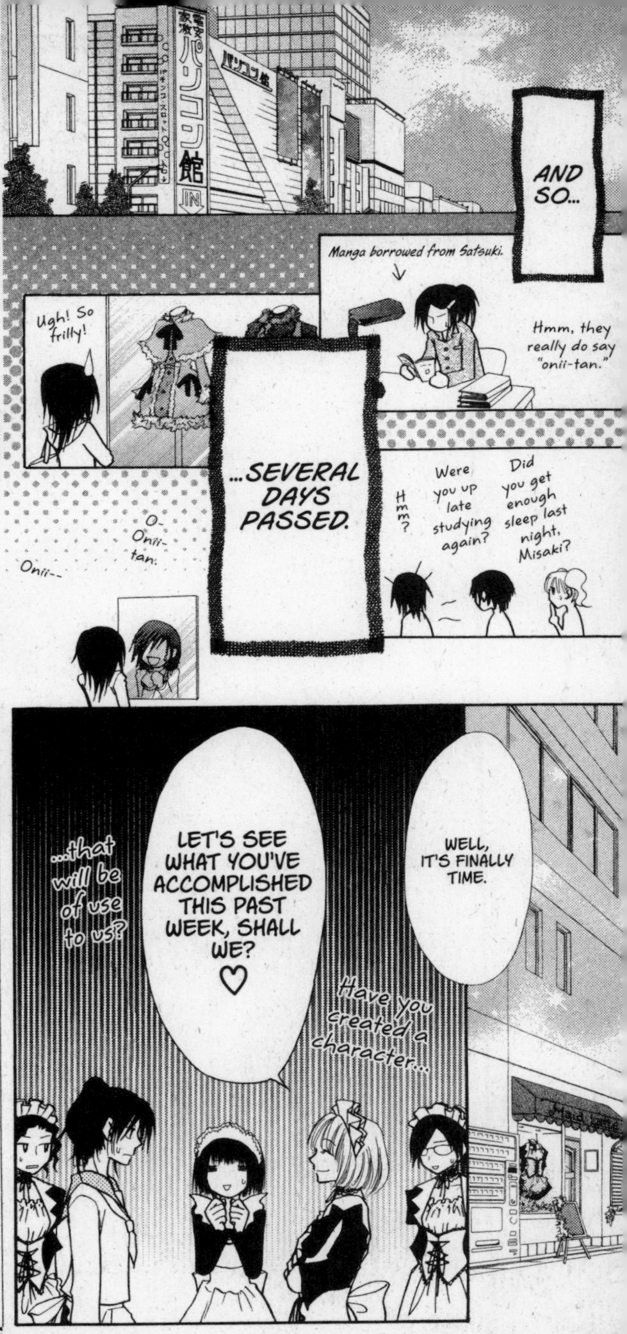
家電激安
パソコン館
パソコン館
IN
AND SO...
Manga borrowed from Satsuki.
Hmm, they really do say "onii-tan."
...SEVERAL DAYS PASSED.
Ugh! So frilly!
Onii--
O-Onii-tan.
Did you get enough sleep last night, Misaki?
Were you up late studying again?
Hmm?
WELL, IT'S FINALLY TIME.
LET'S SEE WHAT YOU'VE ACCOMPLISHED THIS PAST WEEK, SHALL WE? ♡
Have you created a character...
...that will be of use to us?

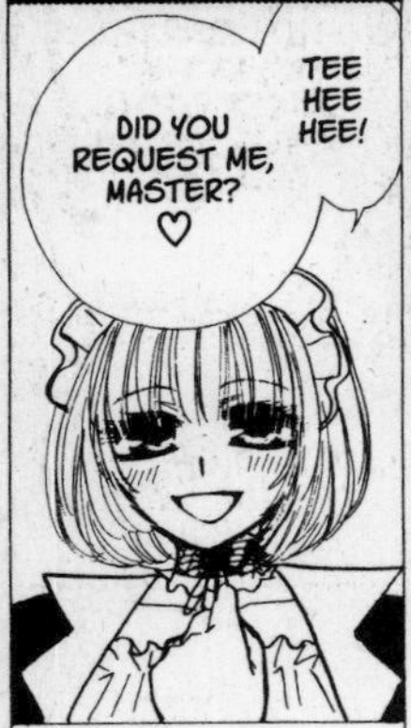
TEE HEE HEE!
DID YOU REQUEST ME, MASTER? ♡

NAME

Honoka ♡

AGE (CLASS)

20

BLOOD TYPE

B

HEIGHT

157 cm (5 ft 2 in)

WEIGHT

46 kg (101 lbs)

SPECIAL SKILLS

Creating characters

LIKES

Fantasy Worlds

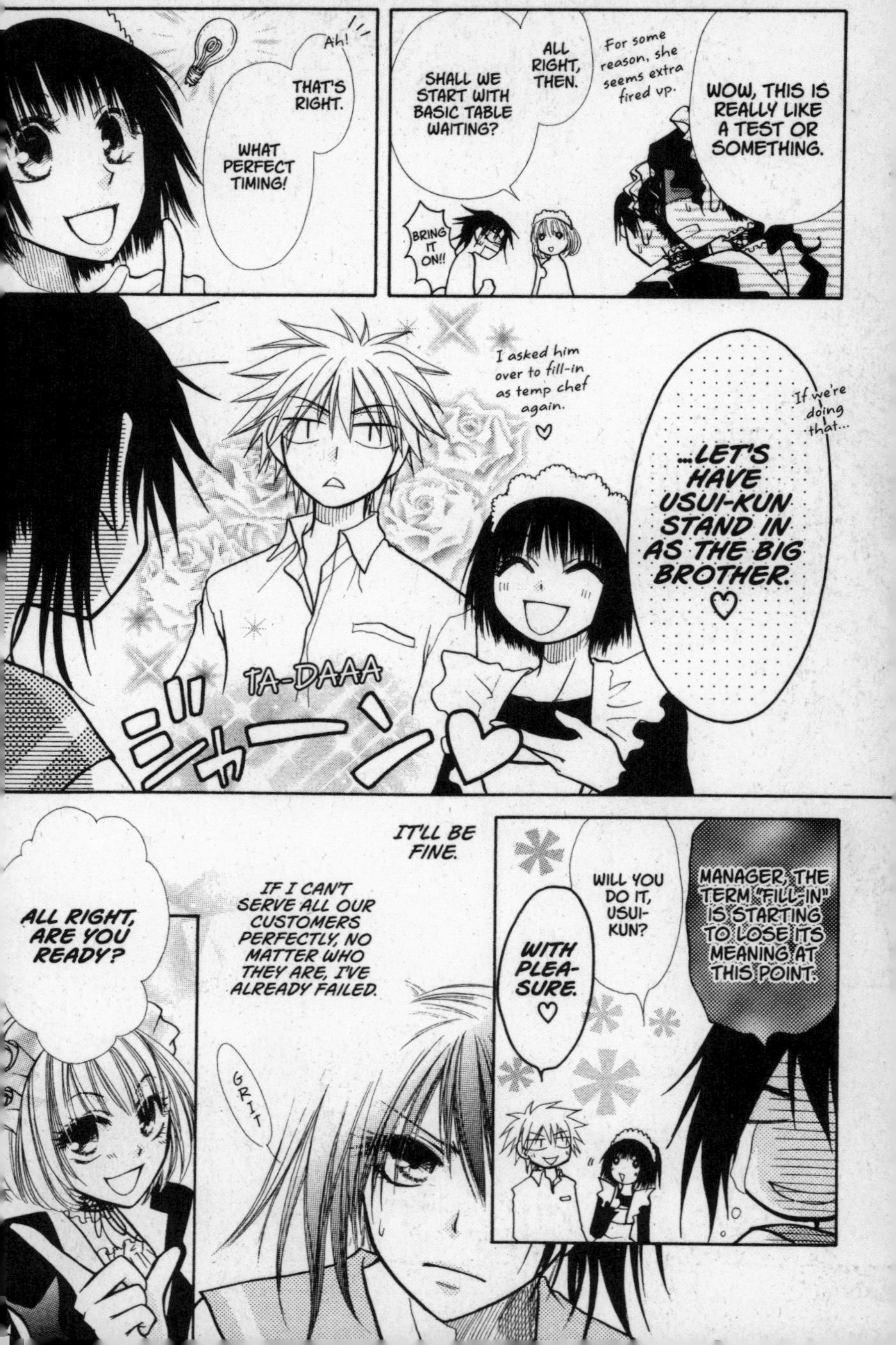
WOW, THIS IS REALLY LIKE A TEST OR SOMETHING.
For some reason, she seems extra fired up.
ALL RIGHT, THEN.
SHALL WE START WITH BASIC TABLE WAITING?
BRING IT ON!!
Ah!
THAT'S RIGHT.
WHAT PERFECT TIMING!
If we're doing that...
...LET'S HAVE USUI-KUN STAND IN AS THE BIG BROTHER. ♡
I asked him over to fill-in as temp chef again. ♡
TA-DAAA
ジャーン
MANAGER, THE TERM "FILL-IN" IS STARTING TO LOSE ITS MEANING AT THIS POINT.
WILL YOU DO IT, USUI-KUN?
WITH PLEA-SURE. ♡
IT'LL BE FINE.
IF I CAN'T SERVE ALL OUR CUSTOMERS PERFECTLY, NO MATTER WHO THEY ARE, I'VE ALREADY FAILED.
GRIT
ALL RIGHT, ARE YOU READY?

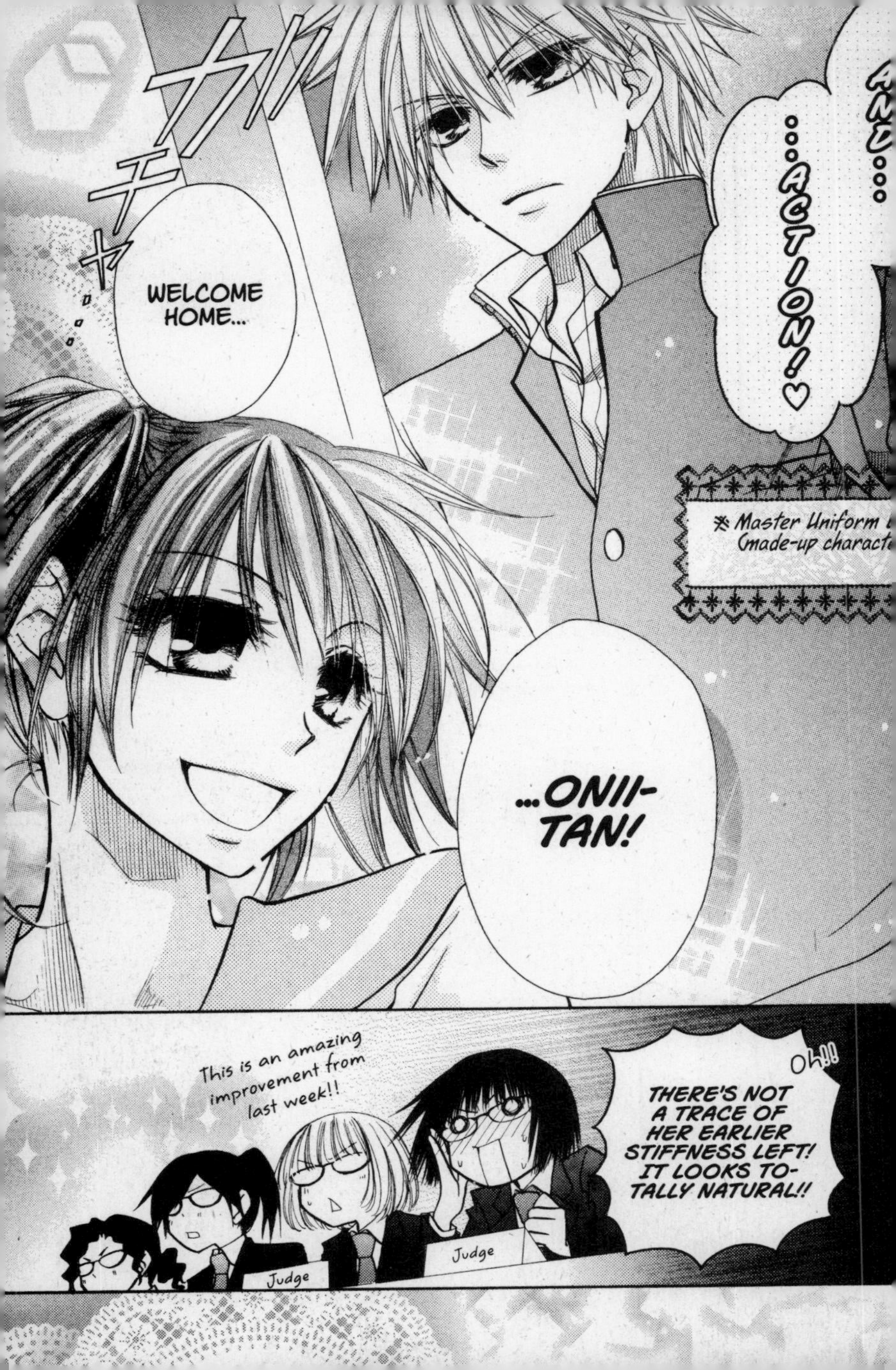
AND...
...ACTION! ♥
※ Master Uniform
(made-up
カッチャ
WELCOME HOME...
...ONII-TAN!
Oh!!
THERE'S NOT A TRACE OF HER EARLIER STIFFNESS LEFT! IT LOOKS TOTALLY NATURAL!!
This is an amazing improvement from last week!!
Judge
Judge

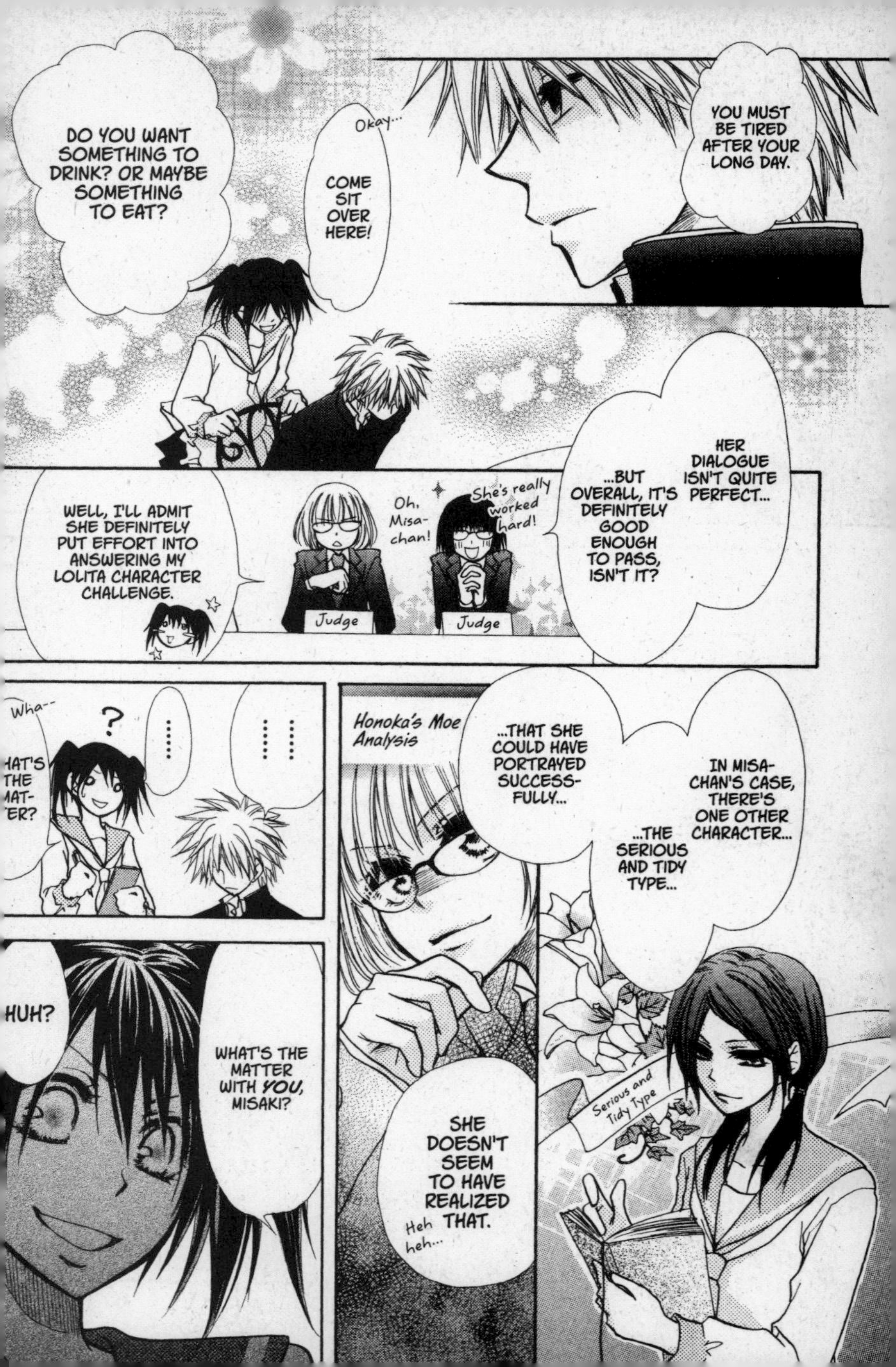
YOU MUST BE TIRED AFTER YOUR LONG DAY.
Okay...
COME SIT OVER HERE!
DO YOU WANT SOMETHING TO DRINK? OR MAYBE SOMETHING TO EAT?
HER DIALOGUE ISN'T QUITE PERFECT...
...BUT OVERALL, IT'S DEFINITELY GOOD ENOUGH TO PASS, ISN'T IT?
She's really worked hard!
Oh, Misa-chan!
Judge
Judge
WELL, I'LL ADMIT SHE DEFINITELY PUT EFFORT INTO ANSWERING MY LOLITA CHARACTER CHALLENGE.
IN MISA-CHAN'S CASE, THERE'S ONE OTHER CHARACTER...
...THE SERIOUS AND TIDY TYPE...
Serious and Tidy Type
Honoka's Moe Analysis
...THAT SHE COULD HAVE PORTRAYED SUCCESSFULLY...
SHE DOESN'T SEEM TO HAVE REALIZED THAT.
Heh heh...
......
......
?
Wha--
HAT'S THE MAT-TER?
WHAT'S THE MATTER WITH *YOU*, MISAKI?
HUH?

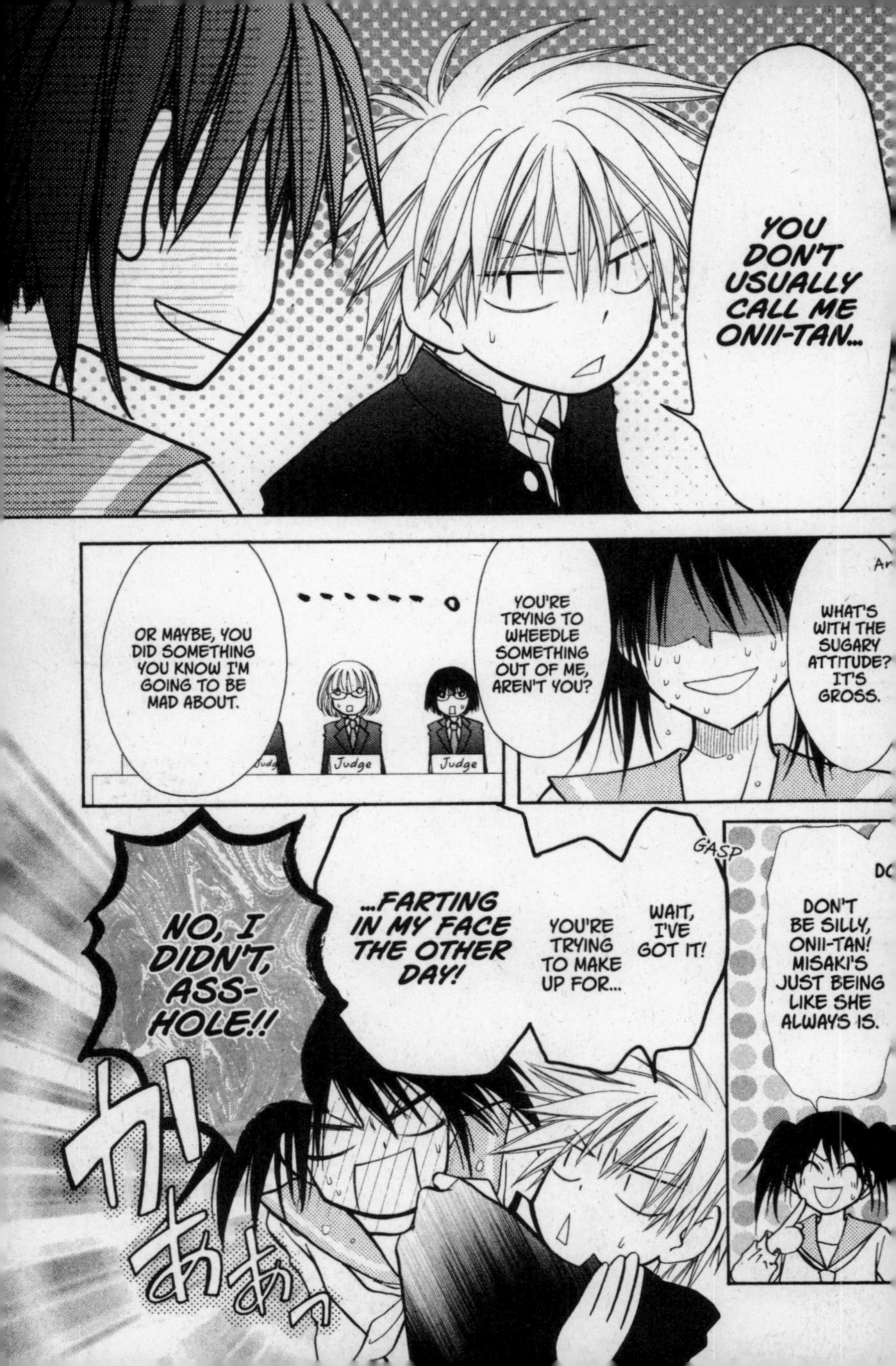

YOU DON'T USUALLY CALL ME ONII-TAN...
WHAT'S WITH THE SUGARY ATTITUDE? IT'S GROSS.
YOU'RE TRYING TO WHEEDLE SOMETHING OUT OF ME, AREN'T YOU?
....
Judge
Judge
OR MAYBE, YOU DID SOMETHING YOU KNOW I'M GOING TO BE MAD ABOUT.
DON'T BE SILLY, ONII-TAN! MISAKI'S JUST BEING LIKE SHE ALWAYS IS.
GASP
WAIT, I'VE GOT IT!
YOU'RE TRYING TO MAKE UP FOR...
...FARTING IN MY FACE THE OTHER DAY!
NO, I DIDN'T, ASS-HOLE!!

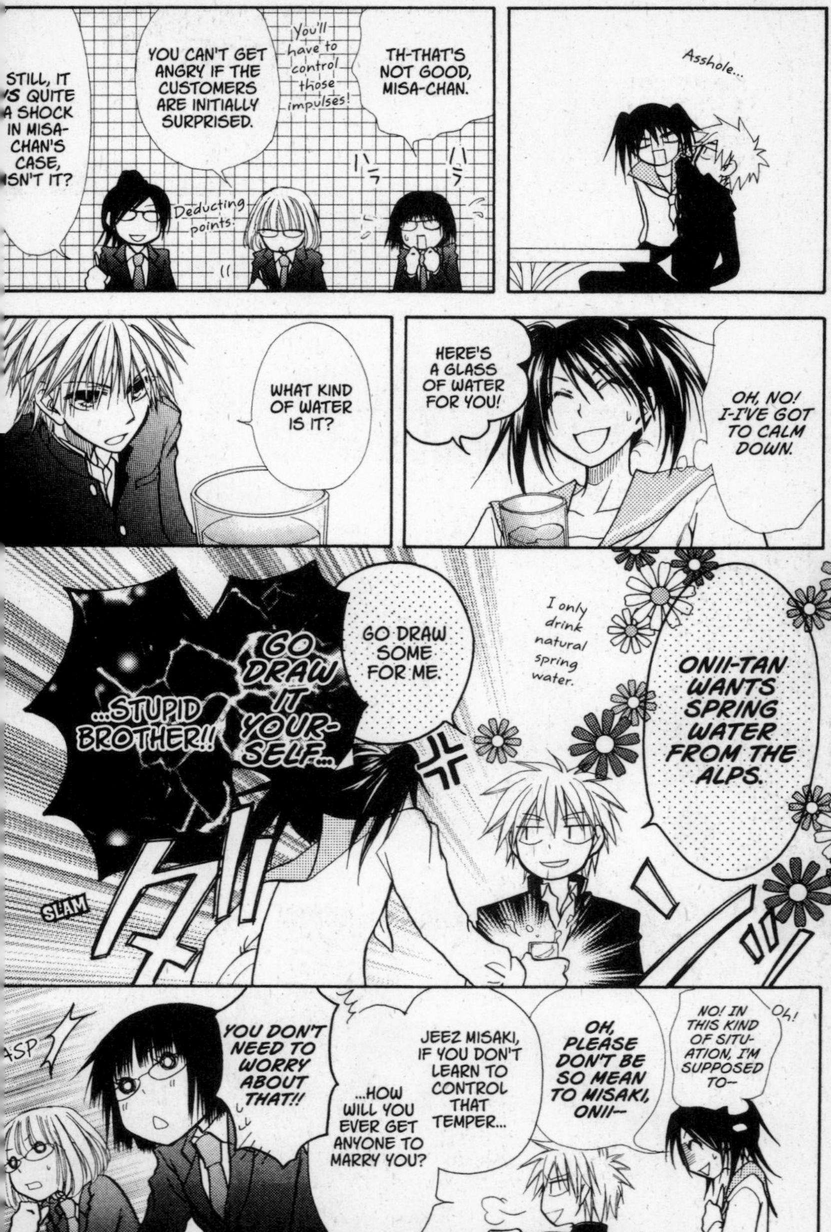
Asshole...
TH-THAT'S NOT GOOD, MISA-CHAN.
You'll have to control those impulses!
YOU CAN'T GET ANGRY IF THE CUSTOMERS ARE INITIALLY SURPRISED.
Deducting points!
STILL, IT 'S QUITE A SHOCK IN MISA-CHAN'S CASE, SN'T IT?
OH, NO! I-I'VE GOT TO CALM DOWN.
HERE'S A GLASS OF WATER FOR YOU!
WHAT KIND OF WATER IS IT?
ONII-TAN WANTS SPRING WATER FROM THE ALPS.
I only drink natural spring water.
GO DRAW SOME FOR ME.
GO DRAW IT YOURSELF...
...STUPID BROTHER!!
SLAM
Oh!
NO! IN THIS KIND OF SITUATION, I'M SUPPOSED TO--
OH, PLEASE DON'T BE SO MEAN TO MISAKI, ONII--
JEEZ MISAKI, IF YOU DON'T LEARN TO CONTROL THAT TEMPER...
...HOW WILL YOU EVER GET ANYONE TO MARRY YOU?
YOU DON'T NEED TO WORRY ABOUT THAT!!
ASP

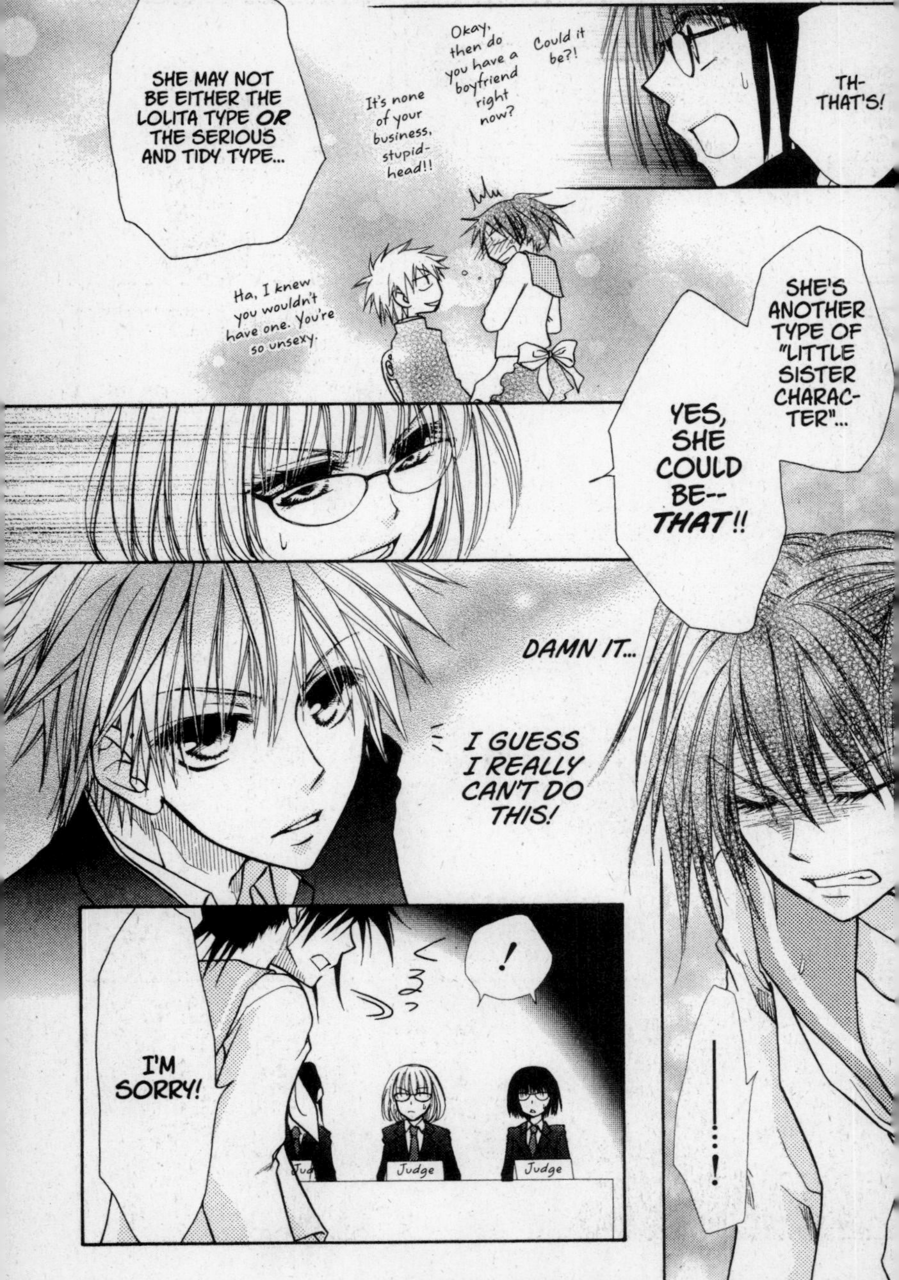
TH- THAT'S!
Could it be?!
Okay, then do you have a boyfriend right now?
It's none of your business, stupid-head!!
Ha, I knew you wouldn't have one. You're so unsexy.
SHE MAY NOT BE EITHER THE LOLITA TYPE *OR* THE SERIOUS AND TIDY TYPE...
SHE'S ANOTHER TYPE OF "LITTLE SISTER CHARACTER"...
YES, SHE COULD BE-- *THAT*!!
DAMN IT...
I GUESS I REALLY CAN'T DO THIS!
......!
!
I'M SORRY!
Judge
Judge

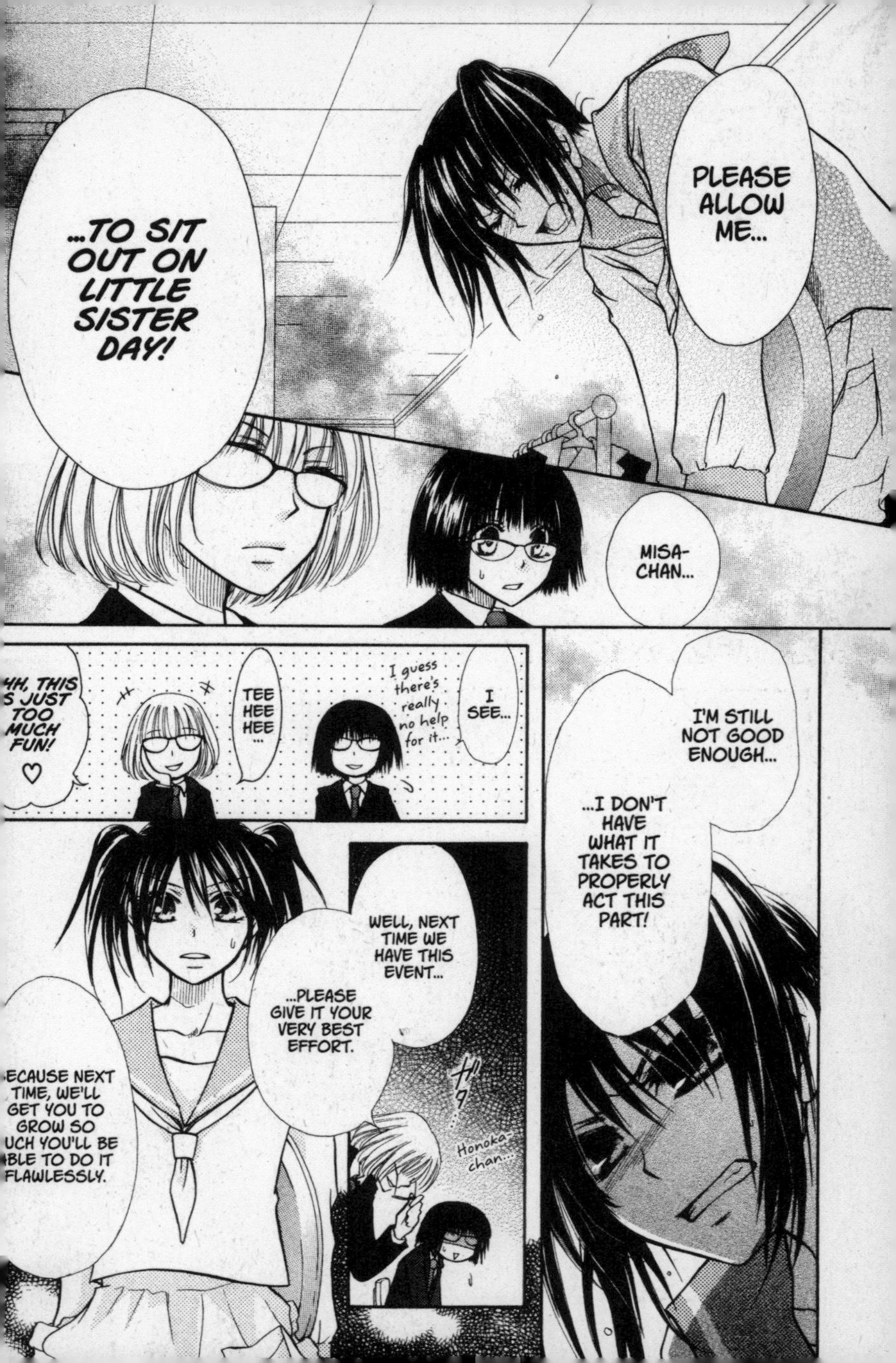
PLEASE ALLOW ME...
...TO SIT OUT ON LITTLE SISTER DAY!
MISA-CHAN...
I'M STILL NOT GOOD ENOUGH...
...I DON'T HAVE WHAT IT TAKES TO PROPERLY ACT THIS PART!
I SEE...
I guess there's really no help for it...
TEE HEE HEE...
HH, THIS S JUST TOO MUCH FUN! ♡
ガク
Honoka-chan...
WELL, NEXT TIME WE HAVE THIS EVENT...
...PLEASE GIVE IT YOUR VERY BEST EFFORT.
ECAUSE NEXT TIME, WE'LL GET YOU TO GROW SO UCH YOU'LL BE BLE TO DO IT FLAWLESSLY.

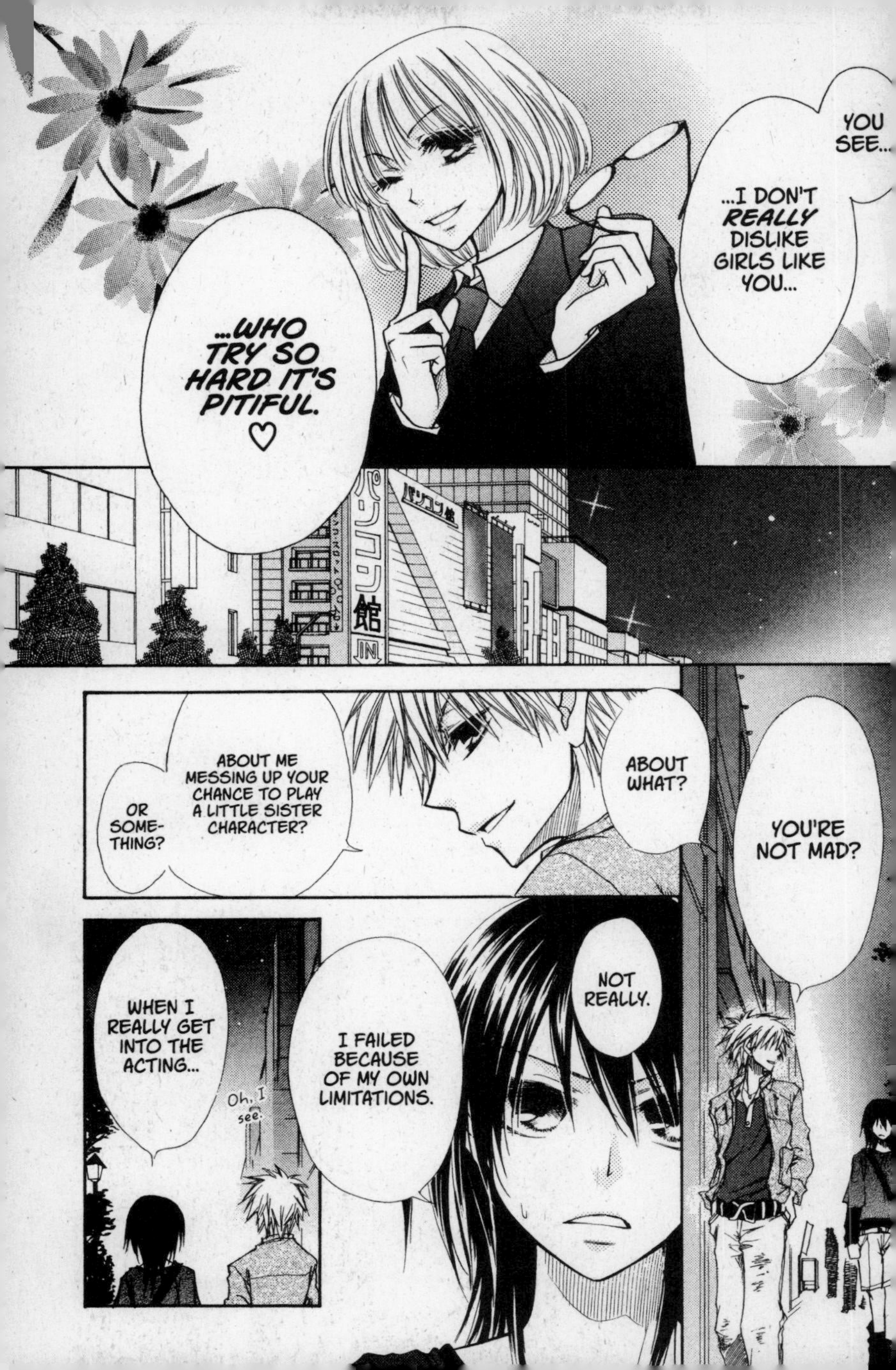
YOU SEE...
...I DON'T *REALLY* DISLIKE GIRLS LIKE YOU...
...WHO TRY SO HARD IT'S PITIFUL. ♡
パソコン館
パソコン館
IN
YOU'RE NOT MAD?
ABOUT WHAT?
ABOUT ME MESSING UP YOUR CHANCE TO PLAY A LITTLE SISTER CHARACTER?
OR SOMETHING?
NOT REALLY.
I FAILED BECAUSE OF MY OWN LIMITATIONS.
Oh, I see.
WHEN I REALLY GET INTO THE ACTING...

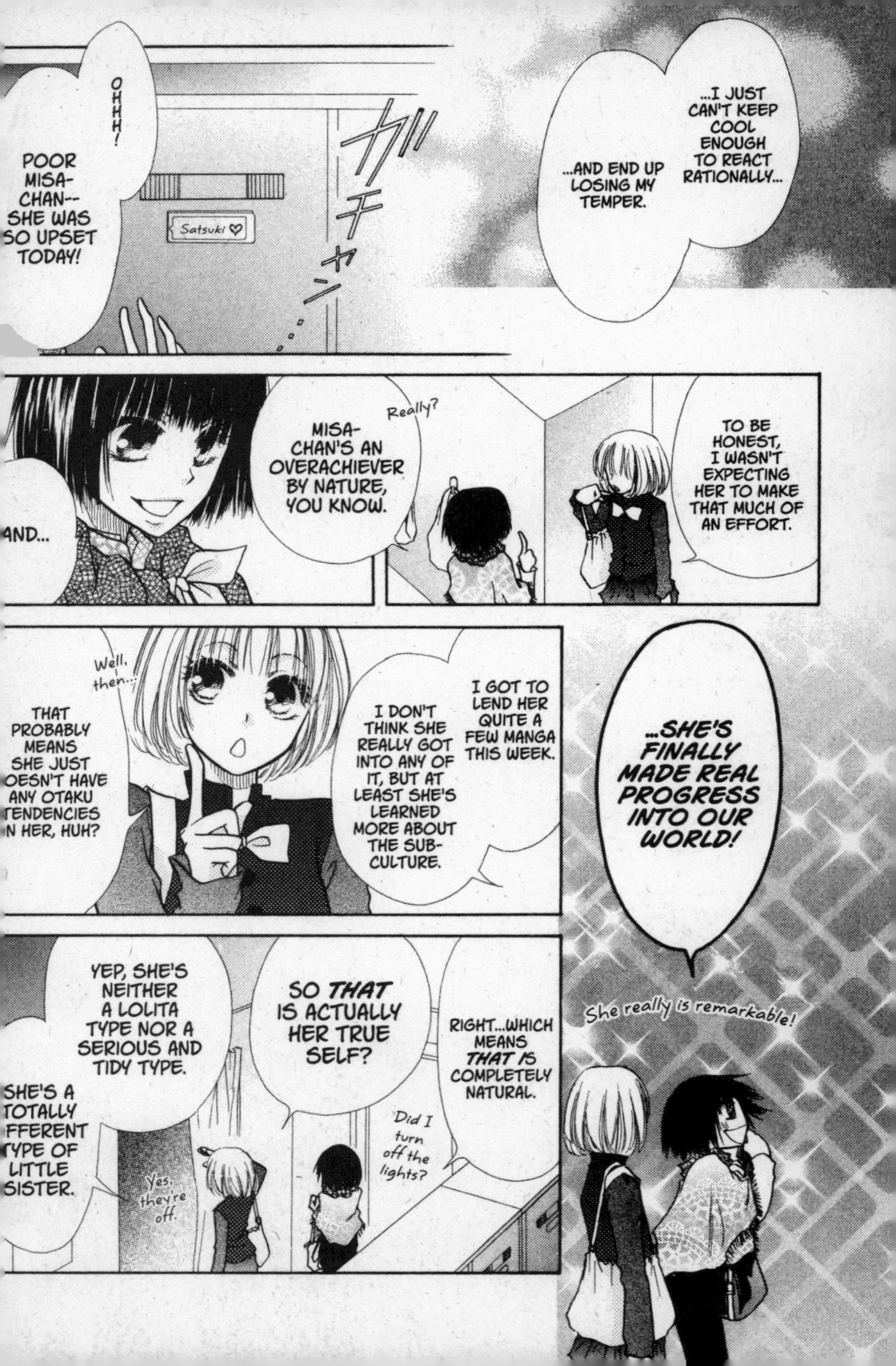

...I JUST CAN'T KEEP COOL ENOUGH TO REACT RATIONALLY...
...AND END UP LOSING MY TEMPER.
ガチャン
OHHH!
POOR MISA-CHAN-- SHE WAS SO UPSET TODAY!
Satsuki ♡
TO BE HONEST, I WASN'T EXPECTING HER TO MAKE THAT MUCH OF AN EFFORT.
Really?
MISA-CHAN'S AN OVERACHIEVER BY NATURE, YOU KNOW.
AND...
...SHE'S FINALLY MADE REAL PROGRESS INTO OUR WORLD!
She really is remarkable!
I GOT TO LEND HER QUITE A FEW MANGA THIS WEEK.
I DON'T THINK SHE REALLY GOT INTO ANY OF IT, BUT AT LEAST SHE'S LEARNED MORE ABOUT THE SUB-CULTURE.
Well, then...
THAT PROBABLY MEANS SHE JUST OESN'T HAVE ANY OTAKU TENDENCIES N HER, HUH?
RIGHT...WHICH MEANS THAT IS COMPLETELY NATURAL.
Did I turn off the lights?
SO THAT IS ACTUALLY HER TRUE SELF?
YEP, SHE'S NEITHER A LOLITA TYPE NOR A SERIOUS AND TIDY TYPE.
SHE'S A TOTALLY FFERENT TYPE OF LITTLE SISTER.
Yes, they're off.

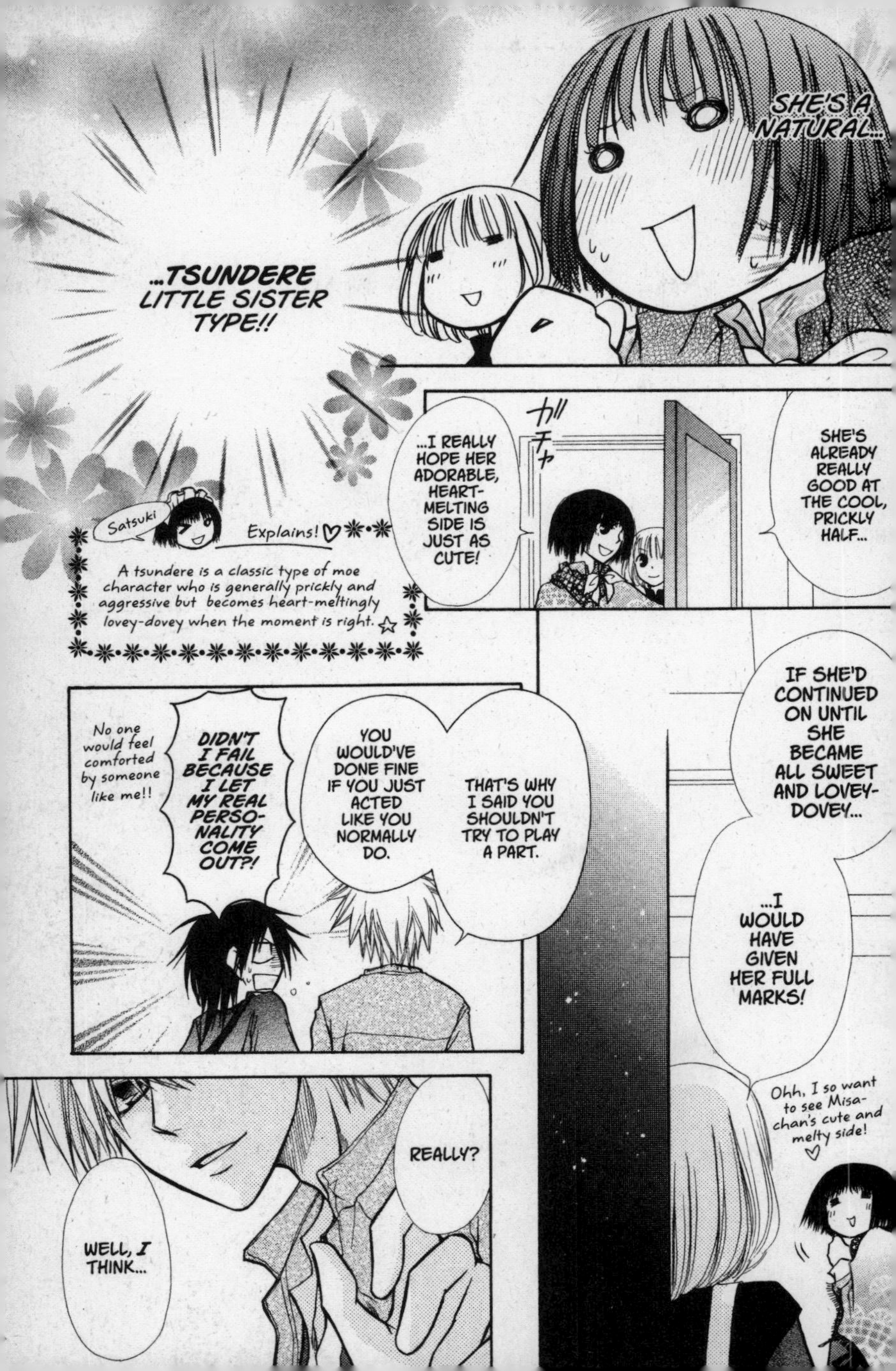
SHE'S A NATURAL...
...TSUNDERE LITTLE SISTER TYPE!!
Satsuki Explains!
A tsundere is a classic type of moe character who is generally prickly and aggressive but becomes heart-meltingly lovey-dovey when the moment is right.
SHE'S ALREADY REALLY GOOD AT THE COOL, PRICKLY HALF...
ガチャ
...I REALLY HOPE HER ADORABLE, HEART-MELTING SIDE IS JUST AS CUTE!
IF SHE'D CONTINUED ON UNTIL SHE BECAME ALL SWEET AND LOVEY-DOVEY...
...I WOULD HAVE GIVEN HER FULL MARKS!
Ohh, I so want to see Misa-chan's cute and melty side!
THAT'S WHY I SAID YOU SHOULDN'T TRY TO PLAY A PART.
YOU WOULD'VE DONE FINE IF YOU JUST ACTED LIKE YOU NORMALLY DO.
DIDN'T I FAIL BECAUSE I LET MY REAL PERSONALITY COME OUT?!
No one would feel comforted by someone like me!!
REALLY?
WELL, I THINK...

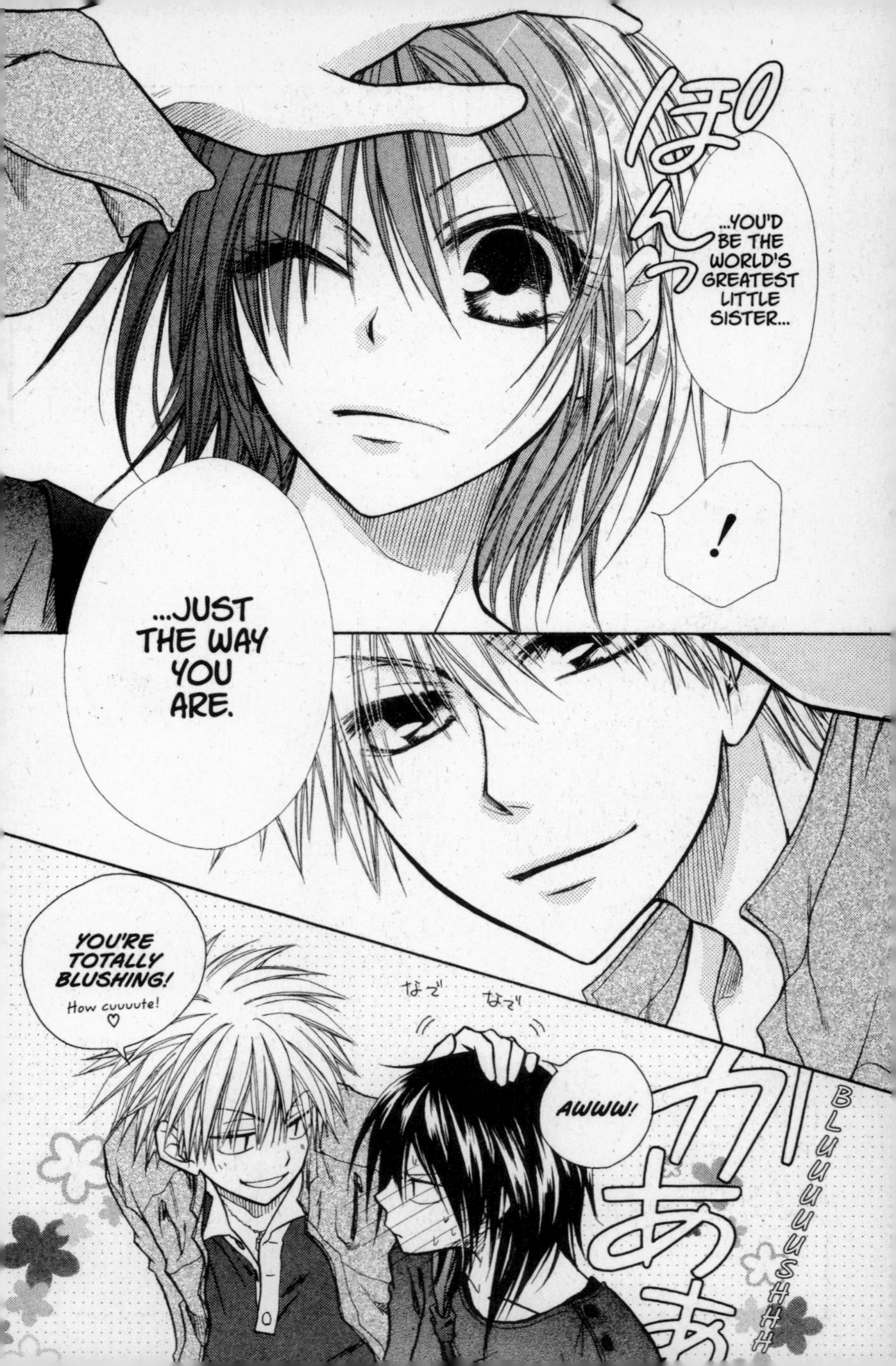
ぽんっ
...YOU'D BE THE WORLD'S GREATEST LITTLE SISTER...
!
...JUST THE WAY YOU ARE.
かあ
BLUUUUUUSHHH
AWWW!
なで なで
YOU'RE TOTALLY BLUSHING!
How cuuuute! ♡

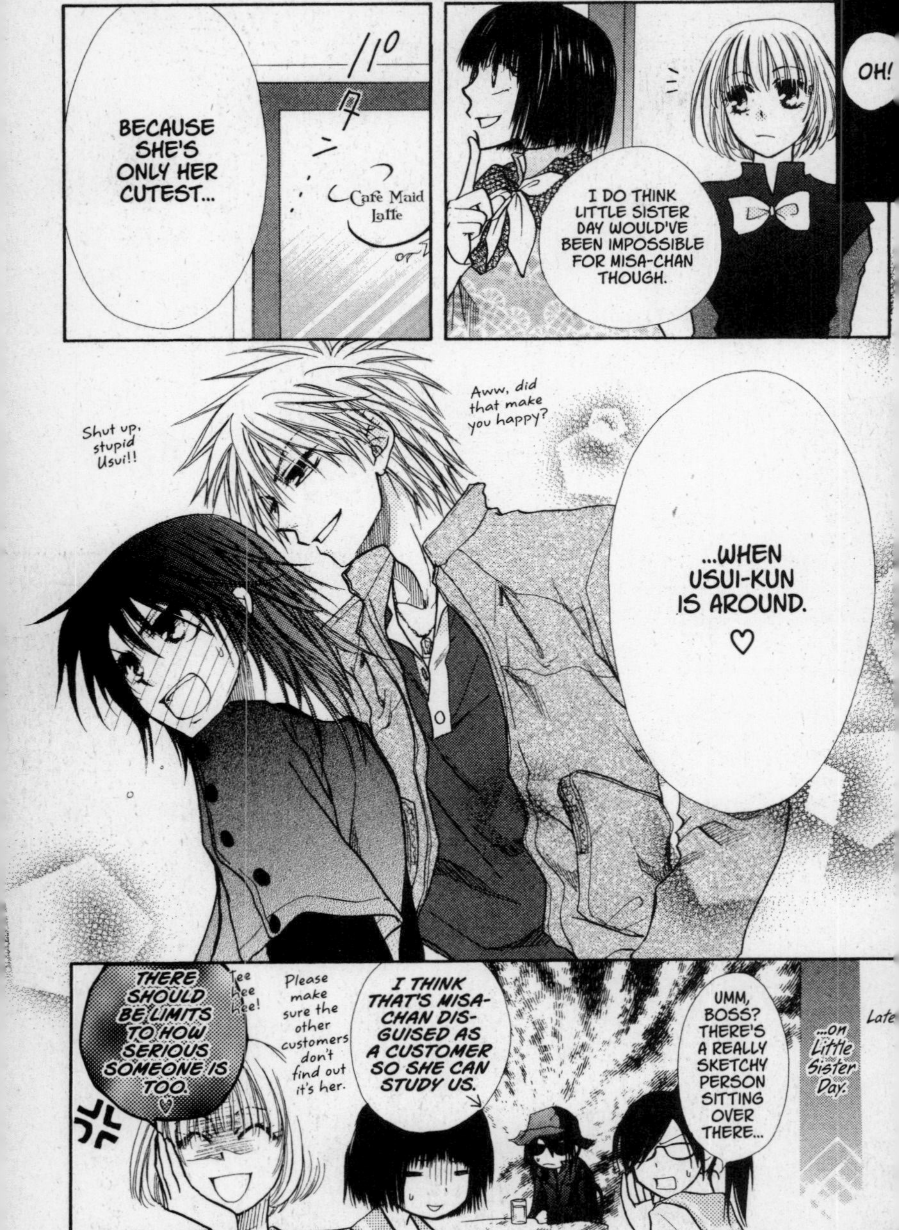
OH!
I DO THINK LITTLE SISTER DAY WOULD'VE BEEN IMPOSSIBLE FOR MISA-CHAN THOUGH.
Café Maid Latte
BECAUSE SHE'S ONLY HER CUTEST...
...WHEN USUI-KUN IS AROUND. ♡
Aww, did that make you happy?
Shut up, stupid Usui!!
Late
...on Little Sister Day.
UMM, BOSS? THERE'S A REALLY SKETCHY PERSON SITTING OVER THERE...
I THINK THAT'S MISA-CHAN DISGUISED AS A CUSTOMER SO SHE CAN STUDY US.
Please make sure the other customers don't find out it's her.
Tee hee hee!
THERE SHOULD BE LIMITS TO HOW SERIOUS SOMEONE IS TOO. ♡

Tea break...

Where Are They Now?

The Bespectacled Koganei of Miyabi Gaoka Academy

Who is Koganei?

First appearance: Volume 2, 5th Course. Koganei is a student at the rich kids' school, Miyabi Gaoka Academy. After stirring up trouble with some Seika students, he demanded an apology from Misaki, but was soundly defeated in a chess match by Usui and ran off with a few parting insults.

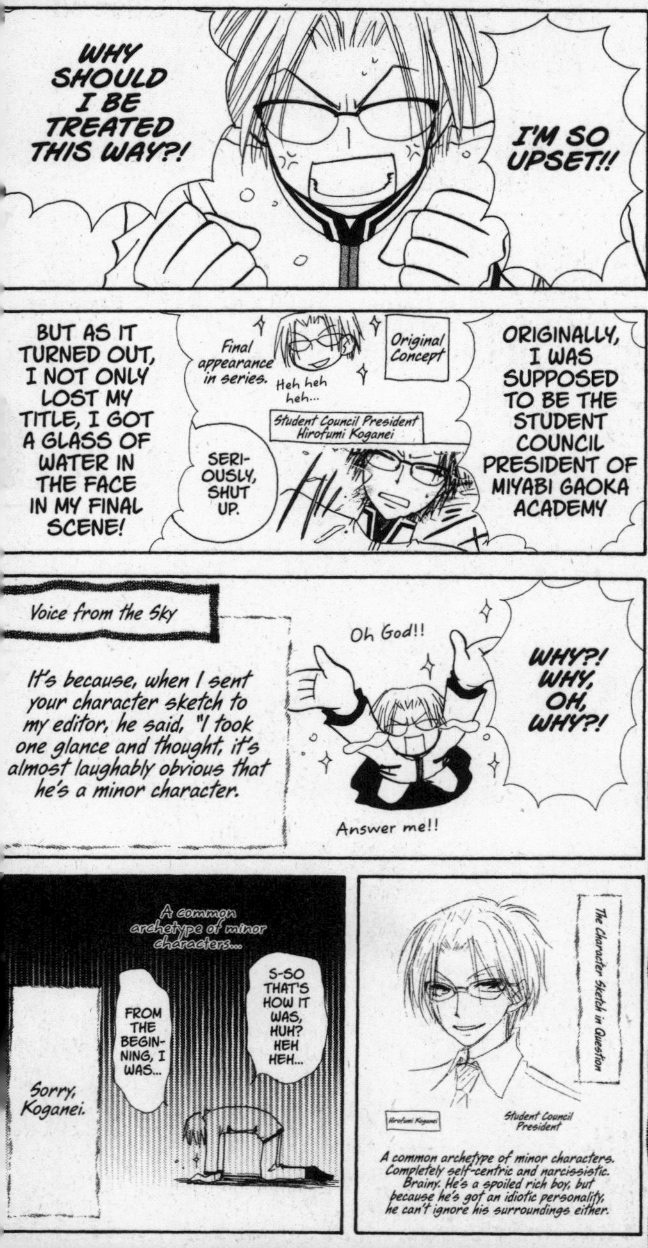
I'M SO UPSET!!
WHY SHOULD I BE TREATED THIS WAY?!
ORIGINALLY, I WAS SUPPOSED TO BE THE STUDENT COUNCIL PRESIDENT OF MIYABI GAOKA ACADEMY
Original Concept
Final appearance in series.
Heh heh heh...
Student Council President Hirofumi Koganei
BUT AS IT TURNED OUT, I NOT ONLY LOST MY TITLE, I GOT A GLASS OF WATER IN THE FACE IN MY FINAL SCENE!
SERIOUSLY, SHUT UP.
WHY?! WHY, OH, WHY?!
Oh God!!
Voice from the Sky
It's because, when I sent your character sketch to my editor, he said, "I took one glance and thought, it's almost laughably obvious that he's a minor character.
Answer me!!
The Character Sketch in Question
Student Council President
Hirofumi Koganei
A common archetype of minor characters. Completely self-centric and narcissistic. Brainy. He's a spoiled rich boy, but because he's got an idiotic personality, he can't ignore his surroundings either.
A common archetype of minor characters...
S-SO THAT'S HOW IT WAS, HUH? HEH HEH...
FROM THE BEGINNING, I WAS...
Sorry, Koganei.

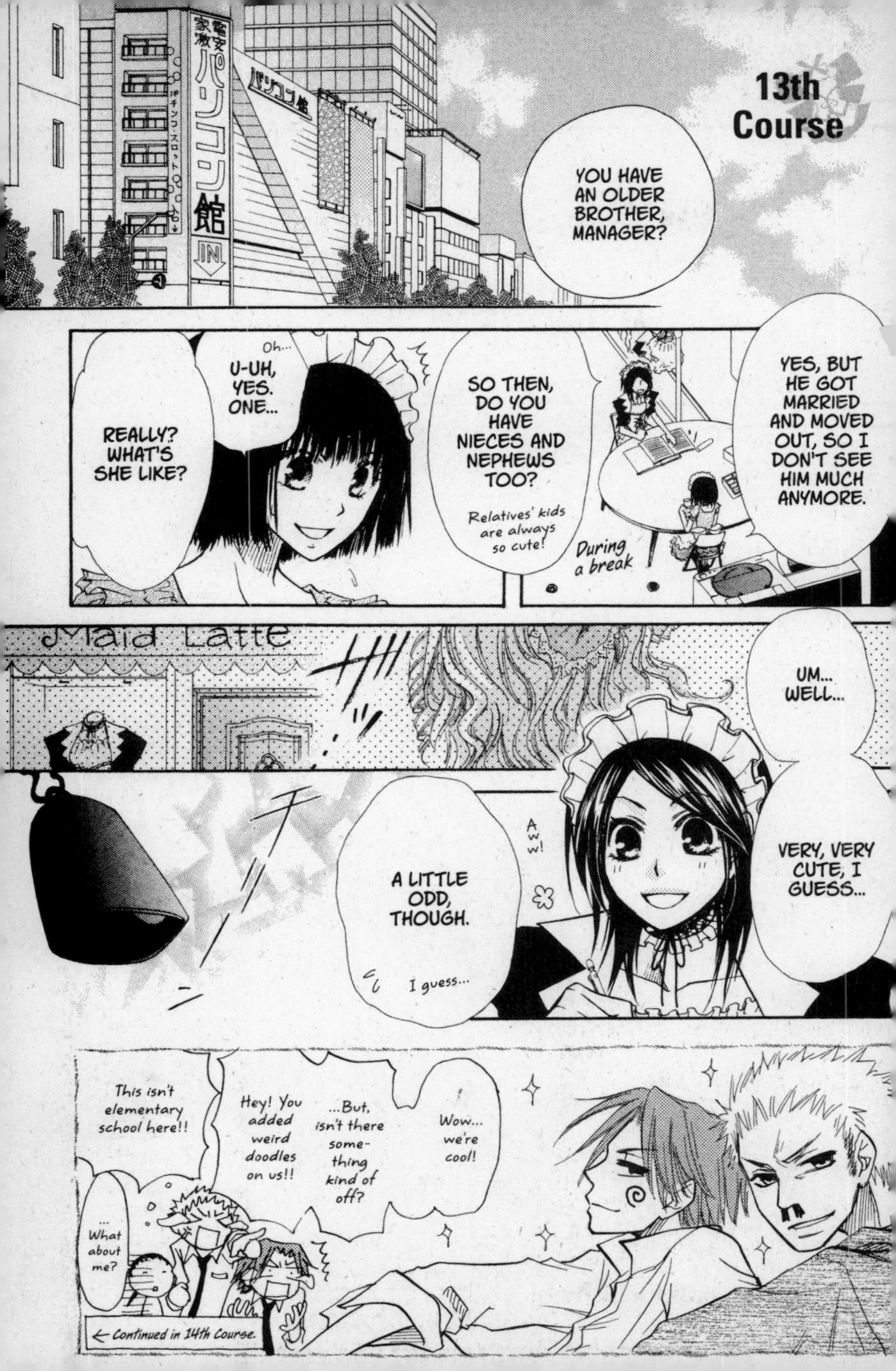

13th Course
YOU HAVE AN OLDER BROTHER, MANAGER?
家電激安
パソコン館
IN
パソコン館
YES, BUT HE GOT MARRIED AND MOVED OUT, SO I DON'T SEE HIM MUCH ANYMORE.
During a break
SO THEN, DO YOU HAVE NIECES AND NEPHEWS TOO?
Relatives' kids are always so cute!
Oh...
U-UH, YES. ONE...
REALLY? WHAT'S SHE LIKE?
UM... WELL...
VERY, VERY CUTE, I GUESS...
Maid Latte
Aww!
A LITTLE ODD, THOUGH.
I guess...
Wow... we're cool!
...But, isn't there something kind of off?
Hey! You added weird doodles on us!!
This isn't elementary school here!!
...What about me?

← Continued in 14th Course.

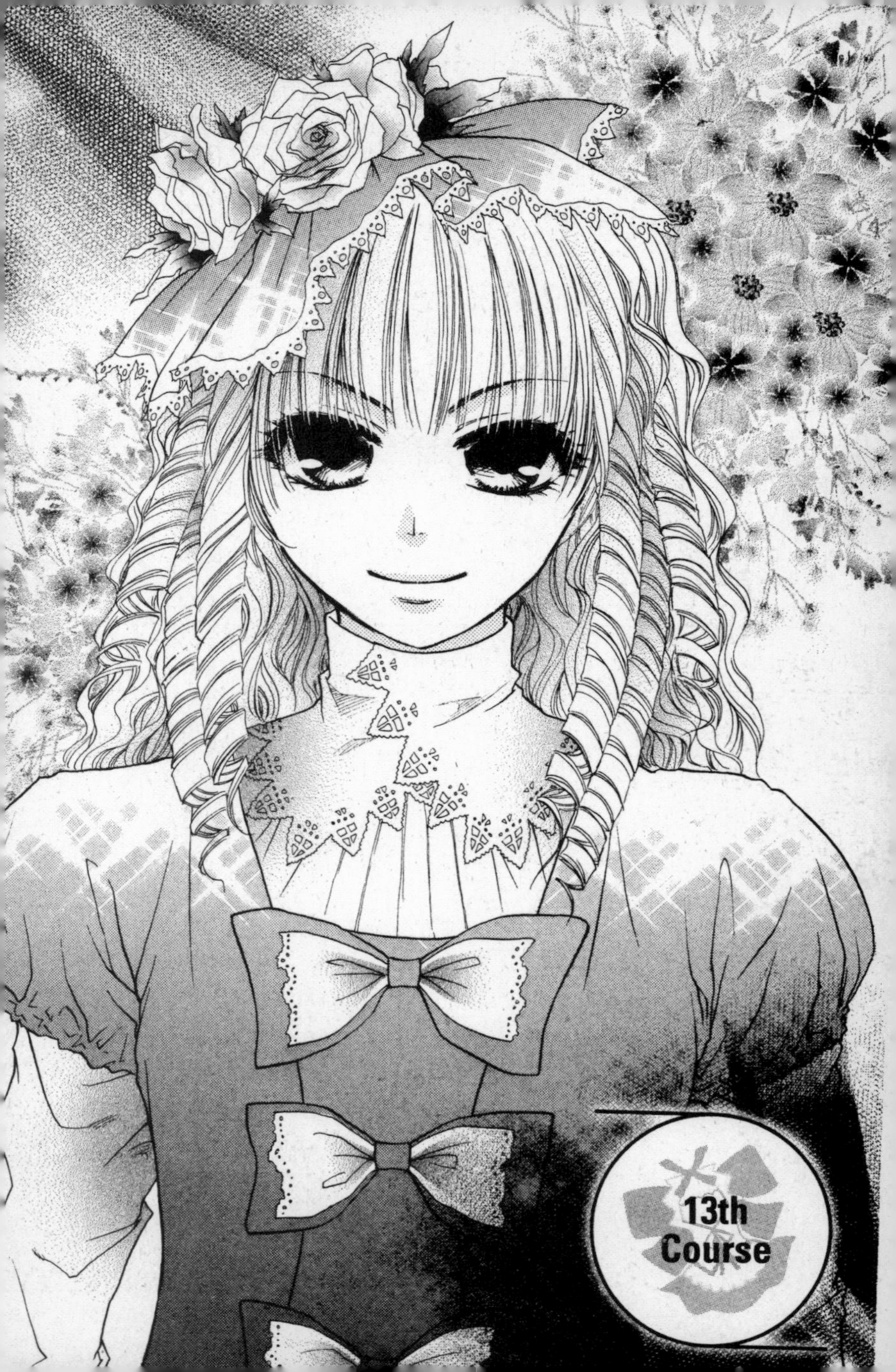
13th
Course

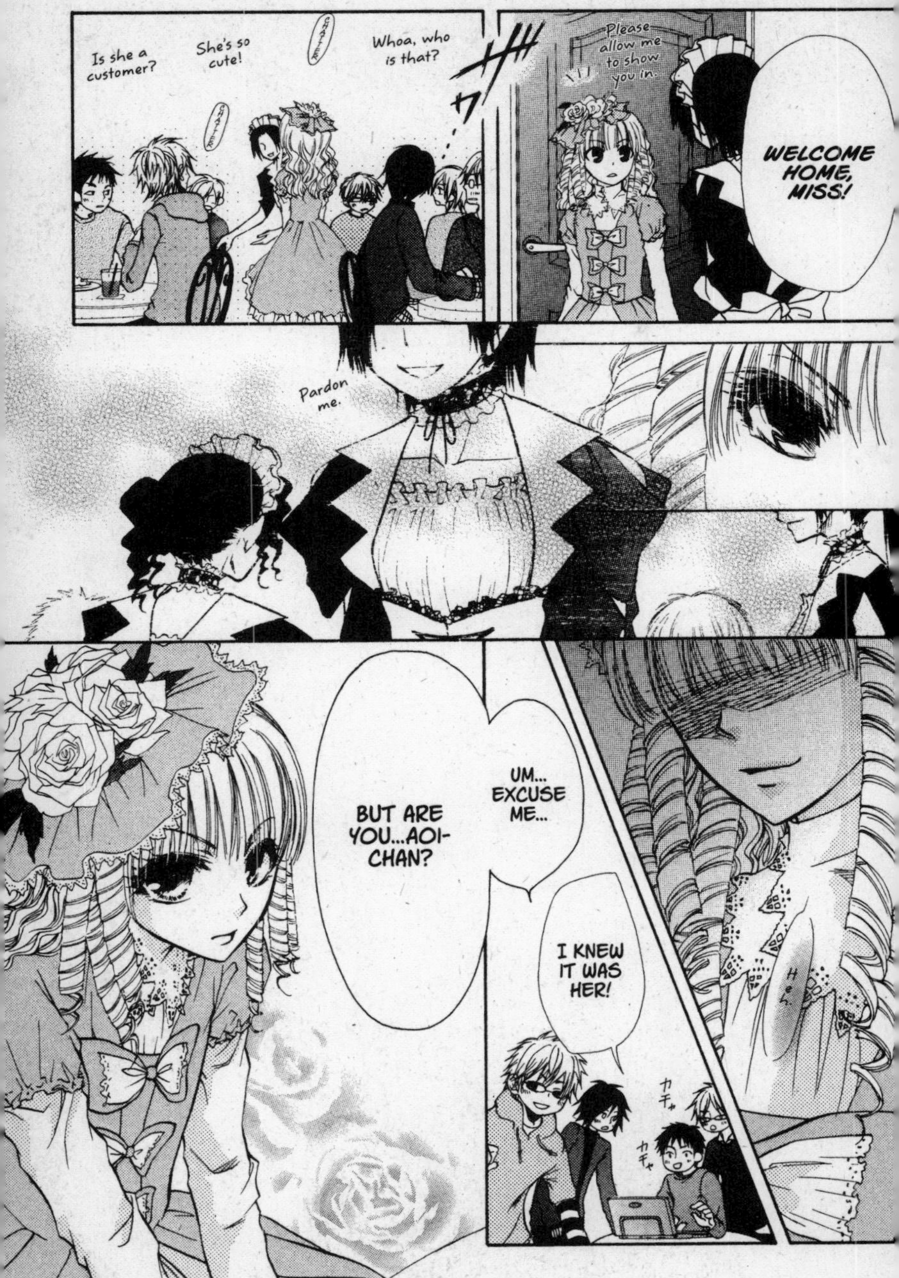
WELCOME HOME, MISS!
Please allow me to show you in.
ガ
Whoa, who is that?
CHATTER
She's so cute!
CHATTER
Is she a customer?
Pardon me.
He...
I KNEW IT WAS HER!
カチャ
カチャ
UM... EXCUSE ME...
BUT ARE YOU...AOI-CHAN?

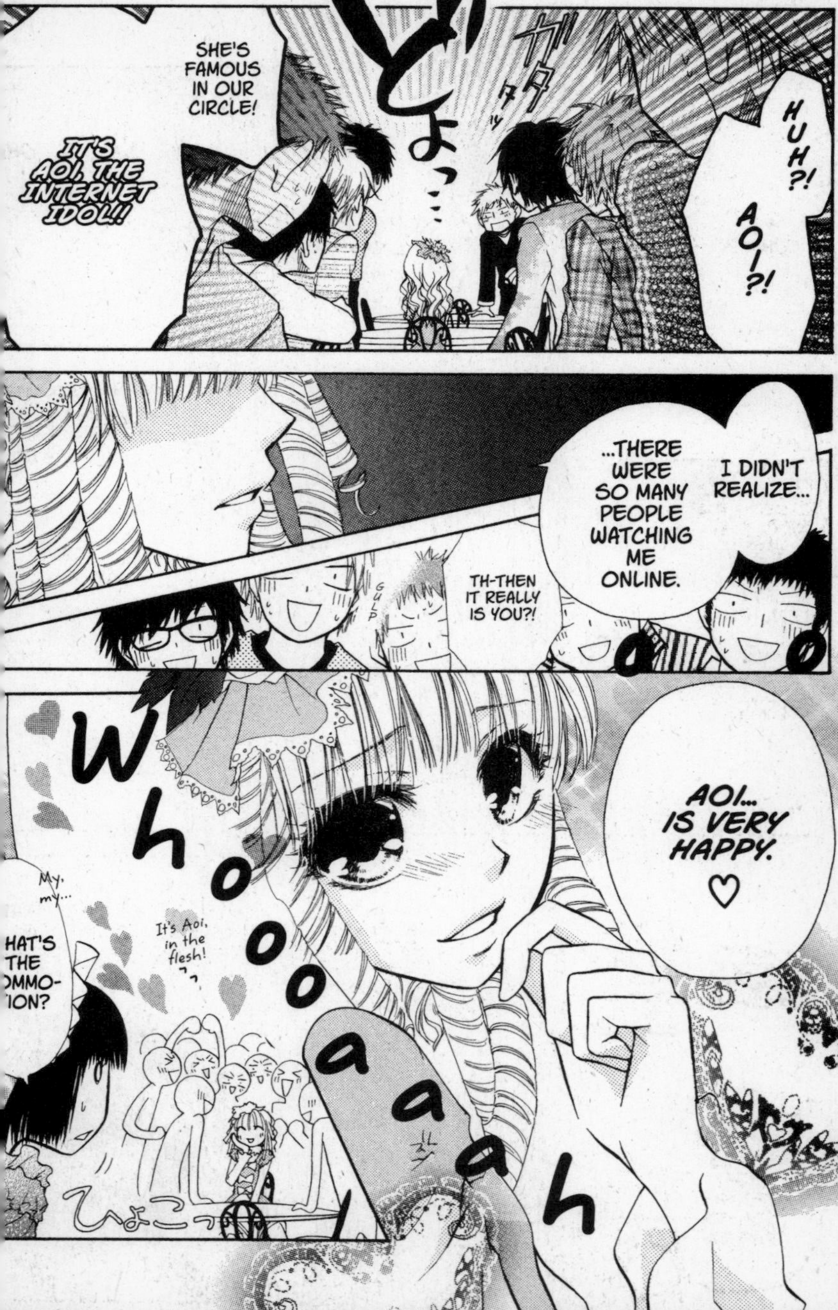
HUH?! AOI?!
どよっ…
ガタッ
SHE'S FAMOUS IN OUR CIRCLE!
IT'S AOI, THE INTERNET IDOL!!
I DIDN'T REALIZE...
...THERE WERE SO MANY PEOPLE WATCHING ME ONLINE.
TH-THEN IT REALLY IS YOU?!
GULP
AOI... IS VERY HAPPY. ♡
Whoooaaaah
It's Aoi, in the flesh!
My, my...
HAT'S THE OMMO- ION?
ひよこっ

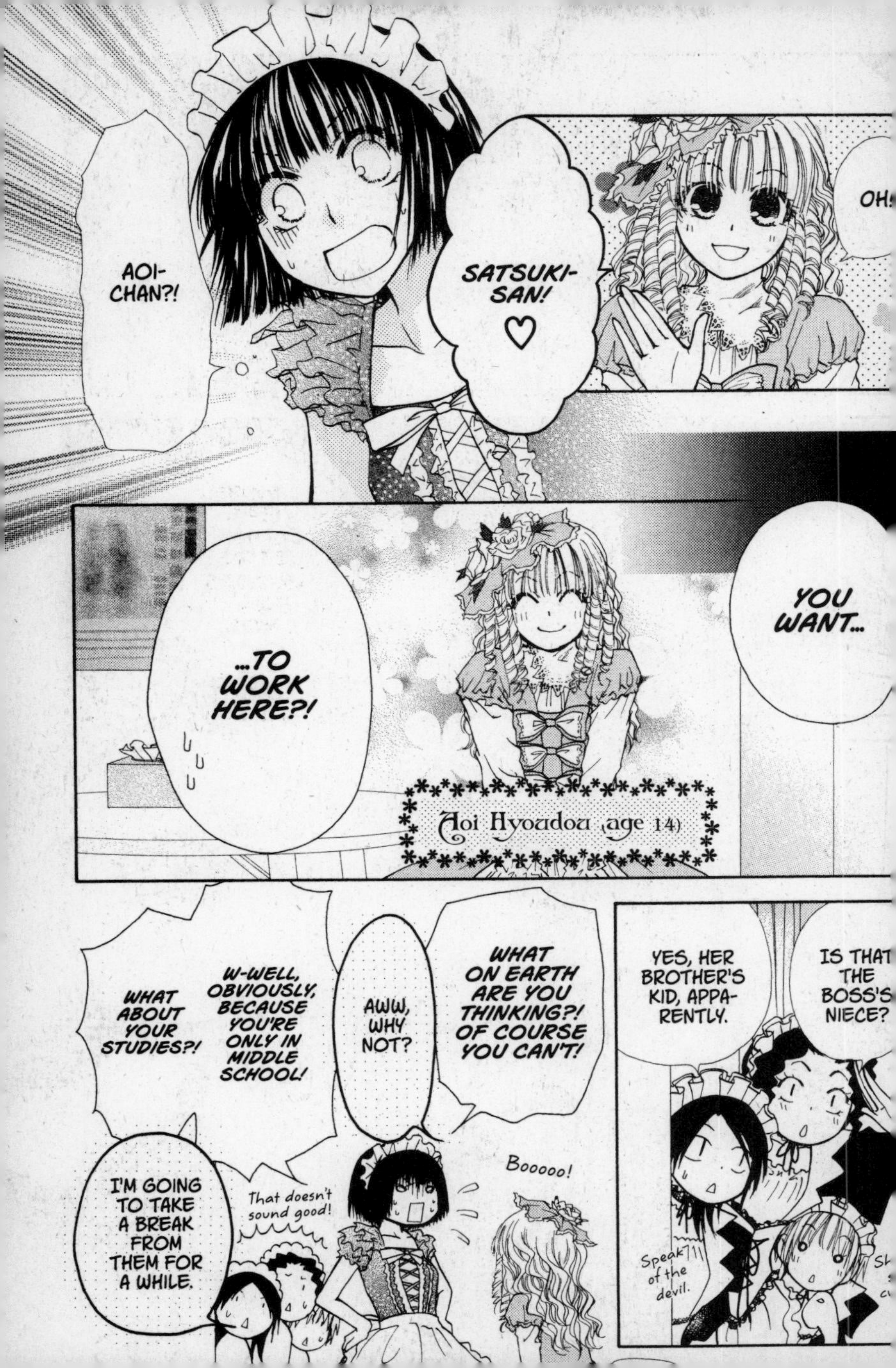
OH!
SATSUKI-SAN! ♡
AOI-CHAN?!
YOU WANT...
...TO WORK HERE?!
Aoi Hyoudou (age 14)
IS THAT THE BOSS'S NIECE?
YES, HER BROTHER'S KID, APPA-RENTLY.
Speak of the devil.
WHAT ON EARTH ARE YOU THINKING?! OF COURSE YOU CAN'T!
AWW, WHY NOT?
W-WELL, OBVIOUSLY, BECAUSE YOU'RE ONLY IN MIDDLE SCHOOL!
WHAT ABOUT YOUR STUDIES?!
Booooo!
I'M GOING TO TAKE A BREAK FROM THEM FOR A WHILE.
That doesn't sound good!

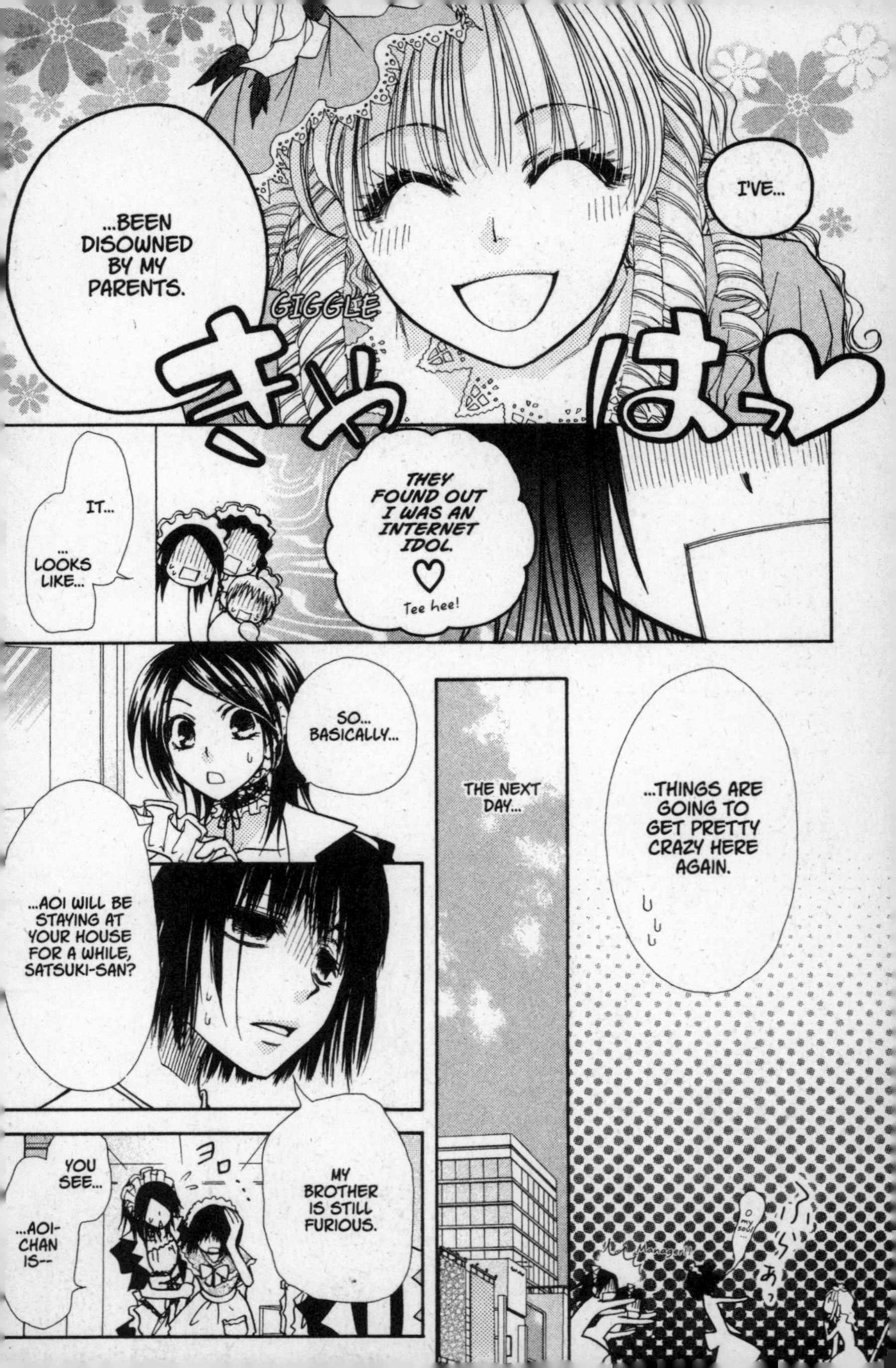
I'VE...
...BEEN DISOWNED BY MY PARENTS.
GIGGLE
きゃはっ♥
THEY FOUND OUT I WAS AN INTERNET IDOL. ♥
Tee hee!
IT...
...LOOKS LIKE...
...THINGS ARE GOING TO GET PRETTY CRAZY HERE AGAIN.
O my soul!
Manager!!
THE NEXT DAY...
SO... BASICALLY...
...AOI WILL BE STAYING AT YOUR HOUSE FOR A WHILE, SATSUKI-SAN?
MY BROTHER IS STILL FURIOUS.
YOU SEE...
...AOI-CHAN IS--

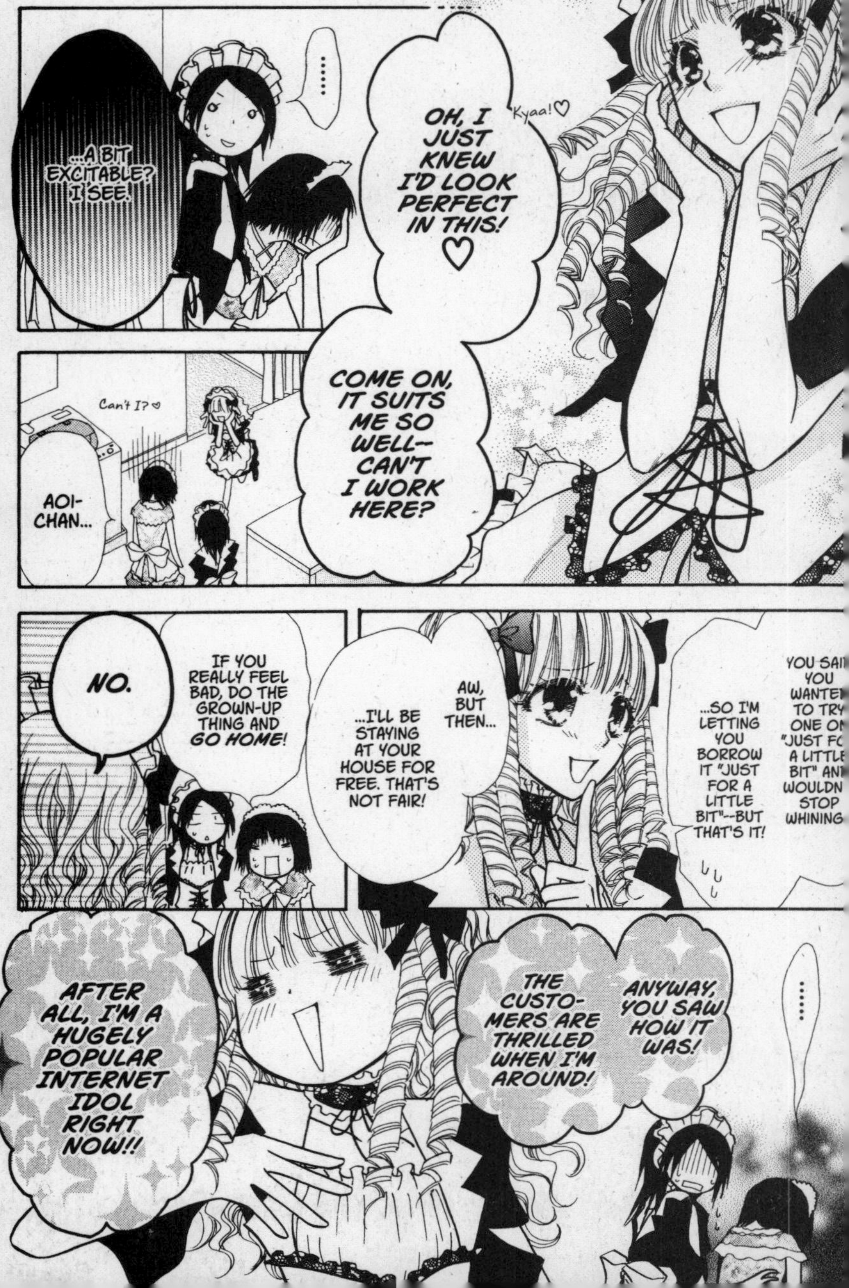
Kyaa!♡
OH, I JUST KNEW I'D LOOK PERFECT IN THIS! ♡
COME ON, IT SUITS ME SO WELL--CAN'T I WORK HERE?
......
...A BIT EXCITABLE? I SEE.
Can't I?♡
AOI-CHAN...
YOU SAI YOU WANTE TO TRY ONE ON "JUST FO A LITTLE BIT" AN WOULDN STOP WHINING
...SO I'M LETTING YOU BORROW IT "JUST FOR A LITTLE BIT"--BUT THAT'S IT!
AW, BUT THEN...
...I'LL BE STAYING AT YOUR HOUSE FOR FREE. THAT'S NOT FAIR!
IF YOU REALLY FEEL BAD, DO THE GROWN-UP THING AND GO HOME!
NO.
......
ANYWAY, YOU SAW HOW IT WAS!
THE CUSTO-MERS ARE THRILLED WHEN I'M AROUND!
AFTER ALL, I'M A HUGELY POPULAR INTERNET IDOL RIGHT NOW!!

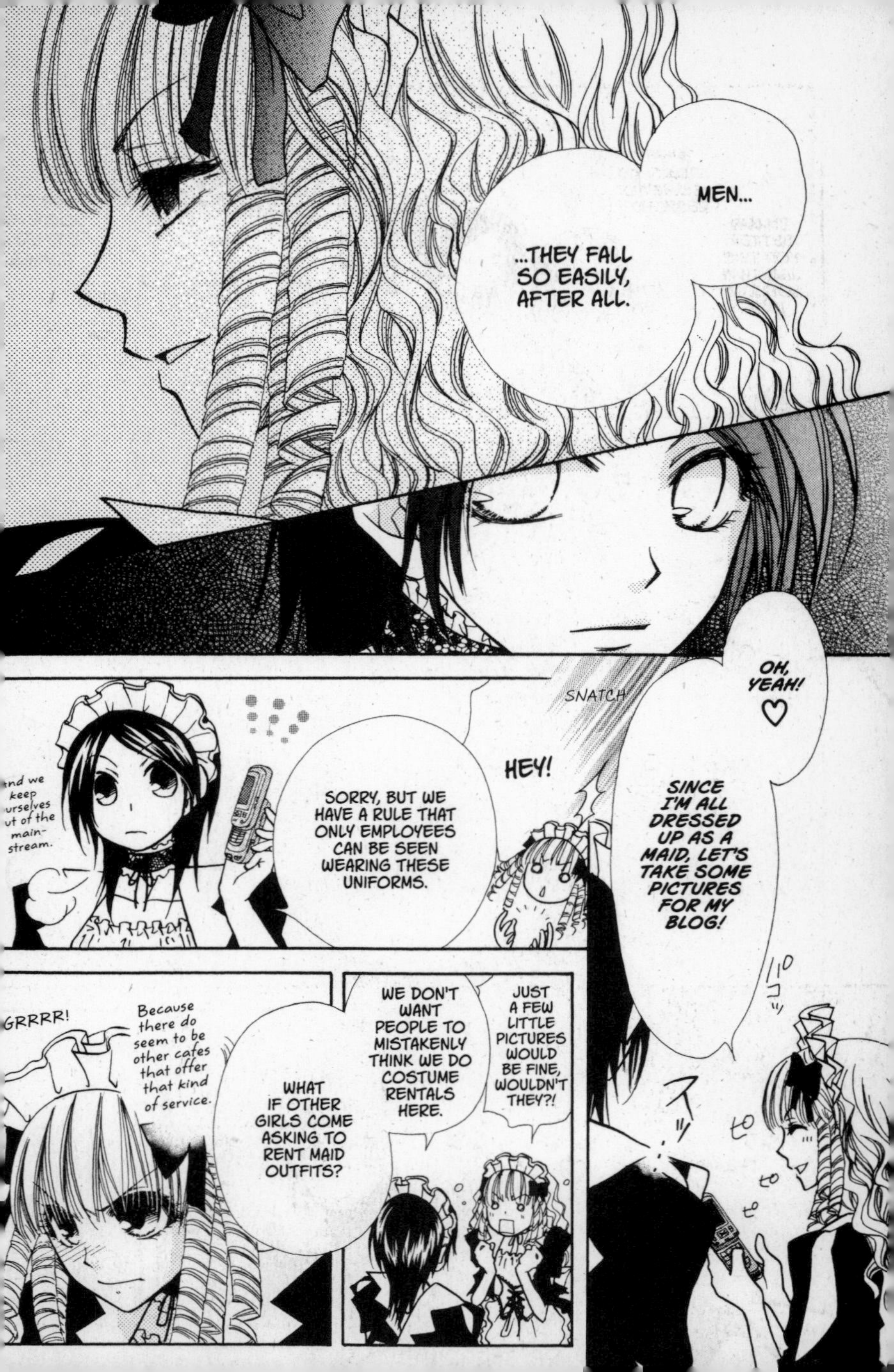
MEN...
...THEY FALL SO EASILY, AFTER ALL.
OH, YEAH! ♥
SINCE I'M ALL DRESSED UP AS A MAID, LET'S TAKE SOME PICTURES FOR MY BLOG!
SNATCH
HEY!
SORRY, BUT WE HAVE A RULE THAT ONLY EMPLOYEES CAN BE SEEN WEARING THESE UNIFORMS.
nd we keep urselves ut of the main-stream.
JUST A FEW LITTLE PICTURES WOULD BE FINE, WOULDN'T THEY?!
WE DON'T WANT PEOPLE TO MISTAKENLY THINK WE DO COSTUME RENTALS HERE.
WHAT IF OTHER GIRLS COME ASKING TO RENT MAID OUTFITS?
GRRRR!
Because there do seem to be other cafes that offer that kind of service.

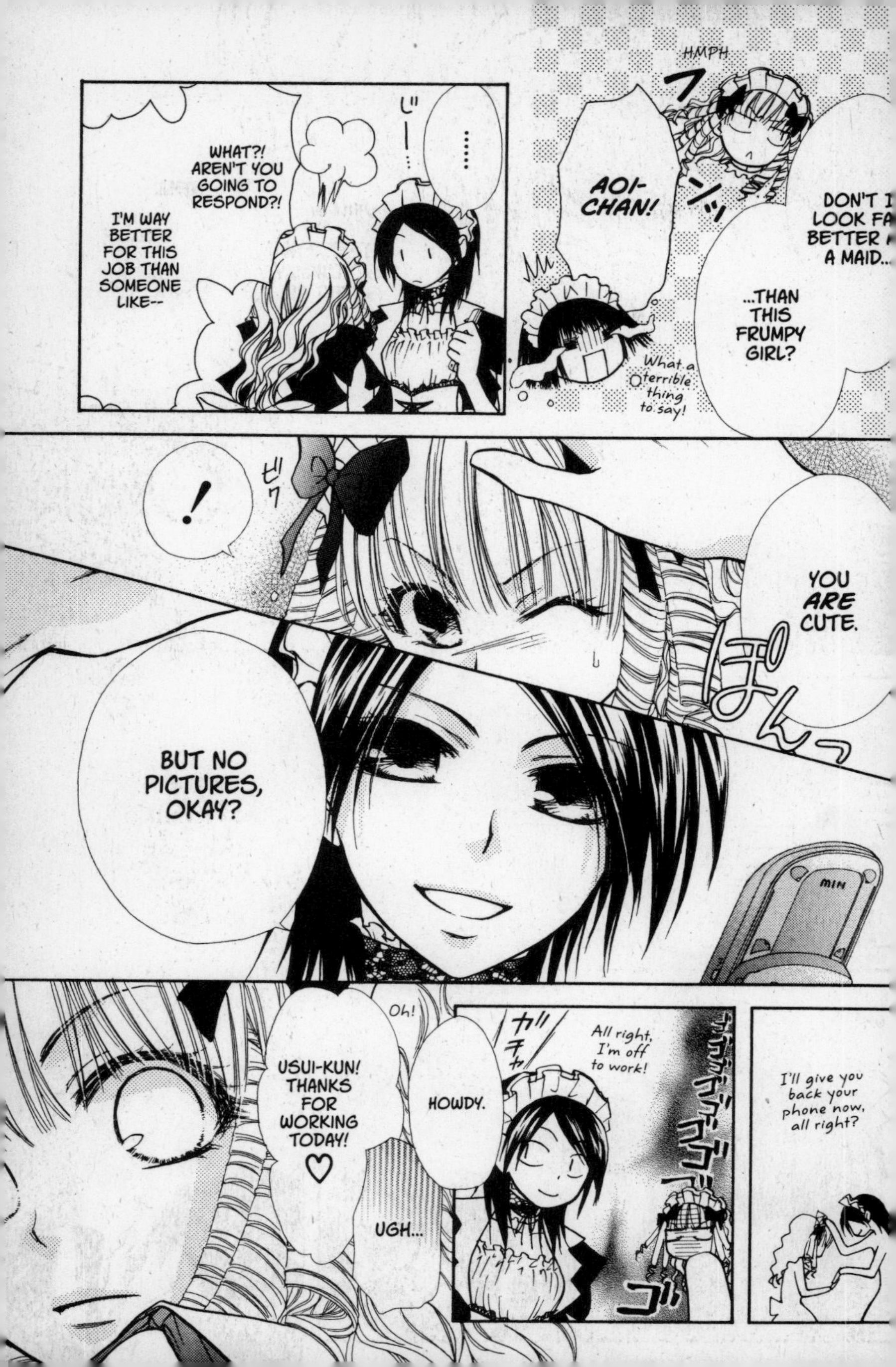
HMPH
DON'T I LOOK FA BETTER A MAID...
...THAN THIS FRUMPY GIRL?
AOI-CHAN!
What a terrible thing to say!
......
じー
WHAT?! AREN'T YOU GOING TO RESPOND?!
I'M WAY BETTER FOR THIS JOB THAN SOMEONE LIKE--
YOU ARE CUTE.
ぽんっ
!
ビク
BUT NO PICTURES, OKAY?
MIN
I'll give you back your phone now, all right?
All right, I'm off to work!
ガチャ
Oh!
HOWDY.
USUI-KUN! THANKS FOR WORKING TODAY! ♡
UGH...

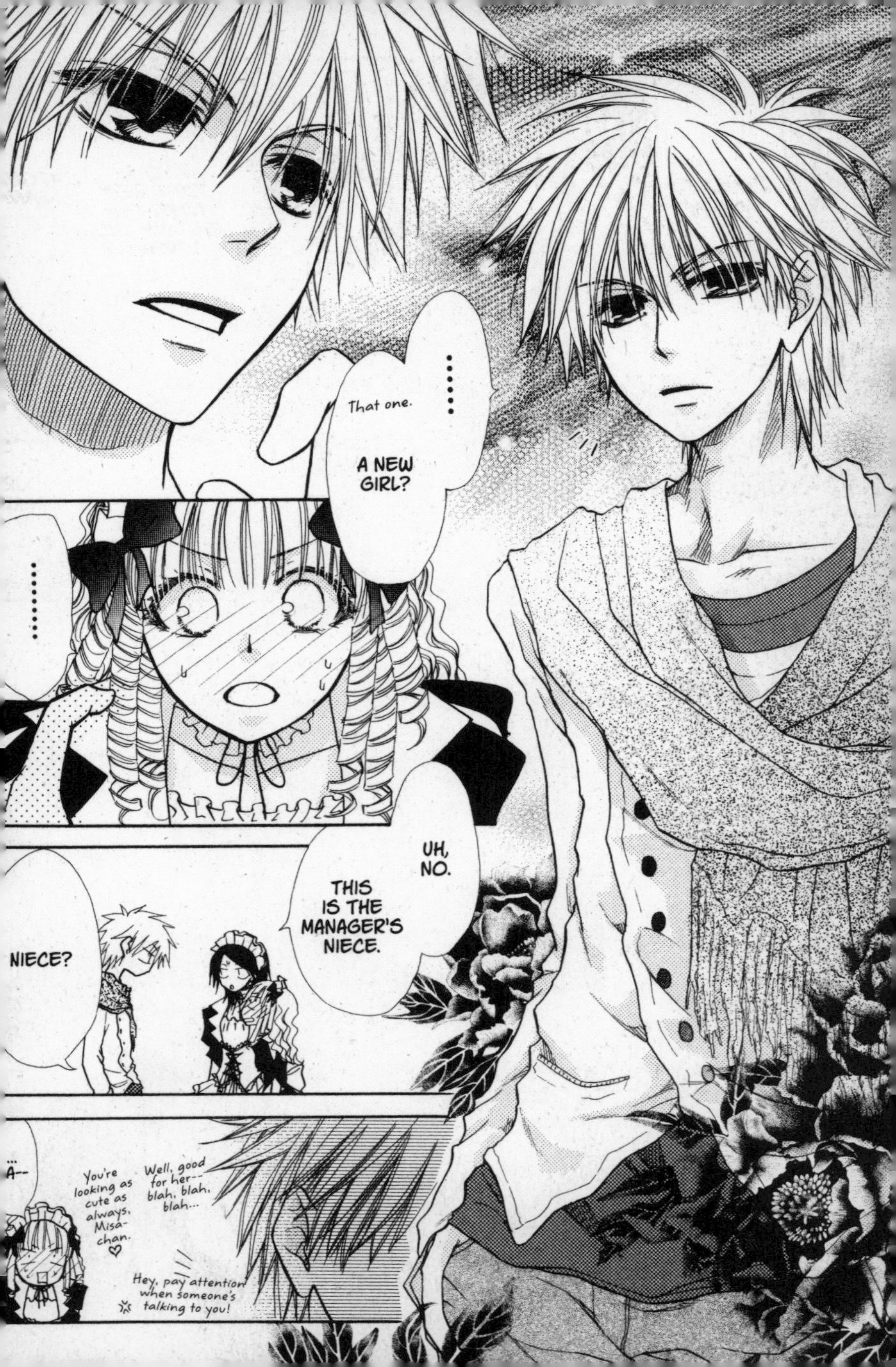
......
That one.
A NEW GIRL?
......
UH, NO.
THIS IS THE MANAGER'S NIECE.
NIECE?
Hey, pay attention when someone's talking to you!
Well, good for her-- blah, blah, blah...
You're looking as cute as always, Misa-chan. ♡
... A--

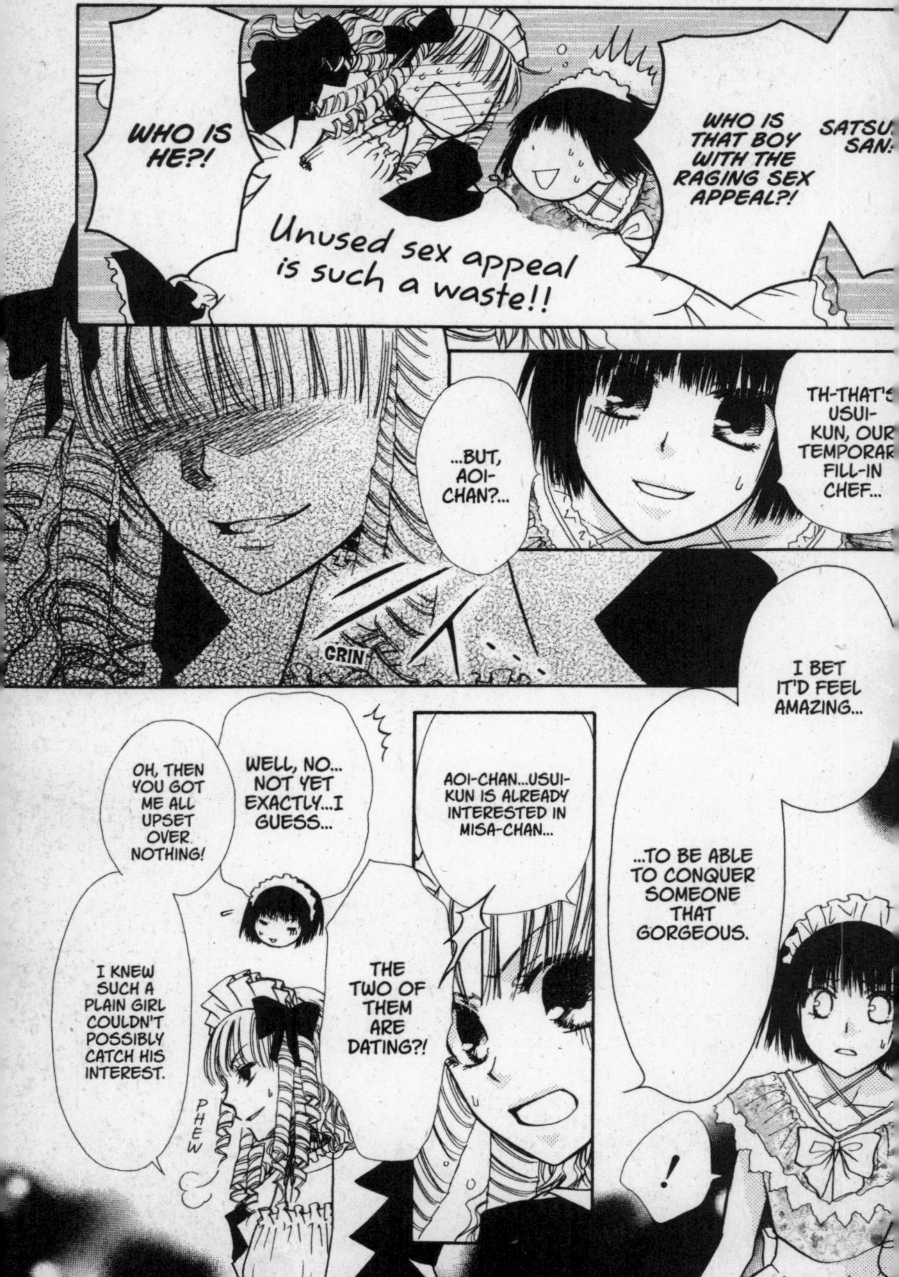
SATSU SAN!
WHO IS THAT BOY WITH THE RAGING SEX APPEAL?!
WHO IS HE?!
Unused sex appeal is such a waste!!
TH-THAT'S USUI-KUN, OUR TEMPORAR FILL-IN CHEF...
...BUT, AOI-CHAN?...
GRIN
I BET IT'D FEEL AMAZING...
...TO BE ABLE TO CONQUER SOMEONE THAT GORGEOUS.
!
AOI-CHAN...USUI-KUN IS ALREADY INTERESTED IN MISA-CHAN...
THE TWO OF THEM ARE DATING?!
WELL, NO... NOT YET EXACTLY...I GUESS...
OH, THEN YOU GOT ME ALL UPSET OVER NOTHING!
I KNEW SUCH A PLAIN GIRL COULDN'T POSSIBLY CATCH HIS INTEREST.
PHEW

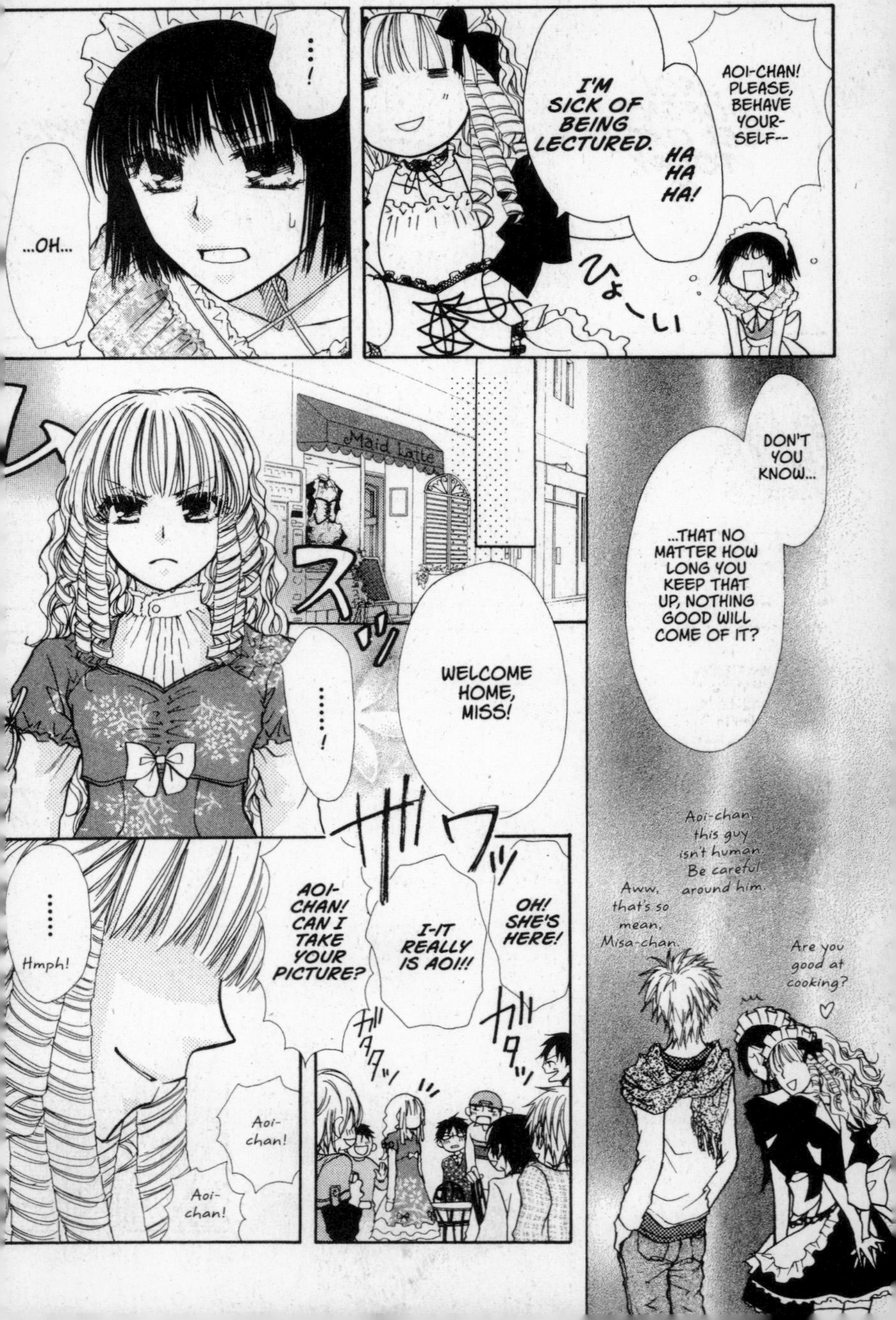
AOI-CHAN! PLEASE, BEHAVE YOURSELF--
I'M SICK OF BEING LECTURED.
HA HA HA!
ひょ〜い
...!
...OH...
DON'T YOU KNOW...
...THAT NO MATTER HOW LONG YOU KEEP THAT UP, NOTHING GOOD WILL COME OF IT?
Aoi-chan, this guy isn't human. Be careful around him.
Aww, that's so mean, Misa-chan.
Are you good at cooking?
Maid Latte
スッ
WELCOME HOME, MISS!
......!
ザワッ
OH! SHE'S HERE!
I-IT REALLY IS AOI!!
AOI-CHAN! CAN I TAKE YOUR PICTURE?
ガタッ
ガタタッ
Aoi-chan!
Aoi-chan!
......
Hmph!

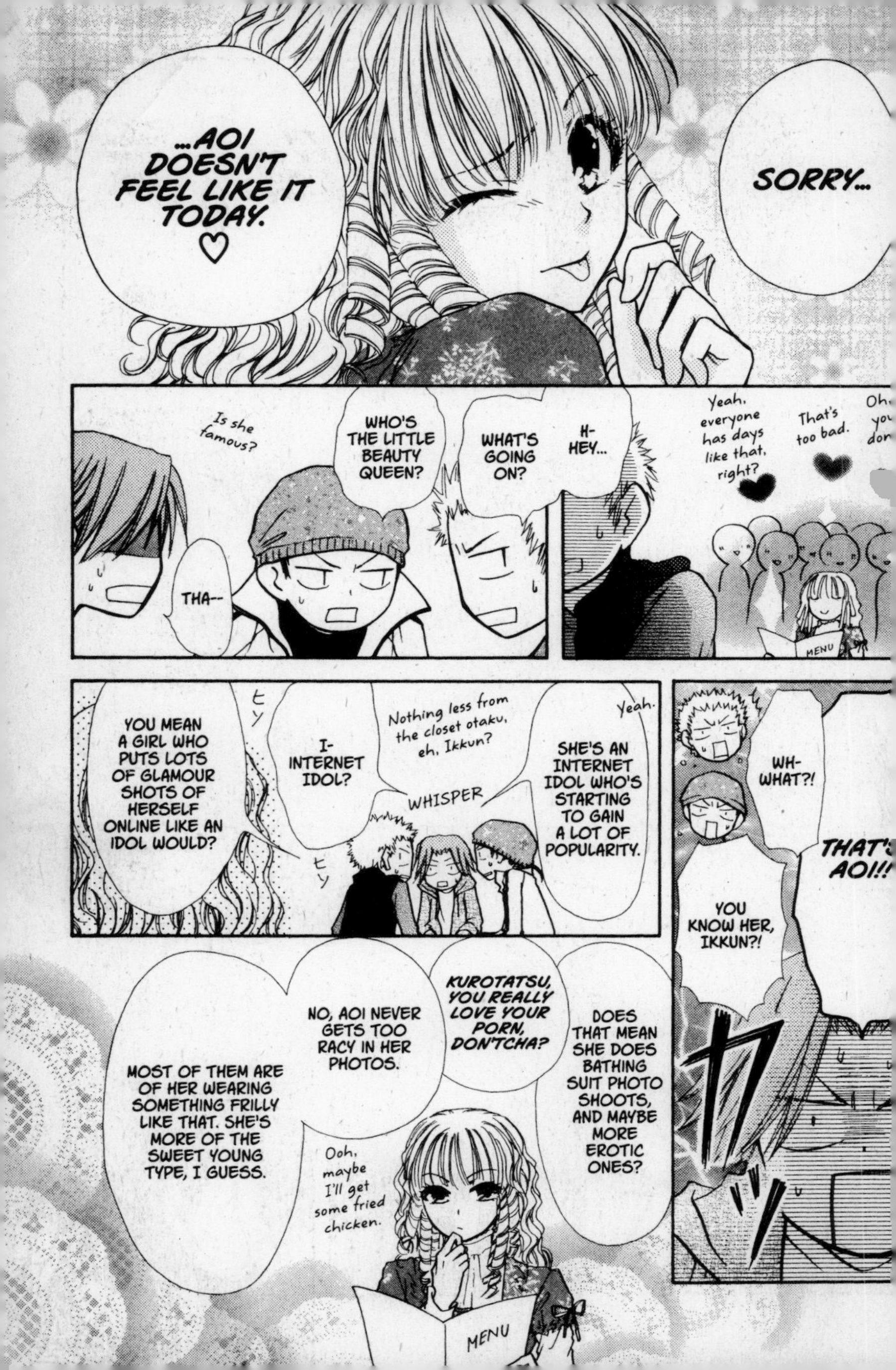
SORRY...
...AOI DOESN'T FEEL LIKE IT TODAY. ♡
That's too bad.
Yeah, everyone has days like that, right?
MENU
H- HEY...
WHAT'S GOING ON?
WHO'S THE LITTLE BEAUTY QUEEN?
Is she famous?
THA--
WH- WHAT?!
THAT'S AOI!!
YOU KNOW HER, IKKUN?!
Yeah.
SHE'S AN INTERNET IDOL WHO'S STARTING TO GAIN A LOT OF POPULARITY.
Nothing less from the closet otaku, eh, Ikkun?
I- INTERNET IDOL?
WHISPER
YOU MEAN A GIRL WHO PUTS LOTS OF GLAMOUR SHOTS OF HERSELF ONLINE LIKE AN IDOL WOULD?
ヒソ
ヒソ
DOES THAT MEAN SHE DOES BATHING SUIT PHOTO SHOOTS, AND MAYBE MORE EROTIC ONES?
KUROTATSU, YOU REALLY LOVE YOUR PORN, DON'TCHA?
NO, AOI NEVER GETS TOO RACY IN HER PHOTOS.
MOST OF THEM ARE OF HER WEARING SOMETHING FRILLY LIKE THAT. SHE'S MORE OF THE SWEET YOUNG TYPE, I GUESS.
Ooh, maybe I'll get some fried chicken.
MENU

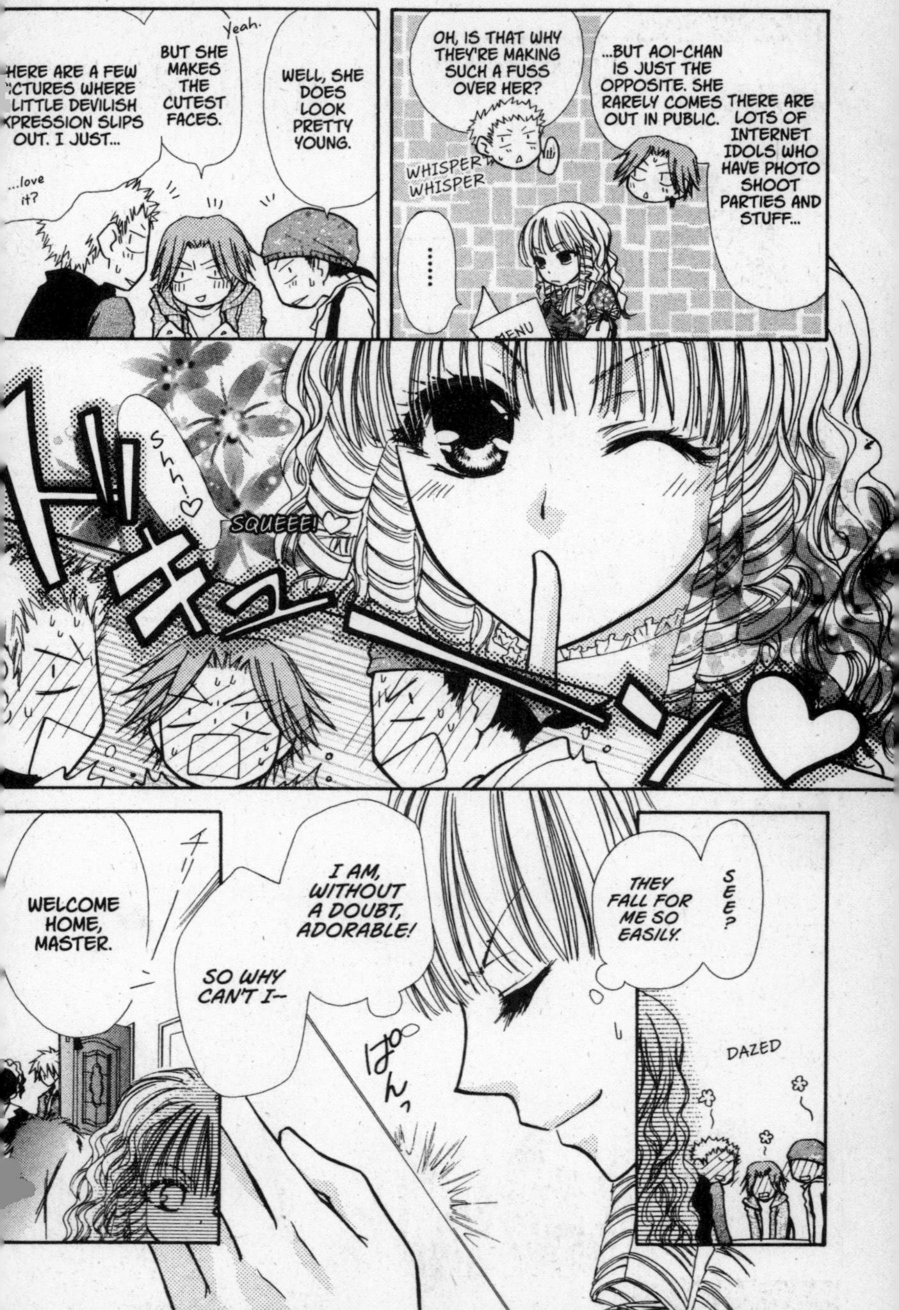
THERE ARE LOTS OF INTERNET IDOLS WHO HAVE PHOTO SHOOT PARTIES AND STUFF...
...BUT AOI-CHAN IS JUST THE OPPOSITE. SHE RARELY COMES OUT IN PUBLIC.
OH, IS THAT WHY THEY'RE MAKING SUCH A FUSS OVER HER?
WHISPER WHISPER
......
MENU
WELL, SHE DOES LOOK PRETTY YOUNG.
Yeah.
BUT SHE MAKES THE CUTEST FACES.
HERE ARE A FEW ICTURES WHERE LITTLE DEVILISH XPRESSION SLIPS OUT. I JUST...
...love it?
Shhh~♡
SQUEEE!♡
SEE?
THEY FALL FOR ME SO EASILY.
DAZED
I AM, WITHOUT A DOUBT, ADORABLE!
SO WHY CAN'T I--
WELCOME HOME, MASTER.

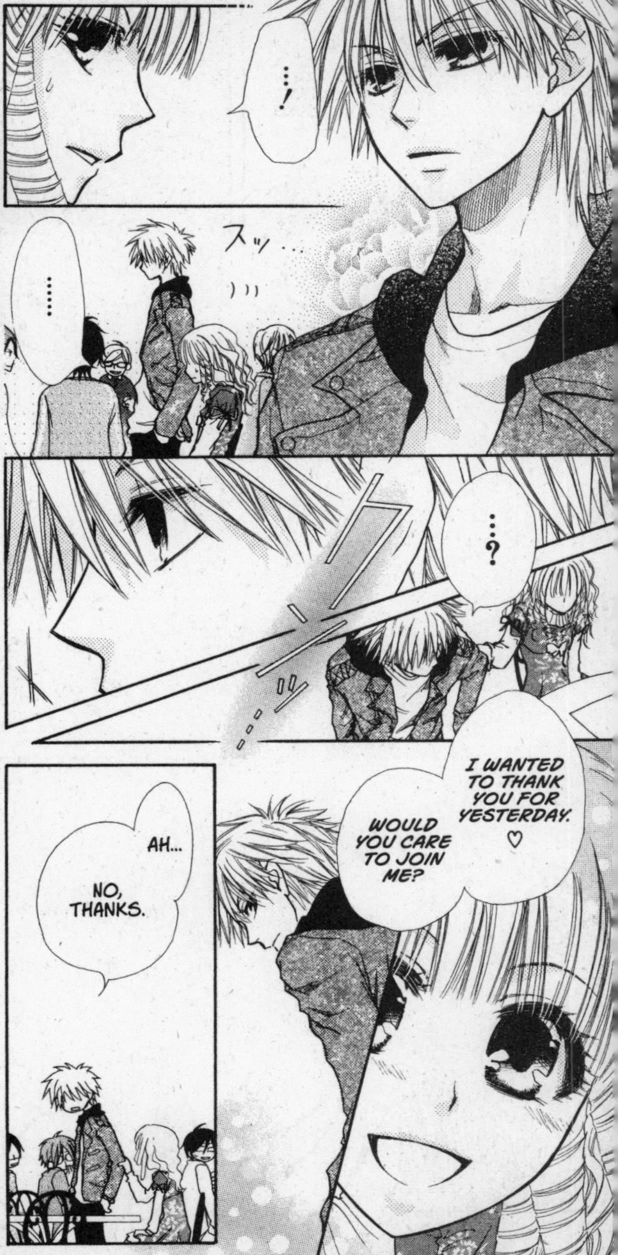
…!
スッ…
……
…?
I WANTED TO THANK YOU FOR YESTERDAY. ♡
WOULD YOU CARE TO JOIN ME?
AH...
NO, THANKS.

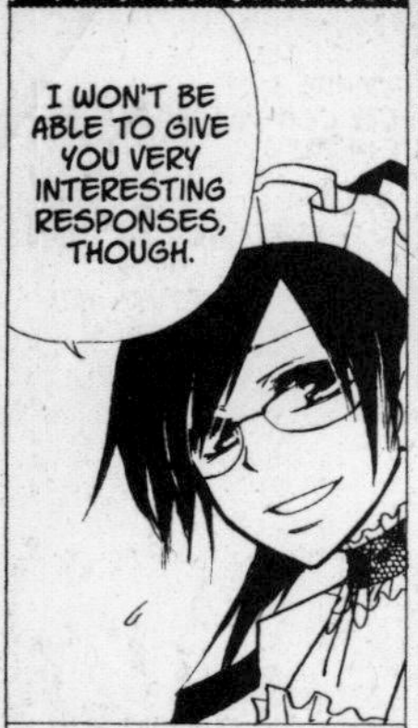
I WON'T BE ABLE TO GIVE YOU VERY INTERESTING RESPONSES, THOUGH.

NAME

Subaru

AGE (CLASS)

22

BLOOD TYPE

A

HEIGHT

164 cm
(5 ft 4 in)

WEIGHT

52 kg (115 lbs)

SPECIAL SKILLS

English

LIKES

Her Savings Account

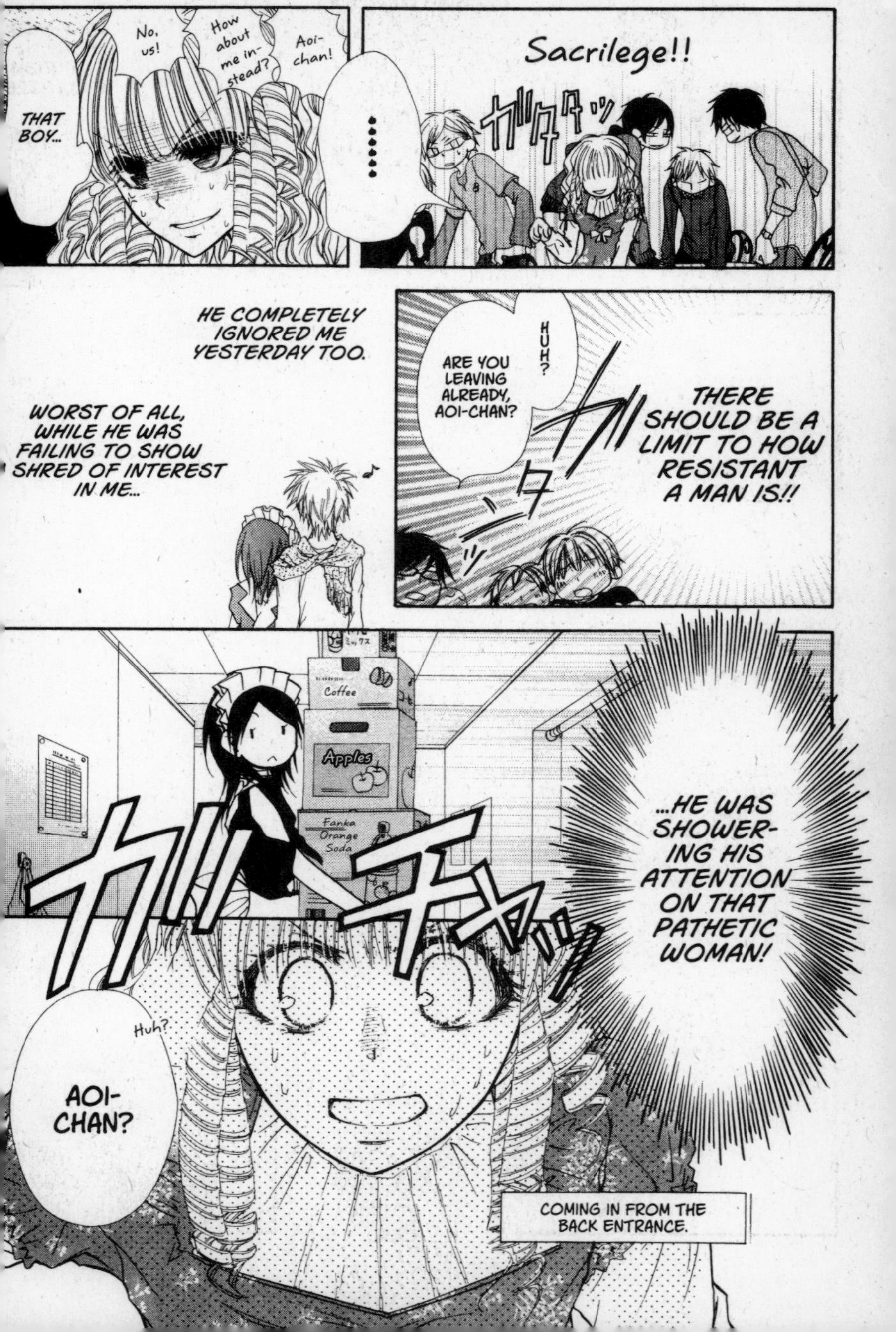

Sacrilege!!
ガタタッ
......
Aoi-chan!
How about me instead?
No, us!
THAT BOY...
HUH?
ARE YOU LEAVING ALREADY, AOI-CHAN?
ガタッ
THERE SHOULD BE A LIMIT TO HOW RESISTANT A MAN IS!!
HE COMPLETELY IGNORED ME YESTERDAY TOO.
WORST OF ALL, WHILE HE WAS FAILING TO SHOW SHRED OF INTEREST IN ME...
...HE WAS SHOWERING HIS ATTENTION ON THAT PATHETIC WOMAN!
Coffee
Apples
Fanka Orange Soda
ガチャッ
Huh?
AOI-CHAN?
COMING IN FROM THE BACK ENTRANCE.

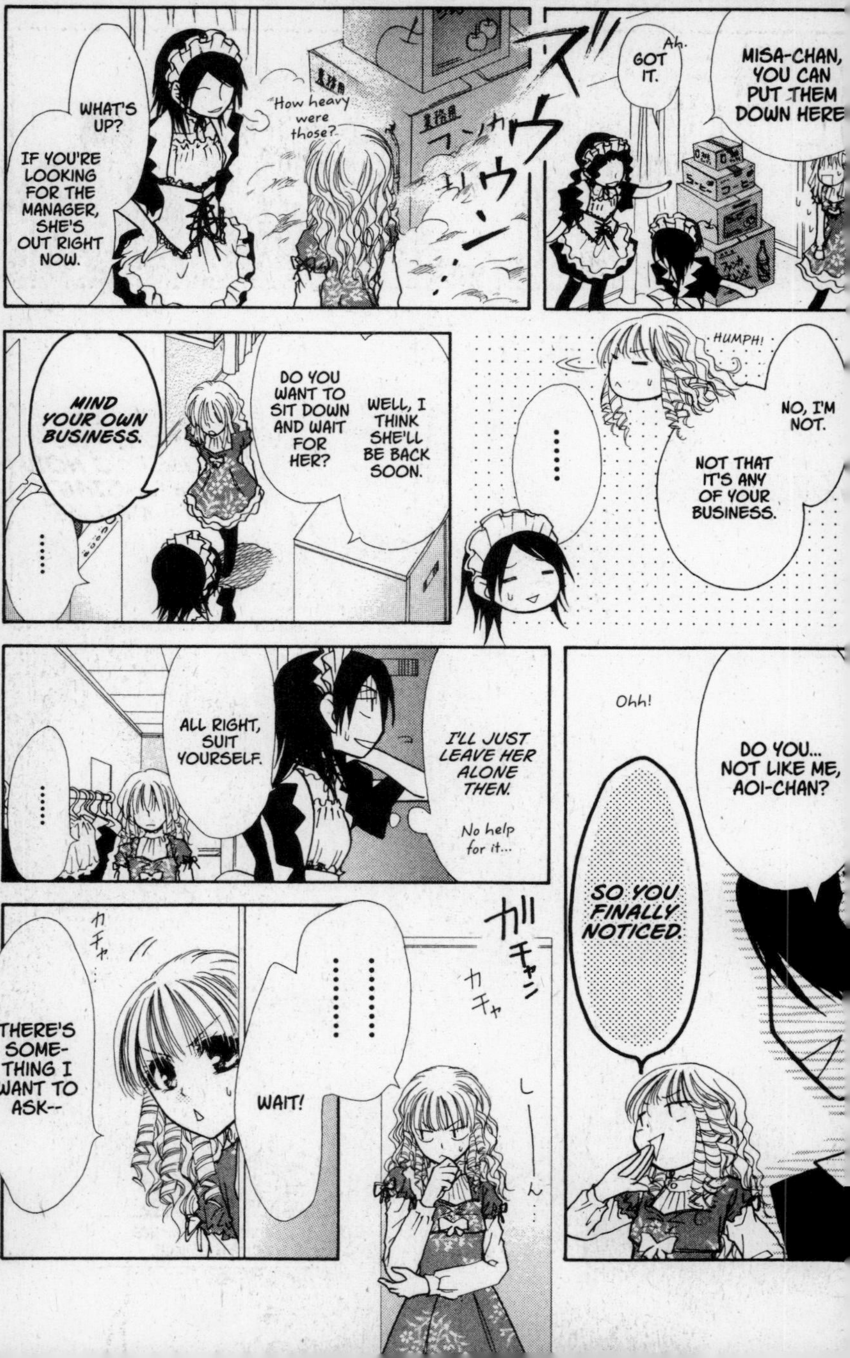
MISA-CHAN, YOU CAN PUT THEM DOWN HERE
Ah. GOT IT.
How heavy were those?
WHAT'S UP?
IF YOU'RE LOOKING FOR THE MANAGER, SHE'S OUT RIGHT NOW.
HUMPH!
NO, I'M NOT.
NOT THAT IT'S ANY OF YOUR BUSINESS.
......
WELL, I THINK SHE'LL BE BACK SOON.
DO YOU WANT TO SIT DOWN AND WAIT FOR HER?
MIND YOUR OWN BUSINESS.
......
DO YOU... NOT LIKE ME, AOI-CHAN?
Ohh!
SO YOU FINALLY NOTICED.
I'LL JUST LEAVE HER ALONE THEN.
No help for it...
ALL RIGHT, SUIT YOURSELF.
......
ガチャン
カチャ
......
WAIT!
THERE'S SOMETHING I WANT TO ASK--

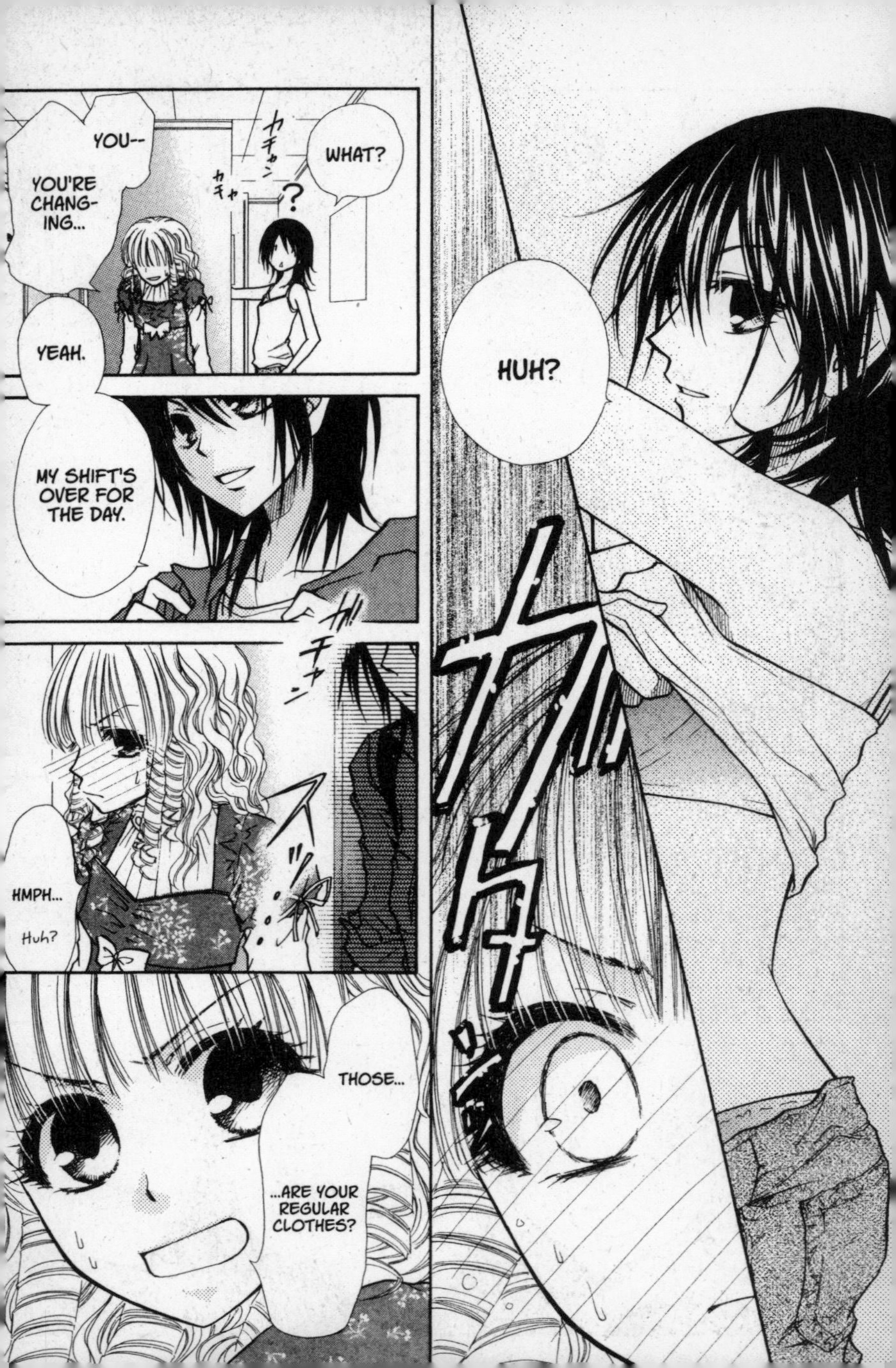
HUH?
WHAT?
カチャン
カチャ
?
YOU--
YOU'RE CHANGING...
YEAH.
MY SHIFT'S OVER FOR THE DAY.
ガチャン
HMPH...
Huh?
THOSE...
...ARE YOUR REGULAR CLOTHES?

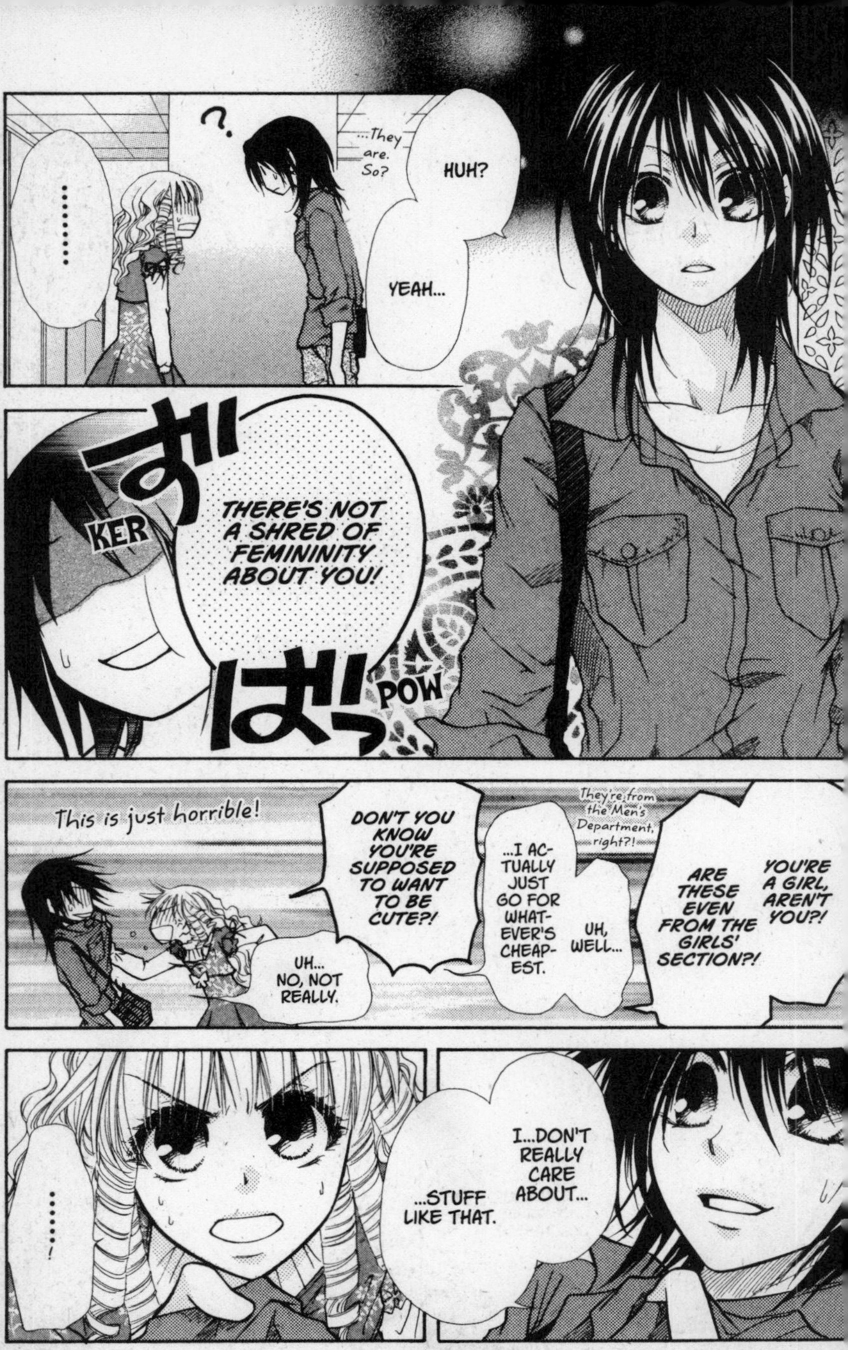
HUH?
...They are. So?
YEAH...
?
....
THERE'S NOT A SHRED OF FEMININITY ABOUT YOU!
KER
POW
YOU'RE A GIRL, AREN'T YOU?!
ARE THESE EVEN FROM THE GIRLS' SECTION?!
They're from the Men's Department, right?!
UH, WELL...
...I ACTUALLY JUST GO FOR WHATEVER'S CHEAPEST.
DON'T YOU KNOW YOU'RE SUPPOSED TO WANT TO BE CUTE?!
UH... NO, NOT REALLY.
This is just horrible!
I...DON'T REALLY CARE ABOUT...
...STUFF LIKE THAT.
......!

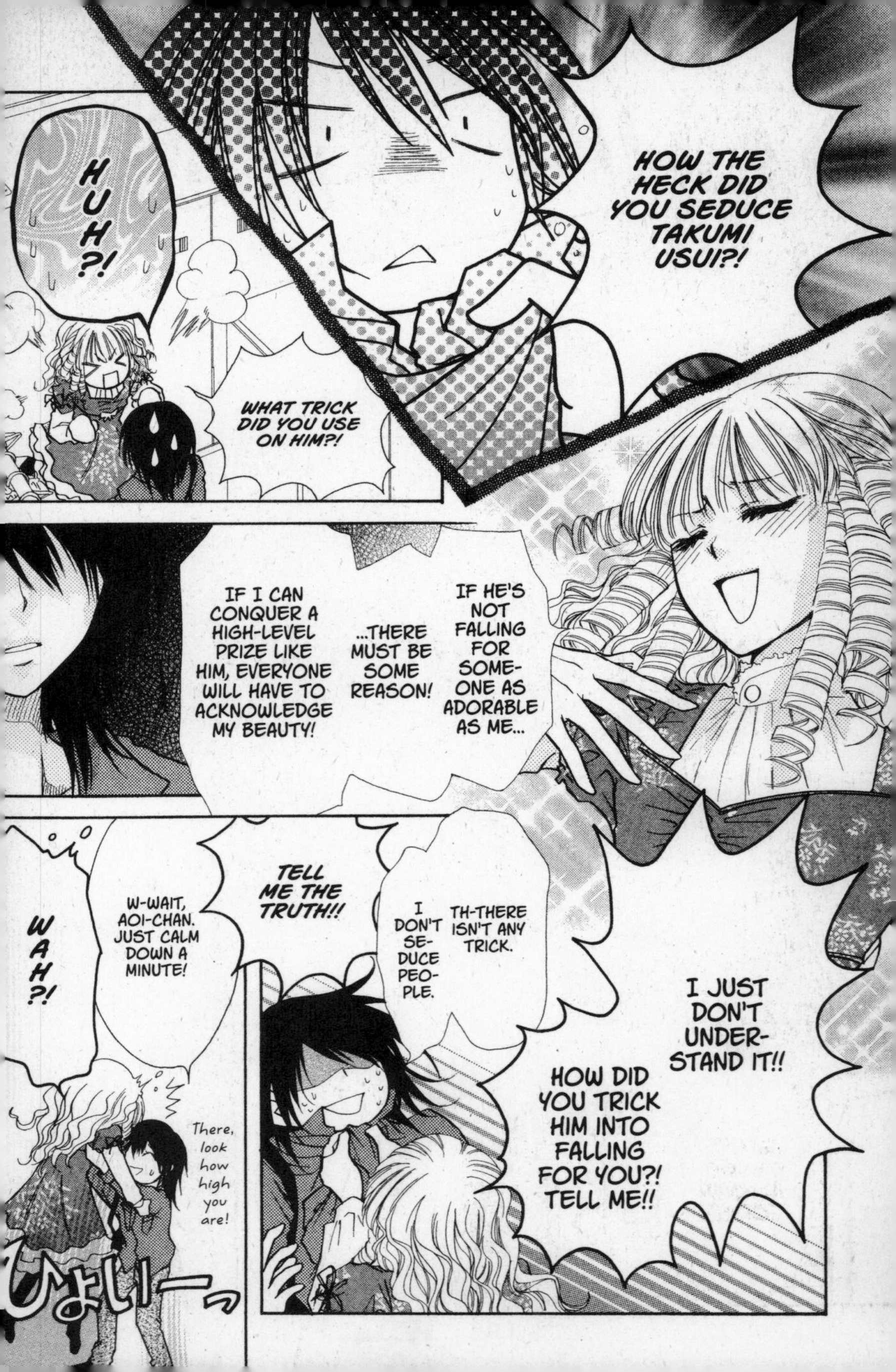
HOW THE HECK DID YOU SEDUCE TAKUMI USUI?!
HUH?!
WHAT TRICK DID YOU USE ON HIM?!
IF HE'S NOT FALLING FOR SOME-ONE AS ADORABLE AS ME...
...THERE MUST BE SOME REASON!
IF I CAN CONQUER A HIGH-LEVEL PRIZE LIKE HIM, EVERYONE WILL HAVE TO ACKNOWLEDGE MY BEAUTY!
I JUST DON'T UNDER-STAND IT!!
HOW DID YOU TRICK HIM INTO FALLING FOR YOU?! TELL ME!!
TH-THERE ISN'T ANY TRICK.
I DON'T SE-DUCE PEO-PLE.
TELL ME THE TRUTH!!
W-WAIT, AOI-CHAN. JUST CALM DOWN A MINUTE!
WAH?!
There, look how high you are!
ひょいーっ

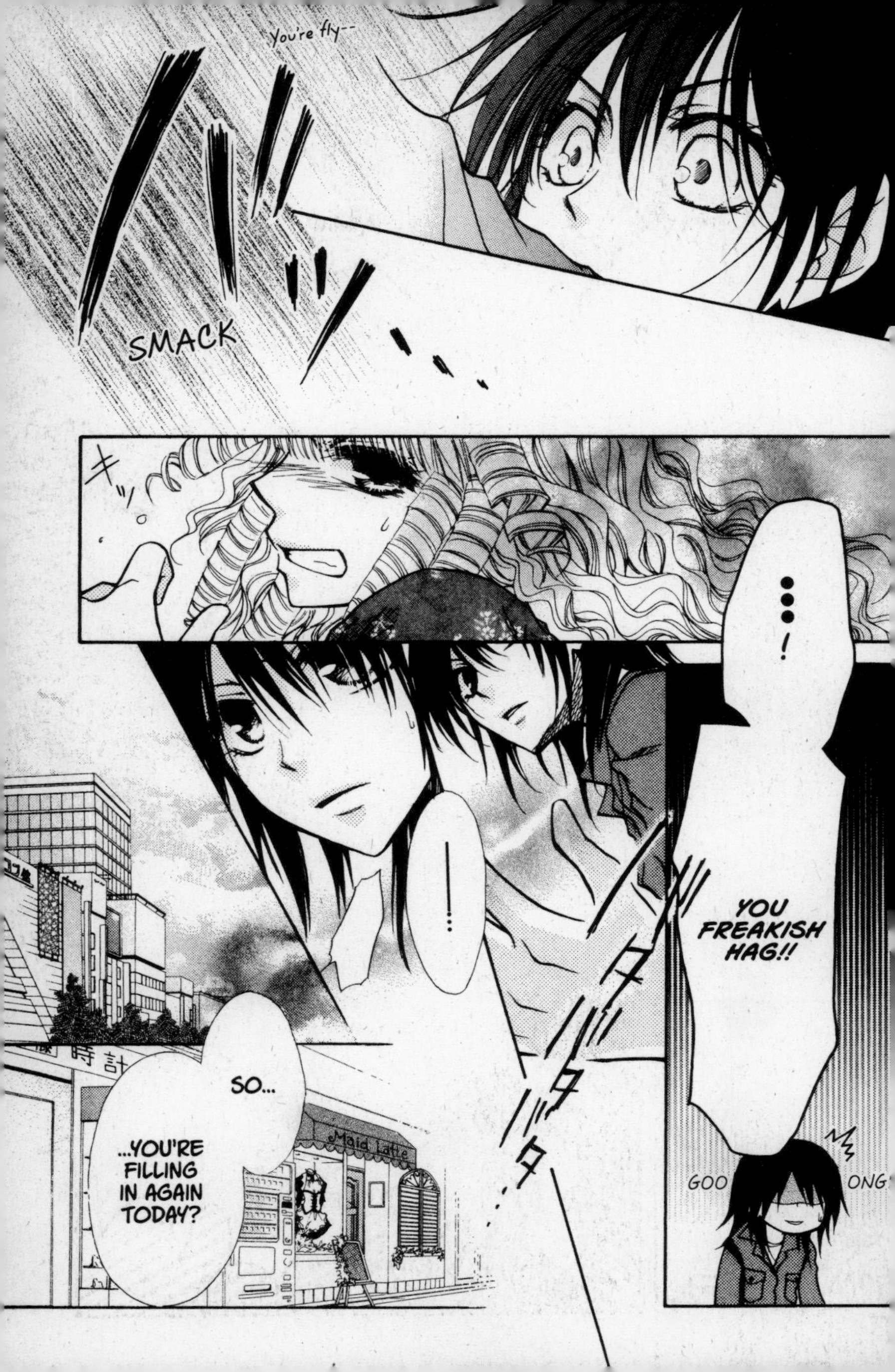

You're fly--
SMACK
...!
キッ
YOU FREAKISH HAG!!
GOO ONG
...!
バタバタ
時計
Maid Latte
SO...
...YOU'RE FILLING IN AGAIN TODAY?

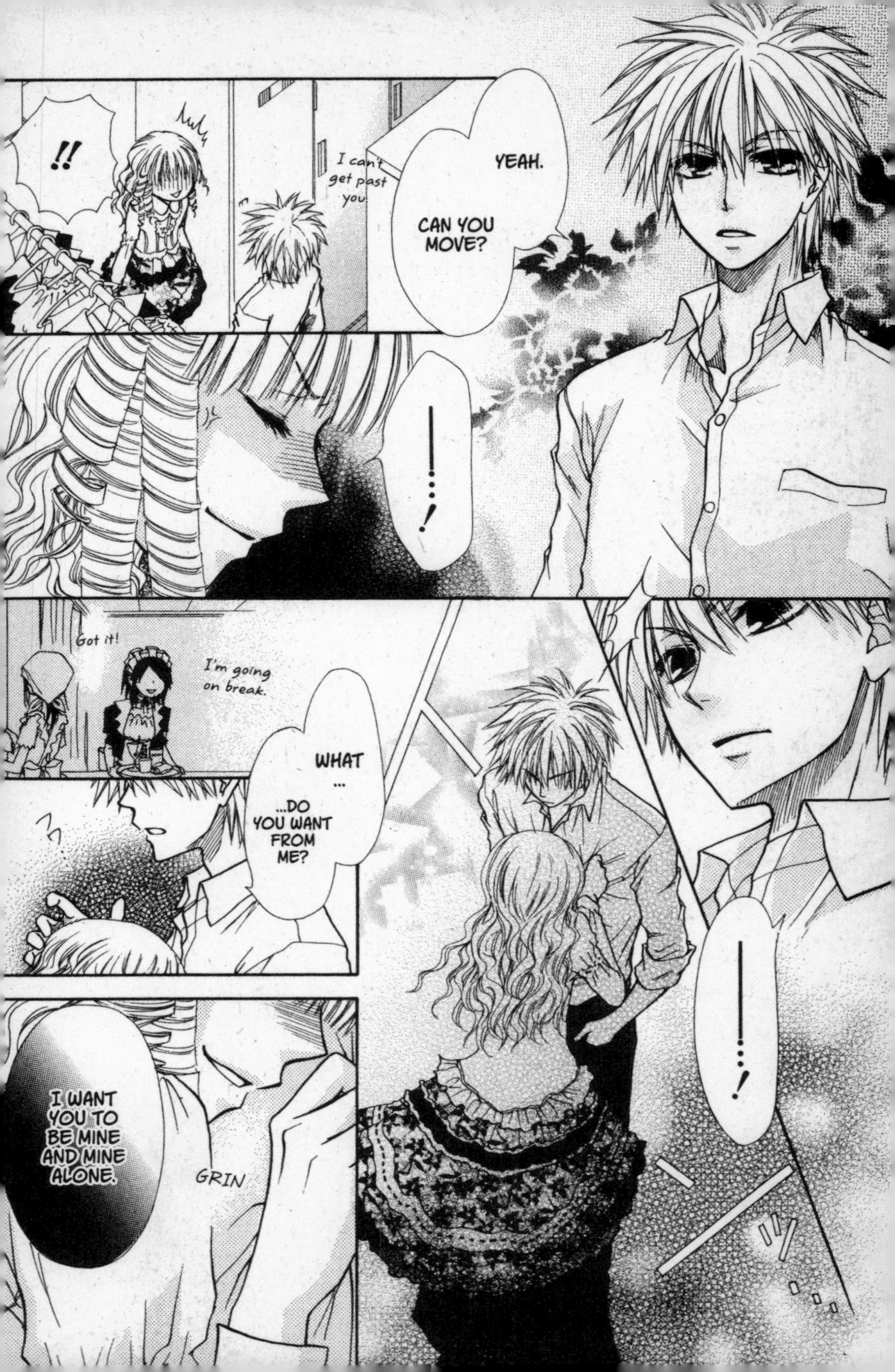

YEAH.
CAN YOU MOVE?
I can't get past you.
!!
...!
...!
I'm going on break.
Got it!
WHAT ...
...DO YOU WANT FROM ME?
I WANT YOU TO BE MINE AND MINE ALONE.
GRIN

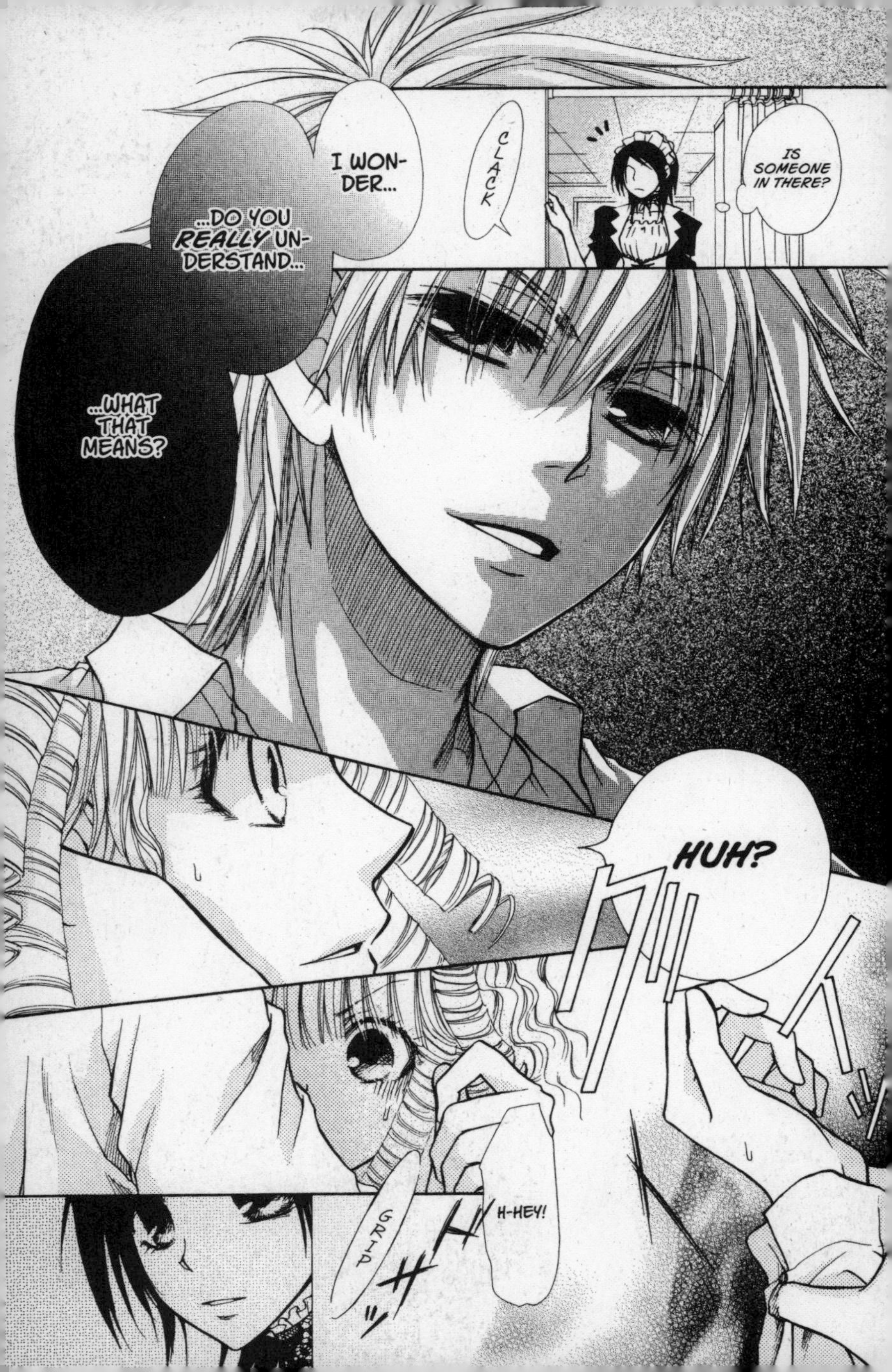
IS SOMEONE IN THERE?
CLACK
I WON-DER...
...DO YOU REALLY UN-DERSTAND...
...WHAT THAT MEANS?
HUH?
H-HEY!
GRIP

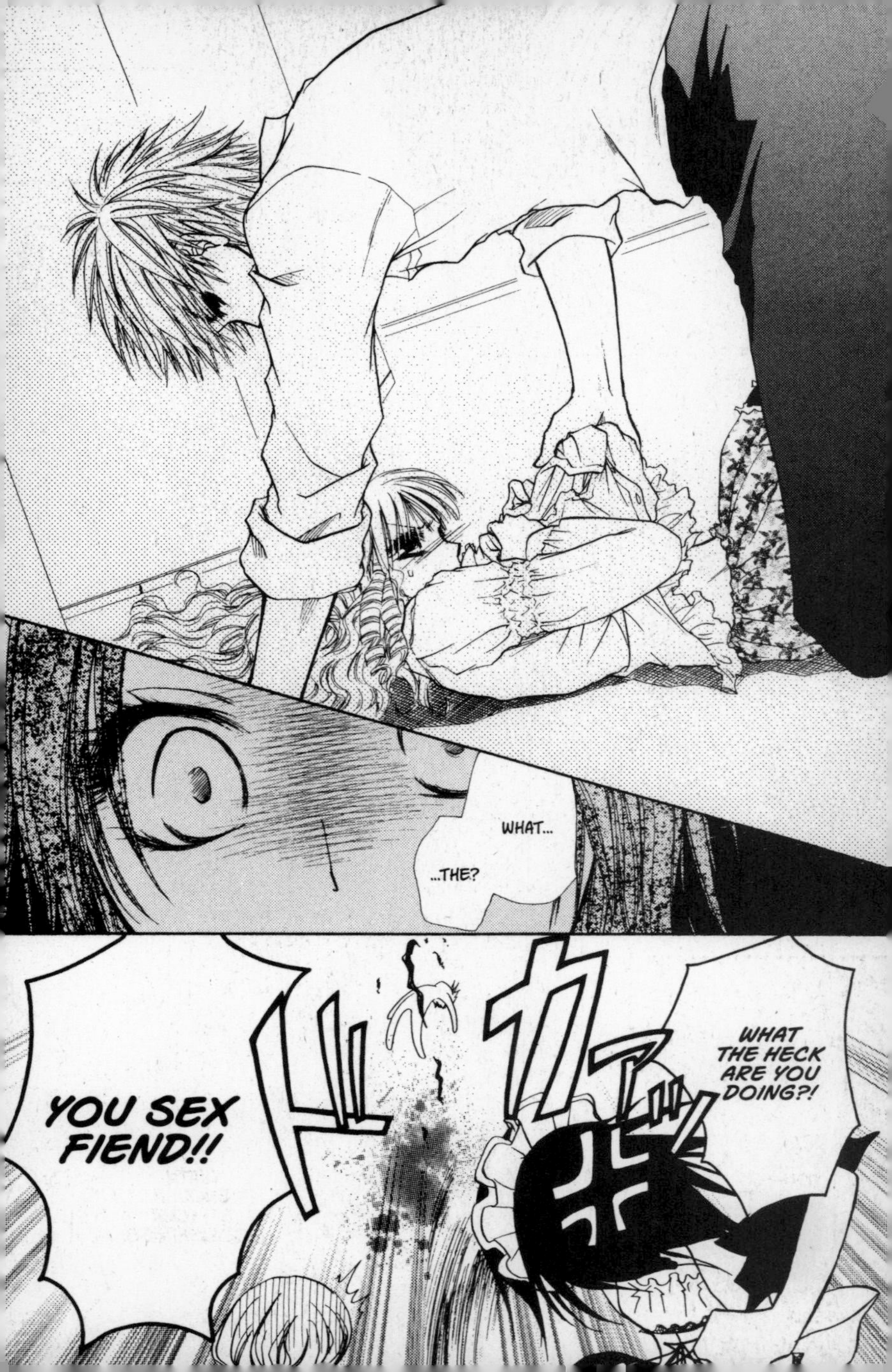
WHAT...
...THE?
WHAT THE HECK ARE YOU DOING?!
YOU SEX FIEND!!

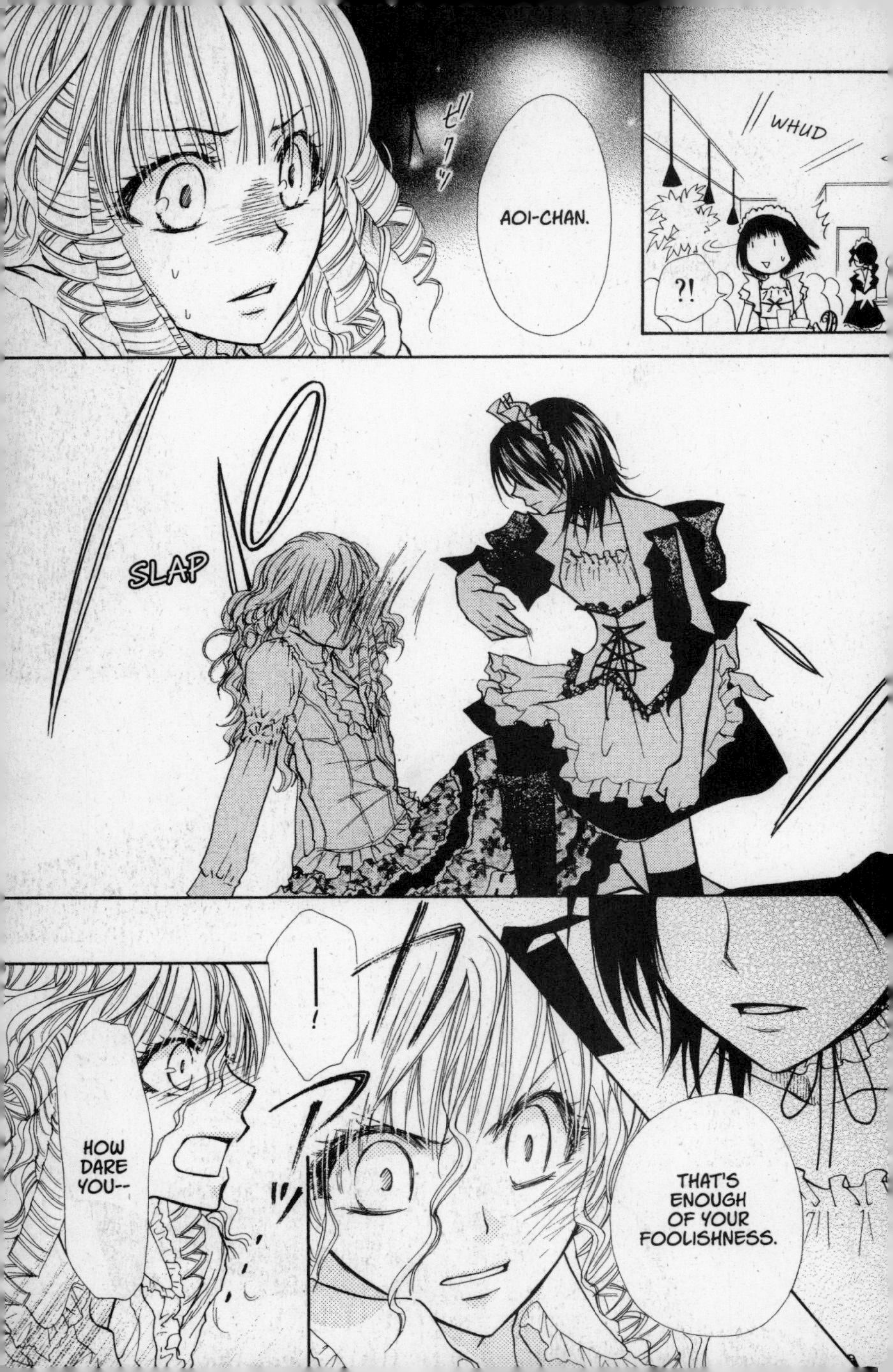
WHUD
?!
ビクッ
AOI-CHAN.
SLAP
THAT'S ENOUGH OF YOUR FOOLISHNESS.
!
HOW DARE YOU--

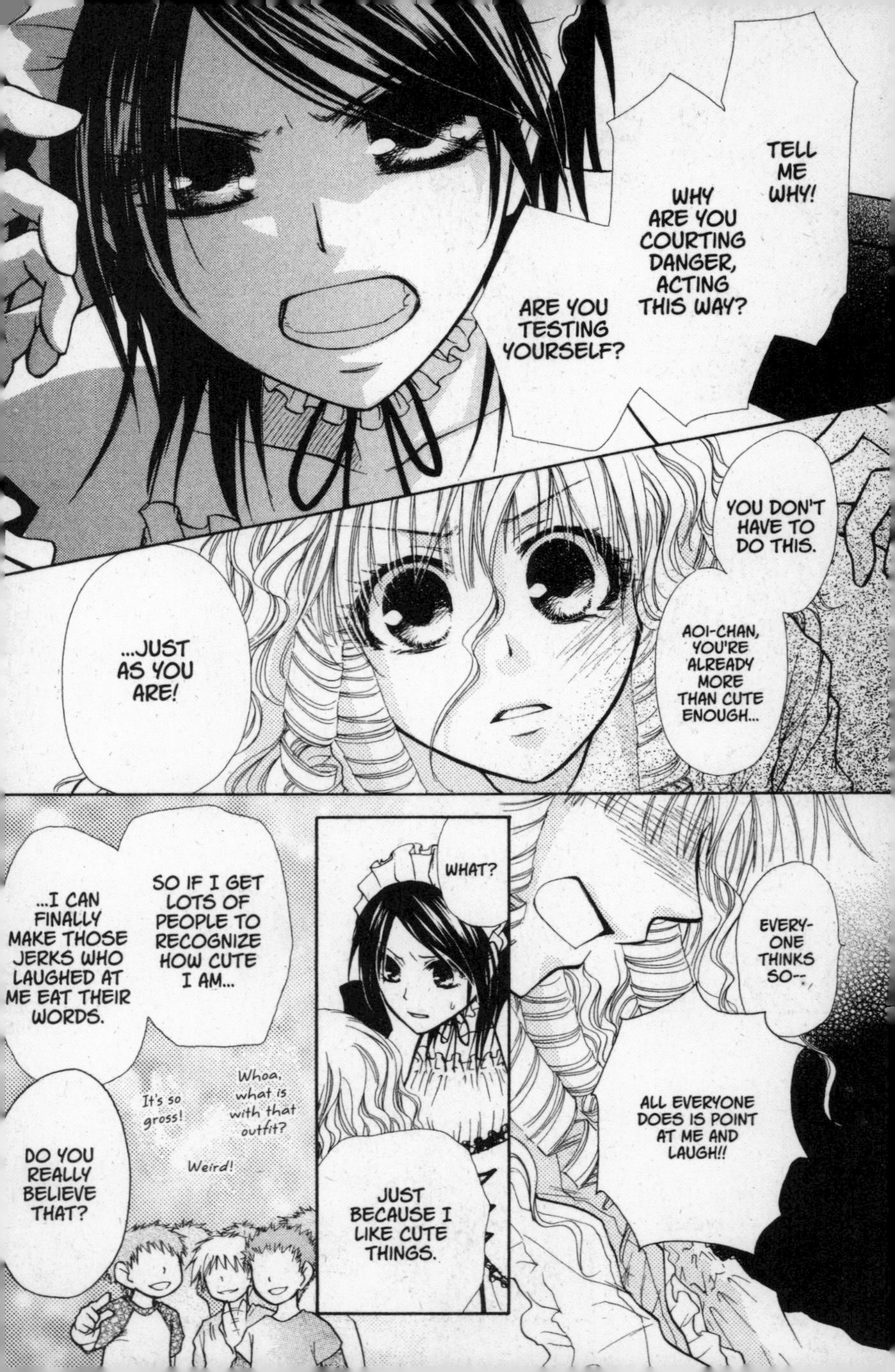
TELL ME WHY!
WHY ARE YOU COURTING DANGER, ACTING THIS WAY?
ARE YOU TESTING YOURSELF?
YOU DON'T HAVE TO DO THIS.
AOI-CHAN, YOU'RE ALREADY MORE THAN CUTE ENOUGH...
...JUST AS YOU ARE!
EVERY-ONE THINKS SO--,
ALL EVERYONE DOES IS POINT AT ME AND LAUGH!!
WHAT?
JUST BECAUSE I LIKE CUTE THINGS.
SO IF I GET LOTS OF PEOPLE TO RECOGNIZE HOW CUTE I AM...
...I CAN FINALLY MAKE THOSE JERKS WHO LAUGHED AT ME EAT THEIR WORDS.
Whoa, what is with that outfit?
It's so gross!
Weird!
DO YOU REALLY BELIEVE THAT?

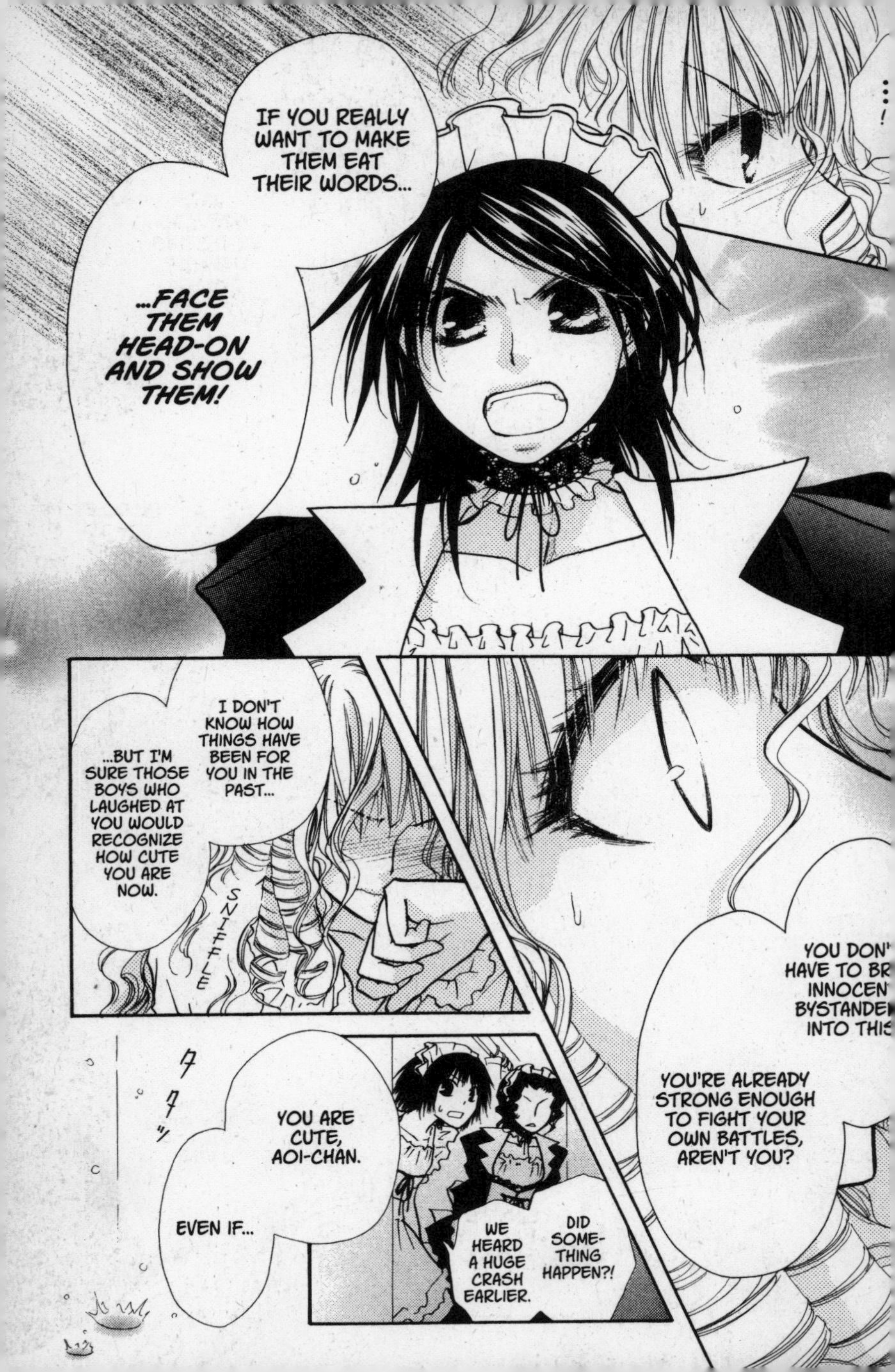
...!
IF YOU REALLY WANT TO MAKE THEM EAT THEIR WORDS...
...FACE THEM HEAD-ON AND SHOW THEM!
YOU DON' HAVE TO BR INNOCEN BYSTANDE INTO THIS
YOU'RE ALREADY STRONG ENOUGH TO FIGHT YOUR OWN BATTLES, AREN'T YOU?
I DON'T KNOW HOW THINGS HAVE BEEN FOR YOU IN THE PAST...
...BUT I'M SURE THOSE BOYS WHO LAUGHED AT YOU WOULD RECOGNIZE HOW CUTE YOU ARE NOW.
SNIFFLE
DID SOME-THING HAPPEN?!
WE HEARD A HUGE CRASH EARLIER.
タタッ
YOU ARE CUTE, AOI-CHAN.
EVEN IF...

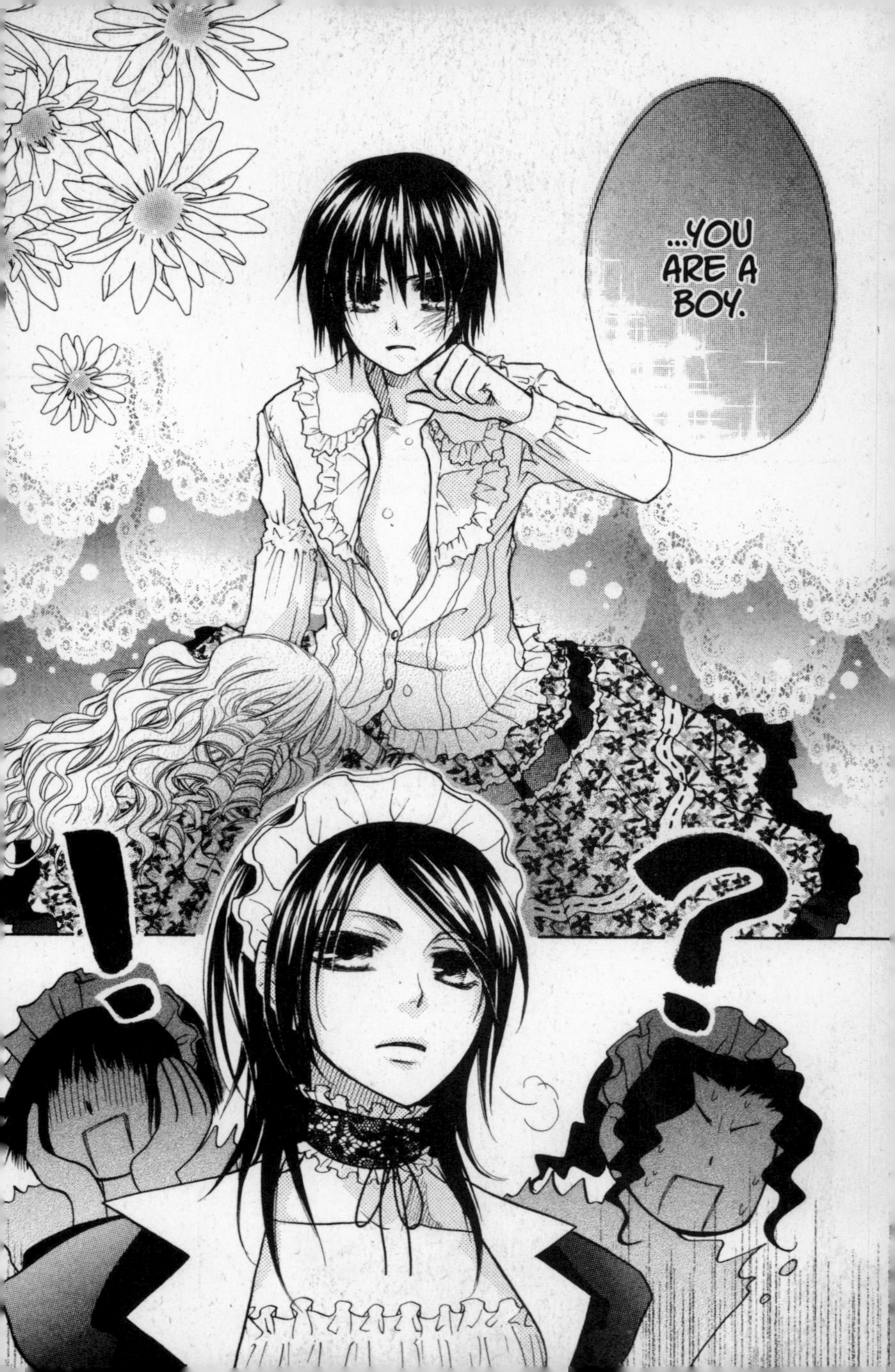
...YOU ARE A BOY.

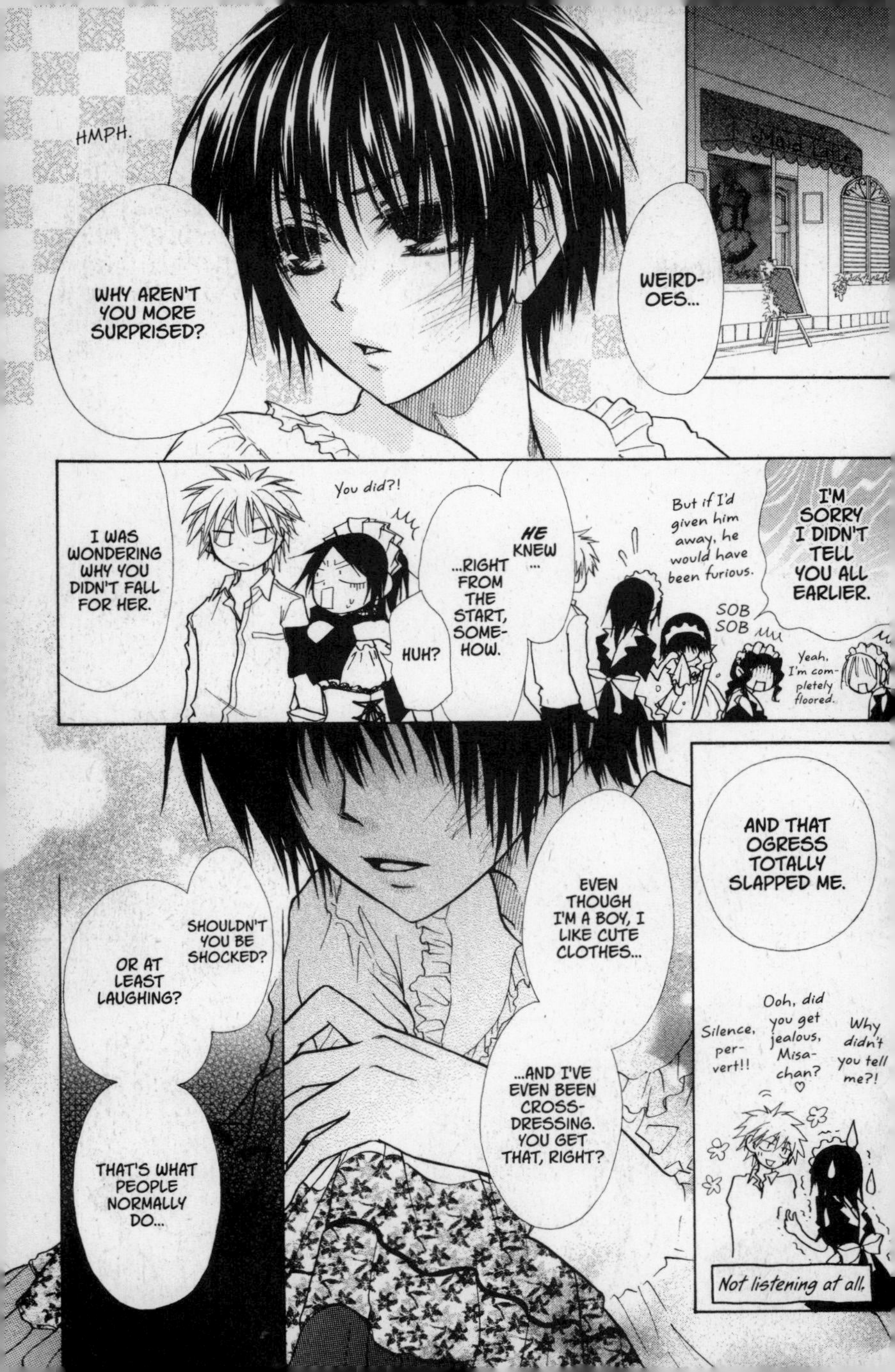
WEIRD-OES...
HMPH.
WHY AREN'T YOU MORE SURPRISED?
I'M SORRY I DIDN'T TELL YOU ALL EARLIER.
Yeah, I'm completely floored.
But if I'd given him away, he would have been furious.
SOB SOB
HE KNEW...
...RIGHT FROM THE START, SOMEHOW.
You did?!
HUH?
I WAS WONDERING WHY YOU DIDN'T FALL FOR HER.
AND THAT OGRESS TOTALLY SLAPPED ME.
Why didn't you tell me?!
Ooh, did you get jealous, Misa-chan?
Silence, pervert!!
Not listening at all.
EVEN THOUGH I'M A BOY, I LIKE CUTE CLOTHES...
...AND I'VE EVEN BEEN CROSS-DRESSING. YOU GET THAT, RIGHT?
SHOULDN'T YOU BE SHOCKED?
OR AT LEAST LAUGHING?
THAT'S WHAT PEOPLE NORMALLY DO...

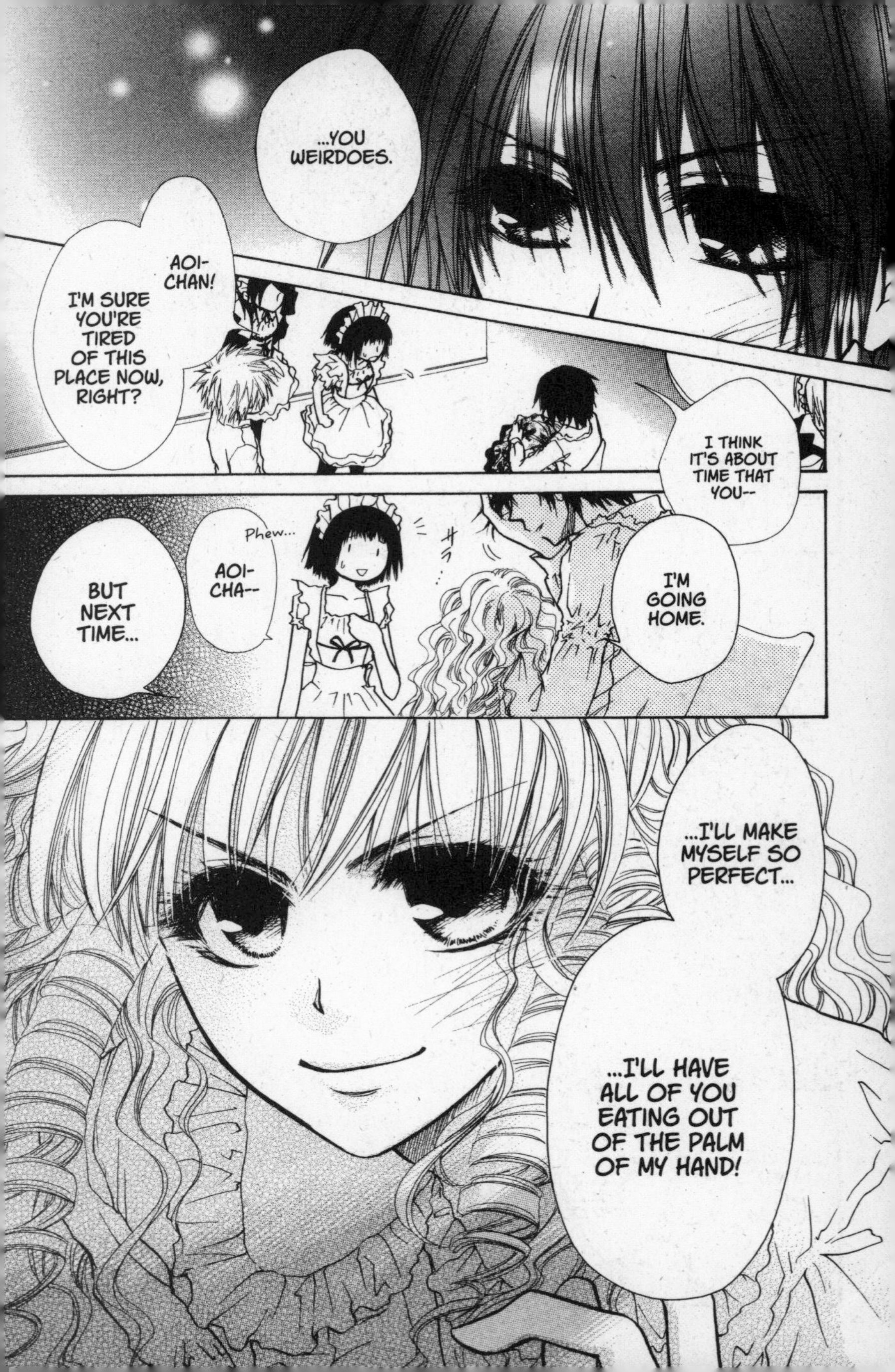
...YOU WEIRDOES.
AOI-CHAN! I'M SURE YOU'RE TIRED OF THIS PLACE NOW, RIGHT?
I THINK IT'S ABOUT TIME THAT YOU--
I'M GOING HOME.
AOI-CHA--
Phew...
BUT NEXT TIME...
...I'LL MAKE MYSELF SO PERFECT...
...I'LL HAVE ALL OF YOU EATING OUT OF THE PALM OF MY HAND!

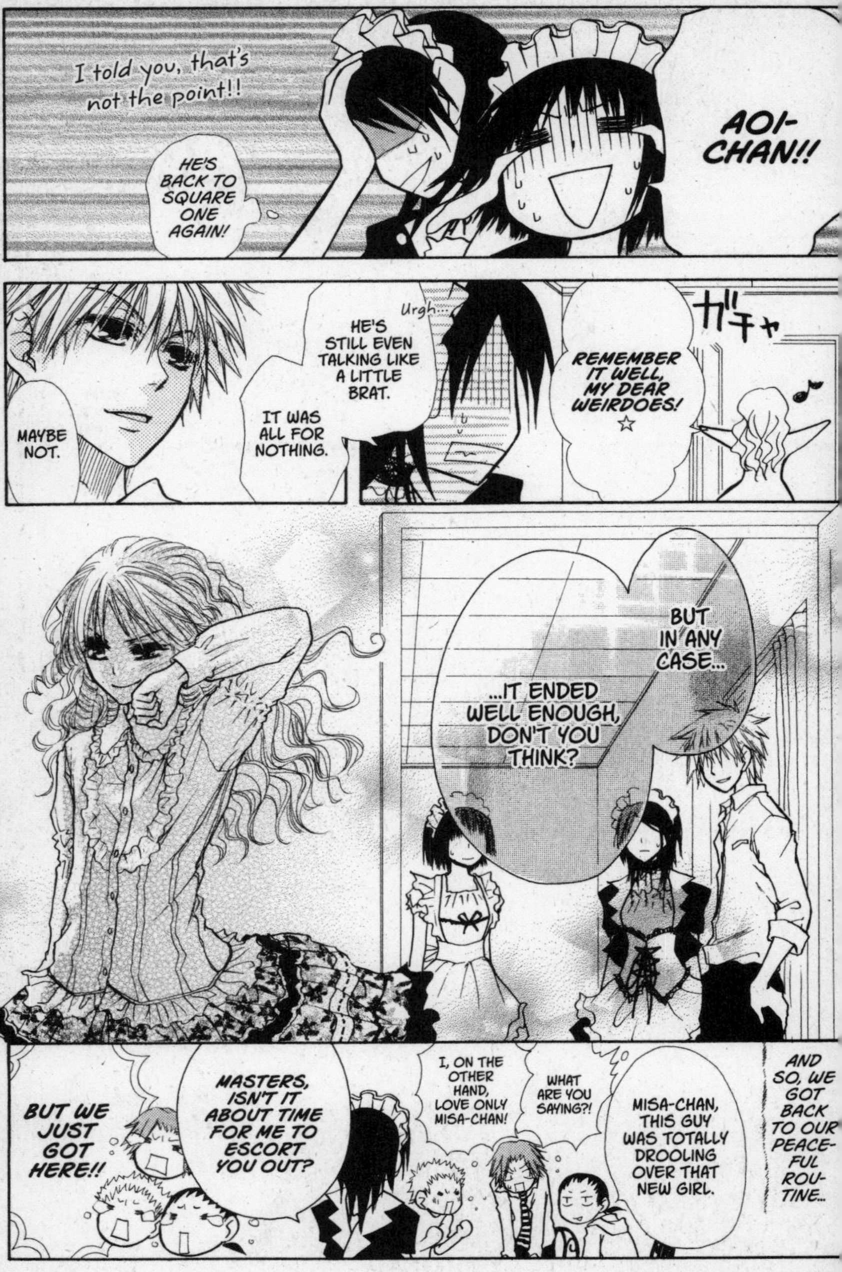
AOI-CHAN!!
HE'S BACK TO SQUARE ONE AGAIN!
I told you, that's not the point!!
ガチャ
REMEMBER IT WELL, MY DEAR WEIRDOES! ☆
Urgh...
HE'S STILL EVEN TALKING LIKE A LITTLE BRAT.
IT WAS ALL FOR NOTHING.
MAYBE NOT.
BUT IN ANY CASE...
...IT ENDED WELL ENOUGH, DON'T YOU THINK?
AND SO, WE GOT BACK TO OUR PEACE-FUL ROU-TINE...
MISA-CHAN, THIS GUY WAS TOTALLY DROOLING OVER THAT NEW GIRL.
WHAT ARE YOU SAYING?!
I, ON THE OTHER HAND, LOVE ONLY MISA-CHAN!
MASTERS, ISN'T IT ABOUT TIME FOR ME TO ESCORT YOU OUT?
BUT WE JUST GOT HERE!!

re's a little something I dug out from the time en they first announced that Maid Sama! would be a rialized manga rather than a one-shot story. After I und them, I stared at them for a long time thinking, sui's really been the same since the beginning." I und myself getting all swept up in the memories.

Excavated!

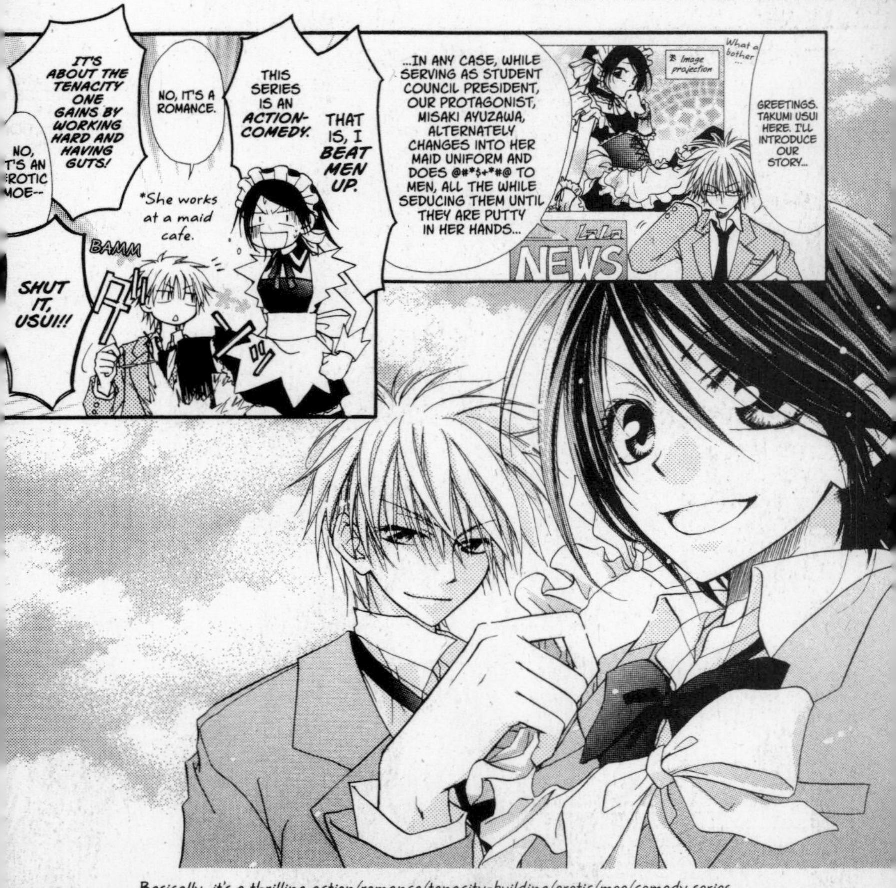
What a bother...
GREETINGS. TAKUMI USUI HERE. I'LL INTRODUCE OUR STORY...
Image projection
...IN ANY CASE, WHILE SERVING AS STUDENT COUNCIL PRESIDENT, OUR PROTAGONIST, MISAKI AYUZAWA, ALTERNATELY CHANGES INTO HER MAID UNIFORM AND DOES @#*$+*#@ TO MEN, ALL THE WHILE SEDUCING THEM UNTIL THEY ARE PUTTY IN HER HANDS...
LaLa NEWS
THIS SERIES IS AN ACTION-COMEDY.
THAT IS, I BEAT MEN UP.
NO, IT'S A ROMANCE.
IT'S ABOUT THE TENACITY ONE GAINS BY WORKING HARD AND HAVING GUTS!
NO, T'S AN EROTIC MOE--
*She works at a maid cafe.
BAMM
SHUT IT, USUI!!

Basically, it's a thrilling action/romance/tenacity-building/erotic/moe/comedy series.

14th Course

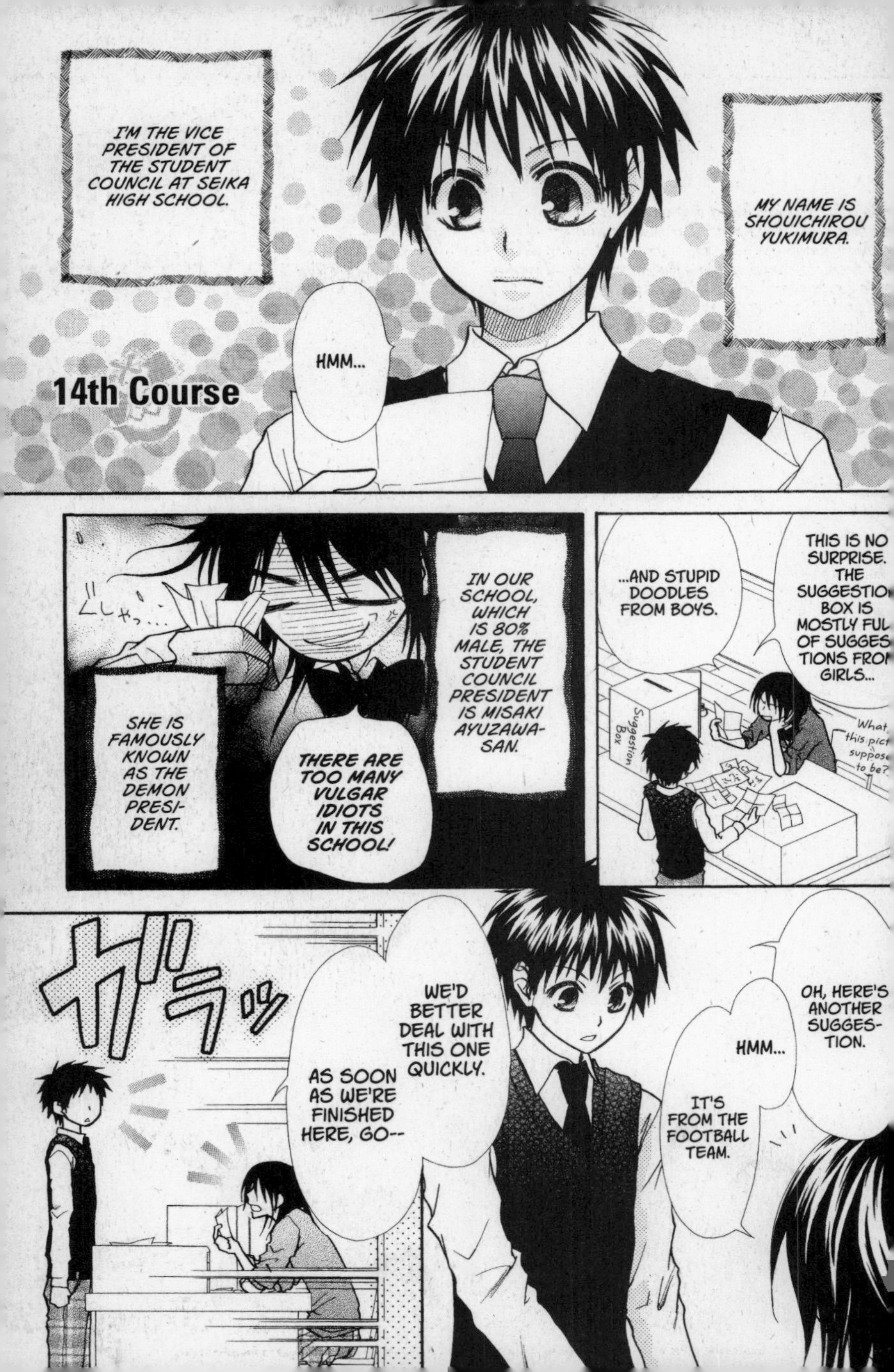

MY NAME IS SHOUICHIROU YUKIMURA.
I'M THE VICE PRESIDENT OF THE STUDENT COUNCIL AT SEIKA HIGH SCHOOL.
HMM...
THIS IS NO SURPRISE. THE SUGGESTIO BOX IS MOSTLY FUL OF SUGGESTIONS FRO GIRLS...
...AND STUPID DOODLES FROM BOYS.
What this pict suppose to be?
Suggestion Box
IN OUR SCHOOL, WHICH IS 80% MALE, THE STUDENT COUNCIL PRESIDENT IS MISAKI AYUZAWA-SAN.
ぐしゃっ...
THERE ARE TOO MANY VULGAR IDIOTS IN THIS SCHOOL!
SHE IS FAMOUSLY KNOWN AS THE DEMON PRESIDENT.
OH, HERE'S ANOTHER SUGGESTION.
HMM...
IT'S FROM THE FOOTBALL TEAM.
WE'D BETTER DEAL WITH THIS ONE QUICKLY.
AS SOON AS WE'RE FINISHED HERE, GO--
ガラッ

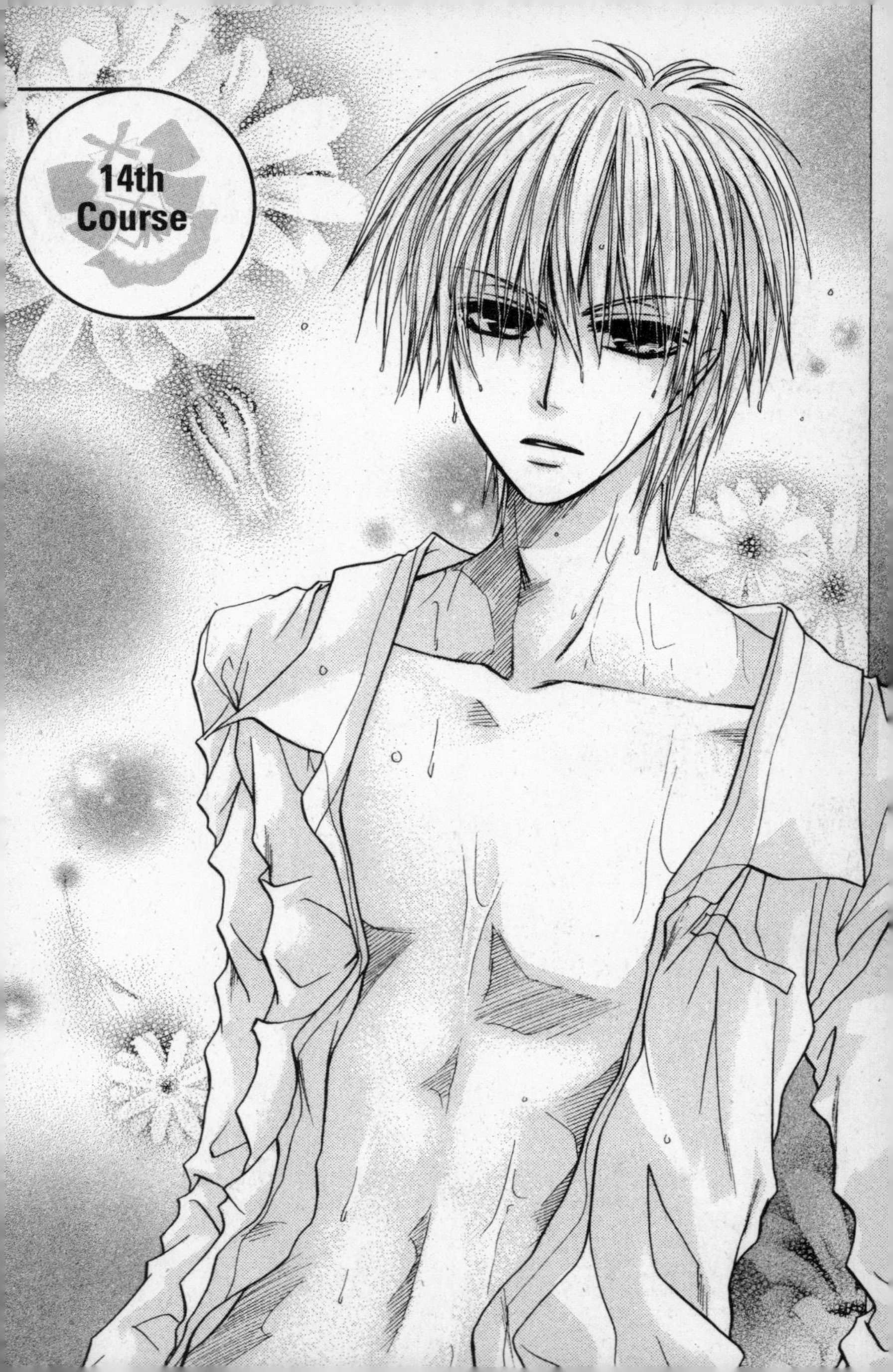
14th
Course

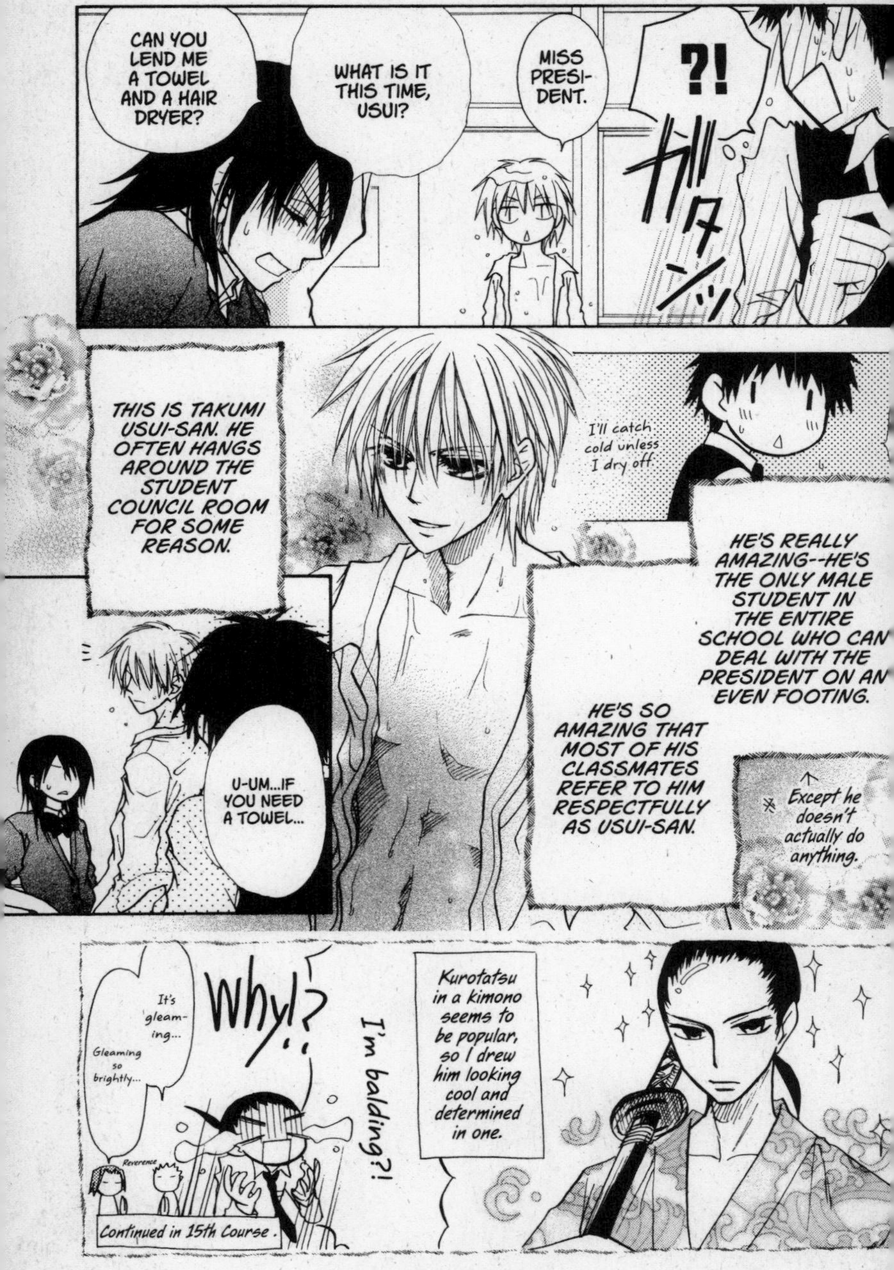
?!
ガタンッ
MISS PRESI-DENT.
WHAT IS IT THIS TIME, USUI?
CAN YOU LEND ME A TOWEL AND A HAIR DRYER?
I'll catch cold unless I dry off.
THIS IS TAKUMI USUI-SAN. HE OFTEN HANGS AROUND THE STUDENT COUNCIL ROOM FOR SOME REASON.
HE'S REALLY AMAZING--HE'S THE ONLY MALE STUDENT IN THE ENTIRE SCHOOL WHO CAN DEAL WITH THE PRESIDENT ON AN EVEN FOOTING.
HE'S SO AMAZING THAT MOST OF HIS CLASSMATES REFER TO HIM RESPECTFULLY AS USUI-SAN.
※ Except he doesn't actually do anything.
U-UM...IF YOU NEED A TOWEL...
Kurotatsu in a kimono seems to be popular, so I drew him looking cool and determined in one.
I'm balding?!
Why!?
It's gleam-ing...
Gleaming so brightly...
Reverence
Continued in 15th Course.

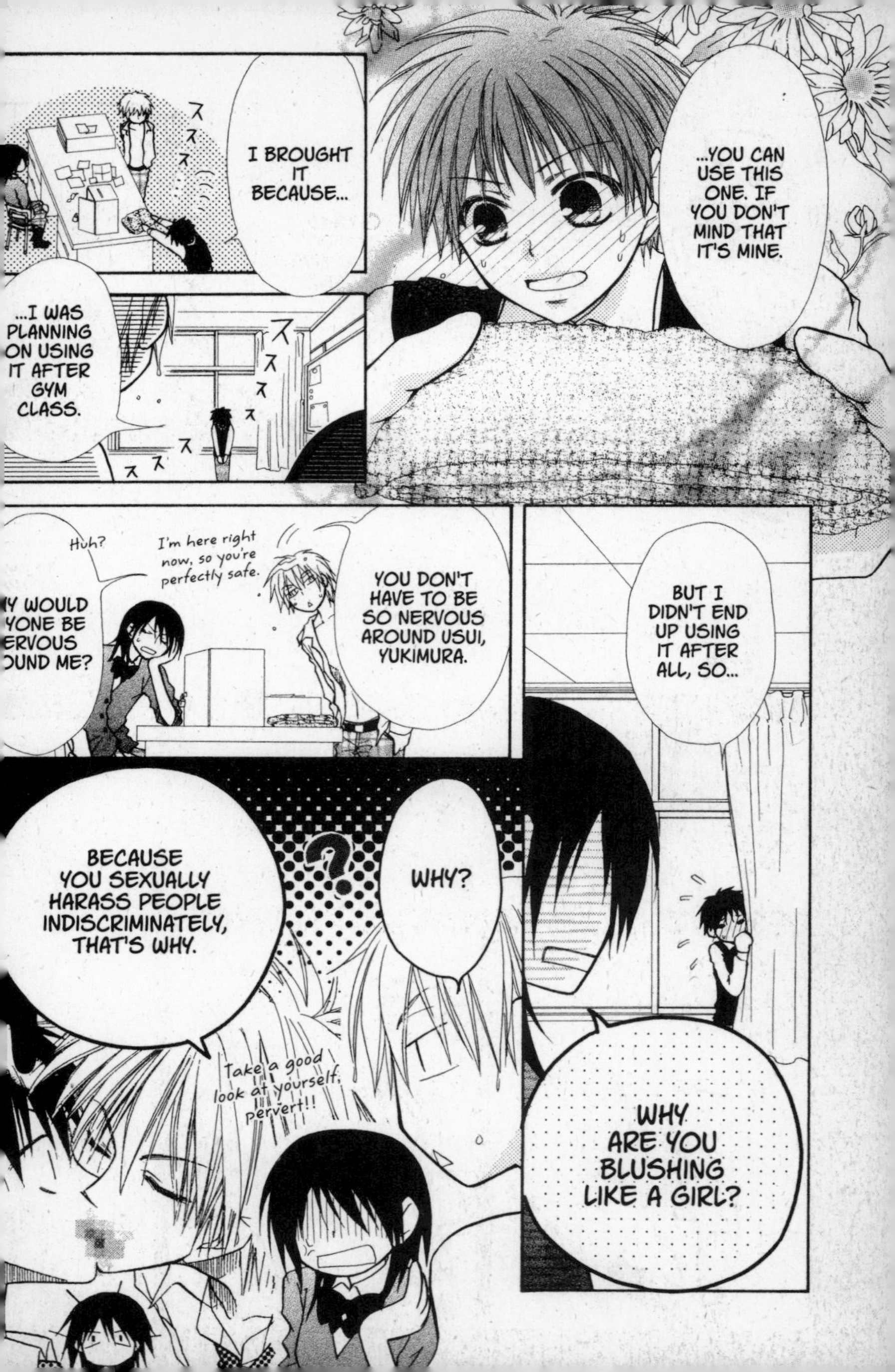
...YOU CAN USE THIS ONE. IF YOU DON'T MIND THAT IT'S MINE.
I BROUGHT IT BECAUSE...
ススス
...I WAS PLANNING ON USING IT AFTER GYM CLASS.
スススススス
BUT I DIDN'T END UP USING IT AFTER ALL, SO...
WHY ARE YOU BLUSHING LIKE A GIRL?
YOU DON'T HAVE TO BE SO NERVOUS AROUND USUI, YUKIMURA.
I'm here right now, so you're perfectly safe.
Huh?
Y WOULD YONE BE ERVOUS OUND ME?
WHY?
BECAUSE YOU SEXUALLY HARASS PEOPLE INDISCRIMINATELY, THAT'S WHY.
Take a good look at yourself, pervert!!

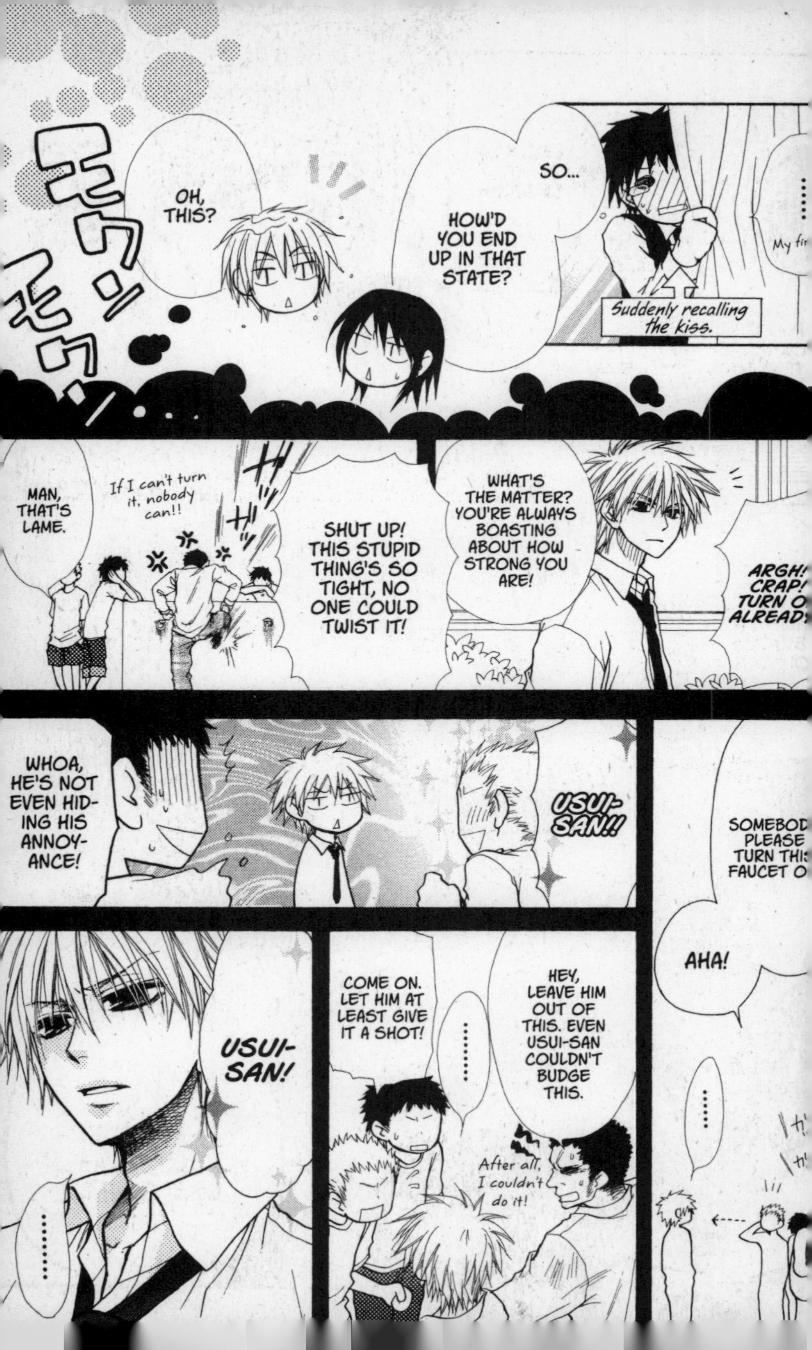
......
SO...
HOW'D YOU END UP IN THAT STATE?
Suddenly recalling the kiss.
OH, THIS?
ARGH! CRAP! TURN O ALREAD
WHAT'S THE MATTER? YOU'RE ALWAYS BOASTING ABOUT HOW STRONG YOU ARE!
SHUT UP! THIS STUPID THING'S SO TIGHT, NO ONE COULD TWIST IT!
If I can't turn it, nobody can!!
MAN, THAT'S LAME.
SOMEBOD PLEASE TURN THIS FAUCET O
AHA!
......
USUI-SAN!!
WHOA, HE'S NOT EVEN HIDING HIS ANNOYANCE!
HEY, LEAVE HIM OUT OF THIS. EVEN USUI-SAN COULDN'T BUDGE THIS.
After all, I couldn't do it!
COME ON. LET HIM AT LEAST GIVE IT A SHOT!
......
USUI-SAN!
......

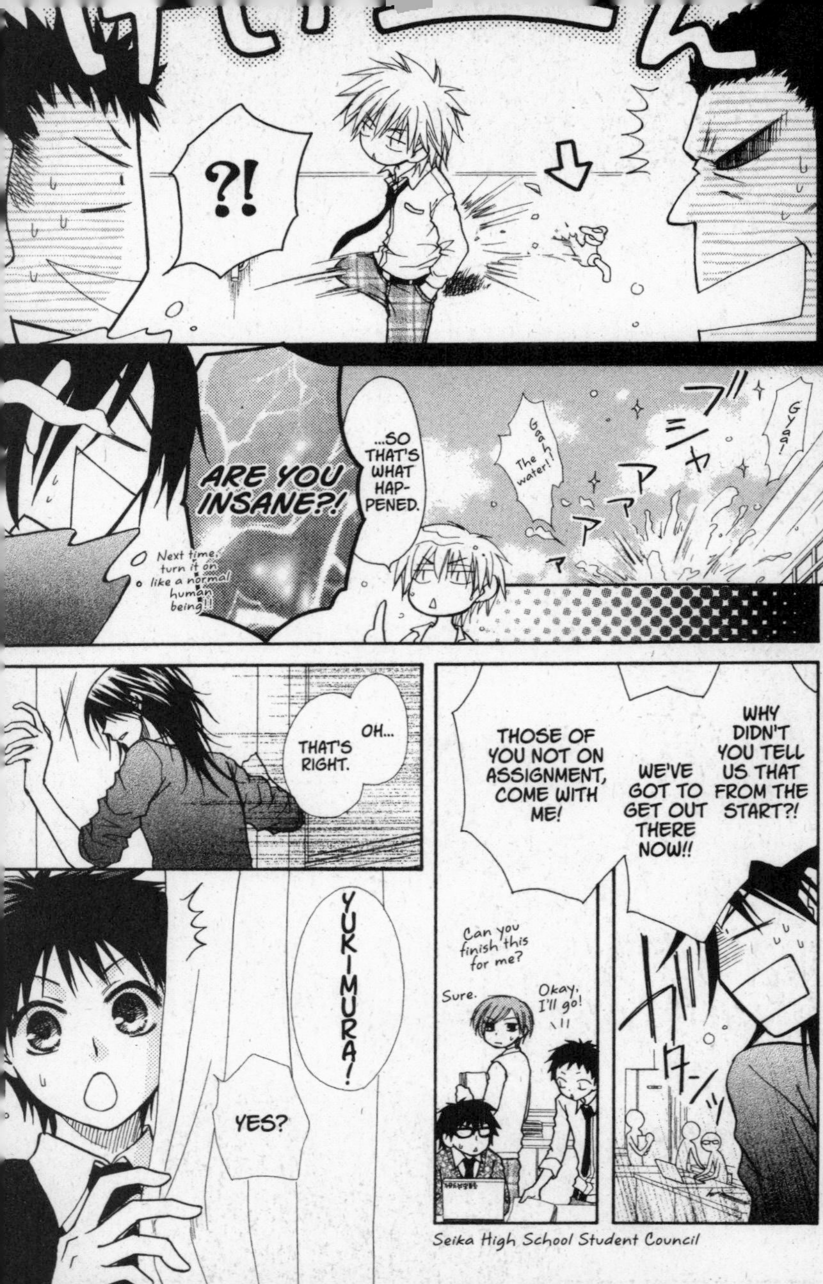

?!
Gyaa!
ブシャアアアア
Gaah The water!!
...SO THAT'S WHAT HAP-PENED.
ARE YOU INSANE?!
Next time, turn it on like a normal human being!!
WHY DIDN'T YOU TELL US THAT FROM THE START?!
WE'VE GOT TO GET OUT THERE NOW!!
THOSE OF YOU NOT ON ASSIGNMENT, COME WITH ME!
ガターンッ
Okay, I'll go!
Sure.
Can you finish this for me?
OH... THAT'S RIGHT.
YUKIMURA!
YES?

Seika High School Student Council

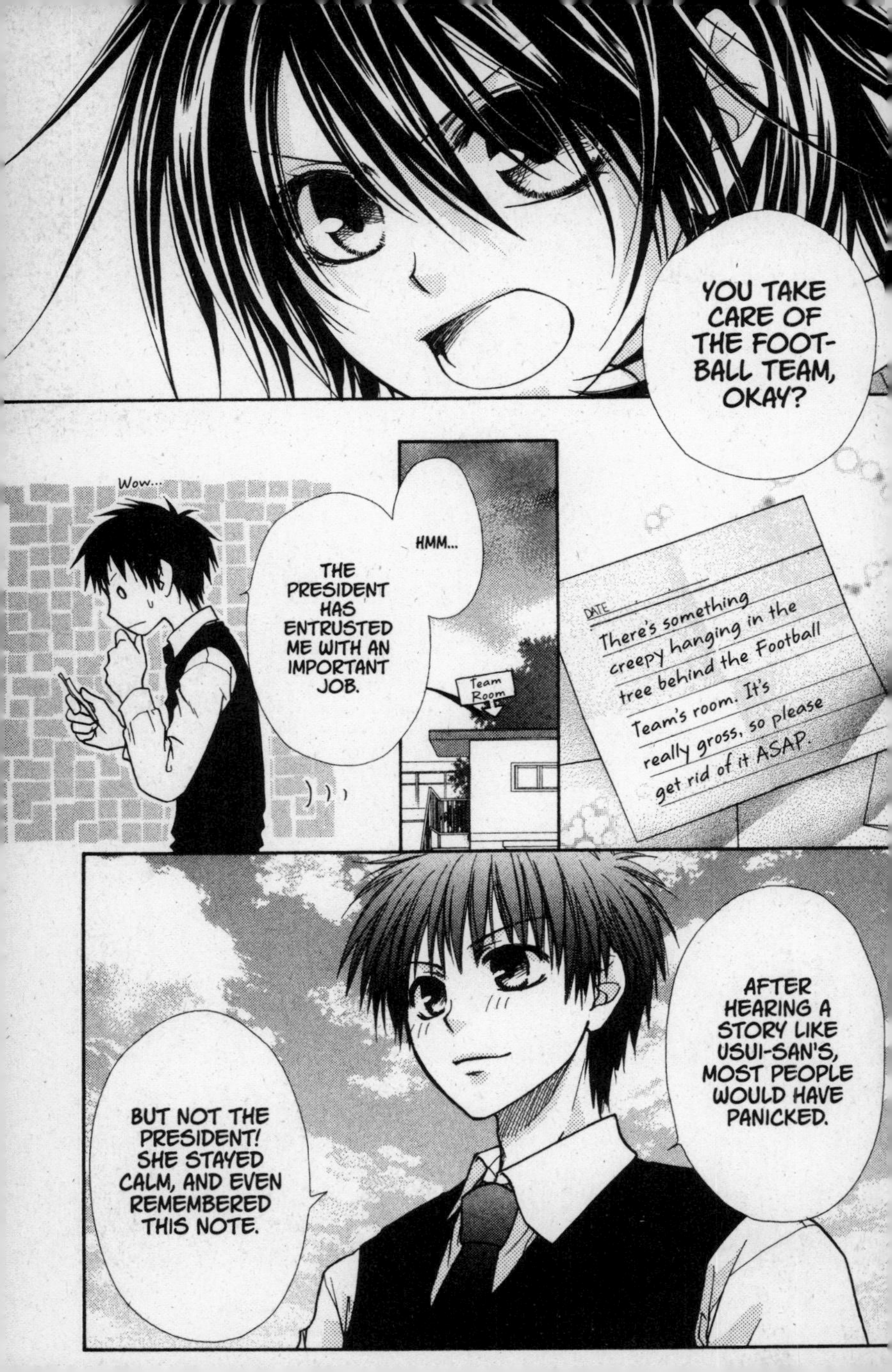
YOU TAKE CARE OF THE FOOT-BALL TEAM, OKAY?
DATE
There's something creepy hanging in the tree behind the Football Team's room. It's really gross, so please get rid of it ASAP.
Team Room
HMM...
THE PRESIDENT HAS ENTRUSTED ME WITH AN IMPORTANT JOB.
Wow...
AFTER HEARING A STORY LIKE USUI-SAN'S, MOST PEOPLE WOULD HAVE PANICKED.
BUT NOT THE PRESIDENT! SHE STAYED CALM, AND EVEN REMEMBERED THIS NOTE.

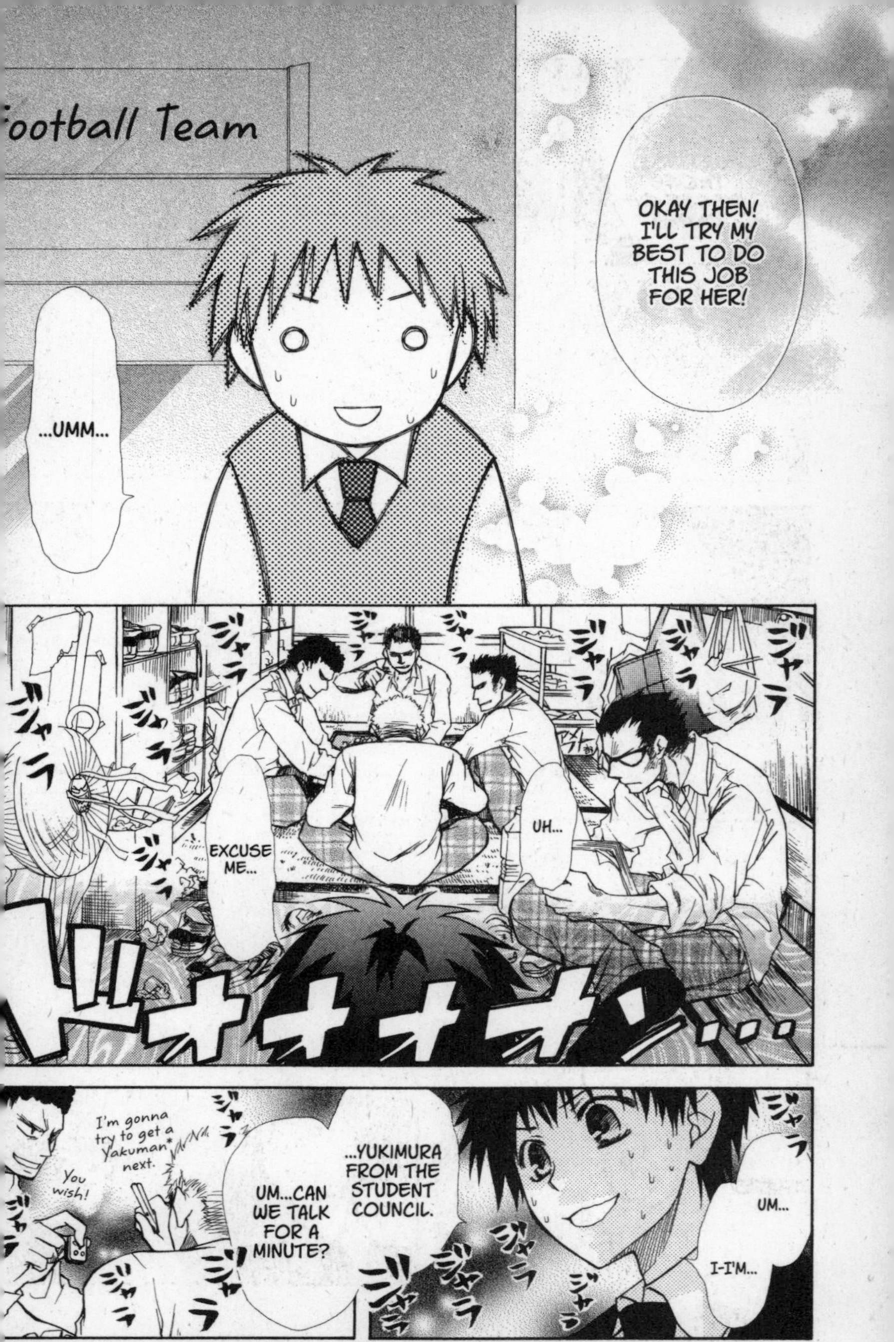
ootball Team
OKAY THEN! I'LL TRY MY BEST TO DO THIS JOB FOR HER!
...UMM...
ジャラ
UH...
EXCUSE ME...
UM...
I-I'M...
...YUKIMURA FROM THE STUDENT COUNCIL.
UM...CAN WE TALK FOR A MINUTE?
I'm gonna try to get a Yakuman* next.
You wish!

TE: A "yakuman" is a win worth 32,000 points in the game of Mahjong.

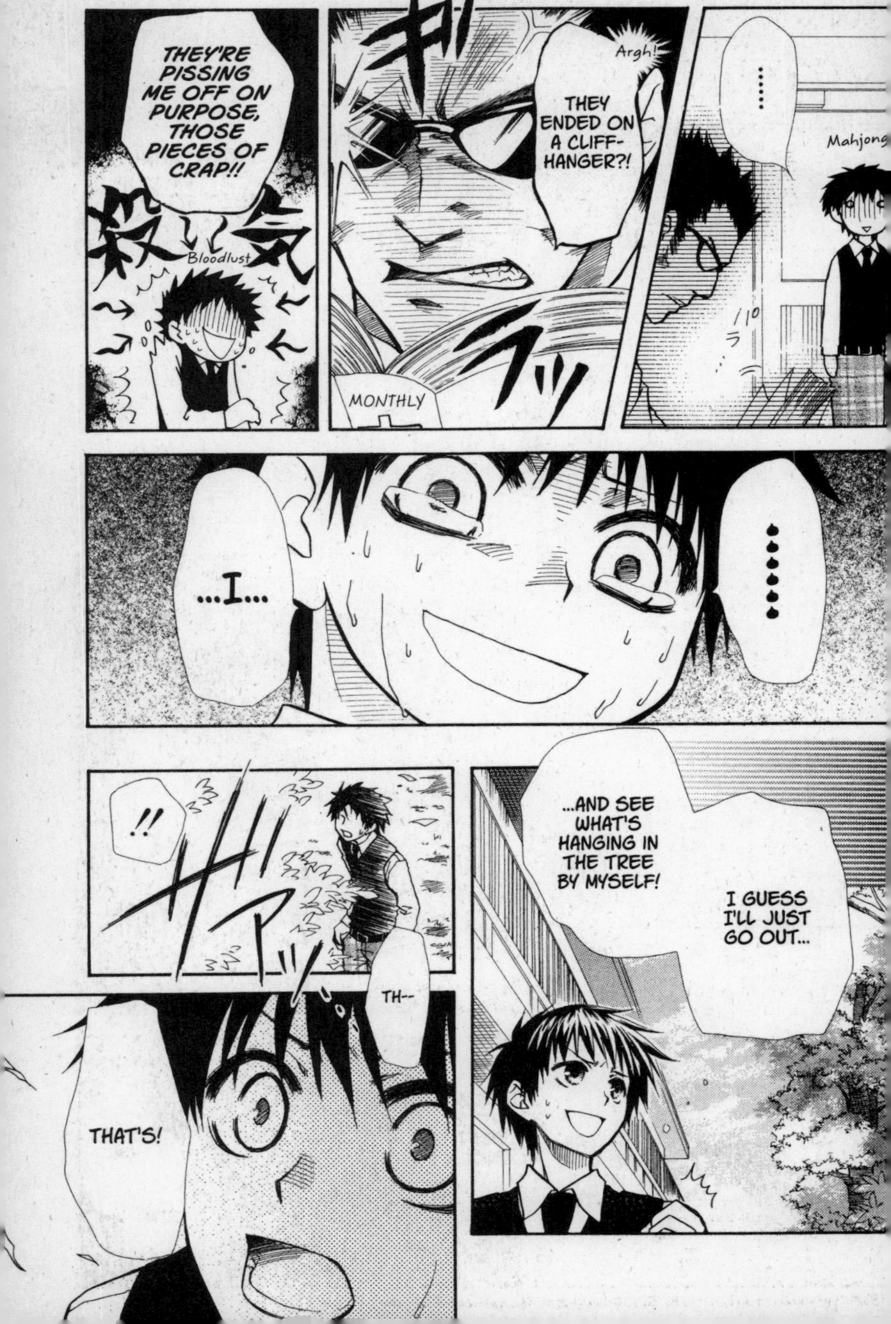
......
Mahjong
Argh!
THEY ENDED ON A CLIFF-HANGER?!
MONTHLY
THEY'RE PISSING ME OFF ON PURPOSE, THOSE PIECES OF CRAP!!
Bloodlust
......
...I...
I GUESS I'LL JUST GO OUT...
...AND SEE WHAT'S HANGING IN THE TREE BY MYSELF!
!!
TH--
THAT'S!

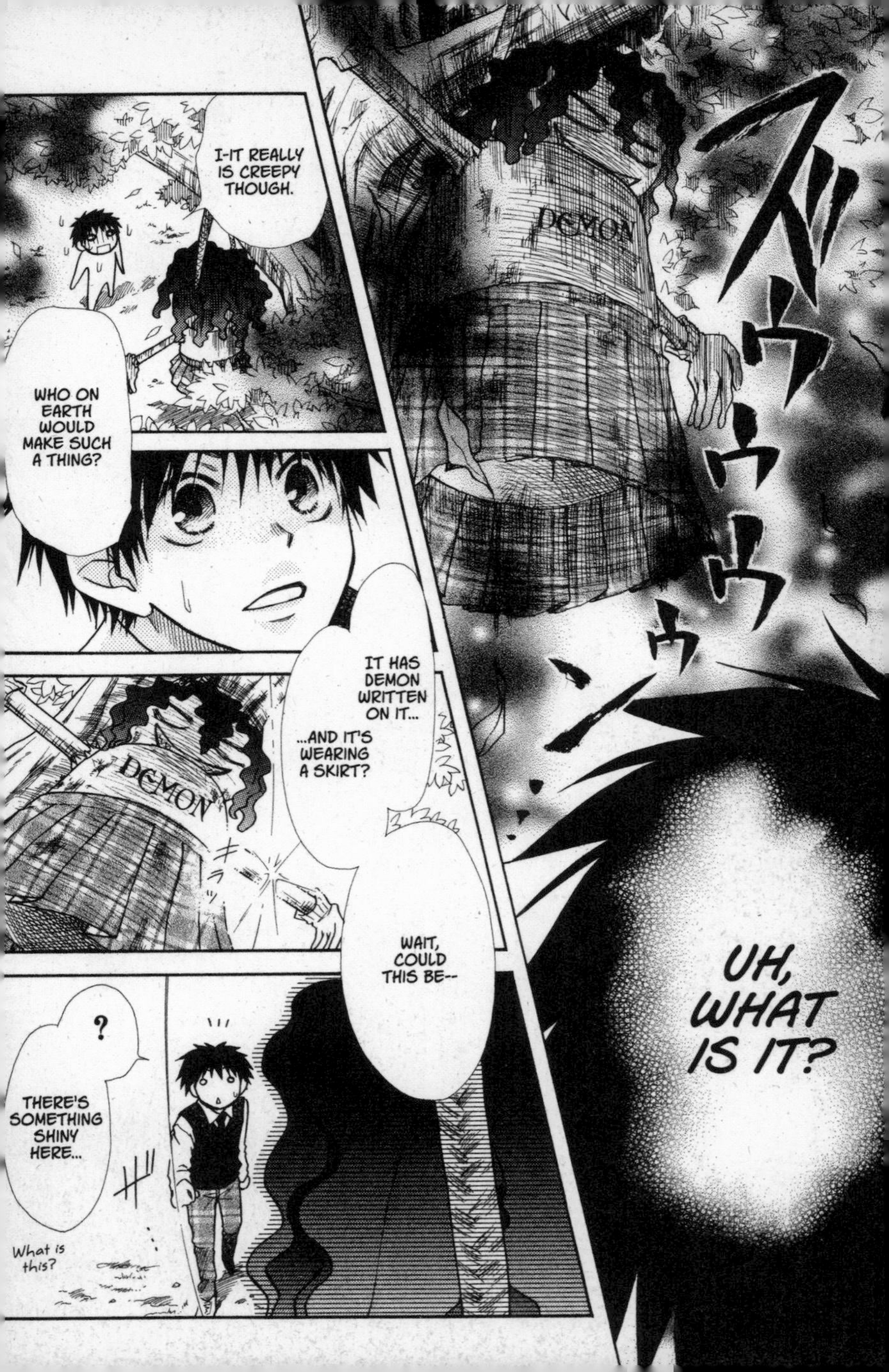
ズリウウウウウ
UH, WHAT IS IT?
I-IT REALLY IS CREEPY THOUGH.
WHO ON EARTH WOULD MAKE SUCH A THING?
DEMON
IT HAS DEMON WRITTEN ON IT...
...AND IT'S WEARING A SKIRT?
DEMON
キラッ
WAIT, COULD THIS BE--
?
THERE'S SOMETHING SHINY HERE...
What is this?

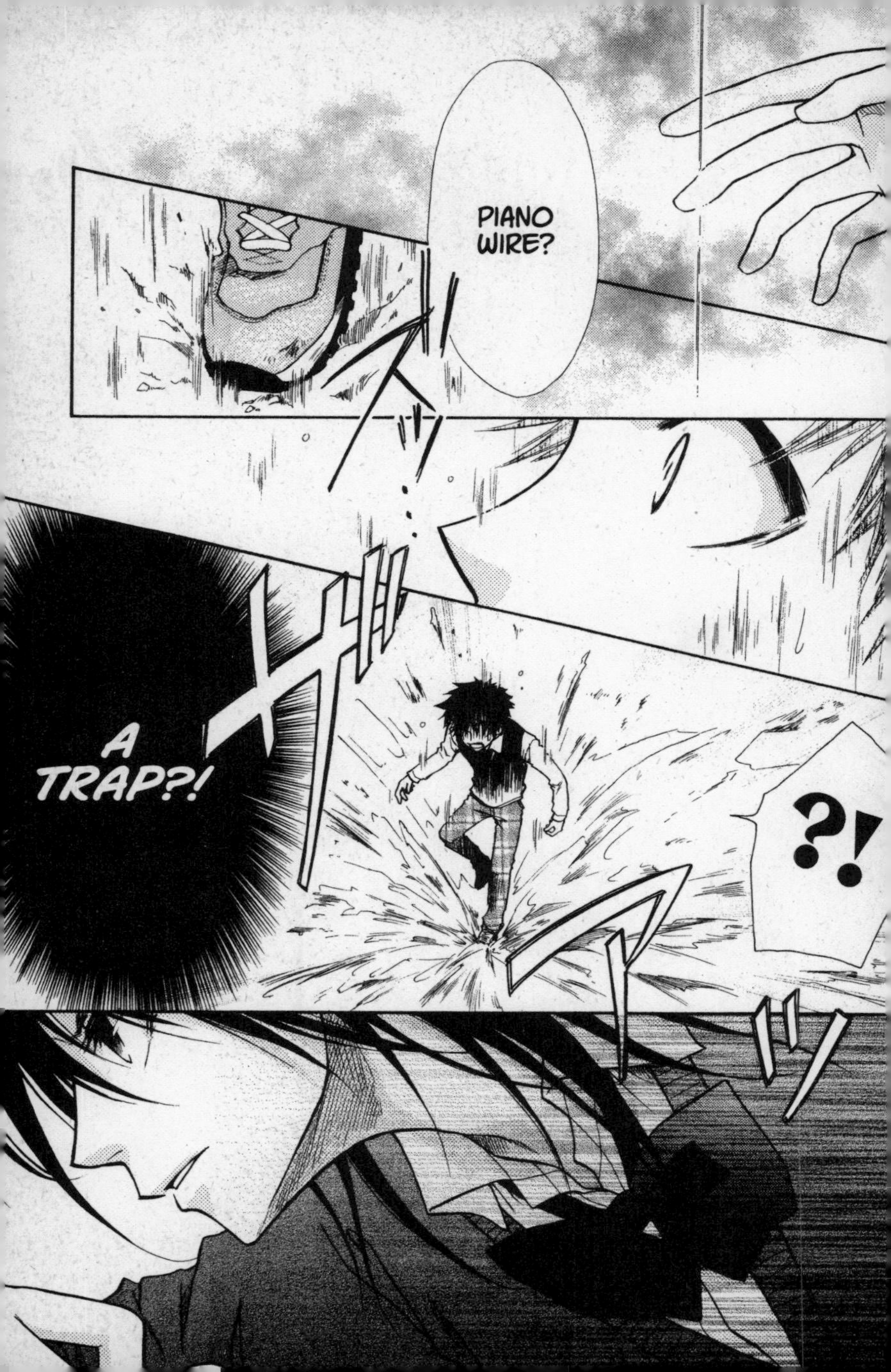
PIANO WIRE?
?!
A TRAP?!

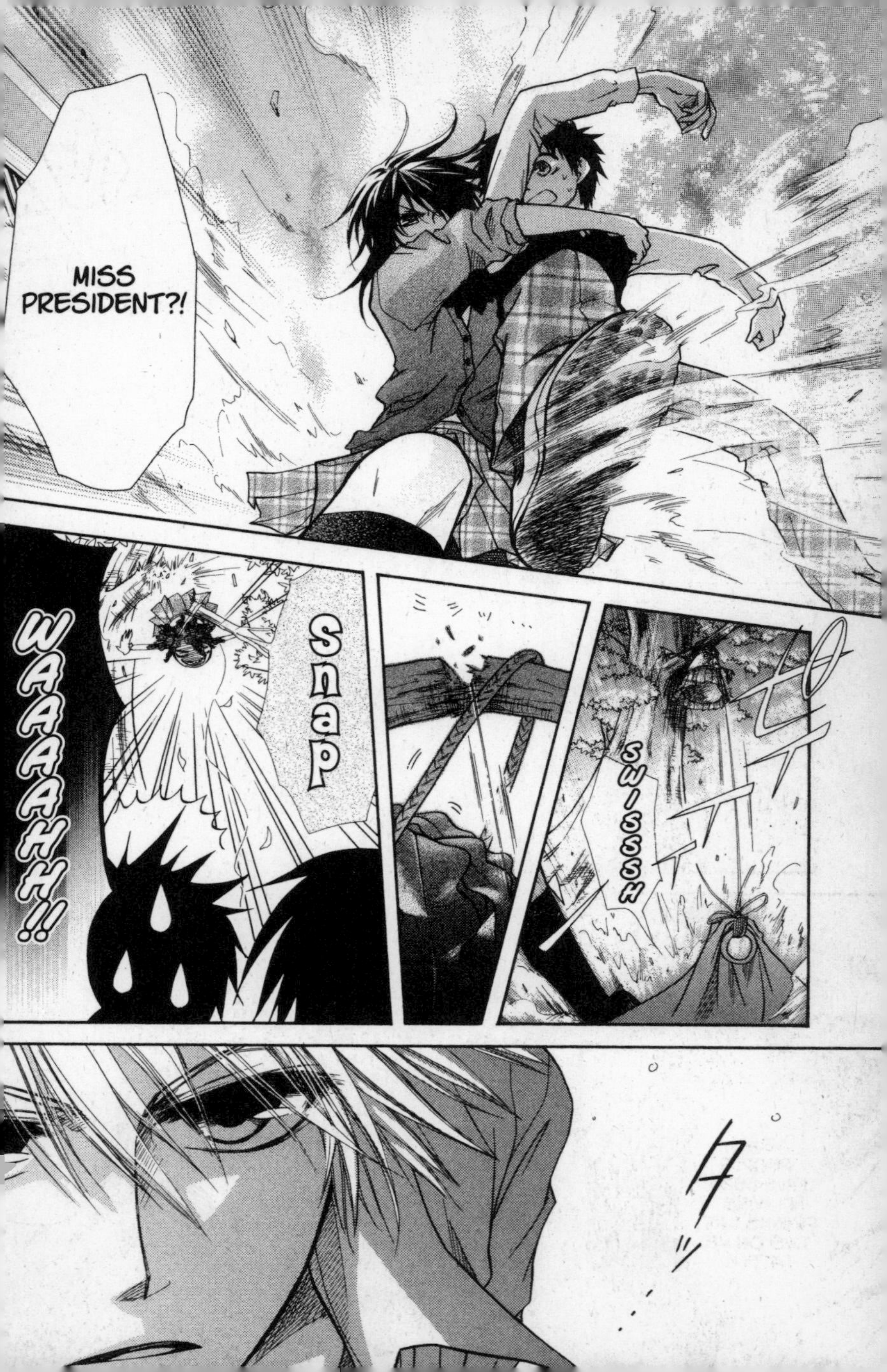
MISS PRESIDENT?!
SWISSSH
snap
WAAAAAAHH!!

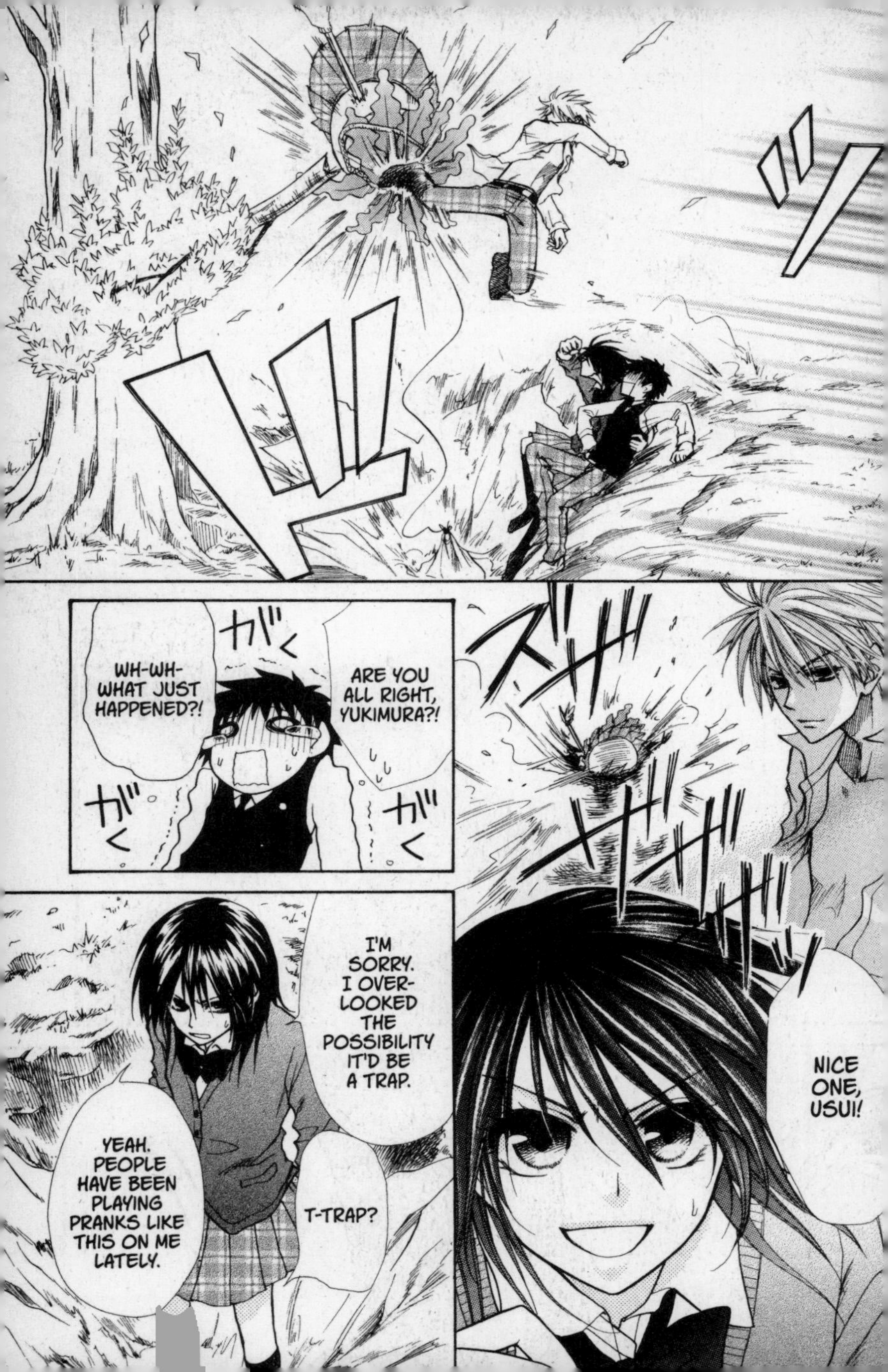
ARE YOU ALL RIGHT, YUKIMURA?!
がく
WH-WH-WHAT JUST HAPPENED?!
がく
がく
NICE ONE, USUI!
I'M SORRY. I OVERLOOKED THE POSSIBILITY IT'D BE A TRAP.
T-TRAP?
YEAH. PEOPLE HAVE BEEN PLAYING PRANKS LIKE THIS ON ME LATELY.

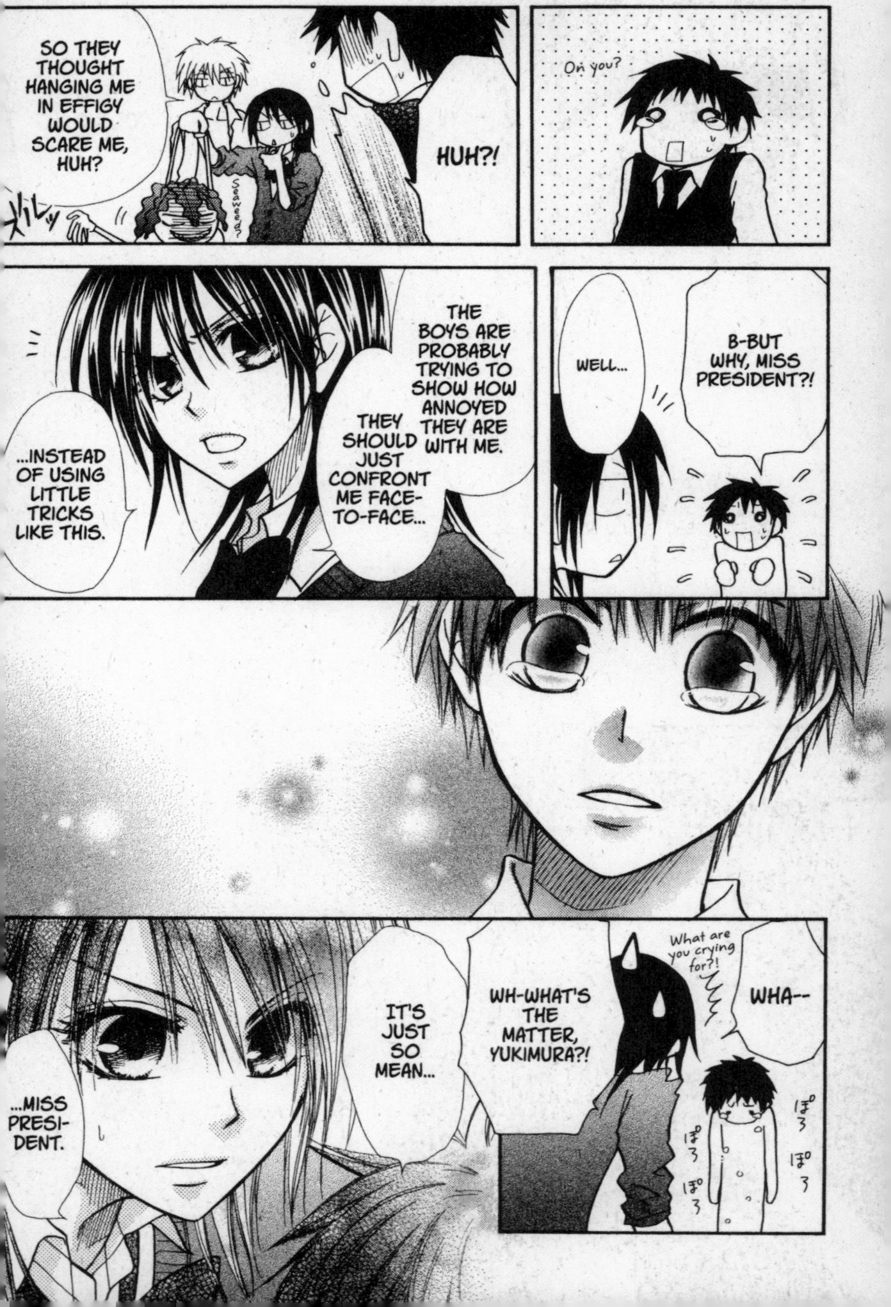
On you?
HUH?!
SO THEY THOUGHT HANGING ME IN EFFIGY WOULD SCARE ME, HUH?
Seaweed?
B-BUT WHY, MISS PRESIDENT?!
WELL...
THE BOYS ARE PROBABLY TRYING TO SHOW HOW ANNOYED THEY ARE WITH ME.
THEY SHOULD JUST CONFRONT ME FACE-TO-FACE...
...INSTEAD OF USING LITTLE TRICKS LIKE THIS.
WHA--
What are you crying for?!
WH-WHAT'S THE MATTER, YUKIMURA?!
ぽろ ぽろ
ぽろ ぽろ
IT'S JUST SO MEAN...
...MISS PRESIDENT.

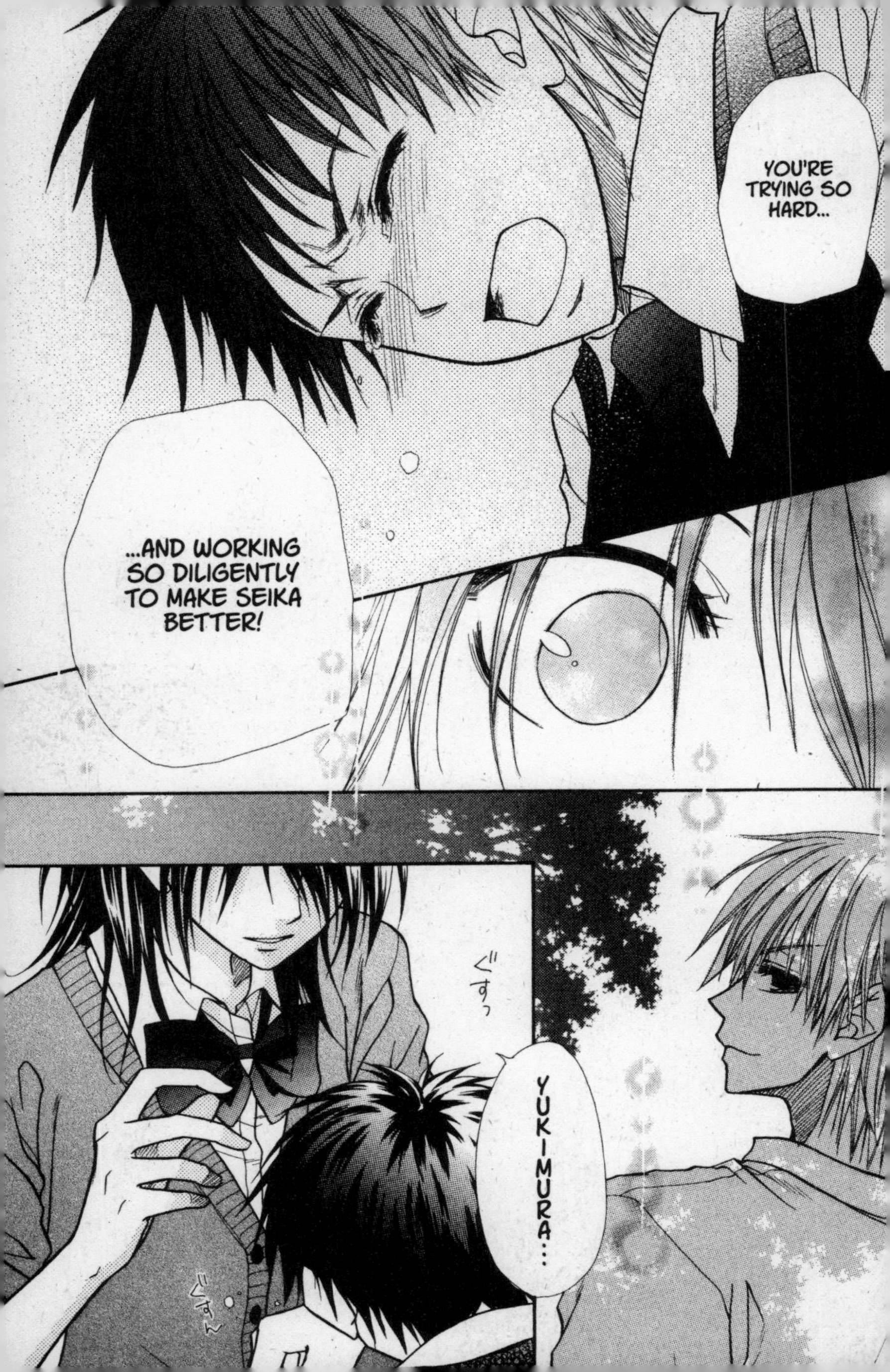
YOU'RE TRYING SO HARD...
...AND WORKING SO DILIGENTLY TO MAKE SEIKA BETTER!
ぐすっ
YUKIMURA...
ぐすん

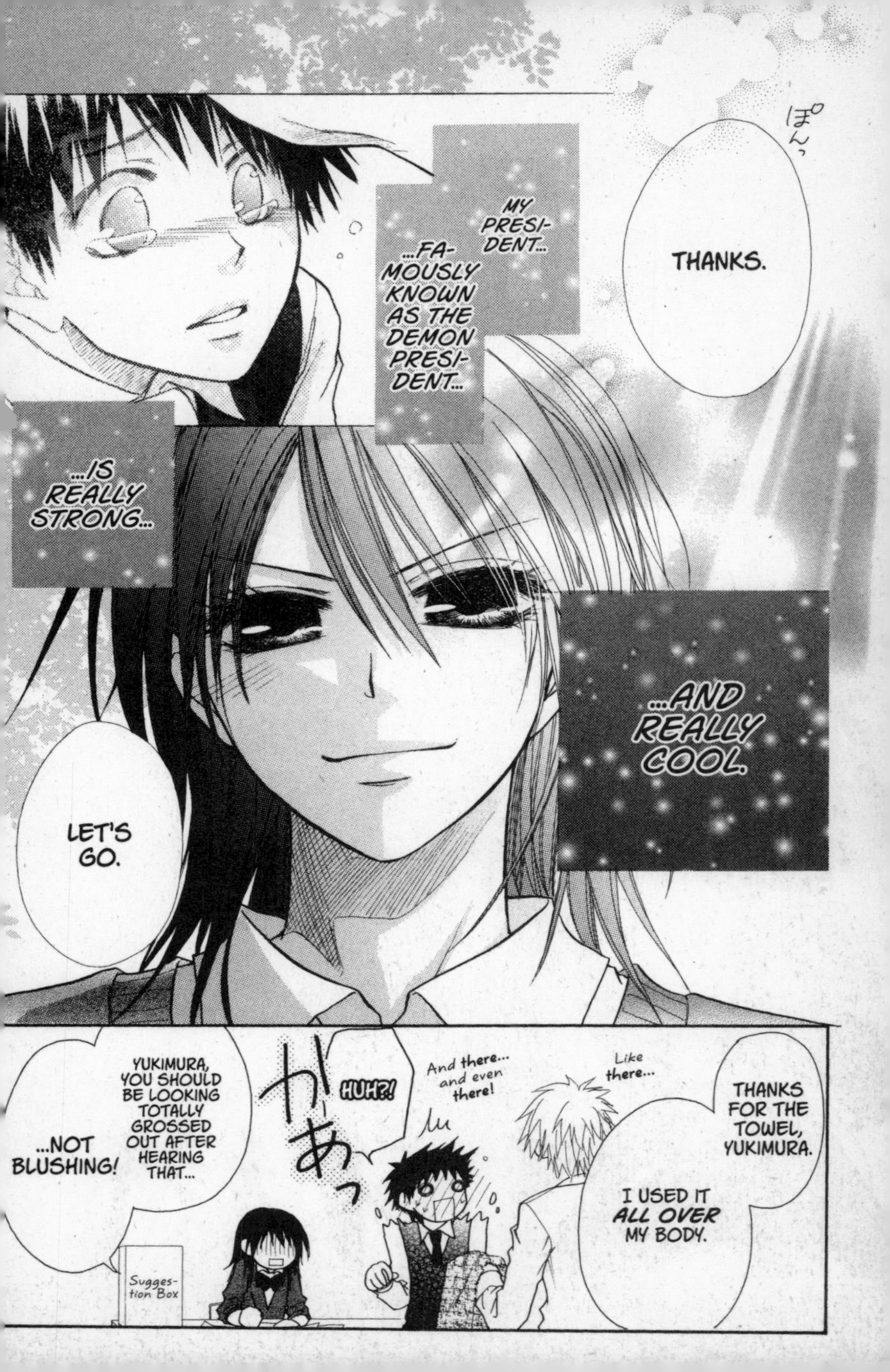
ぽんっ
THANKS.
MY PRESIDENT...
...FAMOUSLY KNOWN AS THE DEMON PRESIDENT...
...IS REALLY STRONG...
...AND REALLY COOL.
LET'S GO.
THANKS FOR THE TOWEL, YUKIMURA.
I USED IT ALL OVER MY BODY.
Like there...
And there... and even there!
HUH?!
かぁっ
YUKIMURA, YOU SHOULD BE LOOKING TOTALLY GROSSED OUT AFTER HEARING THAT...
...NOT BLUSHING!
Sugges-tion Box

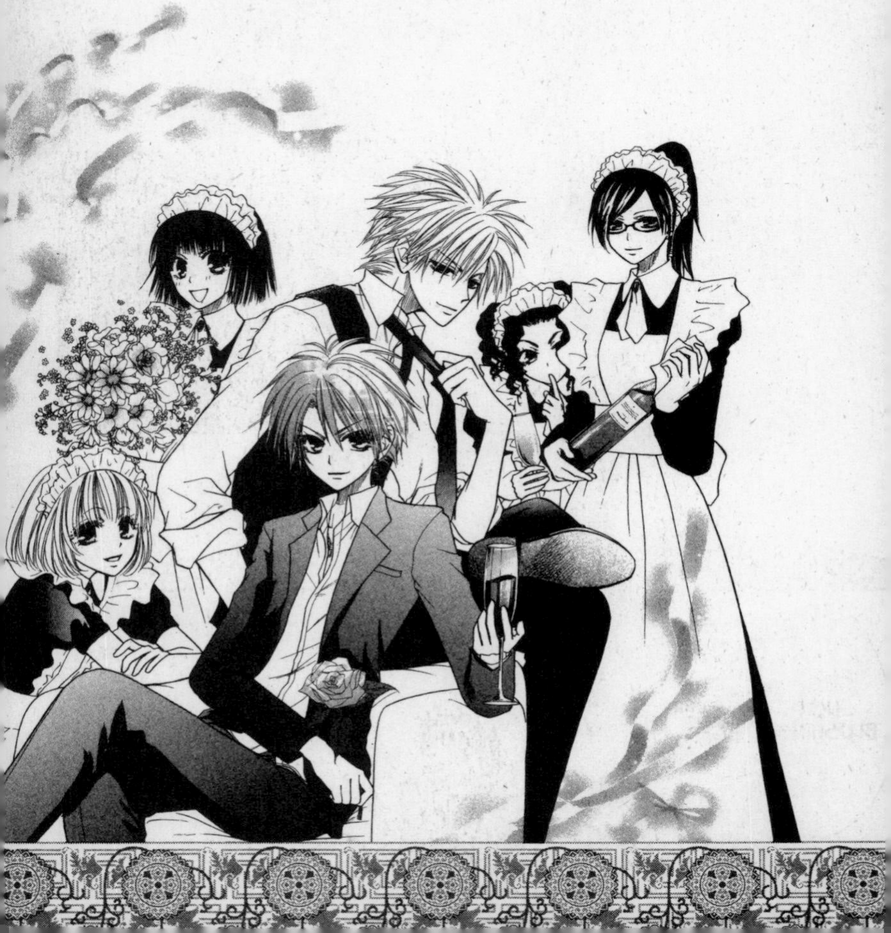

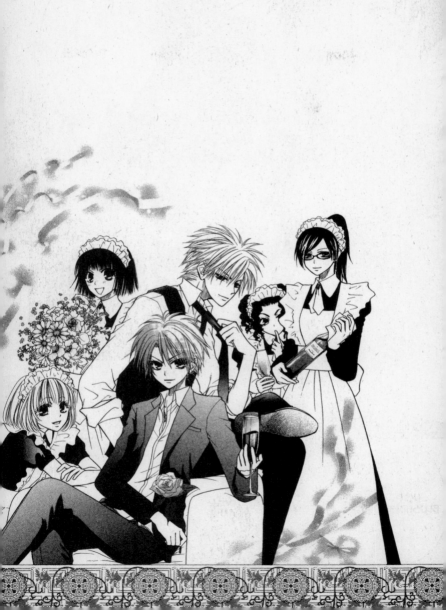

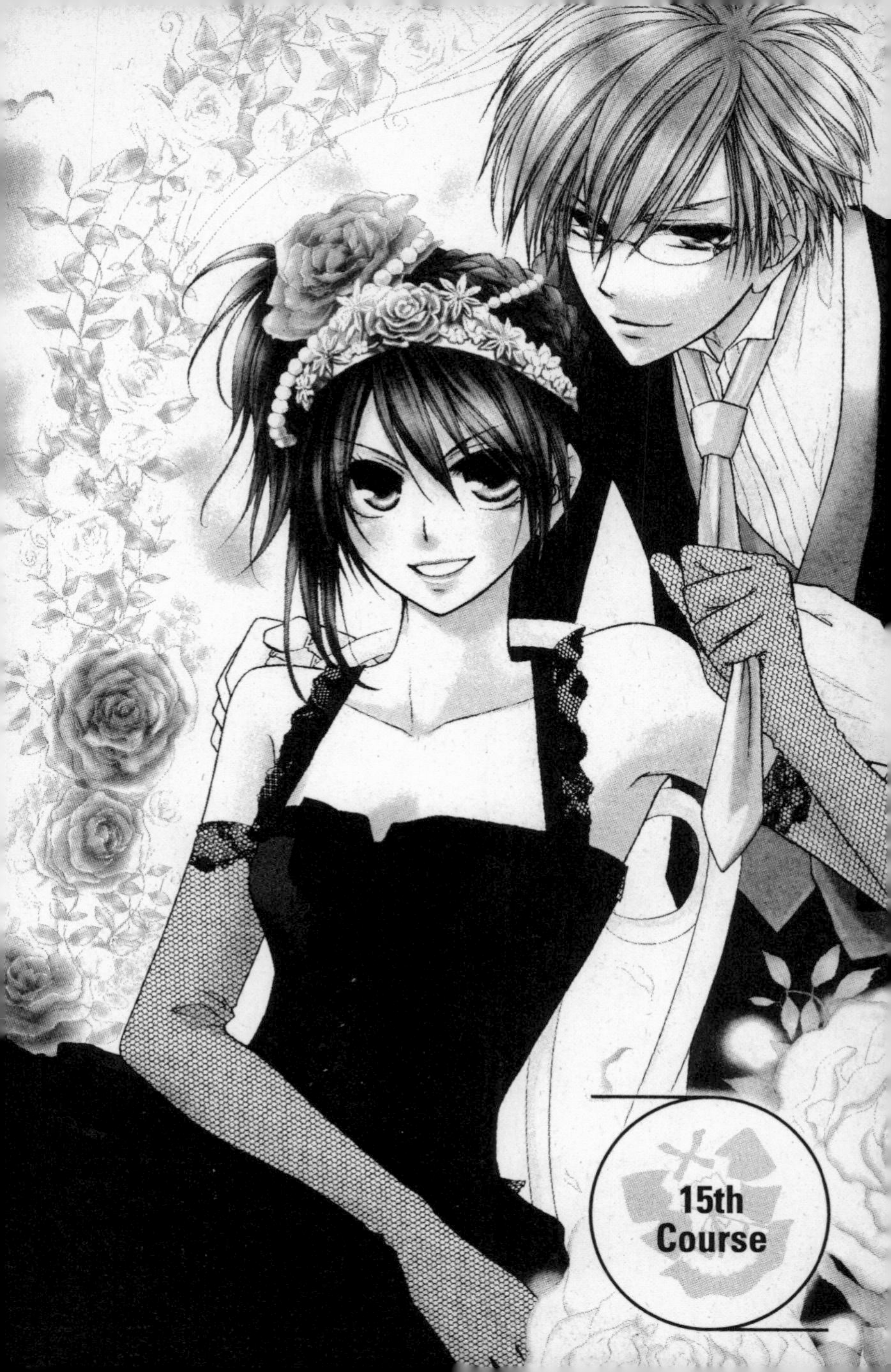
15th
Course

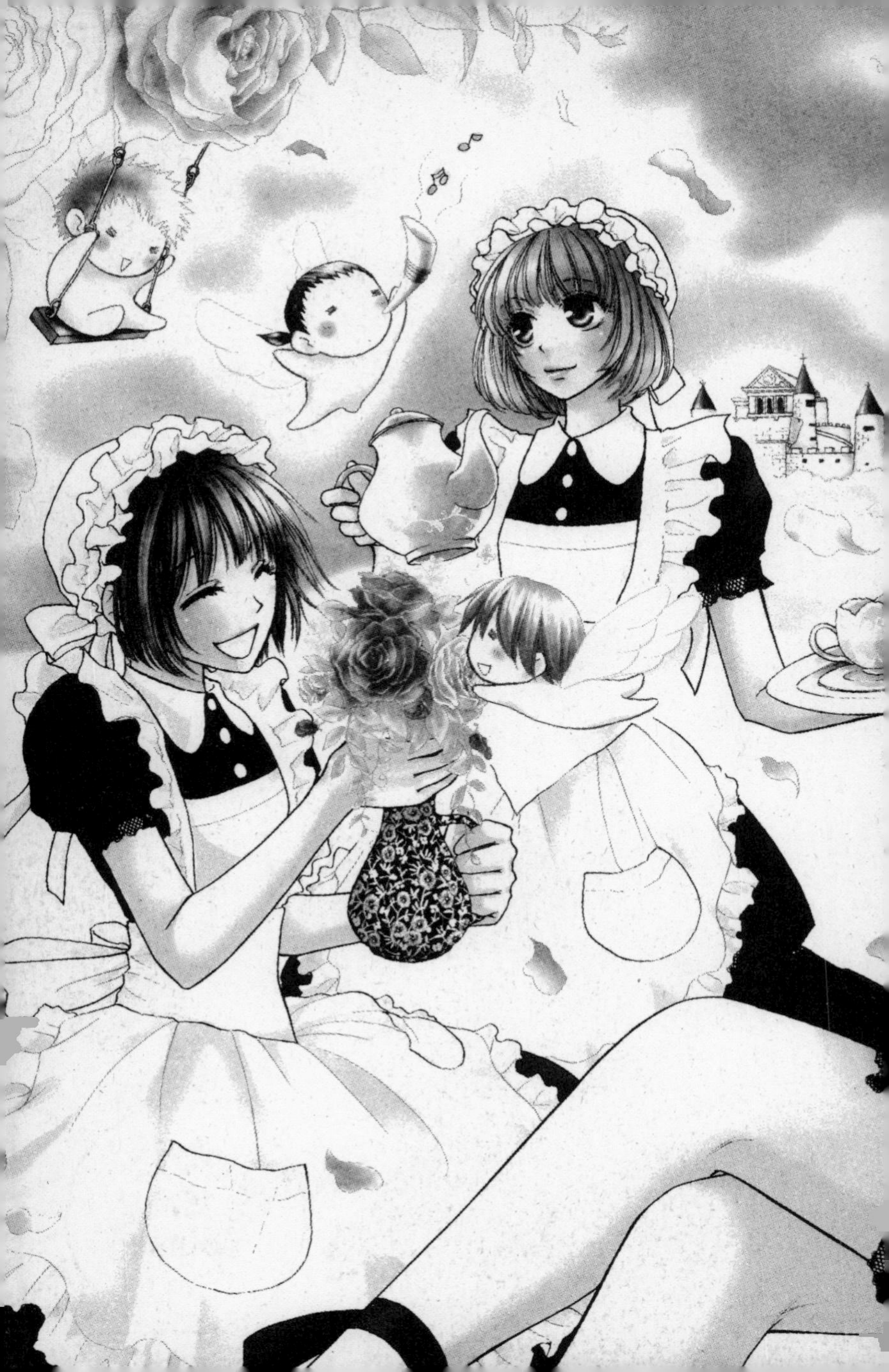

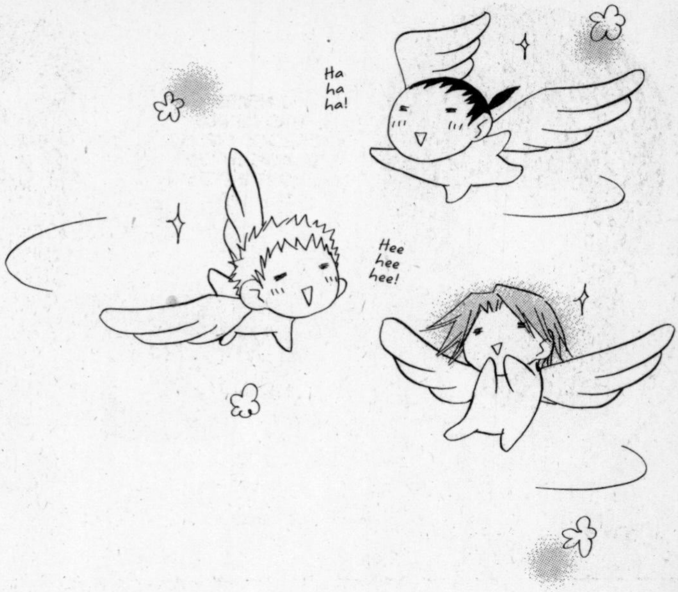
Ha ha ha!
Hee hee hee!

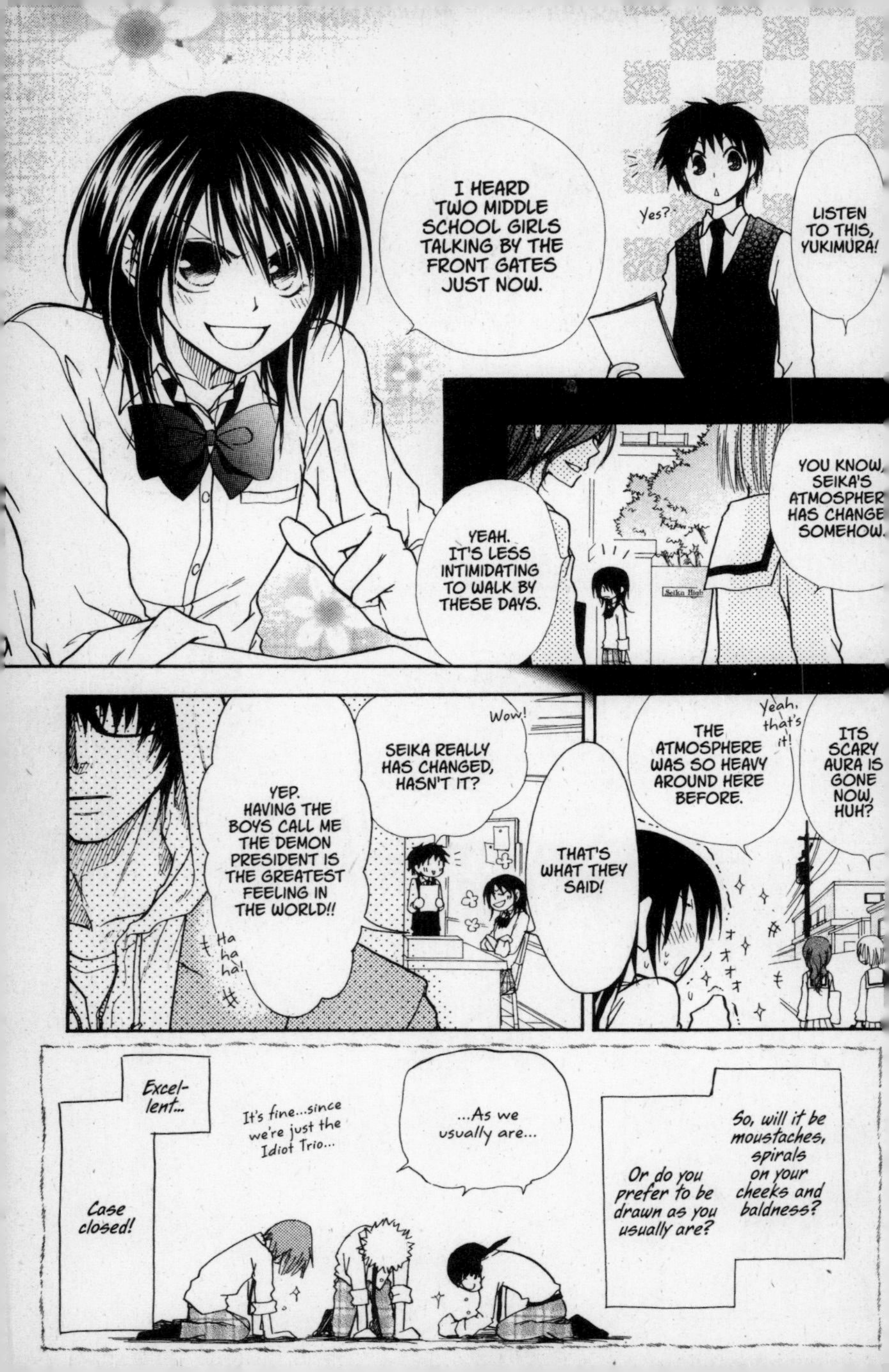
LISTEN TO THIS, YUKIMURA!
Yes?
I HEARD TWO MIDDLE SCHOOL GIRLS TALKING BY THE FRONT GATES JUST NOW.
YOU KNOW, SEIKA'S ATMOSPHER HAS CHANGE SOMEHOW.
YEAH. IT'S LESS INTIMIDATING TO WALK BY THESE DAYS.
Seika High
ITS SCARY AURA IS GONE NOW, HUH?
Yeah, that's it!
THE ATMOSPHERE WAS SO HEAVY AROUND HERE BEFORE.
THAT'S WHAT THEY SAID!
SEIKA REALLY HAS CHANGED, HASN'T IT?
Wow!
YEP. HAVING THE BOYS CALL ME THE DEMON PRESIDENT IS THE GREATEST FEELING IN THE WORLD!!
Ha ha ha!
So, will it be moustaches, spirals on your cheeks and baldness?
Or do you prefer to be drawn as you usually are?
...As we usually are...
It's fine...since we're just the Idiot Trio...
Excel-lent...
Case closed!

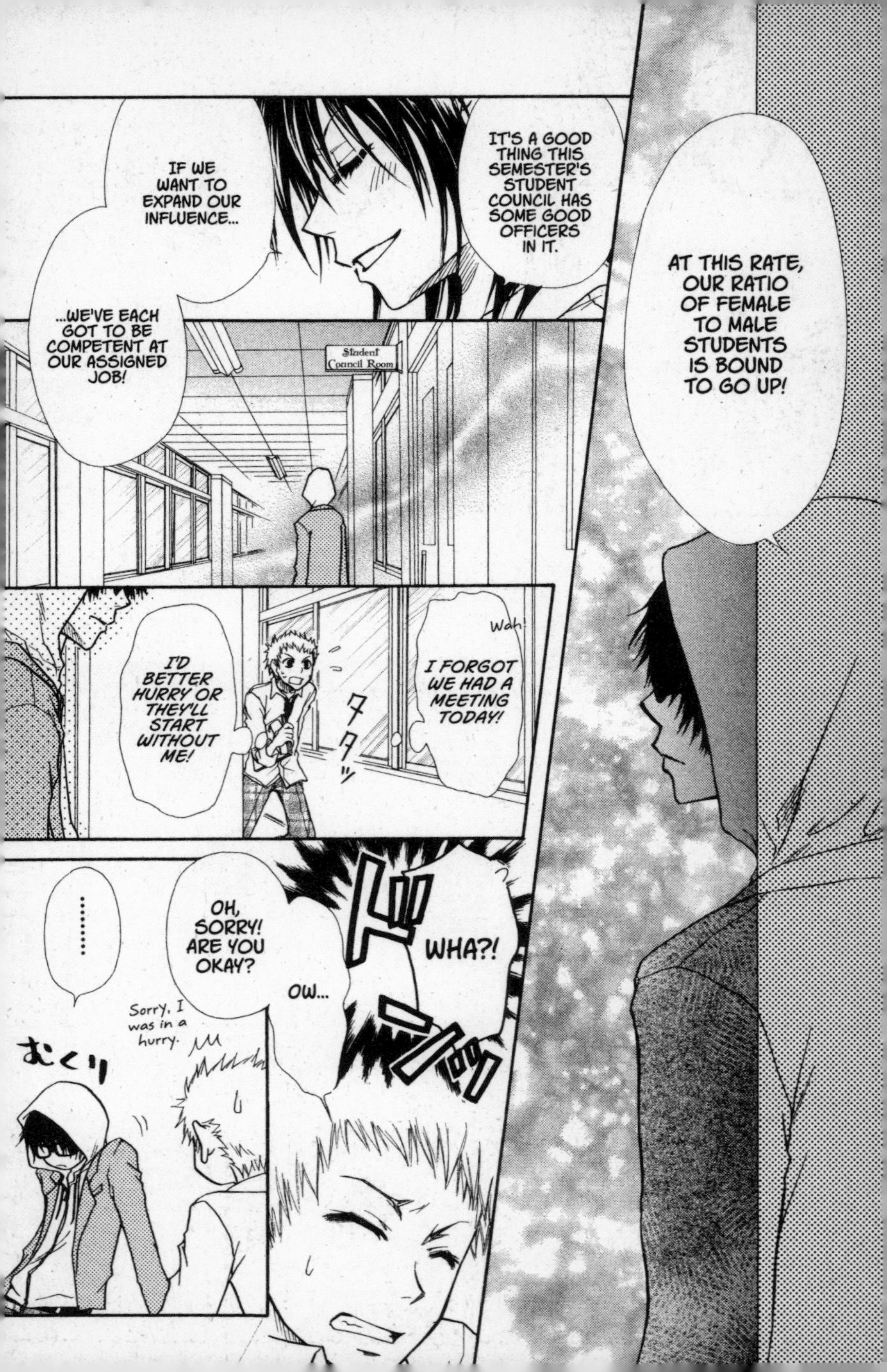
AT THIS RATE, OUR RATIO OF FEMALE TO MALE STUDENTS IS BOUND TO GO UP!
IT'S A GOOD THING THIS SEMESTER'S STUDENT COUNCIL HAS SOME GOOD OFFICERS IN IT.
IF WE WANT TO EXPAND OUR INFLUENCE...
...WE'VE EACH GOT TO BE COMPETENT AT OUR ASSIGNED JOB!
Student Council Room
Wah!
I FORGOT WE HAD A MEETING TODAY!
タタッ
I'D BETTER HURRY OR THEY'LL START WITHOUT ME!
WHA?!
OW...
OH, SORRY! ARE YOU OKAY?
....
Sorry, I was in a hurry.
むくり

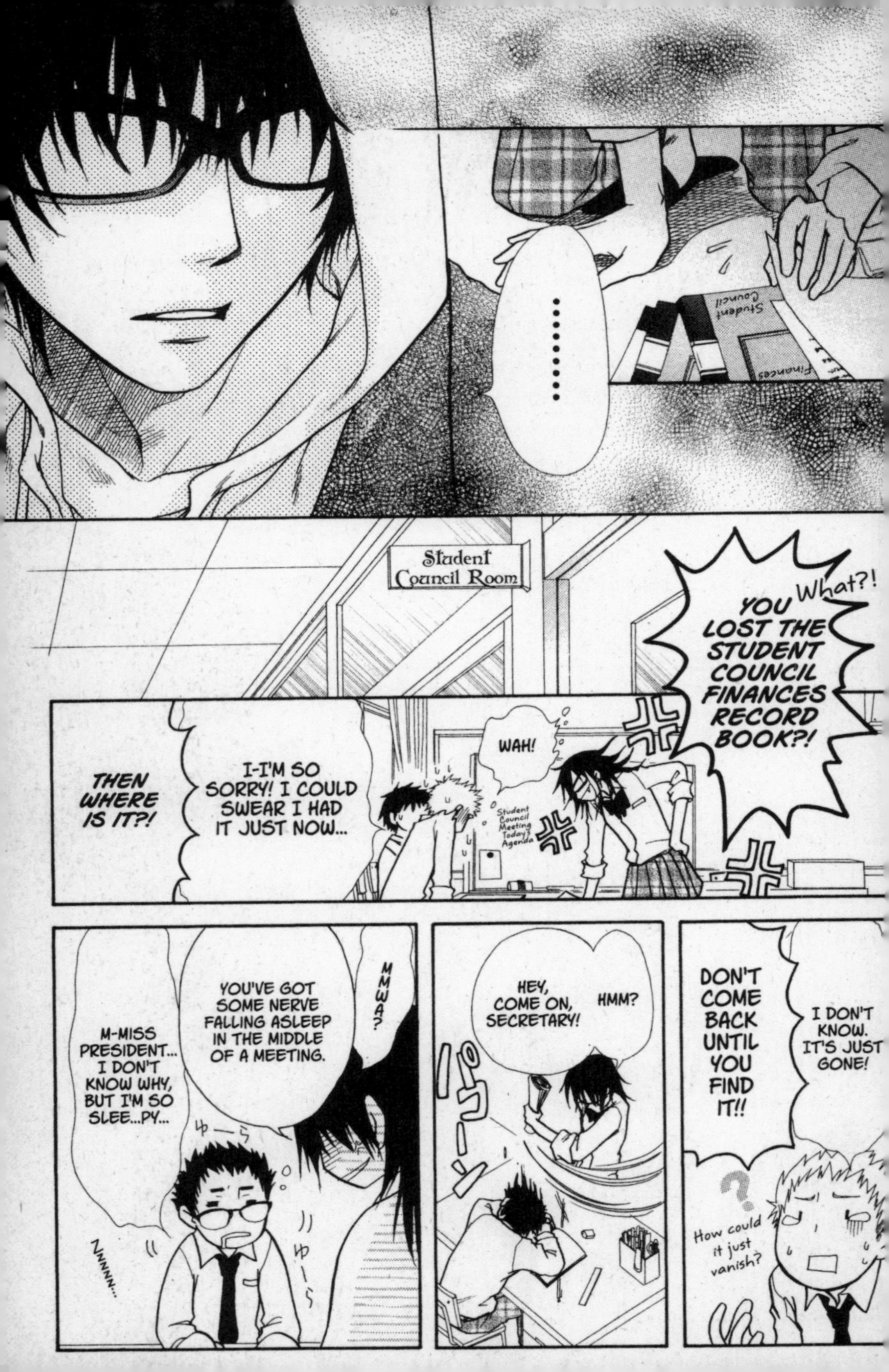

Student Council Finances
......
Student Council Room
What?!
YOU LOST THE STUDENT COUNCIL FINANCES RECORD BOOK?!
WAH!
Student Council Meeting Today's Agenda
I-I'M SO SORRY! I COULD SWEAR I HAD IT JUST NOW...
THEN WHERE IS IT?!
I DON'T KNOW. IT'S JUST GONE!
DON'T COME BACK UNTIL YOU FIND IT!!
How could it just vanish?
HMM?
HEY, COME ON, SECRETARY!
MMWA?
YOU'VE GOT SOME NERVE FALLING ASLEEP IN THE MIDDLE OF A MEETING.
M-MISS PRESIDENT... I DON'T KNOW WHY, BUT I'M SO SLEE...PY...
ゆーら
ゆーら
ZNNNNN...

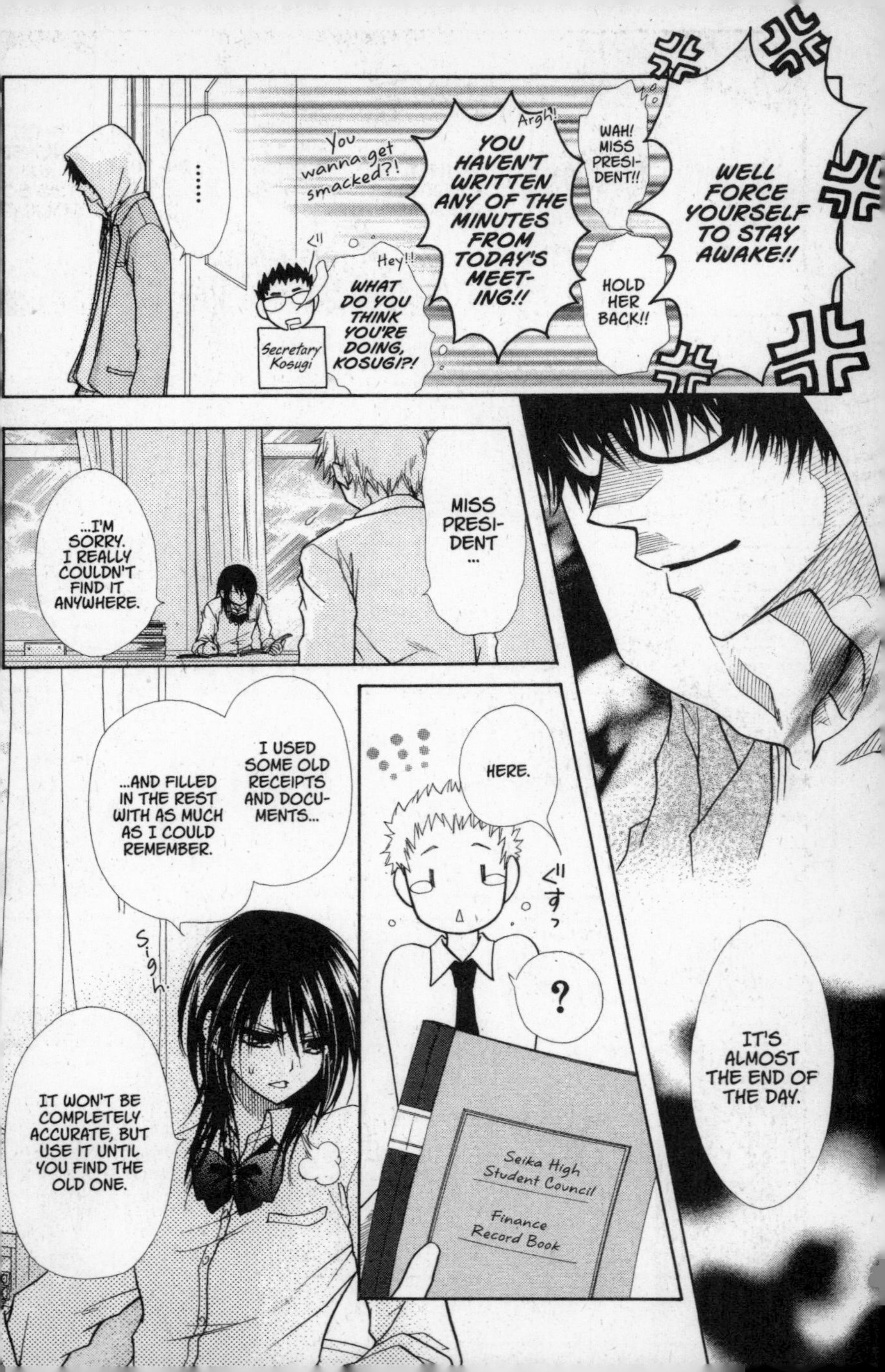
WELL FORCE YOURSELF TO STAY AWAKE!!
WAH! MISS PRESIDENT!!
HOLD HER BACK!!
Argh!!
YOU HAVEN'T WRITTEN ANY OF THE MINUTES FROM TODAY'S MEETING!!
Hey!!
WHAT DO YOU THINK YOU'RE DOING, KOSUGI?!
You wanna get smacked?!
Secretary Kosugi
......
IT'S ALMOST THE END OF THE DAY.
MISS PRESIDENT ...
...I'M SORRY. I REALLY COULDN'T FIND IT ANYWHERE.
HERE.
?
Seika High Student Council
Finance Record Book
I USED SOME OLD RECEIPTS AND DOCUMENTS...
...AND FILLED IN THE REST WITH AS MUCH AS I COULD REMEMBER.
Sigh
IT WON'T BE COMPLETELY ACCURATE, BUT USE IT UNTIL YOU FIND THE OLD ONE.

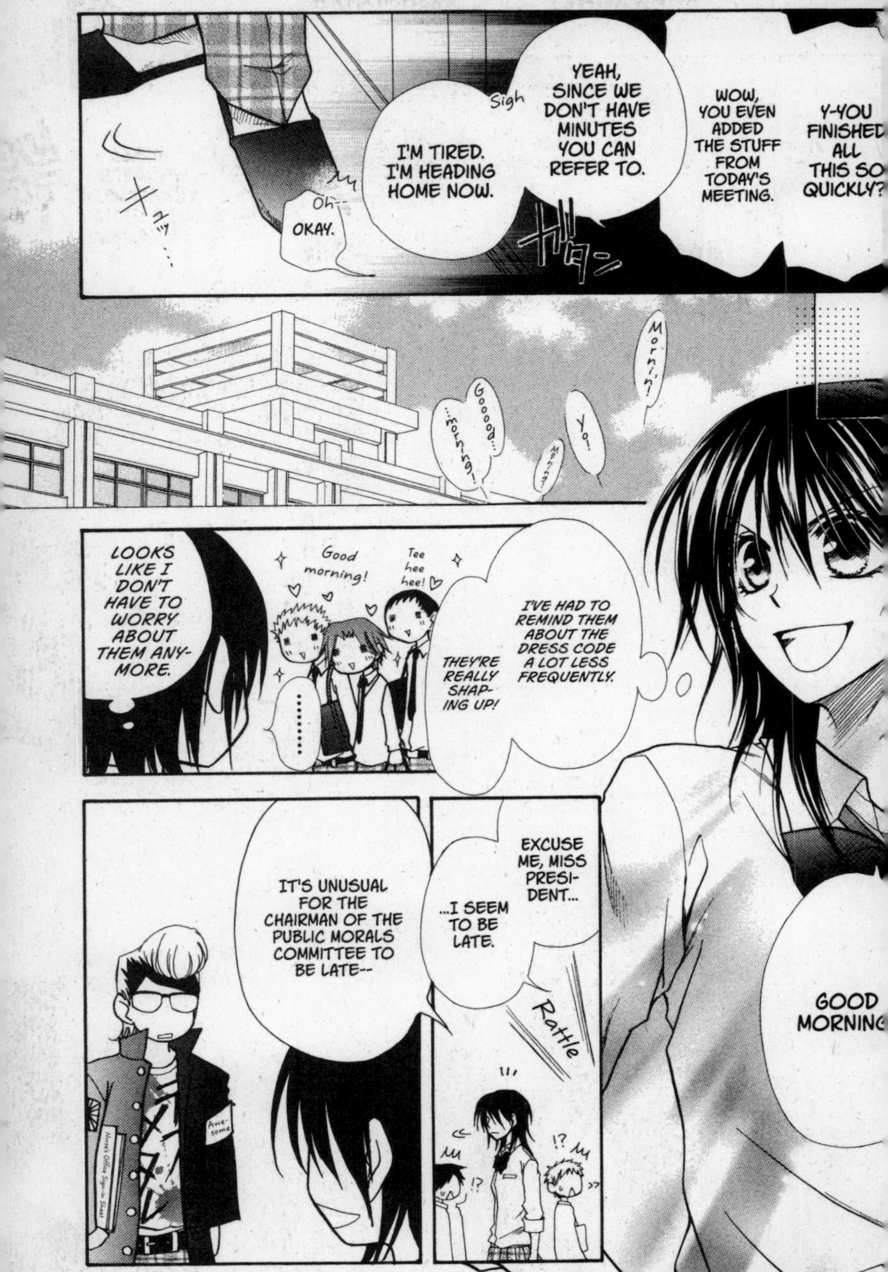
Y-YOU FINISHED ALL THIS SO QUICKLY?
WOW, YOU EVEN ADDED THE STUFF FROM TODAY'S MEETING.
YEAH, SINCE WE DON'T HAVE MINUTES YOU CAN REFER TO.
Sigh
I'M TIRED. I'M HEADING HOME NOW.
Oh-- OKAY.
Mornin'!
Yo!
Morning!
Gooood... ...morning!
GOOD MORNING
I'VE HAD TO REMIND THEM ABOUT THE DRESS CODE A LOT LESS FREQUENTLY.
THEY'RE REALLY SHAPING UP!
Tee hee hee!
Good morning!
....
LOOKS LIKE I DON'T HAVE TO WORRY ABOUT THEM ANYMORE.
EXCUSE ME, MISS PRESIDENT...
...I SEEM TO BE LATE.
Rattle
IT'S UNUSUAL FOR THE CHAIRMAN OF THE PUBLIC MORALS COMMITTEE TO BE LATE--
Awe-some
Nurse's Office Sign-in Sheet

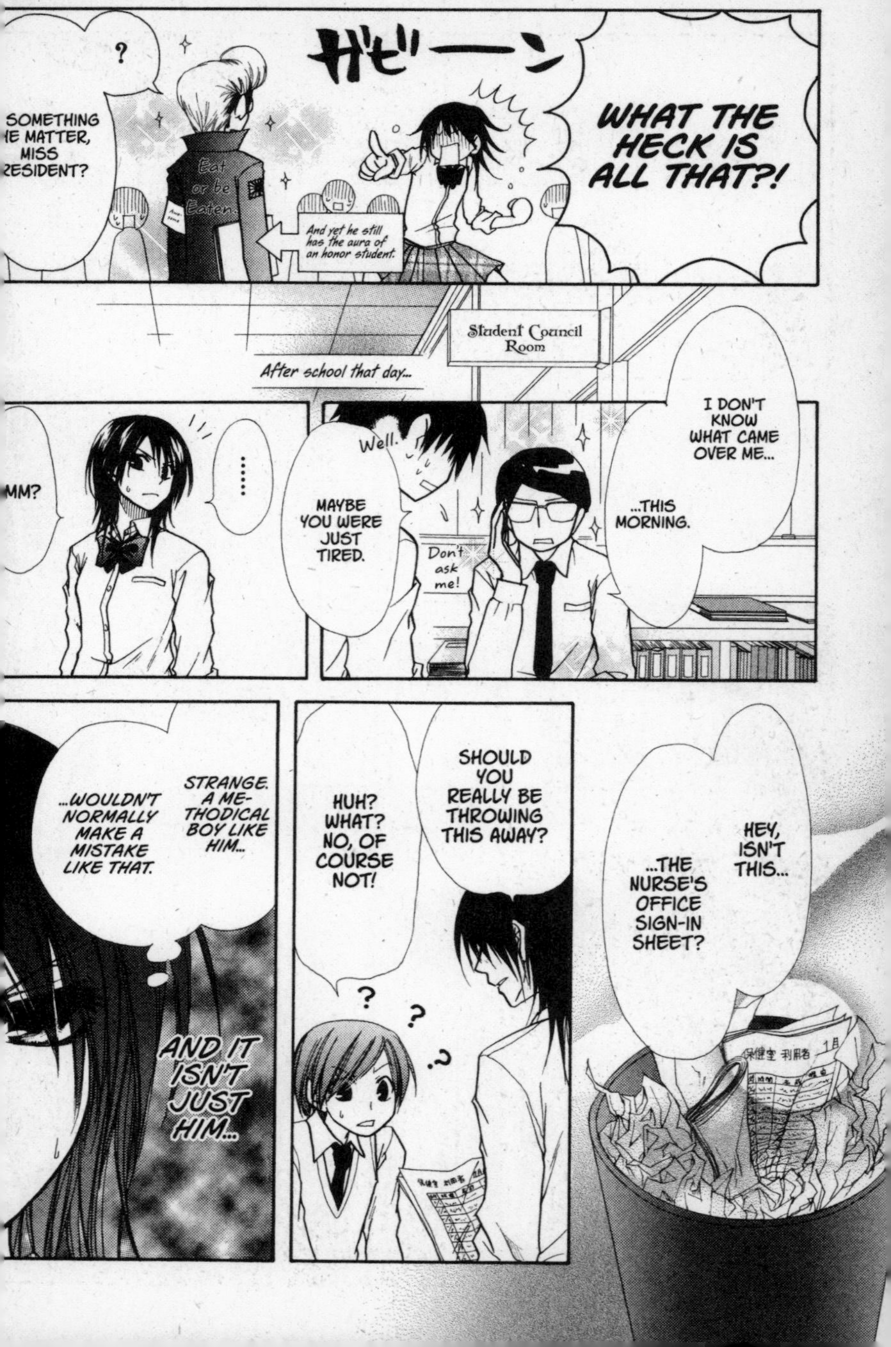
ガビーン
WHAT THE HECK IS ALL THAT?!
?
SOMETHING HE MATTER, MISS RESIDENT?
Eat or be Eaten
And yet he still has the aura of an honor student.
Student Council Room
After school that day...
I DON'T KNOW WHAT CAME OVER ME...
...THIS MORNING.
Well.
MAYBE YOU WERE JUST TIRED.
Don't ask me!
......
MM?
HEY, ISN'T THIS...
...THE NURSE'S OFFICE SIGN-IN SHEET?
SHOULD YOU REALLY BE THROWING THIS AWAY?
HUH? WHAT? NO, OF COURSE NOT!
STRANGE. A METHODICAL BOY LIKE HIM...
...WOULDN'T NORMALLY MAKE A MISTAKE LIKE THAT.
AND IT ISN'T JUST HIM...

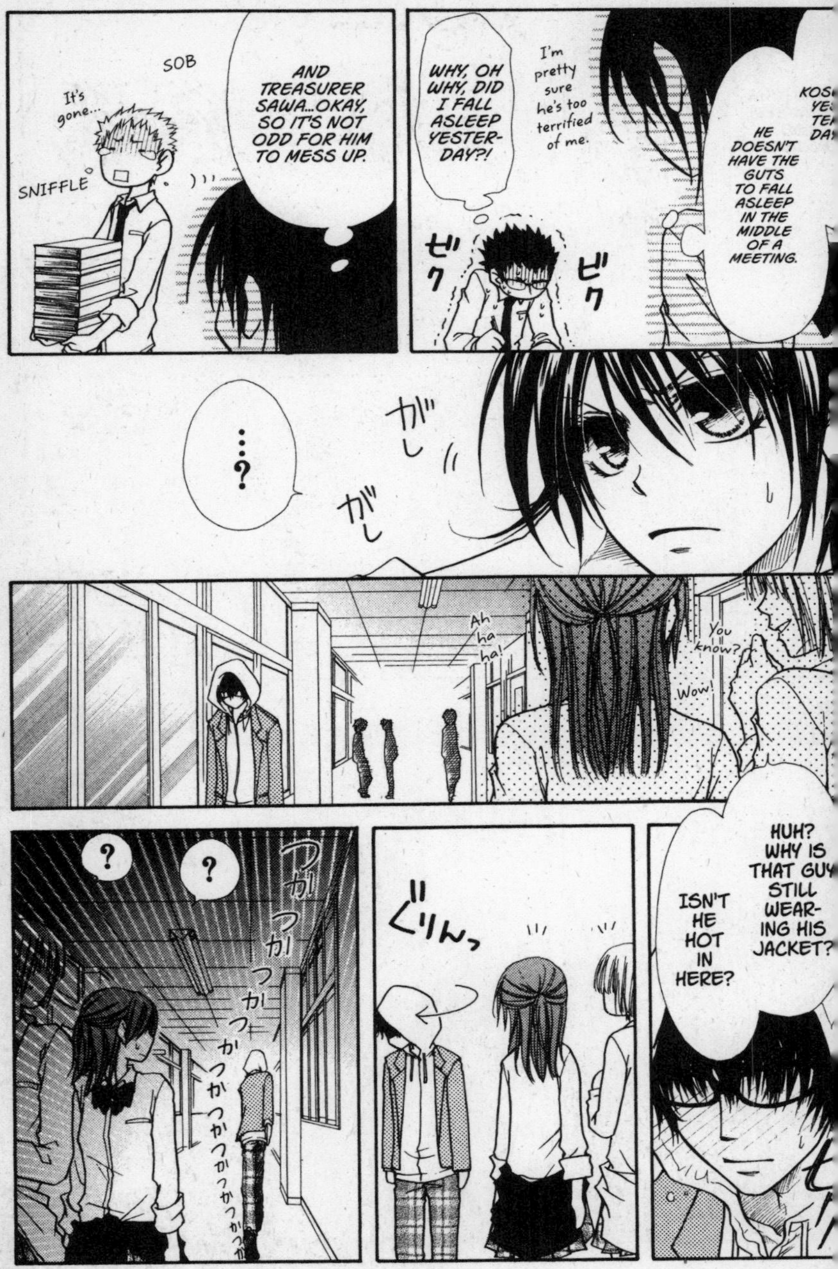
HE DOESN'T HAVE THE GUTS TO FALL ASLEEP IN THE MIDDLE OF A MEETING.
WHY, OH WHY, DID I FALL ASLEEP YESTER-DAY?!
I'm pretty sure he's too terrified of me.
ビク
AND TREASURER SAWA...OKAY, SO IT'S NOT ODD FOR HIM TO MESS UP.
SOB
It's gone...
SNIFFLE
...?
がし
がし
You know?
Wow!
Ah ha ha!
HUH? WHY IS THAT GUY STILL WEARING HIS JACKET?
ISN'T HE HOT IN HERE?
ぐりんっ
?
?
つかつかつかつかつかつかつかつかつかつかつか

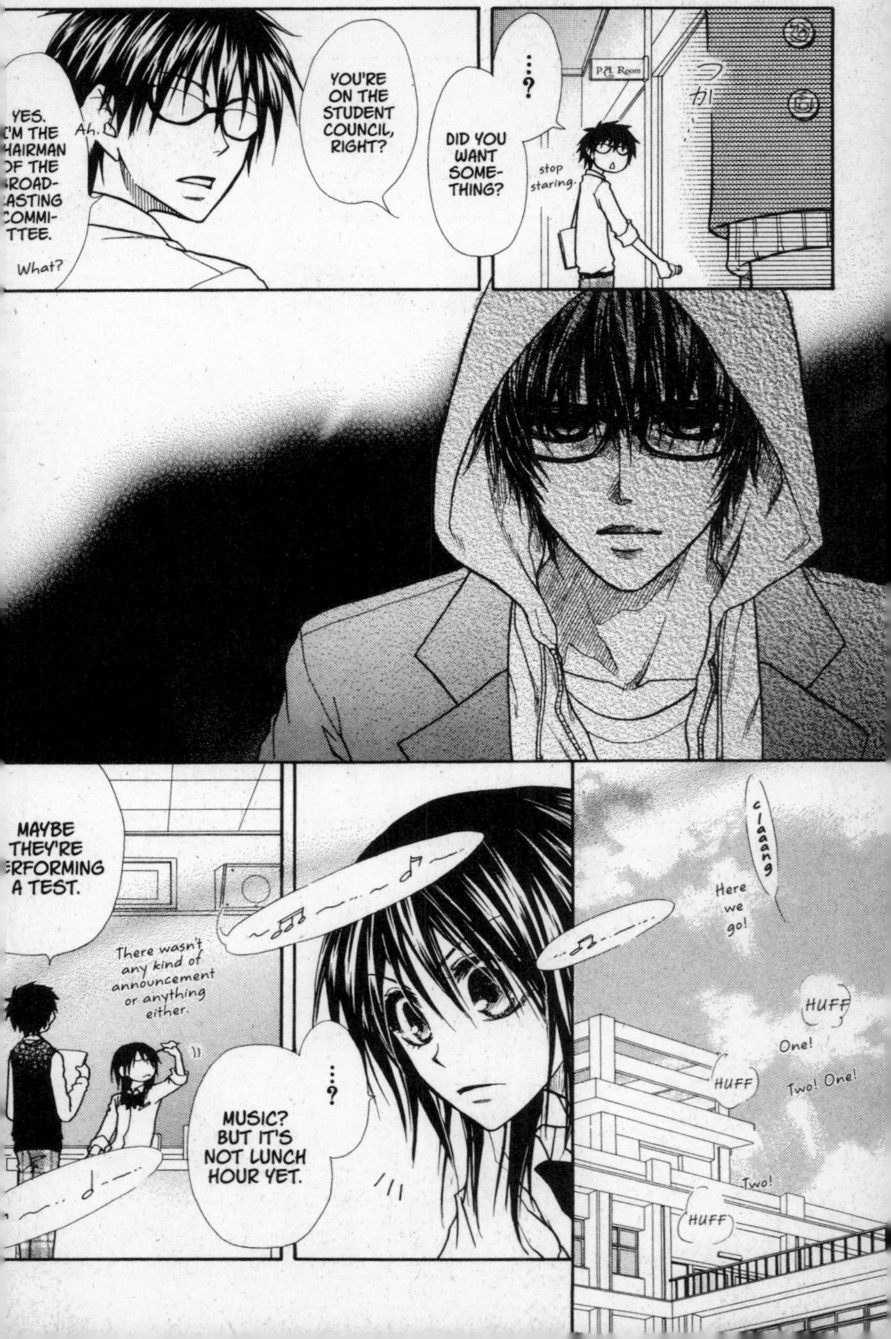
P.A. Room
...?
DID YOU WANT SOMETHING?
stop staring.
YOU'RE ON THE STUDENT COUNCIL, RIGHT?
Ah.
YES. 'M THE HAIRMAN OF THE ROAD-CASTING COMMI-TTEE.
What?
claaang
Here we go!
HUFF
One!
HUFF
Two! One!
Two!
HUFF
...?
MUSIC? BUT IT'S NOT LUNCH HOUR YET.
MAYBE THEY'RE ERFORMING A TEST.
There wasn't any kind of announcement or anything either.

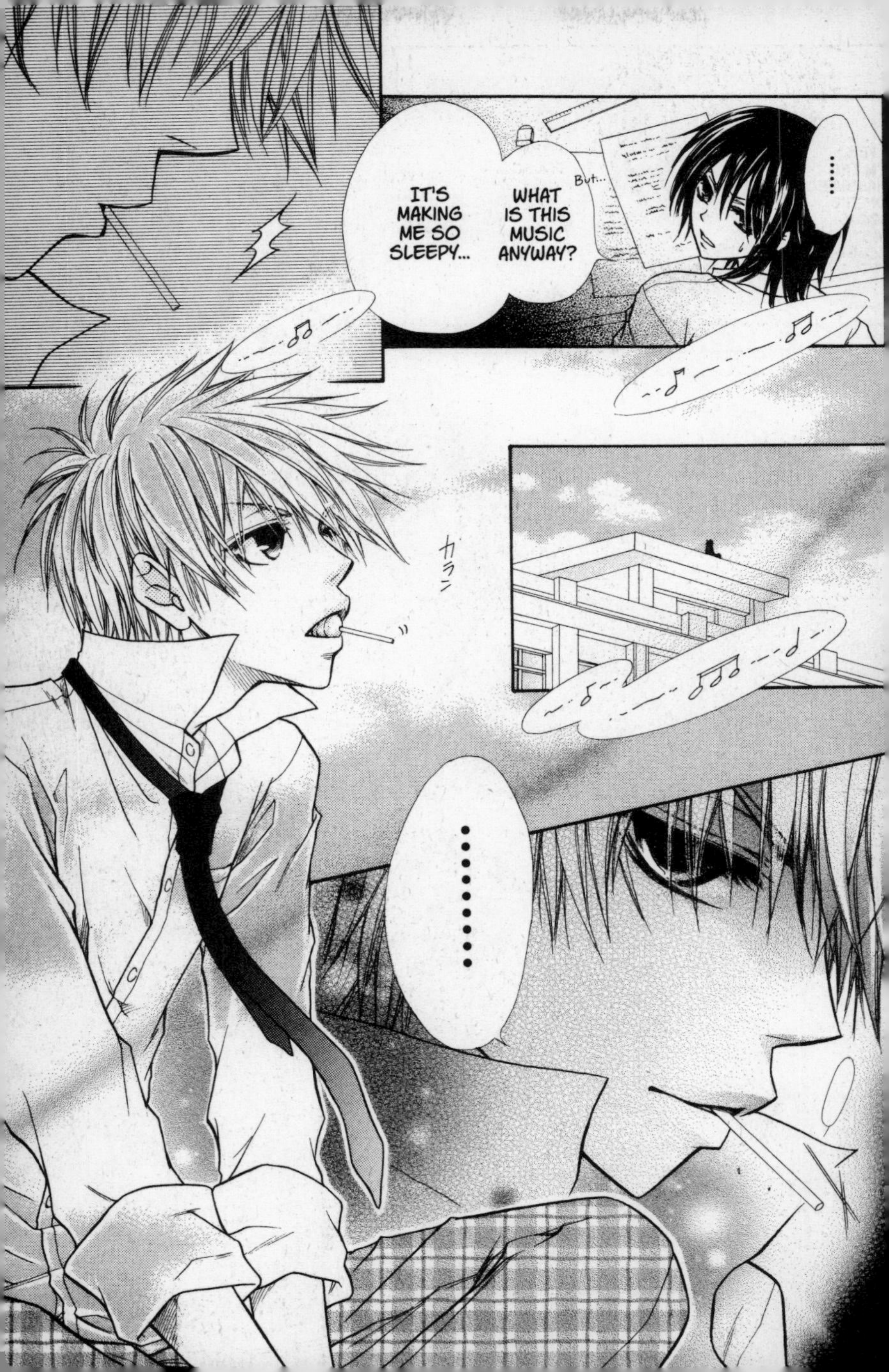

.....
But...
WHAT IS THIS MUSIC ANYWAY?
IT'S MAKING ME SO SLEEPY...
カラン
....

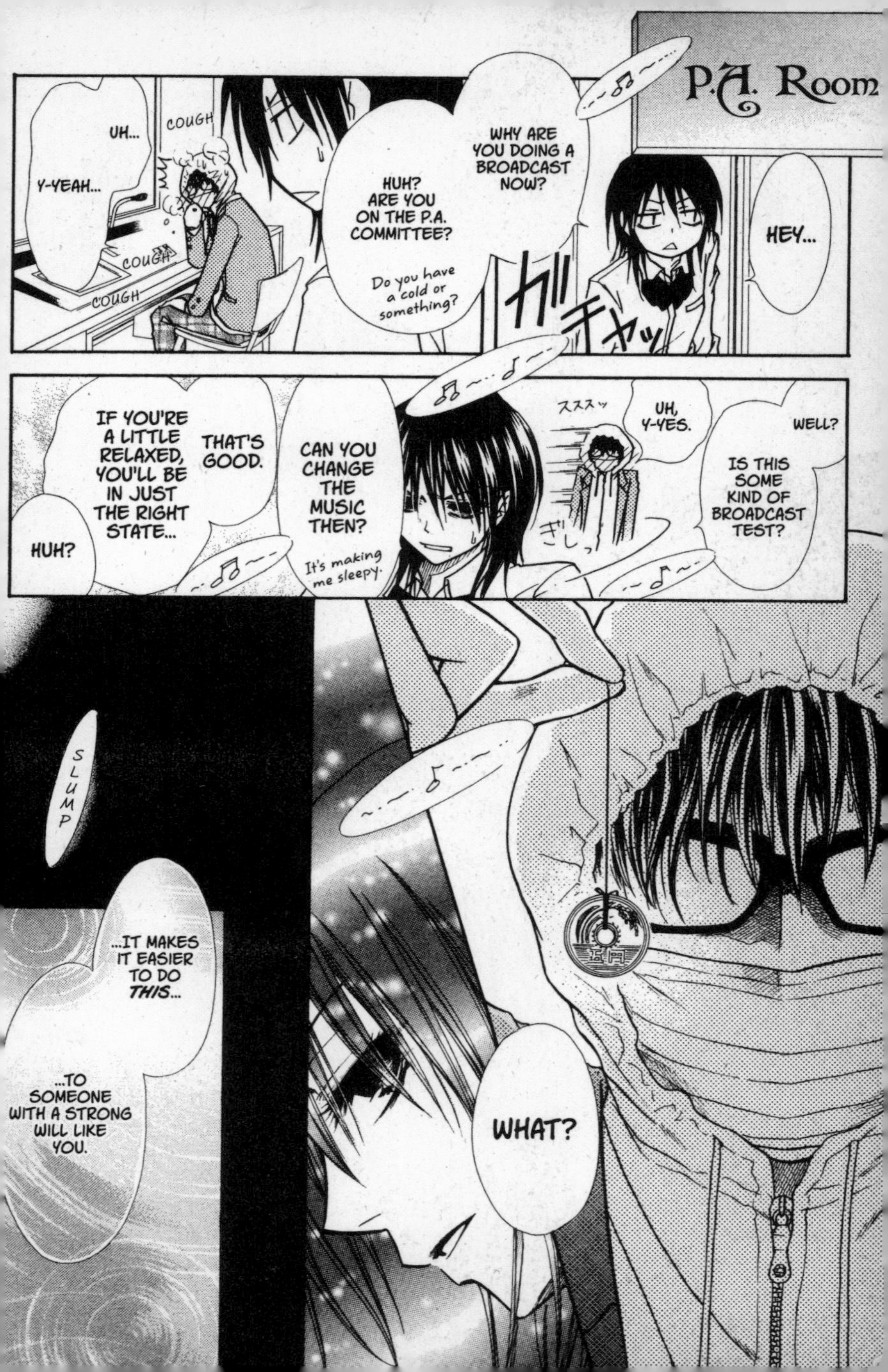
P.A. Room
HEY...
ガチャッ
WHY ARE YOU DOING A BROADCAST NOW?
HUH? ARE YOU ON THE P.A. COMMITTEE?
Do you have a cold or something?
COUGH
COUGH
COUGH
UH...
Y-YEAH...
WELL?
IS THIS SOME KIND OF BROADCAST TEST?
UH, Y-YES.
スススッ
ぎしっ
CAN YOU CHANGE THE MUSIC THEN?
It's making me sleepy.
THAT'S GOOD.
IF YOU'RE A LITTLE RELAXED, YOU'LL BE IN JUST THE RIGHT STATE...
HUH?
WHAT?
五円
...IT MAKES IT EASIER TO DO THIS...
...TO SOMEONE WITH A STRONG WILL LIKE YOU.
SLUMP

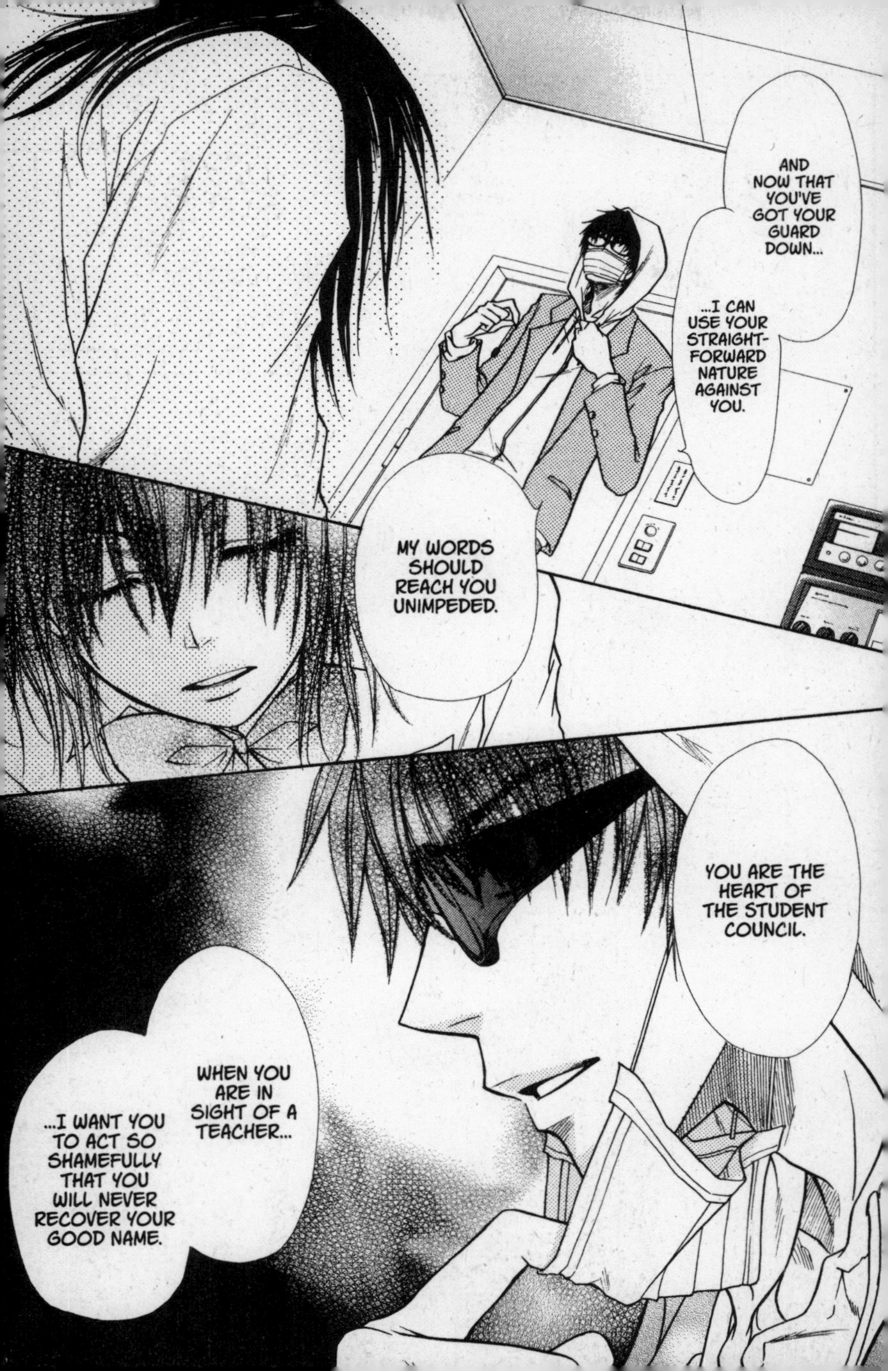
AND NOW THAT YOU'VE GOT YOUR GUARD DOWN...
...I CAN USE YOUR STRAIGHT-FORWARD NATURE AGAINST YOU.
MY WORDS SHOULD REACH YOU UNIMPEDED.
YOU ARE THE HEART OF THE STUDENT COUNCIL.
WHEN YOU ARE IN SIGHT OF A TEACHER...
...I WANT YOU TO ACT SO SHAMEFULLY THAT YOU WILL NEVER RECOVER YOUR GOOD NAME.

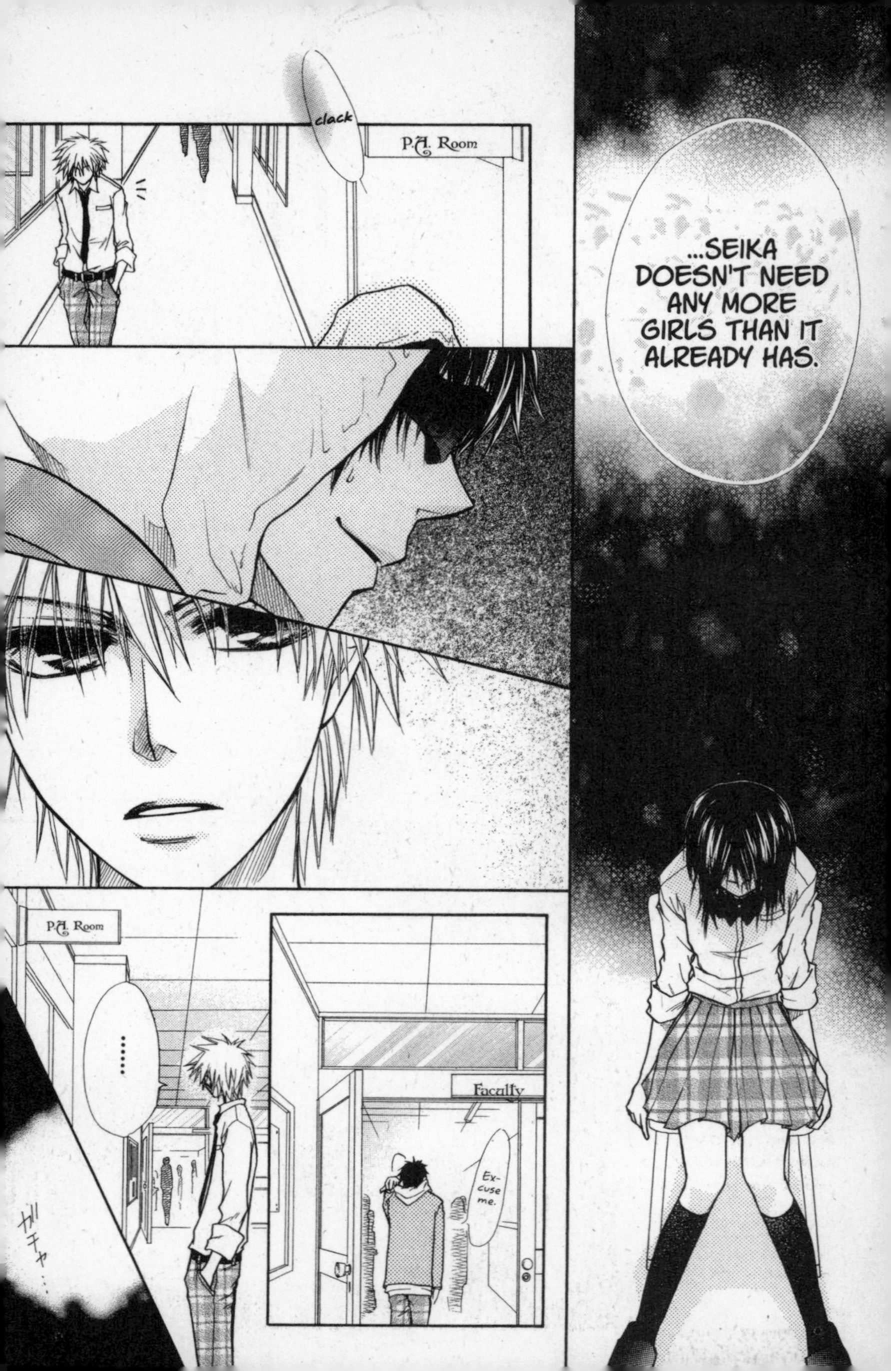
...SEIKA DOESN'T NEED ANY MORE GIRLS THAN IT ALREADY HAS.
clack
P.A. Room
Faculty
Ex-cuse me.
P.A. Room
......
ガチャ...

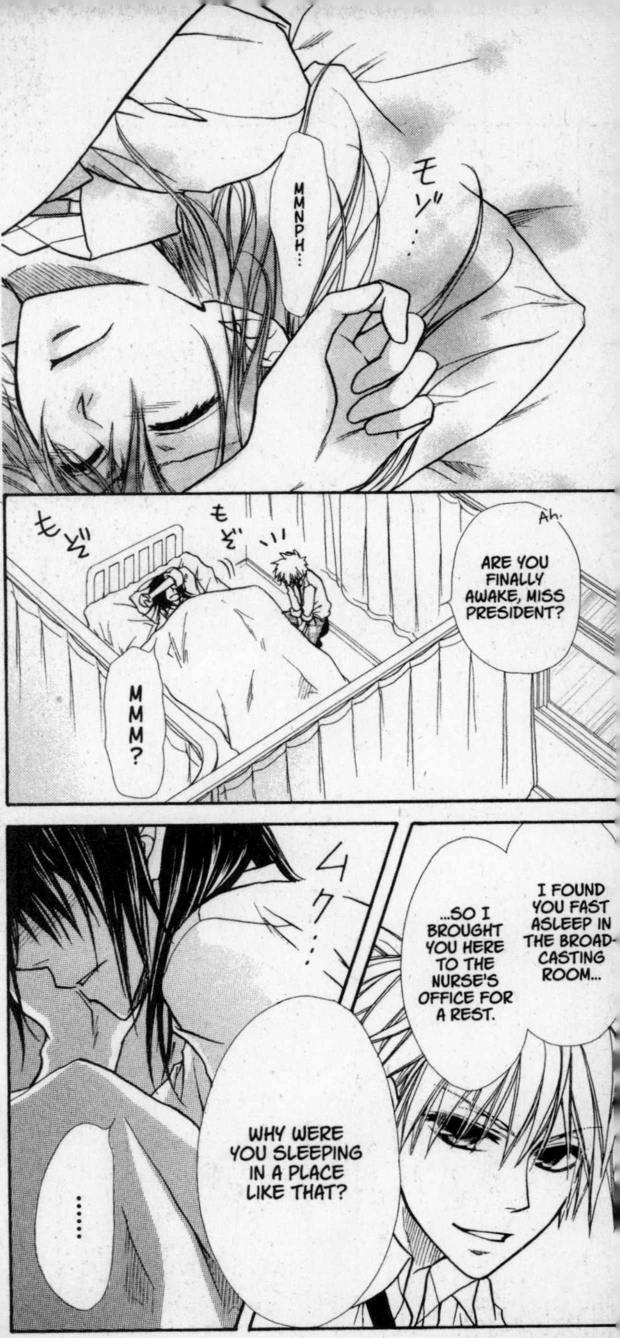
モゾ…
MMNPH…
もぞ
もぞ
Ah.
ARE YOU FINALLY AWAKE, MISS PRESIDENT?
MMM?
I FOUND YOU FAST ASLEEP IN THE BROAD-CASTING ROOM…
…SO I BROUGHT YOU HERE TO THE NURSE'S OFFICE FOR A REST.
WHY WERE YOU SLEEPING IN A PLACE LIKE THAT?
ムク…
……

Thank You!

Hello, I'm Fujiwara.

Thank you again for reading this strangely titled manga!

Maid Sama! has been running for about a year now, and I've gotten many fan letters.

I'm thrilled to receive every single one of them, but the ones that include fan artwork of my characters--which I can see you all have put so much heartfelt effort into--really raise my spirits! They make me so happy! It's interesting to see that Usui is smiling slyly in most of them! And that Misaki is angry in most of them! It looks like you all definitely understand their personalities!

Even if a letter doesn't have sketches in it, it still makes me smile to read your enthusiastic words, so please do write to me!

Well then, see you again at the end of the volume...

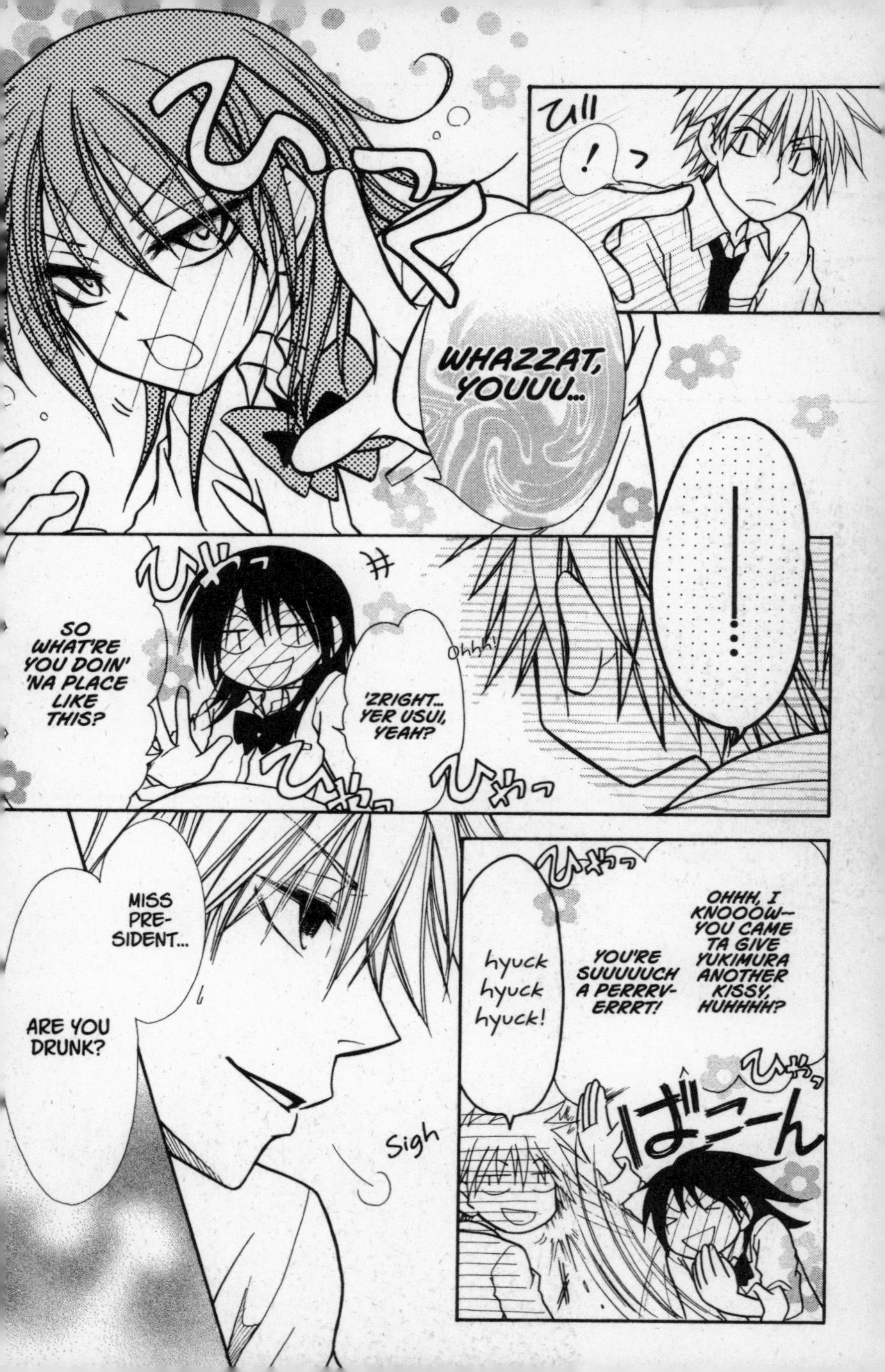

ひ!!
!
WHAZZAT, YOUUU...
!...
Ohhh!
'ZRIGHT... YER USUI, YEAH?
SO WHAT'RE YOU DOIN' 'NA PLACE LIKE THIS?
OHHH, I KNOOOW— YOU CAME TA GIVE YUKIMURA ANOTHER KISSY, HUHHHH?
YOU'RE SUUUUUCH A PERRRV-ERRRT!
hyuck hyuck hyuck!
ばこーん
MISS PRESIDENT...
ARE YOU DRUNK?
Sigh

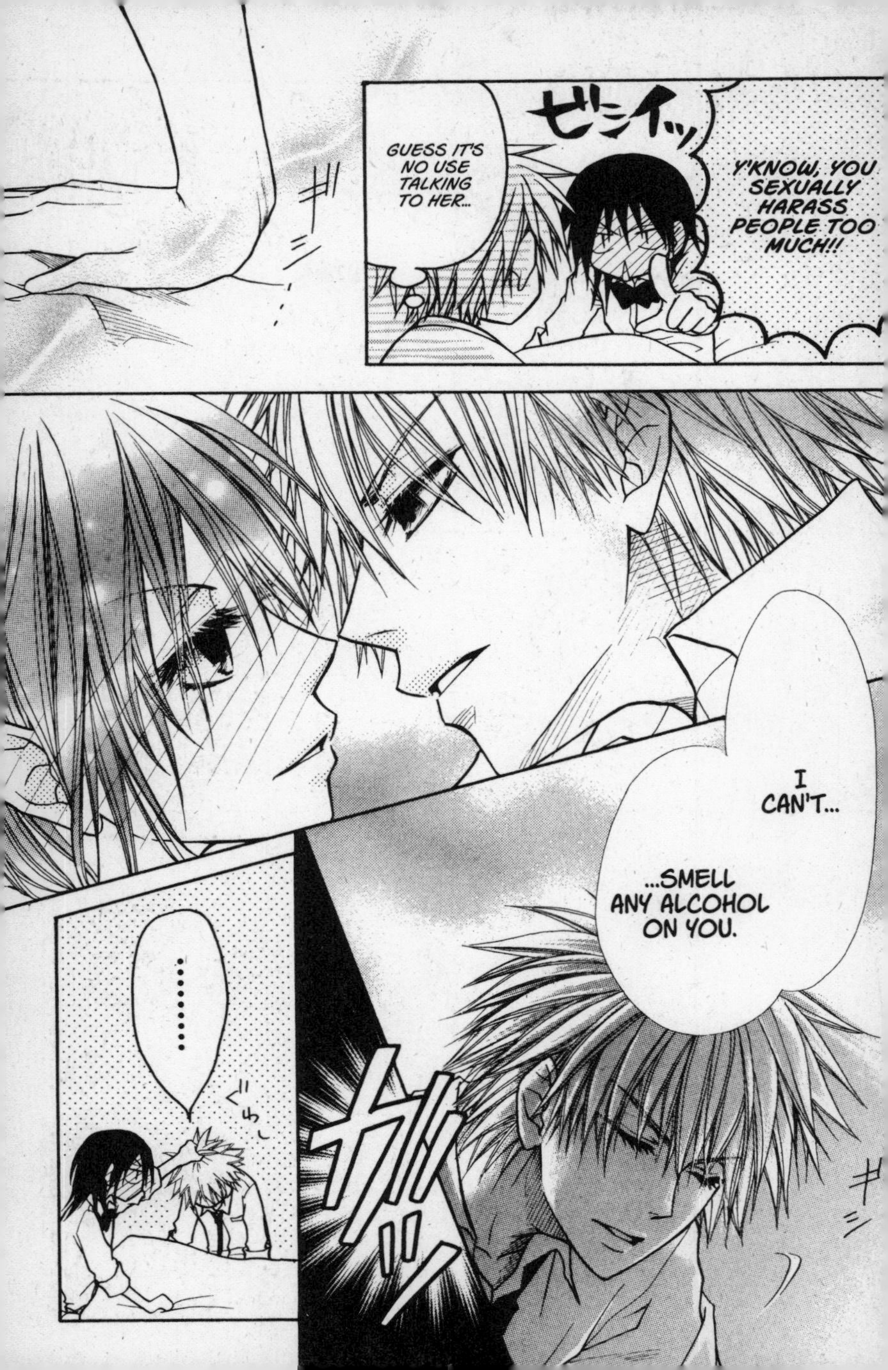
Y'KNOW, YOU SEXUALLY HARASS PEOPLE TOO MUCH!!
GUESS IT'S NO USE TALKING TO HER...
I CAN'T...
...SMELL ANY ALCOHOL ON YOU.
....

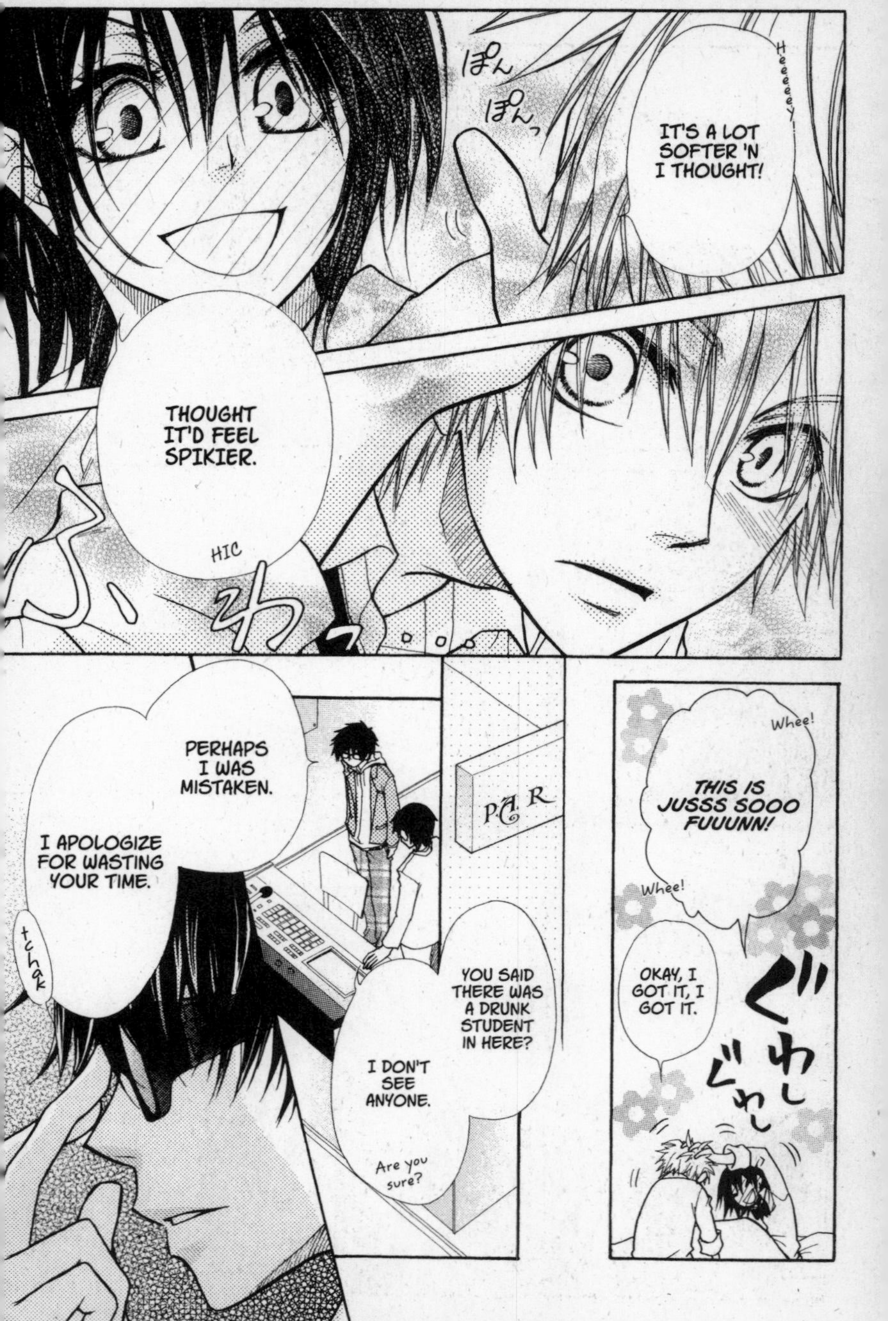
ぽん ぽんっ
Heeeeey!
IT'S A LOT SOFTER 'N I THOUGHT!
THOUGHT IT'D FEEL SPIKIER.
ふわっ
HIC
Whee!
THIS IS JUSSS SOOO FUUUNN!
Whee!
OKAY, I GOT IT, I GOT IT.
P.A.R
YOU SAID THERE WAS A DRUNK STUDENT IN HERE?
I DON'T SEE ANYONE.
Are you sure?
PERHAPS I WAS MISTAKEN.
I APOLOGIZE FOR WASTING YOUR TIME.
tchak

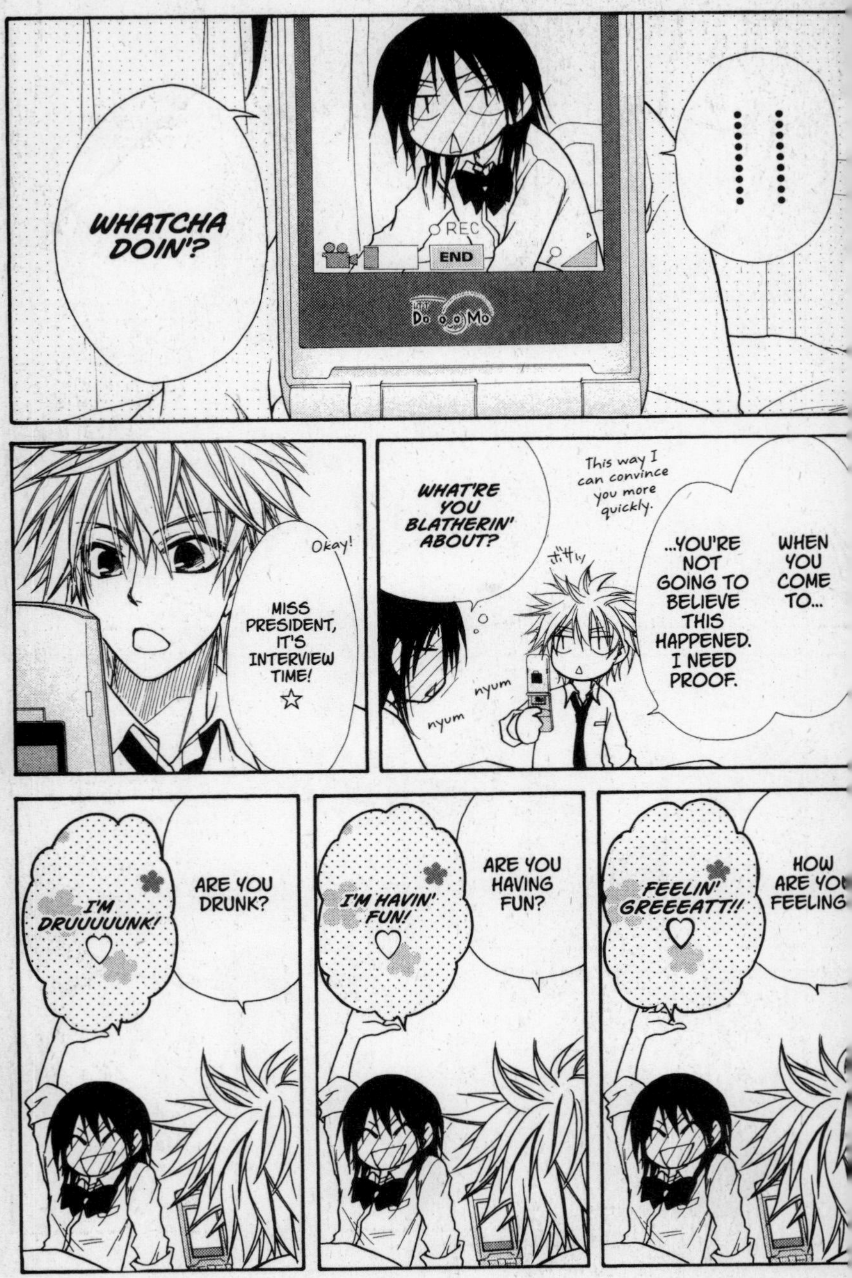
......
WHATCHA DOIN'?
REC
END
WHEN YOU COME TO...
...YOU'RE NOT GOING TO BELIEVE THIS HAPPENED. I NEED PROOF.
This way I can convince you more quickly.
WHAT'RE YOU BLATHERIN' ABOUT?
nyum
nyum
Okay!
MISS PRESIDENT, IT'S INTERVIEW TIME! ☆
HOW ARE YOU FEELING
FEELIN' GREEEATT!! ♡
ARE YOU HAVING FUN?
I'M HAVIN' FUN! ♡
ARE YOU DRUNK?
I'M DRUUUUUNK! ♡

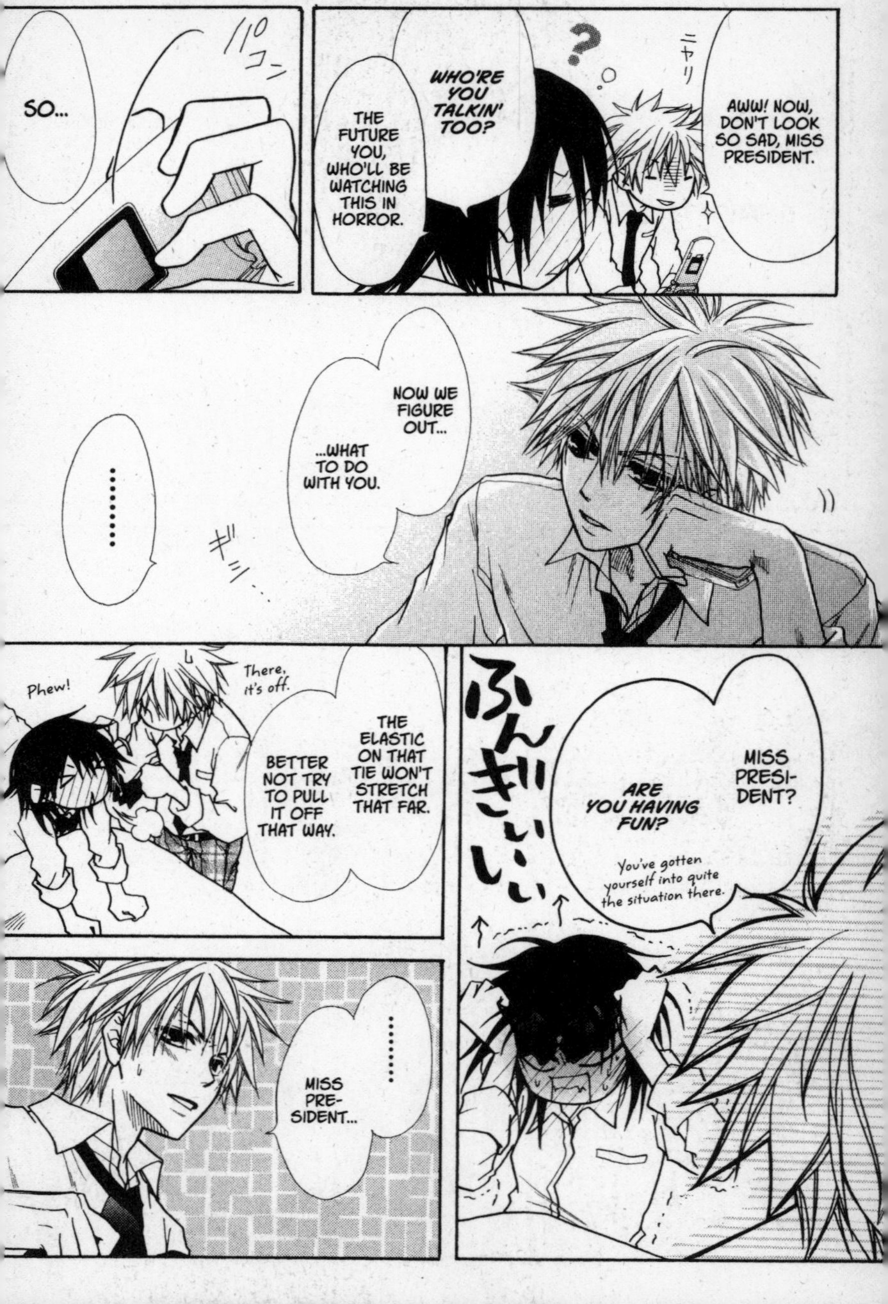
ニヤリ
AWW! NOW, DON'T LOOK SO SAD, MISS PRESIDENT.
?
WHO'RE YOU TALKIN' TOO?
THE FUTURE YOU, WHO'LL BE WATCHING THIS IN HORROR.
パコン
SO...
NOW WE FIGURE OUT...
...WHAT TO DO WITH YOU.
ギシ…
……
ふんぎぃぃぃ
MISS PRESI-DENT?
ARE YOU HAVING FUN?
You've gotten yourself into quite the situation there.
There, it's off.
THE ELASTIC ON THAT TIE WON'T STRETCH THAT FAR.
BETTER NOT TRY TO PULL IT OFF THAT WAY.
Phew!
……
MISS PRE-SIDENT...

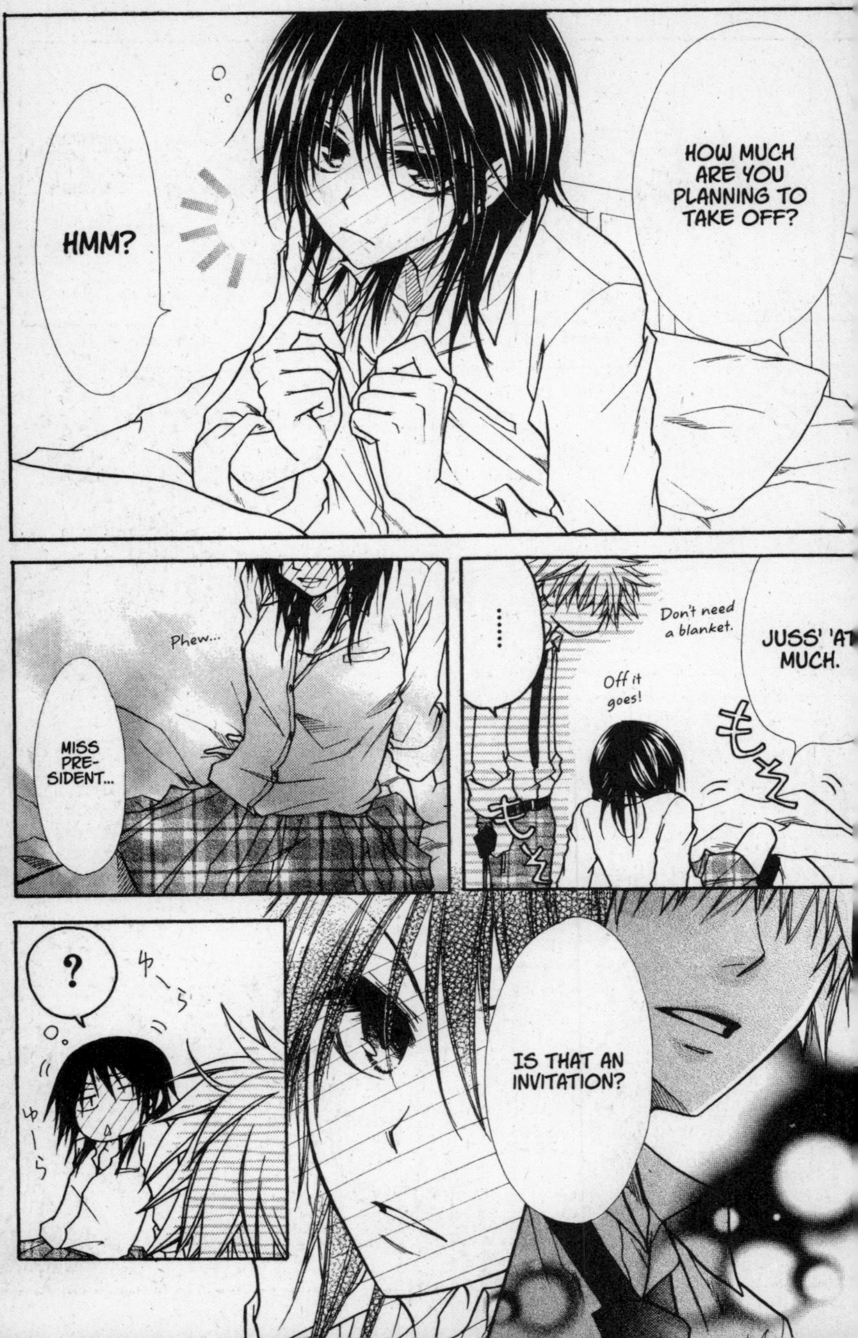
HOW MUCH ARE YOU PLANNING TO TAKE OFF?
HMM?
JUSS' 'AT MUCH.
Don't need a blanket.
Off it goes!
もそ
......
もそ
Phew...
MISS PRESIDENT...
IS THAT AN INVITATION?
?
ゆ～ら
ゆーら

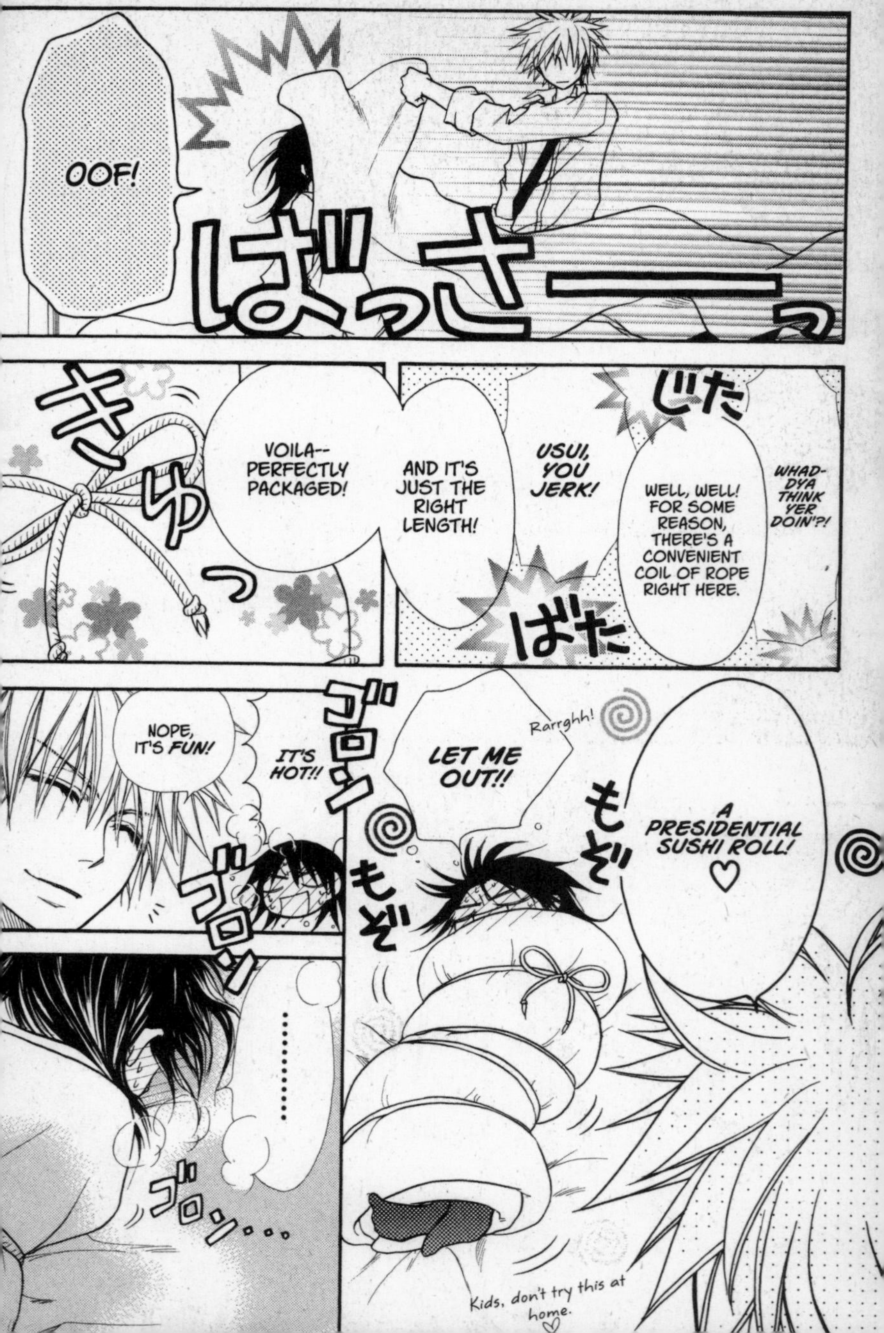
OOF!
ばっさーーっ
じた
WHAD-DYA THINK YER DOIN'?!
WELL, WELL! FOR SOME REASON, THERE'S A CONVENIENT COIL OF ROPE RIGHT HERE.
USUI, YOU JERK!
ばた
AND IT'S JUST THE RIGHT LENGTH!
VOILA-- PERFECTLY PACKAGED!
きゅっ
A PRESIDENTIAL SUSHI ROLL! ♡
もぞ
Rarrghh!
LET ME OUT!!
もぞ
Kids, don't try this at home. ♡
ゴロン
IT'S HOT!!
NOPE, IT'S FUN!
ゴロン
......
ゴロン...

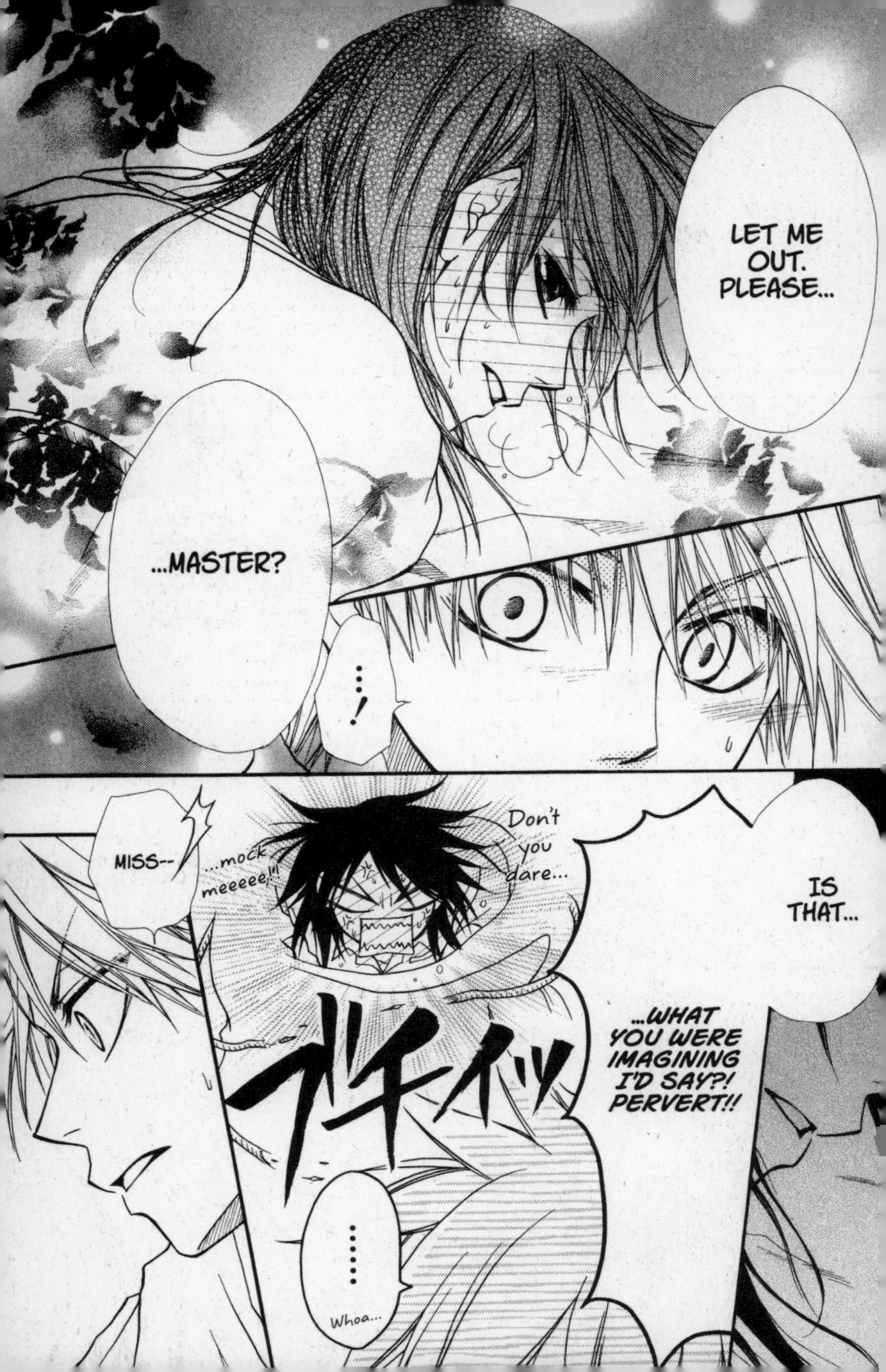
LET ME OUT. PLEASE...
...MASTER?
...!
IS THAT...
...WHAT YOU WERE IMAGINING I'D SAY?! PERVERT!!
Don't you dare...
...mock meeeee!!!
MISS--
ブチイッ
......
Whoa...

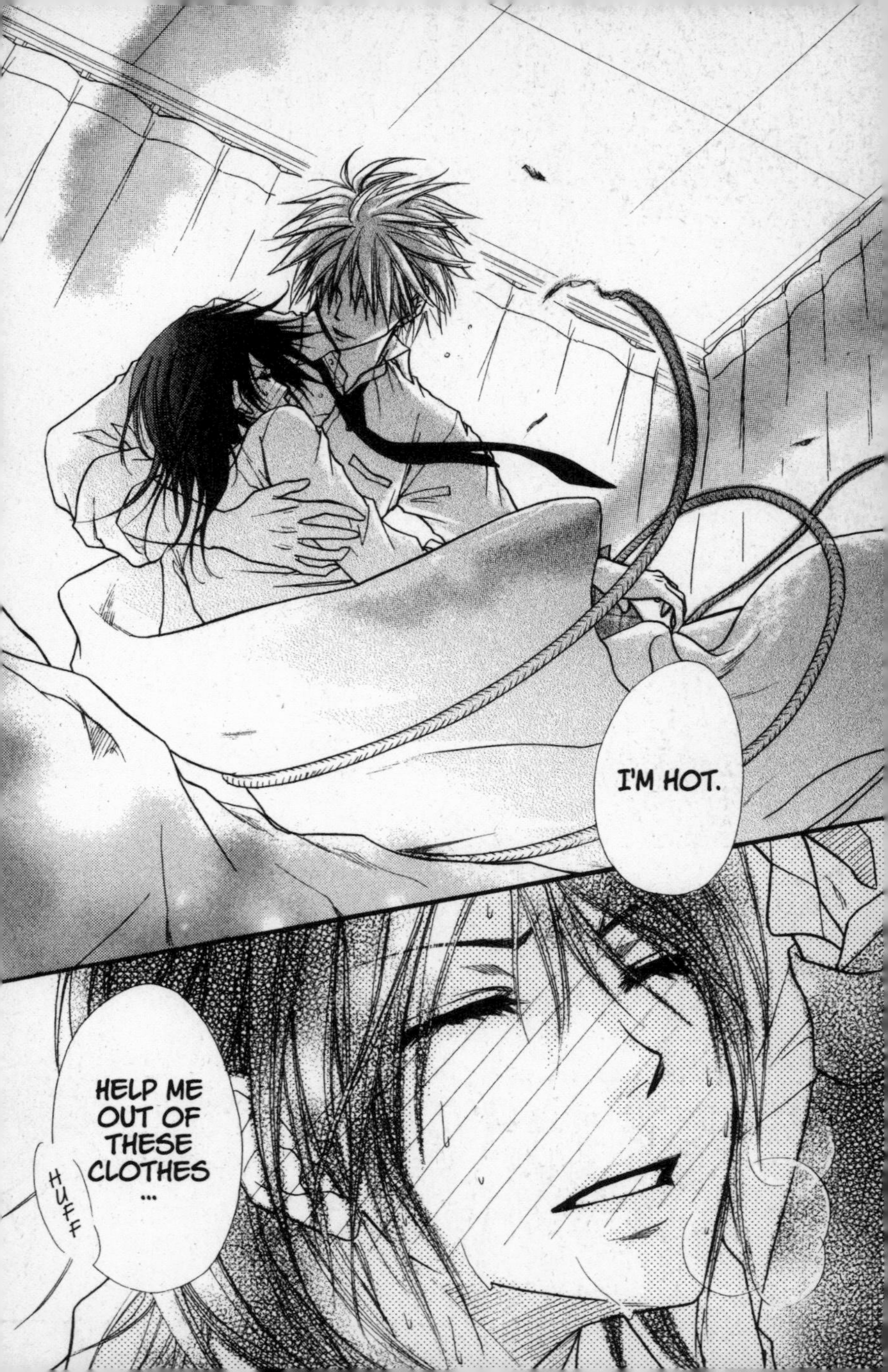
I'M HOT.
HELP ME OUT OF THESE CLOTHES ...
HUFF

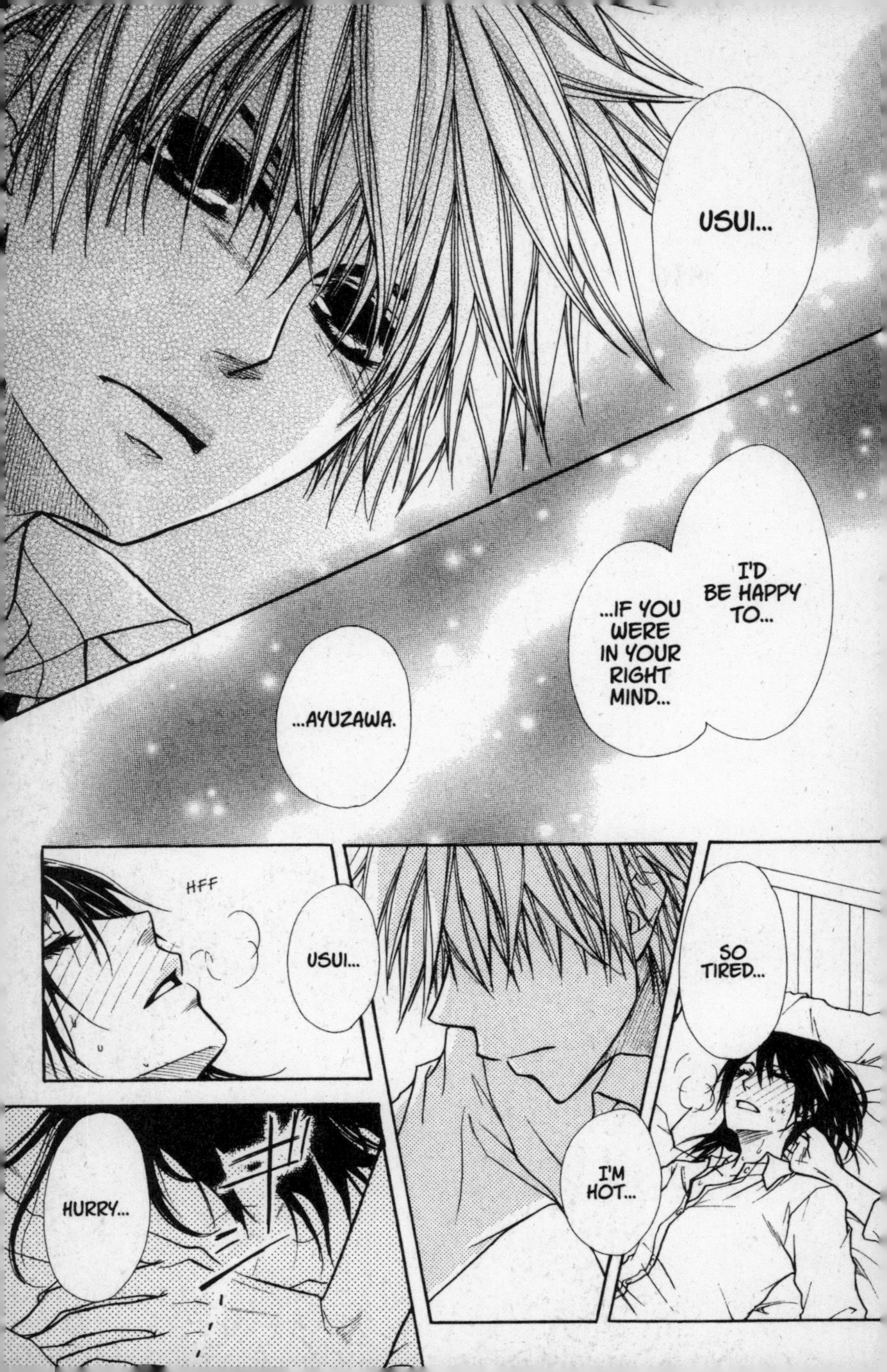
USUI...
I'D BE HAPPY TO...
...IF YOU WERE IN YOUR RIGHT MIND...
...AYUZAWA.
SO TIRED...
I'M HOT...
HFF
USUI...
HURRY...

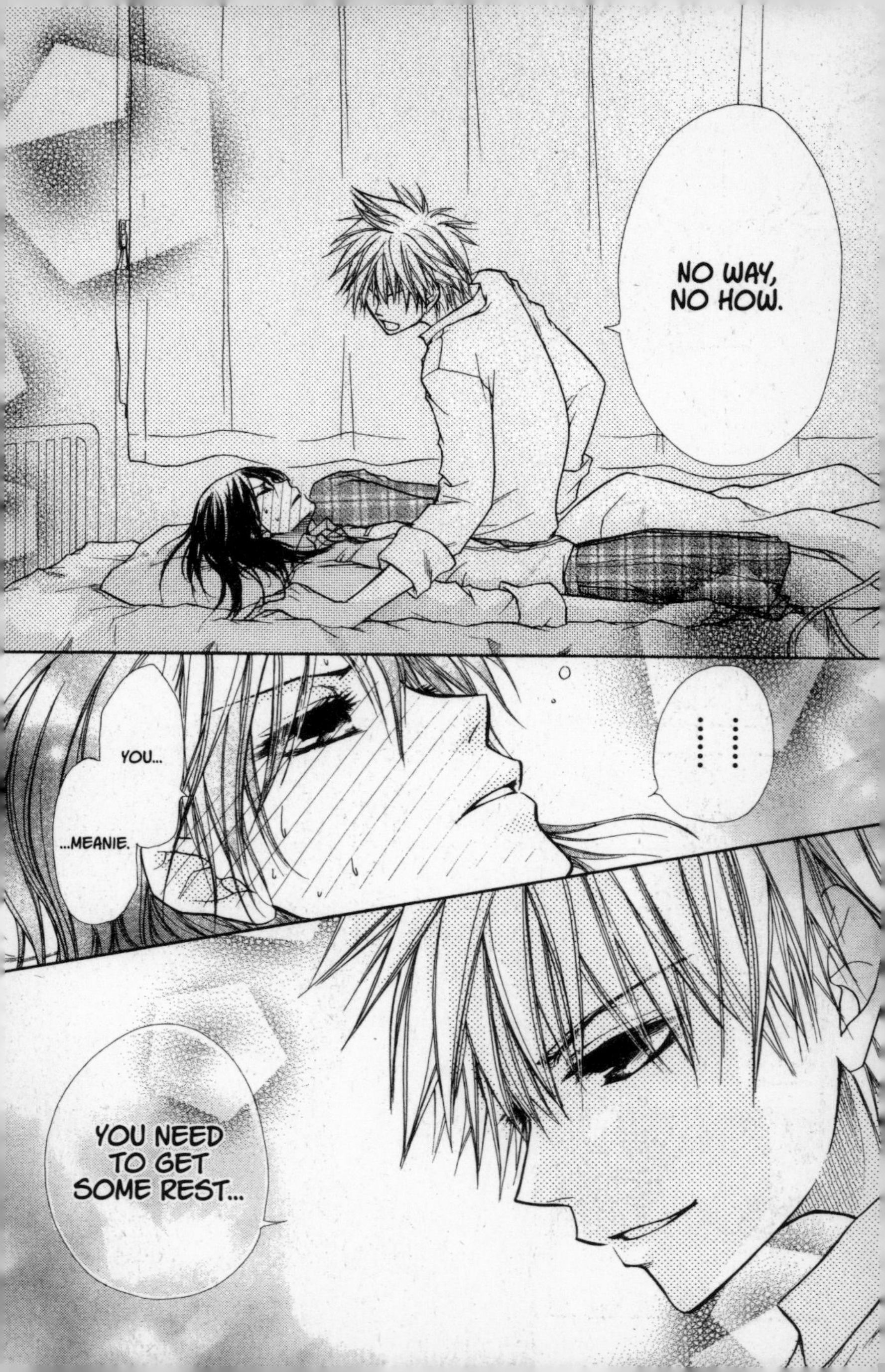
NO WAY, NO HOW.
......
YOU...
...MEANIE.
YOU NEED TO GET SOME REST...

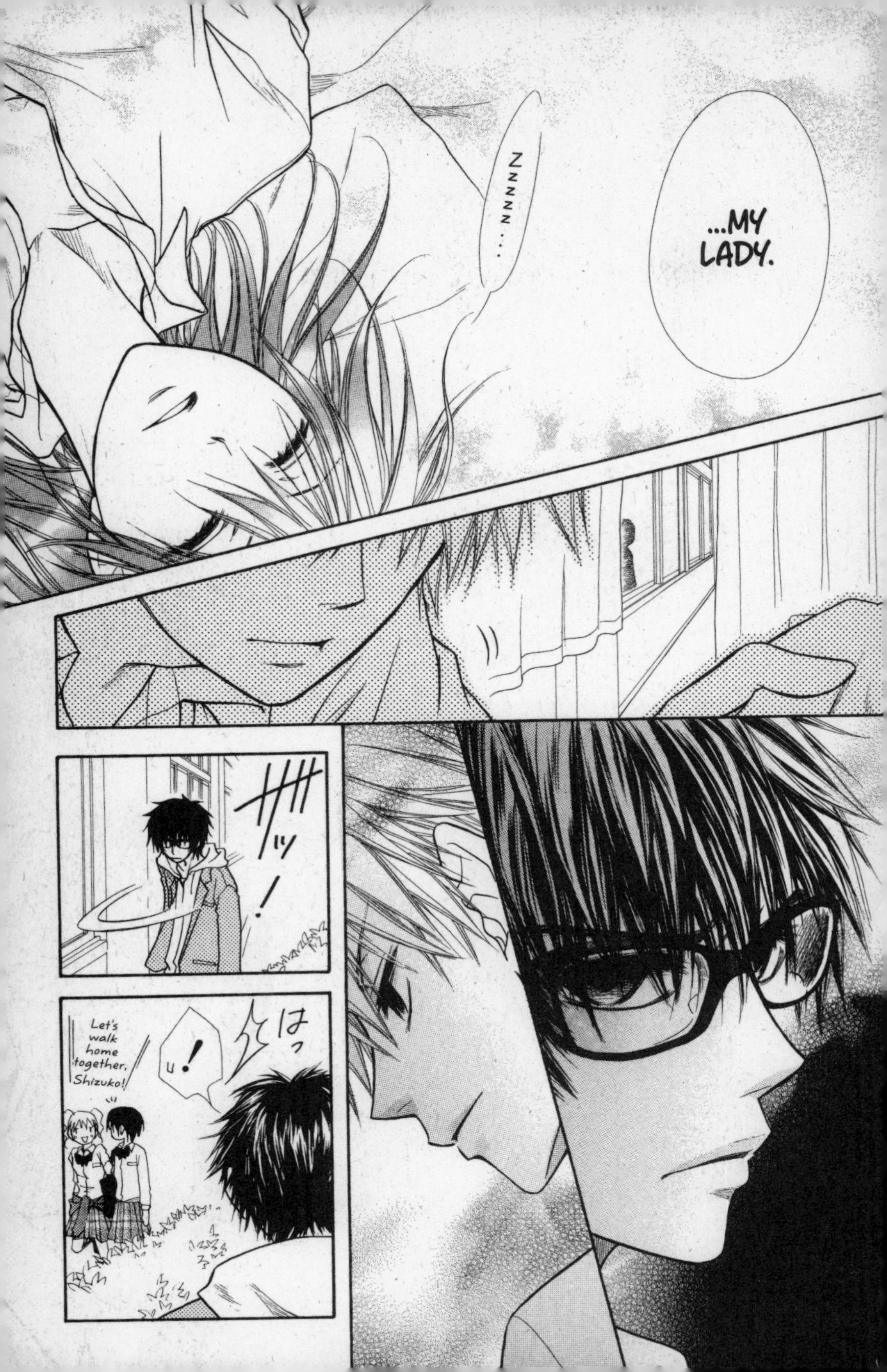
...MY LADY.
Zzzzz...
ザッ!
はっ
!
Let's walk home together, Shizuko!

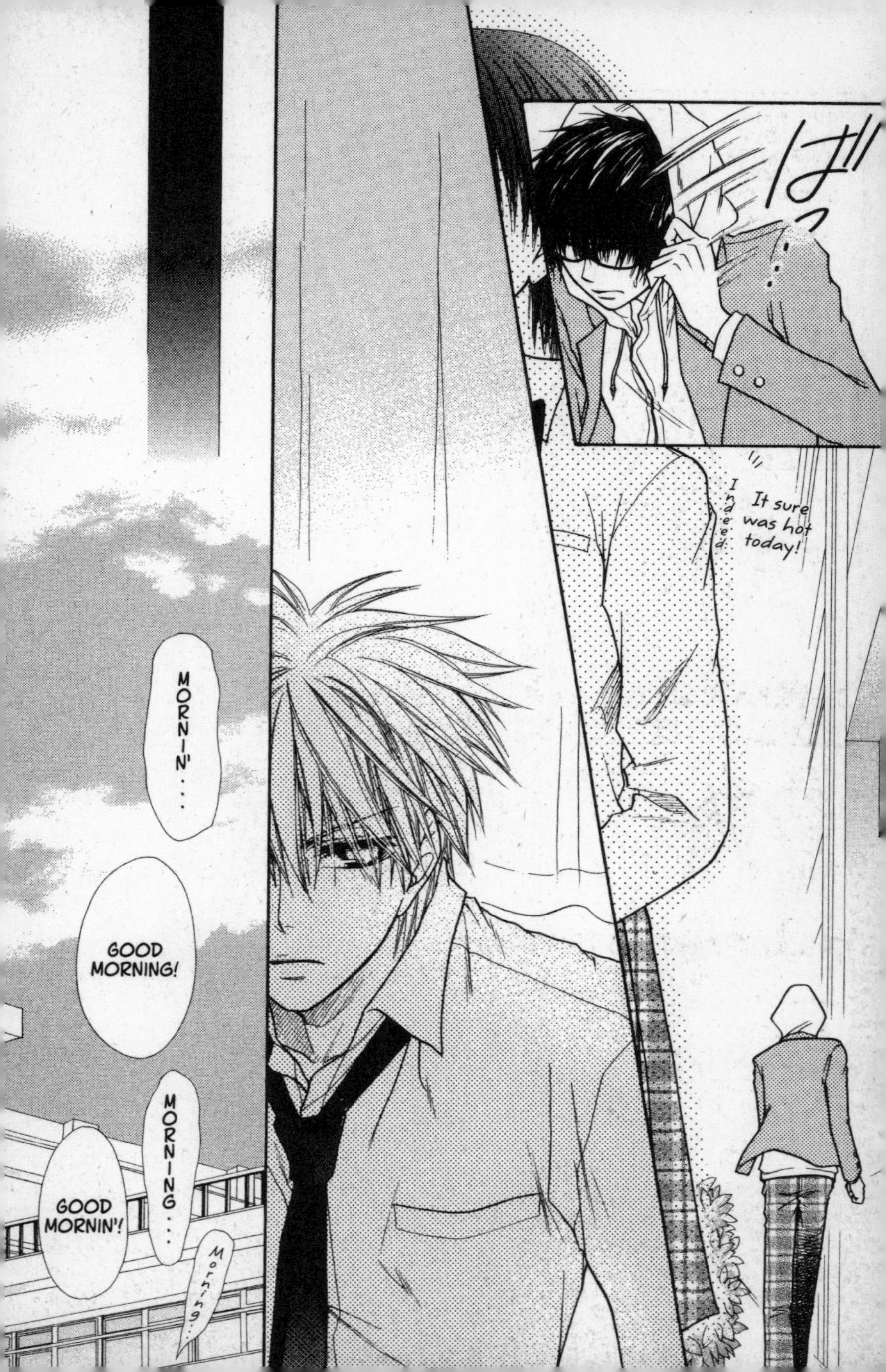

ばっ
It sure was hot today!
Indeed...
MORNIN'...
GOOD MORNING!
MORNING...
GOOD MORNIN'!
Morning...

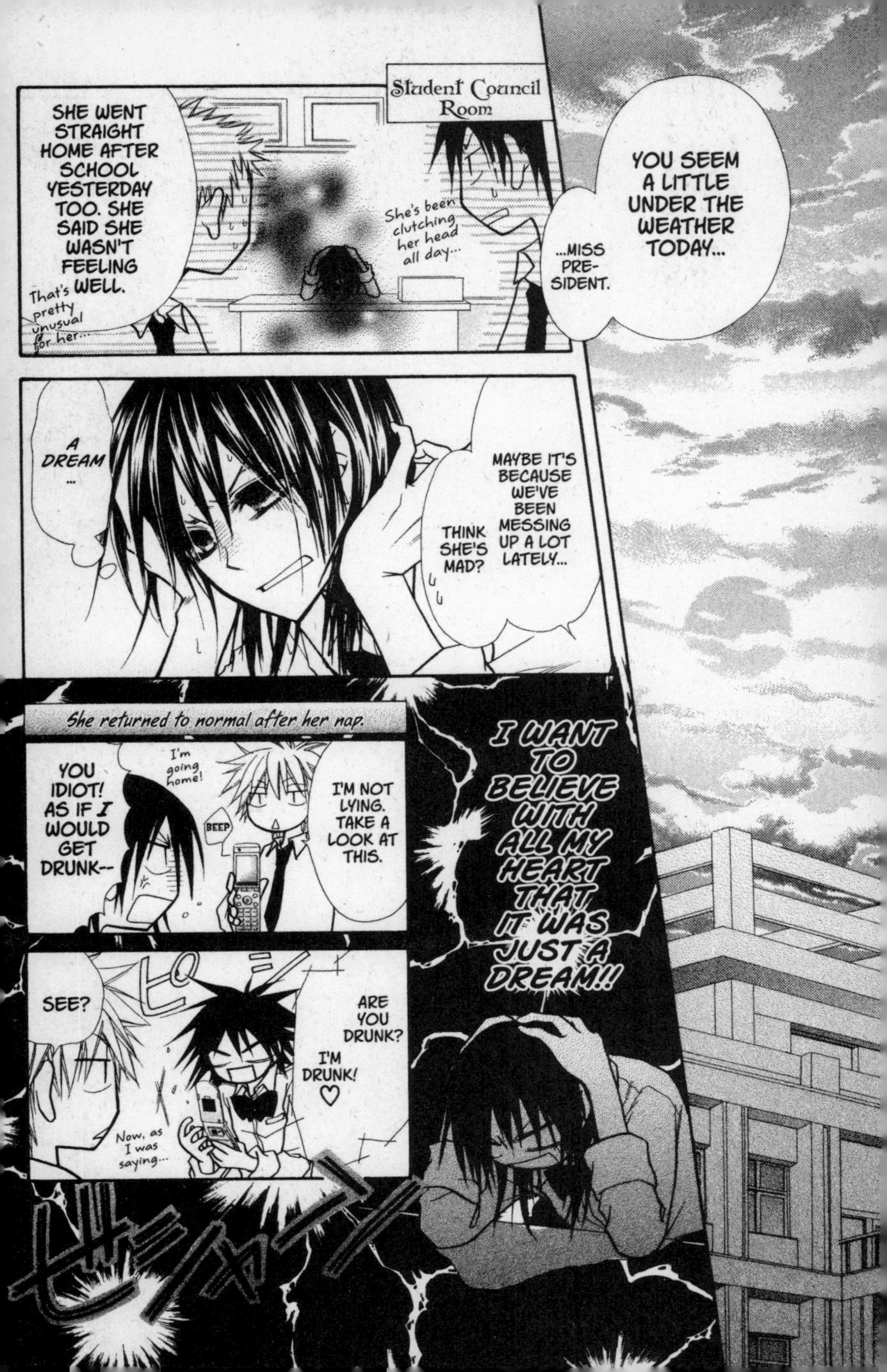
Student Council Room
YOU SEEM A LITTLE UNDER THE WEATHER TODAY...
...MISS PRESIDENT.
She's been clutching her head all day...
SHE WENT STRAIGHT HOME AFTER SCHOOL YESTERDAY TOO. SHE SAID SHE WASN'T FEELING WELL.
That's pretty unusual for her...
MAYBE IT'S BECAUSE WE'VE BEEN MESSING UP A LOT LATELY...
THINK SHE'S MAD?
A DREAM ...
I WANT TO BELIEVE WITH ALL MY HEART THAT IT WAS JUST A DREAM!!
She returned to normal after her nap.
I'M NOT LYING. TAKE A LOOK AT THIS.
I'm going home!
BEEP
YOU IDIOT! AS IF I WOULD GET DRUNK--
ARE YOU DRUNK?
I'M DRUNK! ♡
SEE?
Now, as I was saying...

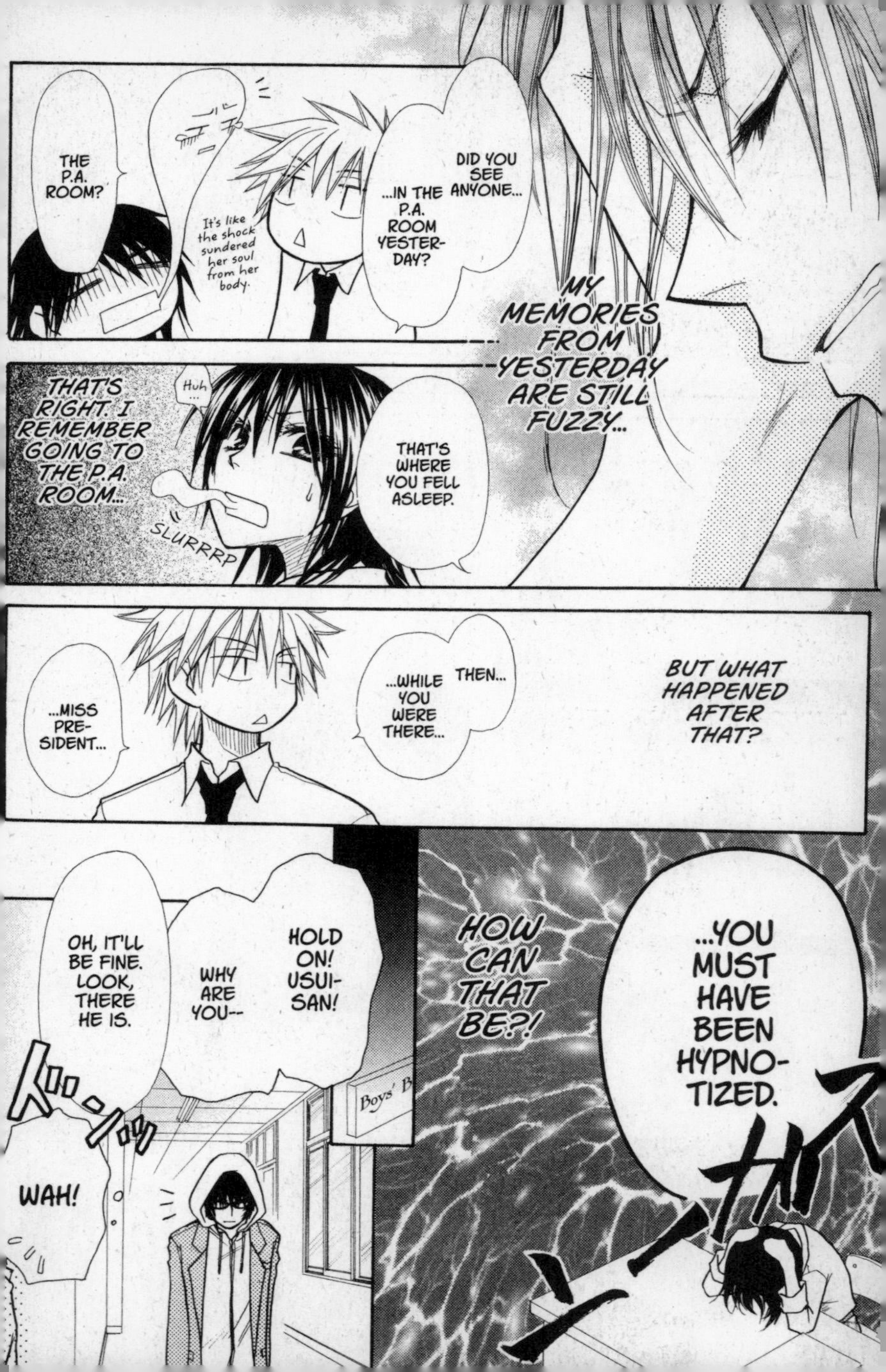

MY MEMORIES FROM YESTERDAY ARE STILL FUZZY...
DID YOU SEE ANYONE...
...IN THE P.A. ROOM YESTERDAY?
It's like the shock sundered her soul from her body.
THE P.A. ROOM?
THAT'S WHERE YOU FELL ASLEEP.
Huh...
THAT'S RIGHT. I REMEMBER GOING TO THE P.A. ROOM...
SLURRRP
BUT WHAT HAPPENED AFTER THAT?
THEN...
...WHILE YOU WERE THERE...
...MISS PRESIDENT...
...YOU MUST HAVE BEEN HYPNOTIZED.
HOW CAN THAT BE?!
HOLD ON! USUI-SAN!
WHY ARE YOU--
OH, IT'LL BE FINE. LOOK, THERE HE IS.
WAH!

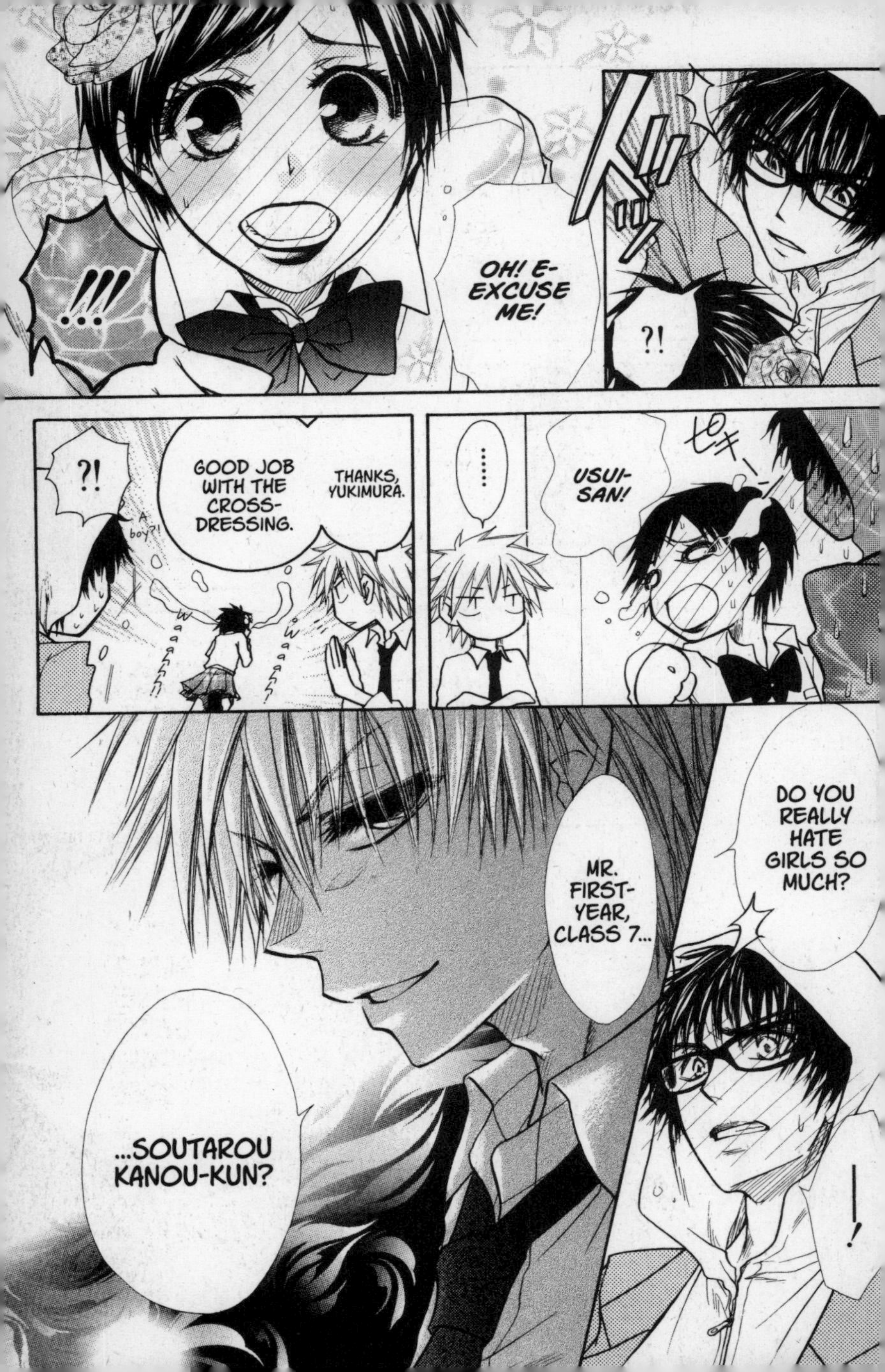
?!
OH! E-EXCUSE ME!
!!!
USUI-SAN!
......
THANKS, YUKIMURA.
GOOD JOB WITH THE CROSS-DRESSING.
?!
A boy?!
DO YOU REALLY HATE GIRLS SO MUCH?
MR. FIRST-YEAR, CLASS 7...
...SOUTAROU KANOU-KUN?
!

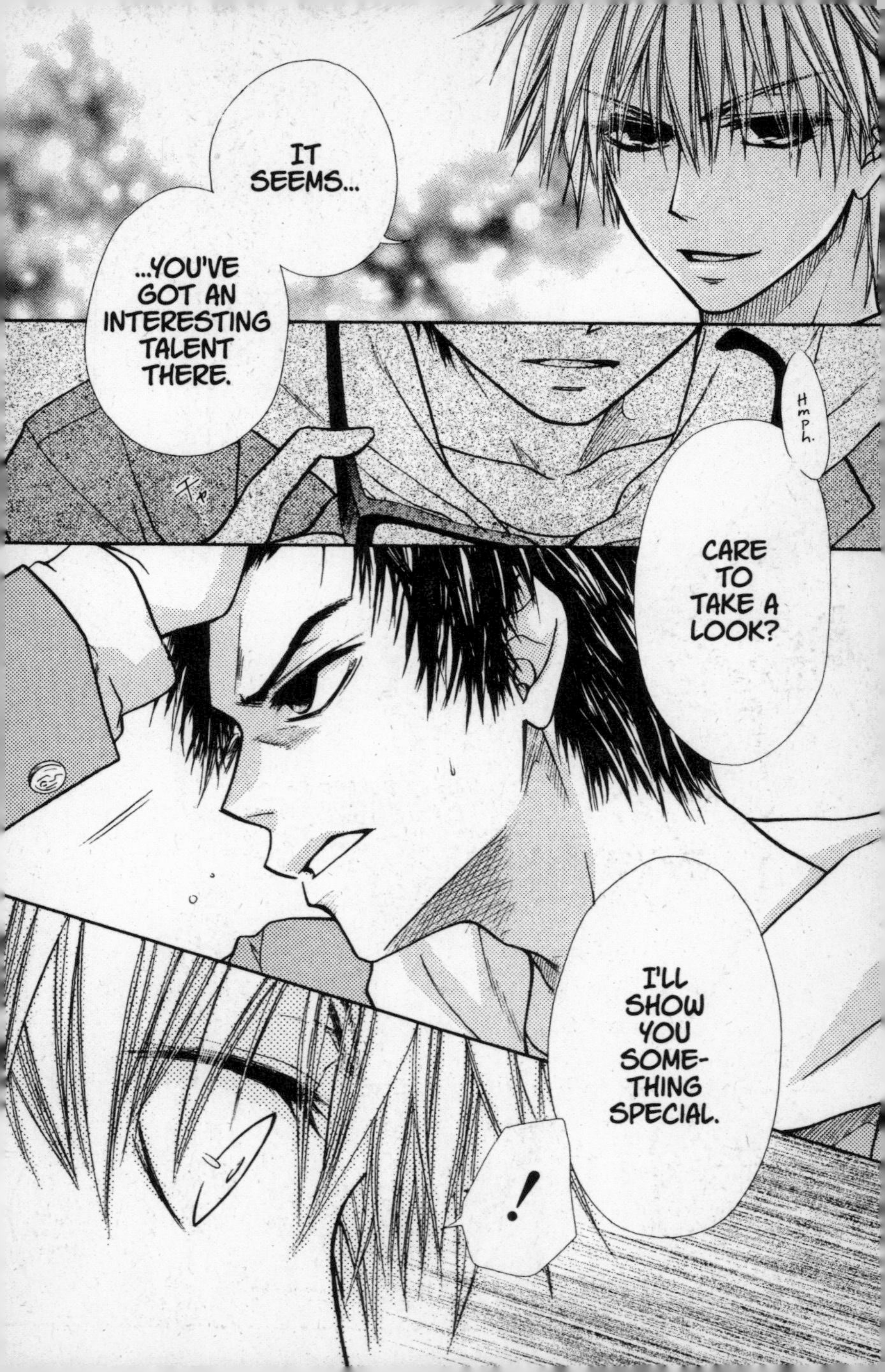
IT SEEMS...
...YOU'VE GOT AN INTERESTING TALENT THERE.
Hmph.
CARE TO TAKE A LOOK?
I'LL SHOW YOU SOME-THING SPECIAL.
!

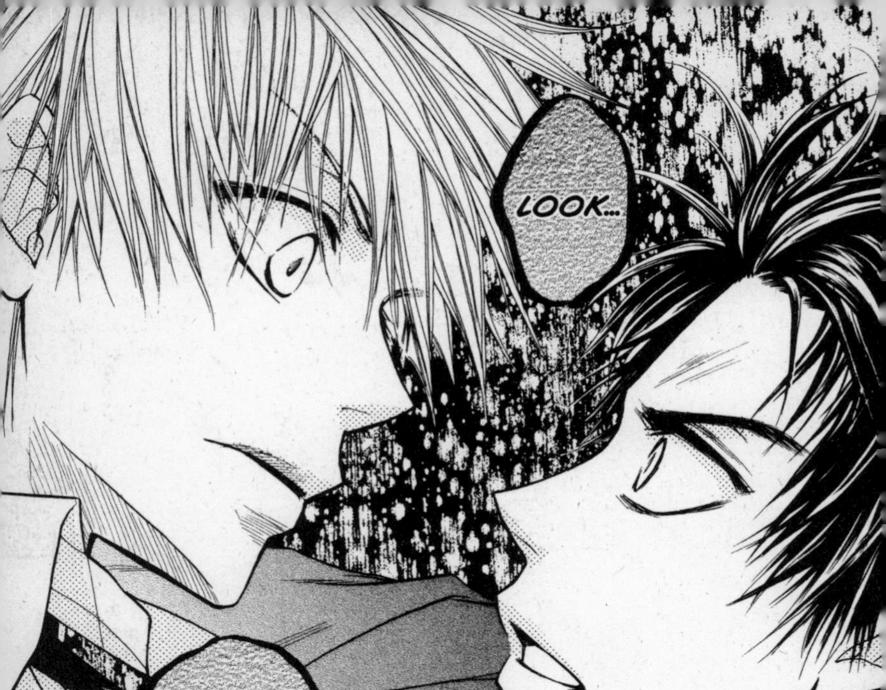
LOOK...
...INTO MY EYES.
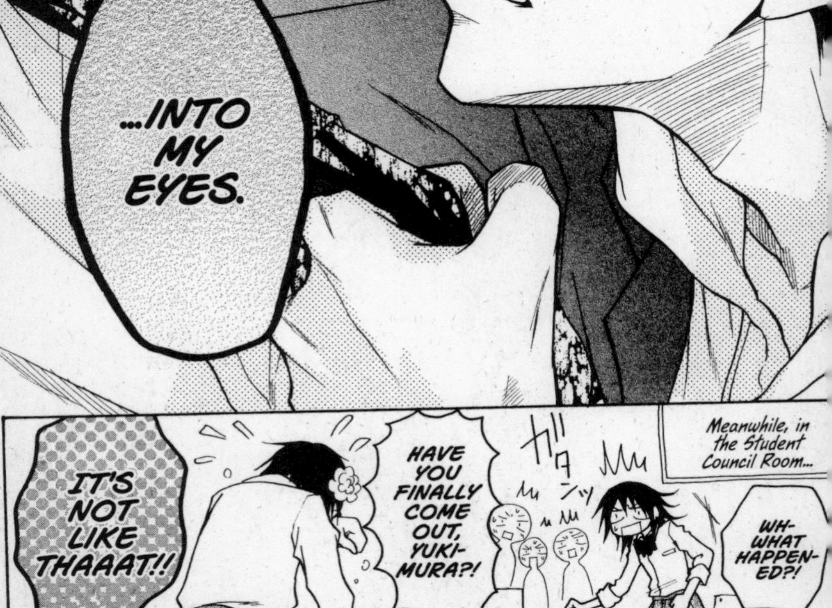
Meanwhile, in the Student Council Room...
WH-WHAT HAPPENED?!
ガタッ
HAVE YOU FINALLY COME OUT, YUKI-MURA?!
IT'S NOT LIKE THAAAT!!

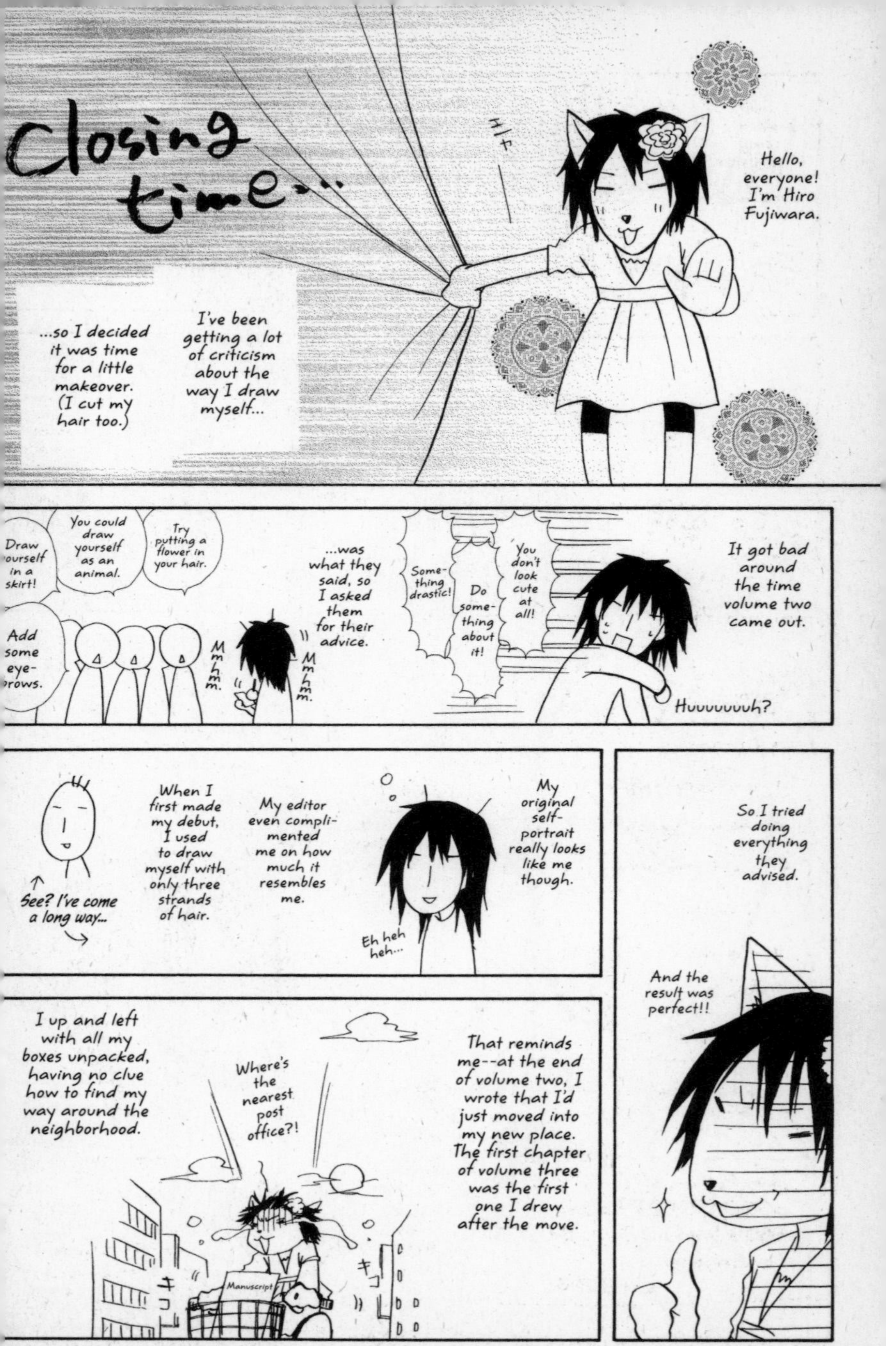

Closing time...
Hello, everyone! I'm Hiro Fujiwara.
I've been getting a lot of criticism about the way I draw myself...
...so I decided it was time for a little makeover. (I cut my hair too.)
It got bad around the time volume two came out.
Huuuuuuuh?
You don't look cute at all!
Do something about it!
Something drastic!
...was what they said, so I asked them for their advice.
Mmhmm.
Mmhmm.
Try putting a flower in your hair.
You could draw yourself as an animal.
Draw ourself in a skirt!
Add some eye-rows.
So I tried doing everything they advised.
And the result was perfect!!
My original self-portrait really looks like me though.
Eh heh heh...
My editor even complimented me on how much it resembles me.
When I first made my debut, I used to draw myself with only three strands of hair.
See? I've come a long way...
That reminds me--at the end of volume two, I wrote that I'd just moved into my new place. The first chapter of volume three was the first one I drew after the move.
Where's the nearest post office?!
キコ
キコ
Manuscript
I up and left with all my boxes unpacked, having no clue how to find my way around the neighborhood.

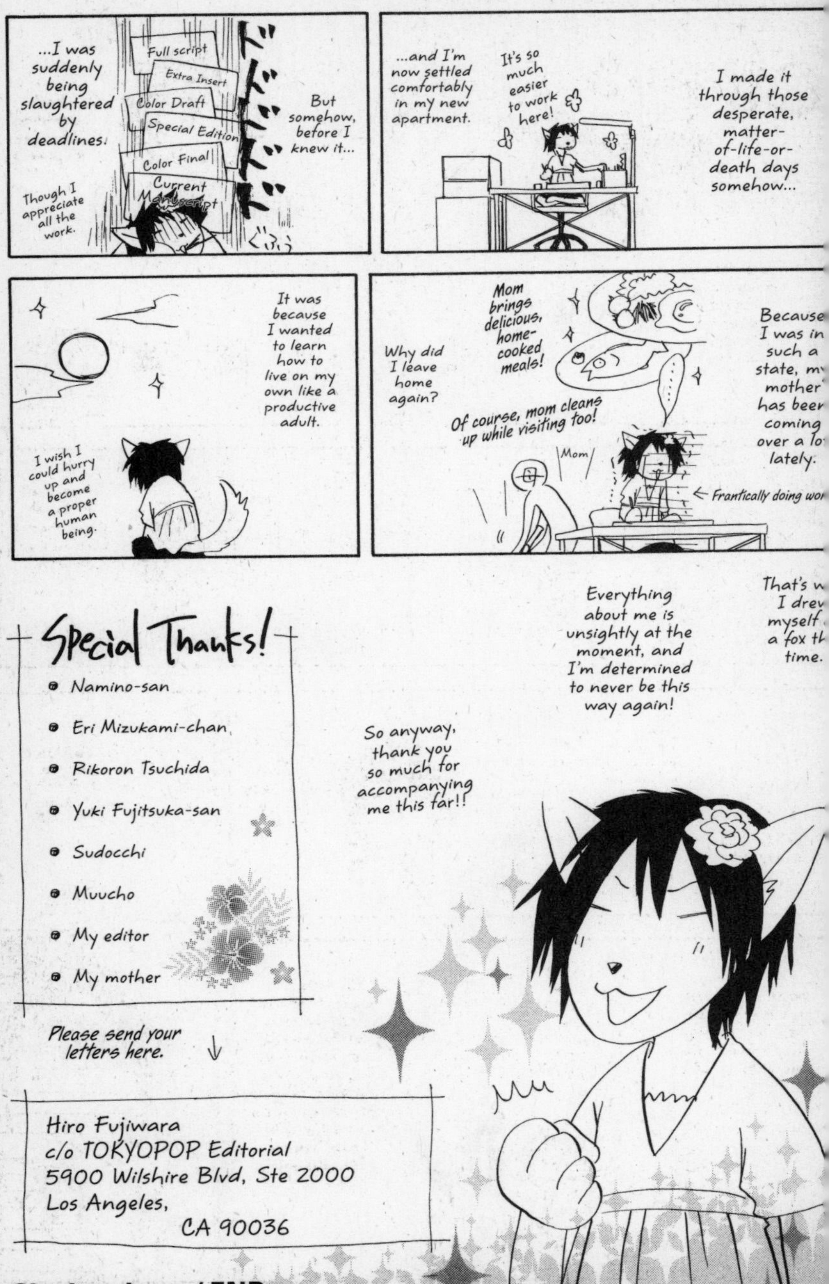
I made it through those desperate, matter-of-life-or-death days somehow...
...and I'm now settled comfortably in my new apartment.
It's so much easier to work here!
But somehow, before I knew it...
...I was suddenly being slaughtered by deadlines.
Full script
Extra Insert
Color Draft
Special Edition
Color Final
Current Manuscript
Though I appreciate all the work.
Because I was in such a state, m mother has bee coming over a lo lately.
Mom brings delicious, home-cooked meals!
Why did I leave home again?
Of course, mom cleans up while visiting too!
Mom
Frantically doing wo
It was because I wanted to learn how to live on my own like a productive adult.
I wish I could hurry up and become a proper human being.
That's w I drew myself a fox th time.
Everything about me is unsightly at the moment, and I'm determined to never be this way again!
So anyway, thank you so much for accompanying me this far!!
Special Thanks!
Namino-san
Eri Mizukami-chan
Rikoron Tsuchida
Yuki Fujitsuka-san
Sudocchi
Muucho
My editor
My mother
Please send your letters here.
Hiro Fujiwara
c/o TOKYOPOP Editorial
5900 Wilshire Blvd, Ste 2000
Los Angeles,
CA 90036

Closing time.../ END

Cafe
Maid
Latte

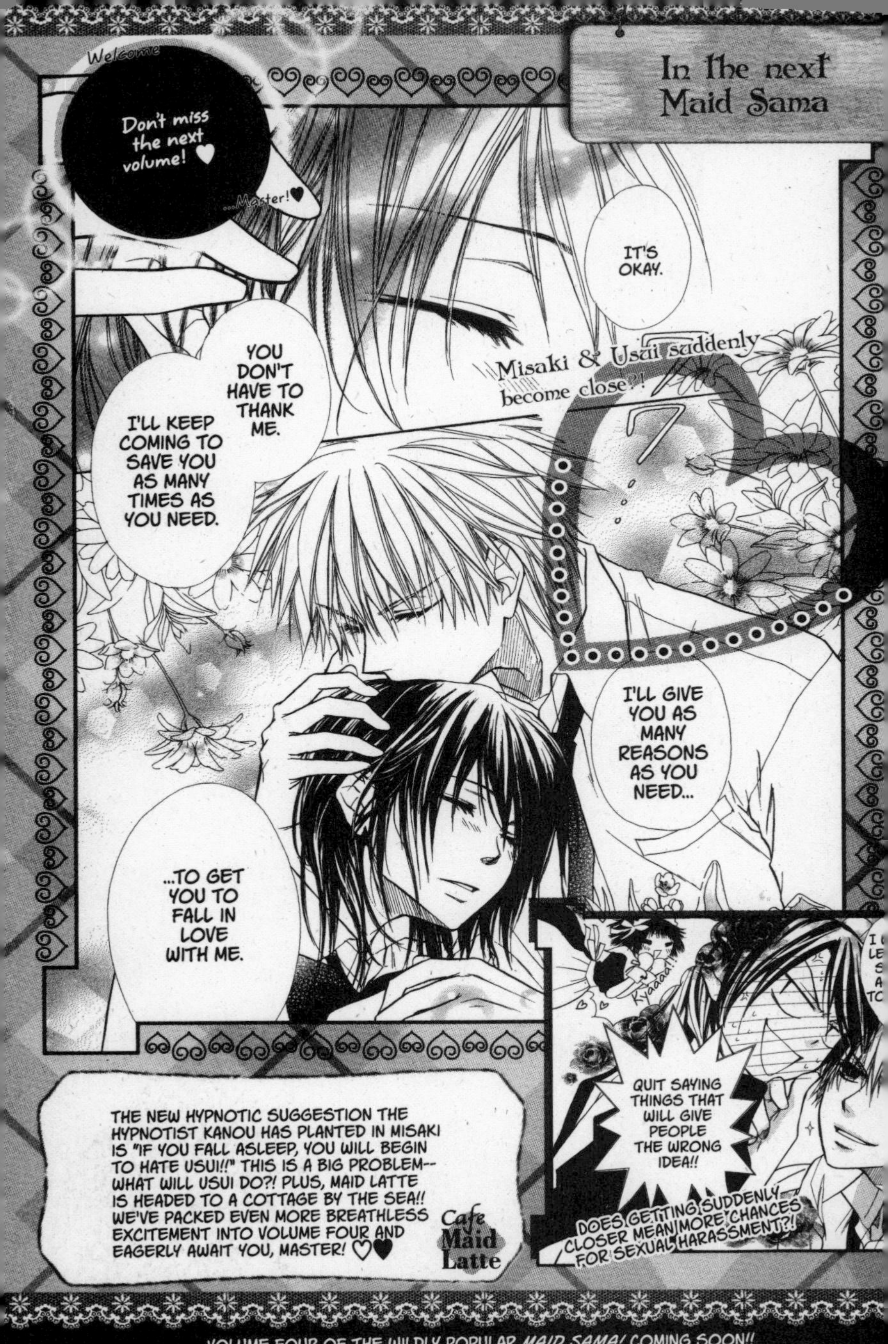
In the next Maid Sama
Welcome
Don't miss the next volume! ♥
...Master!♥
IT'S OKAY.
Misaki & Usui suddenly become close?!
YOU DON'T HAVE TO THANK ME.
I'LL KEEP COMING TO SAVE YOU AS MANY TIMES AS YOU NEED.
I'LL GIVE YOU AS MANY REASONS AS YOU NEED...
...TO GET YOU TO FALL IN LOVE WITH ME.
Kyaaaa!
QUIT SAYING THINGS THAT WILL GIVE PEOPLE THE WRONG IDEA!!
DOES GETTING SUDDENLY CLOSER MEAN MORE CHANCES FOR SEXUAL HARASSMENT?!
THE NEW HYPNOTIC SUGGESTION THE HYPNOTIST KANOU HAS PLANTED IN MISAKI IS "IF YOU FALL ASLEEP, YOU WILL BEGIN TO HATE USUI!!" THIS IS A BIG PROBLEM--WHAT WILL USUI DO?! PLUS, MAID LATTE IS HEADED TO A COTTAGE BY THE SEA!! WE'VE PACKED EVEN MORE BREATHLESS EXCITEMENT INTO VOLUME FOUR AND EAGERLY AWAIT YOU, MASTER! ♡♥
Cafe Maid Latte

VOLUME FOUR OF THE WILDLY POPULAR *MAID SAMA!* COMING SOON!!

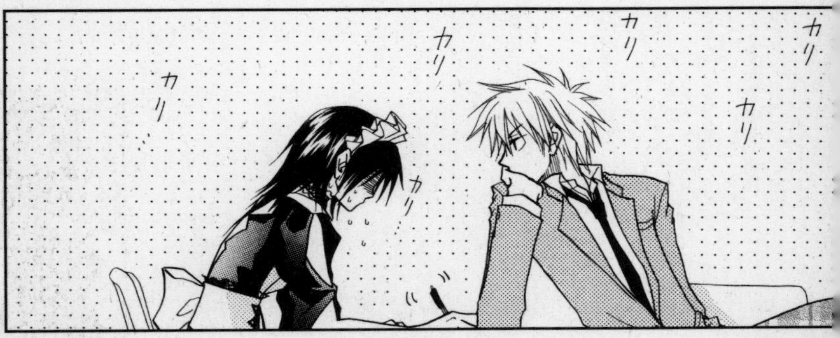
カリ
カリ
カリ
カリ
カリ
カリ

remember
benjamin

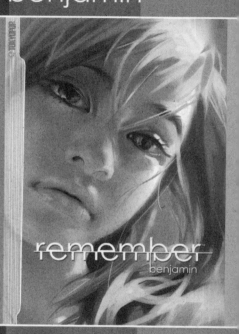

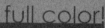

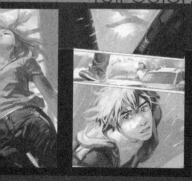

EVERY TEXT COULD BE YOUR LAST

FUTURE DIARY™

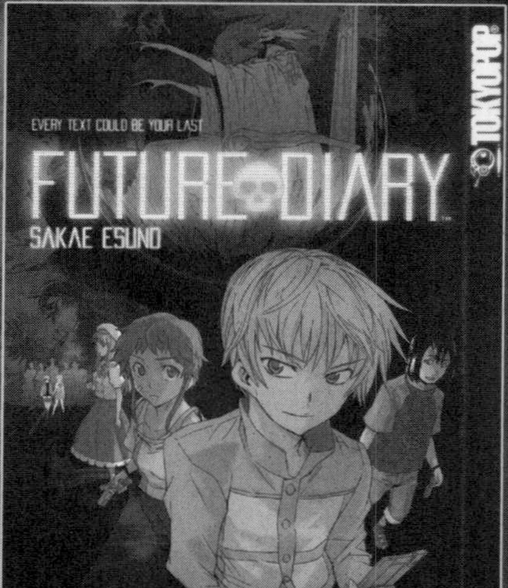
EVERY TEXT COULD BE YOUR LAST
FUTURE DIARY
SAKAE ESUNO
TOKYOPOP
4

Yukiteru is starting out fresh at a new school... or so he thought... Right along with his new classmates, Yukiteru finds himself ambushed by the mysterious Diary Holder Tenth!

"ESUNO'S ART IS SPRIGHTLY, SWEET AND DECEPTIVELY INNOCENT."
—***Publishers Weekly***

BE SURE TO VISIT WWW.TOKYOPOP.COM/SHOP FOR EVERYTHING YOU COULD EVER WANT!

Laser cannon!
Jet strike!
atomic Blaster!
Bellybutton missile!
Domo
THE MANGA
Domo™
full color!
HE ENGLISH-LANGUAGE
anga DEBUT
OF THE WORLD-FAMOUS DOMO!
nvading stores everywhere!
EVIEWS, CONTESTS, AND MORE AT WWW.TOKYOPOP.COM/DOMO_MANGA
MO © NHK-TYO 1998-2009. DOMO ANIMATION © DOMO PRODUCTION COMMITTEE. ALL RIGHTS RESERVED. WWW.DOMONATION.COM

Maid Sama!™

The class president has a little secret she's keeping from the sexy bad boy in school...

t's hard to deny this guilty
leasure when it looks like
's having so much fun."
About.com

isaki's troubles with Usui are
r from over! His apparent
elings for her only confuse
isaki right when she most
eeds to be clear-headed.
vo (male) distractions from a
gh-ranked prep school show up
complicate matters, and the
hool sports festival is just
ound the corner, too!
'hat's a tough maid to do?

ANCE

T
TEEN
AGE 13+

Maid Sama!
Hiro Fujiwara
2

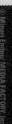

STOP!

This is the back of the book.
You wouldn't want to spoil a great ending!

This book is printed "manga-style," in the authentic Japanese right-to-left format. Since none of the artwork has been flipped or altered, readers get to experience the story just as the creator intended. You've been asking for it, so TOKYOPOP® delivered: authentic, hot-off-the-press, and far more fun!

DIRECTIONS

If this is your first time reading manga-style, here's a quick guide to help you understand how it works.

It's easy... just start in the top right panel and follow the numbers. Have fun, and look for more 100% authentic manga from TOKYOPOP®!